THE ROADS TO RUSSIA

United States Lend-Lease to the Soviet Union

THE ROADS

TO RUSSIA

UNITED STATES LEND-LEASE
TO THE SOVIET UNION

ROBERT HUHN JONES
With a Foreword by Edgar L. Erickson

UNIVERSITY OF OKLAHOMA PRESS : NORMAN

BY ROBERT HUHN JONES

The Civil War in the Northwest (Norman, 1960)
The Centennial Years (with Fred A. Shannon) (Garden City, 1967)

THE PUBLICATION OF THIS VOLUME HAS BEEN AIDED BY A GRANT FROM THE FREEDOM STUDY COMMITTEE OF THE UNIVERSITY OF ILLINOIS.

LIBRARY OF CONGRESS CATALOG CARD NUMBER: 68–15679

TO ETHEL, MERTON, AND FRED

All of Whom Left Too Soon

FOREWORD

By Edgar L. Erickson

At the Teheran Conference of December, 1943, Stalin informed his British and American colleagues that "without American production the war would have been lost." On the basis of supplies delivered, the evidence indicates that Stalin on this occasion frankly and accurately evaluated the importance of Lend-Lease to the survival of Russia. Even so, there was a practical motive for so generous a tribute to his Allies: the war was still to be won; the Germans were still deep in Russia; the Lend-Lease supplies were still an absolute necessity for Russia to win the victory and conquests that ultimately she did. Except for sporadic releases in the Russian press, the people of Russia were never really informed during the war of the importance of the Lend-Lease program to their war effort; and as the war drew to a close and Stalin revealed his intentions to deny the Western Allies a voice in the making of the postwar settlements with countries behind what became known as the iron curtain, the depreciation of Lend-Lease for public effect both at home and abroad became the official Soviet propaganda line. Behind a fury of righteous indignation Stalin castigated the United States for terminating Lend-Lease at the end of the war and thereby provided the theme of belittlement that has been echoed by Russian historians. Depreciation took the form of a concerted minimization of both the amount and the importance of Lend-Lease supplies, and of a trumpeting that the main reason that the Allies sent supplies to Russia was to spill Russian blood to save their own and to advance the interests of capitalist imperialism. Khrushchev voiced the latter theme loud and clear, and as World War II recedes farther and farther into the shadows, Russian historians seek to bury Lend-Lease in a potter's field, damned as an evil design of their capitalist enemies.

Russian minimization of the amount of Lend-Lease supplies fails to stand up in the face of statistics. The charge that the Western Allies used Lend-Lease to enable Russia to fight the war for them is more difficult to answer, not because it is true but because it seems logical to a calloused, materialistic world, all the more so since the President and the Committee to Defend America by Aiding the Allies seemed to think they had to use that argument to sell Lend-Lease to the American people. That the saving of American and British lives was a significant consideration is not to be denied, but not in the cruel and selfish light that Russia claims. The Western Allies regarded the war as a team effort in which each player made his maximum contribution to the defeat of a common enemy. They played their roles to the best of their capacities and abilities. Surely the countries that were responsible for abolishing slavery, for founding a commonwealth of free nations, for establishing a United Nations, and for producing a Marshall Plan were capable of materially assisting an ally engaged in a common cause of defeating Nazism for reasons other than base selfishness. The Russian charge is further discredited by the attitude of the United States military chiefs toward Lend-Lease. They vigorously opposed sending aid to Russia because it seriously interfered with American preparation for war. Had the United States been motivated primarily by the selfish purpose attributed to her by Russia, the military chiefs would have welcomed Lend-Lease to Russia. This military opposition never really changed; it was simply silenced by the order of the Commander-in-Chief.

By conservative estimates the United States delivered Lend-Lease materials valued at $10,200,000,000 to Russia between 1941 and 1945. This total does not include the cost of transporting goods, in American planes and ships, from the United States to Russia. The shortest and most hazardous of the sea routes, the run to Murmansk and Archangel, was approximately 4,500 miles, and the longest, the Persian Gulf via the Cape of Good Hope, approximately 15,000 miles. Considering the astronomical total of ton-miles of materials carried at wartime shipping and insurance rates, the service charges alone increased the value of the goods another $700,000,000.

From her larder, the United States sent millions of tons (4,460,-800 long tons) of foodstuffs to Russia, including wheat, flour, meat, eggs, milk, lard, and butter, which kept Russian armies from starving at the very time that the vast heartland of Russian agriculture had been snatched from her by the Nazis. If in 1963, nearly twenty years after the war, Russia with all of her old agricultural lands and countless new acres to draw from had to purchase millions of bushels of wheat from the Western world to feed her people, one can reasonably conclude that the shortage of food in Russia in World War II was so acute that without the American help Russian resistance might have collapsed from want of food alone.

From United States factories and mills went leather, rubber boots, shoes, cloth for uniforms, and blankets in sufficient quantity to boot, clothe, and bed the entire Russian military force. These supplies enabled the Russian soldier to fight the year around: in the bitter cold and snows of winter and in the slush and mud of the spring thaws. From United States munitions plants were sent arms and ammunition in full United States Army ratios, and enough explosive chemicals to manufacture vast amounts of additional munitions. United States wire plants manufactured great quantities of barbed steel wire that the Soviets very likely used effectively in their famous islands of defense, which disrupted the Nazi timetable and helped the Soviets to save Leningrad, Moscow, and Stalingrad.

The victory at Stalingrad halted the German eastward advance in Russia; caught in the dread Russian winter with over-extended supply lines and low morale, the Nazis could not face the overwhelming counterattack of Russian forces well fed, warmly clothed, and adequately armed, thanks in part to Lend-Lease. But the victory at Stalingrad by no means meant that Russia had won her war with Germany. The latter still occupied the Russian heartland, in which were located the major part of prewar Soviet industries as well as farmlands. Weakened as she was industrially, Russia did not have the means to provide the vast quantities of supplies necessary to equip her armies for the task of rolling back the Germans, who still were, early in 1943, over 1,000 miles deep in Russia. The means were provided by Lend-Lease, which by 1943 was delivering a significant tonnage of supplies. United States trucks, jeeps, and reconnaissance cars put the Russian armies on wheels and gave them striking mobility to outrun the Germans. Communications wire and equipment made possible the control of the military movements. United States fighter planes and light bombers, along with their Russian counterparts cleared the Luftwaffe from the skies. United States rails and railroad equipment enabled the Russians to rebuild their railways. United States rubber tires and petroleum kept the trucks rolling and the planes flying. High-grade and specialty steels, aluminum, and other metals, along with top-quality tools and dies, made possible the operation of many Russian war plants. A large number of United States merchant and naval craft made possible Russian participation in the transport of Lend-Lease goods over the Pacific route and Russian defense of her coastal waters. These same factors, ironically, enabled the Soviets swiftly to overrun Eastern Europe in order to establish, in the postwar period, satellite Communist states in that area.

In addition, Lend-Lease supplies, a three months' stockpile, made it possible for the Soviets to act with strength and speed in the Far East. By entering the war in the Pacific, Russia was able to claim the spoils of victory, occupying North Korea and re-annexing the Kuril Islands. A few years later, her position in Manchuria and Korea enabled her to support the Chinese Communists and take advantage of the turmoil and dissatisfaction with the Nationalist faction. In this indirect way, Lend-Lease also adversely affected the Asian settlement.

Although the United States terminated Lend-Lease at the end of the war, Russia had received great assistance to give her a start in postwar recovery. In addition to electric power machinery and a complete rubber tire factory, she acquired a great deal of expert knowledge invaluable for modern postwar development. The equipment she received for drilling and refining gave a tremendous boost to her petroleum industry.

The "big lie" that the Soviet Union seeks to record for posterity with respect to Lend-Lease cannot be permitted to go unanswered. For historians to ignore the challenge is unthinkable, not only in the interest of an accurate recording and interpretation of the facts, but out of respect for the generous, heroic, and even sacrificial efforts of the American people, assisted greatly by the British, in offering and carrying out the Lend-Lease program. For these reasons the Committee on Individual Freedom of the University of Illinois, operating under a grant by the Lilly Endowment Inc., has supported this research by Robert Huhn Jones.

Professor Jones has prepared a documented, objective account of United States Lend-Lease to Russia during World War II. His work represents an exhaustive search of the published official and unofficial sources (American, British, and Russian), and of such unpublished documentary sources of agencies and officials who participated in the Lend-Lease program as have been opened to scholars. He has not endeavored to prove a conclusion set forth in advance of his research. He has gathered his data and written a factual and interpretative account of why and how Lend-Lease became a reality, who the leaders were, the routes by which the supplies were delivered and the trials experienced in getting them to Russia, the amount of the supplies delivered under each of the protocol agreements, the use made of the goods in Russia, the Russian and American opinions of Lend-Lease, and an evaluation of the program. His most difficult problem has been to determine the use made of the supplies, for the Soviet Union denied American liaison officers, except in a few instances, the courtesy of observing how the goods were used. He has been careful to draw only conclusions that can be substantiated by the facts.

PREFACE

This examination of Lend-Lease to Russia was conceived by Professor Edgar L. Erickson of the University of Illinois as a project for Freedom Study Committee research. The Lilly Endowment, Inc., through a generous grant to the committee, made the project possible. The University of Illinois, and the Department of Economics, graciously appointed me Visiting Research Professor for a twelve-month year and Postdoctoral Fellow for a summer, thereby materially assisting in the research for and writing of this book.

The invaluable resources of the fine University of Illinois Library provided a solid base for research in government documents, newspapers, and secondary sources. The National Archives in Washington, D.C.; in Independence, Missouri (the Harry S Truman Library); and especially at Hyde Park, New York (the Franklin D. Roosevelt Library) provided much additional assistance, as did the Library of Congress. The Research Guidance Division of the State Department gave vital assistance. Security clearances from the Army, Navy, and State Department were useful but not essential, since certain categories of records remained closed to me even with such clearance. Fortunately, enough material was readily available and not subject to extended review by clearing agencies to justify the project. It is doubtful that records in closed categories would substantially alter the general outline or conclusions of this book, but the fact that certain records are closed does force the researcher to depend, to a greater degree than is desirable, upon the judgments of teams of "official" historians. Fortunately also, in a government as large and complex as that of the United States, there is often the opportunity to use published records of less directly involved agencies as a cross-check; and, where possible, this has been done. I do not mean to imply that Lend-Lease to Russia is a closed topic with Washington officialdom: it is not. But it is an area of unsettled accounts, an area where negotiations are constantly subject to renewal (realistically or not), and in order not to prejudice these overtures, various categories of information remain closed. This is one of the problems in investigating such recent periods of history.

An additional problem of Russian-language materials and their use was solved by the expeditious labors of Victor Bahmet, a Ukrainian-born graduate assistant, well acquainted with recent Soviet history and historiography. Mr. Bahmet searched through a variety of Russian-language materials, many of them on loan from the Library of Congress, for statistics and information. The problems of Soviet statistics, especially their meaning and use, are well known to those who have occasion to work with them.

Everything considered, this examination of Lend-Lease to Russia is intended as an outline of a very complex subject and by its nature cannot pretend to be definitive. Other historians (economic, military, diplomatic, social, and political) will find many avenues worthy of much more detailed analysis than is given here. The entire history of Lend-Lease, to Great Britain, Latin America, and all other participating nations, presents a host of chapters still to be written.

The constant and thorough review of the manuscript at all stages of completion by Professor Erickson and by Professor Donald L. Kemmerer, also of the University of Illinois, proved tremendously valuable. Professor Frank Freidel of Harvard read the entire manuscript and offered valuable suggestions. Major General John R. Deane, author of *Strange Alliance* (New York,

1947), head of the military mission in Russia during much of World War II, read and commented upon the entire work. These men have materially contributed a great deal, and I cannot fully express my indebtedness to them. In addition, many others, including Elizabeth Drewry at Hyde Park and E. Taylor Parks of the State Department, deserve greater mention and thanks than space permits. I, however, still remain responsible for all errors of fact or judgment.

ROBERT HUHN JONES

Cleveland, Ohio
January 9, 1969

CONTENTS

Foreword by Edgar L. Erickson   *page* *vii*

Preface   *xiii*

ONE   A Garden Hose for the Spreading Fire   3

TWO   Russia's Reverses and Lend-Lease   33

THREE   Moscow Protocol to Master Agreement   70

FOUR   Icebergs and Submarines   97

FIVE   The Washington Protocol   114

SIX   No Easy Road to Russia   139

SEVEN   The Last Two Protocols   165

EIGHT   The Arctic, Allah, and ALSIB   188

NINE   Wheels, Wings, Wrenches, and Wheat   215

TEN   Soviet and American Viewpoints and
        "End-Lease"   240

ELEVEN What Ever Happened to the Garden Hose?   263

Appendix A: Tables

   I. Lend-Lease Shipments to the Soviet Union by
       Time Period, Cargo Type, Route, and Tonnage   272

   II. Aircraft Deliveries to the Soviet Union (by route),
       June 22, 1941–September 20, 1945   277

III.   Aircraft Deliveries to the Soviet Union (by type
       and route), June 22, 1941–Sept. 20, 1945   278

IV.   Vehicles Delivered to the Soviet Union Under the
       Lend-Lease Program   280

V.   Random Exports to the Soviet Union Under the
       Lend-Lease Program   283

VI.   Distribution of Tonnage by Ship Registry (Vessels
       involved in the transfer of Lend-Lease to the
       Soviet Union), June 22, 1941–Sept. 20, 1945   290

VII.   Cargo Shipped from the Western Hemisphere to
       the Soviet Union, June 22, 1941–Sept. 20, 1945   290

VIII. Possible Wartime Uses of Inorganic and Organic
       Chemicals Lend-Leased to Russia in Largest
       Quantities   291

Appendix B: Atomic Espionage and Lend-Lease   293

Appendix C: Chronology of Events   296

Bibliography   303

Index   317

MAPS

The War at a Glance, 1941, and Map 67

Routes to Russia 83

Convoy Routes to North Russia 101

Persian Gulf Routes to Russia 141

The War at a Glance, 1942, and Map 148

Flight Delivery of Aircraft to Russia 157

The War at a Glance, 1943, and Map 190

War at a Glance, 1944–1945, and Maps 198

THE ROADS TO RUSSIA
United States Lend-Lease to the Soviet Union

CHAPTER ONE

A Garden Hose for the Spreading Fire

In 1939, Americans watched the Nazi swastika's somber shadow lengthen across uneasy Europe. It covered Czechoslovakia in March and moved darkly toward Danzig and the Polish Corridor. By 1939 a new and sinister meaning shaded international relationships. Nazi Germany, Fascist Italy, and their Oriental counterpart, militaristic Japan, laughed at international law. They respected only brute strength, treaties became mere paper scraps, and democracy, freedom, and morality became grisly jokes. Through perverted propaganda, their paranoic leaders built powerful and determined combinations and sought world domination as their goal. To such a nightmarish end had Europe come in the twenty-five years since World War I began.

By allying themselves with the Poles, Britain and France at long last sought to stop Germany's mad Führer before he digested Poland as he had Austria and Czechoslovakia. Spurning an alliance with Russia, British and French leaders lost the initiative. The Soviets, suspicious of Western Europe, concluded a nonaggression pact with the Nazis instead. Signed on August 23, 1939, this Russo-German pact in fact isolated luckless Poland. Immediately Adolf Hitler stepped up his barrage of vituperation against the Poles. Then on September 1 he unleashed his Nazi legions, who swept Poland from the map in three weeks. By September 3 the war had spread to Britain and France, as the Germans spurned Anglo-French ultimatums to withdraw from Poland. From the East, with less fanfare but according

3

to Nazi-Soviet agreement, the Russians completed another modern partition of Poland. In the United States on September 5, President Franklin D. Roosevelt invoked his nation's Neutrality Act against the belligerents.

In the autumn and winter of 1939 the belligerents bellowed at each other from the safety of the Maginot and Siegfried lines during a period of relative inaction that Western Europe and the world called the *Sitzkrieg* or the "Phony War." But in Eastern Europe on November 30, 1939, war followed Finland's refusal to cede strategic territory and conclude a mutual assistance pact with the Soviet Union. The valorous Finns commanded American sympathy as they skillfully defended their homeland against Russia. The United States Treasury, prodded by the President, set aside Finland's semiannual debt installment; Congress later voted a moratorium on the account. Congress approved a $10,000,000 loan to the Finns and authorized the Export-Import Bank to extend $20,000,000 more credit, all for nonmilitary supplies. Finnish fighters desperately needed war material at this time, but America was determined not to compromise her neutrality. The United States further demonstrated its distaste for Soviet aggression as Congress nearly severed relations with Russia, appropriating funds for the upkeep of the United States Embassy by three slender votes. The Soviet exhibit at the New York World's Fair, so popular in 1939, vanished in 1940. The League of Nations, emasculated and dying, expelled Russia from membership.

The armistice of March 12, 1940, concluded this first Russo-Finnish episode. Then, as winter warmed to spring in Western Europe, the German war machine roared to life and in a short time crushed Denmark, Norway, Holland, Belgium, and Luxembourg. The French, their Maginot line flanked and pierced, crumbled. The British Expeditionary Force in Belgium and France, cut off and pinned against the Channel, fantastically and heroically escaped to England, but their arms remained on Dunkirk's beaches. On June 10, 1940, the Italian army attacked southern France, and seven days later the French sued for peace. "The bloodthirsty little guttersnipe," as Winston Churchill tagged Hitler, reigned supreme in fortress Europe. During August and September, 1940, under a hail of Nazi bombs, the British girded as best they could for the expected German invasion.

In the East, with the Finns at bay, the Soviets turned to the strategic Baltic states of Estonia, Latvia, and Lithuania. In June, 1940, while the attention of an astonished world fastened on the French collapse, Russia absorbed these three tiny nations. The United States and Great Britain protested vainly. Completing their shield by conquest, Russia next forced Rumania to yield up Bessarabia and northern Bukovina. Hitler and Joseph Stalin, distrustful of each other, partitioned Europe between them. Although Hitler seemed the immediate menace in American eyes, Stalin won no popularity contests.

For almost a year after Poland's division and the spread of war in Europe, the United States sought to walk the tightrope of neutrality and to keep the conflagration from its hemisphere. Haltingly it stepped up its own defenses. By May, 1940, regular-army strength increased to 245,000, the National Guard to 235,-000. The navy kept its main fleet in the Pacific as a warning to restless Japan, but also instituted an Atlantic "neutrality patrol." Circumscribed by the Neutrality Act as amended in November, 1939, the United States could not directly aid the Western allies other than to sell munitions for cash to any who could come and get them and carry them away. To conserve their limited dollar funds, Britain and France at first purchased cautiously. They ordered mostly machine tools and aircraft, sought to build up their own facilities, and considered the United States only as an emergency and reserve supply source. The volume of foreign orders remained small throughout 1939 and early 1940 but served as a stimulus to the American munitions industry.[1]

When the "Phony War" came to a swift and terrible end in

[1] Richard M. Leighton and Robert W. Coakley, *Global Logistics and Strategy, 1940–1943*, 29. Hereafter cited as *Global Logistics*.

5

May, 1940, defensive-minded American military strategists prepared the "Pot of Gold" plan to counter any Axis move toward
Brazil and Latin America. They also drafted the "Rainbow 4"
plan for hemispheric defense, based on the assumption that the
United States and Canada alone would have to face the combined power of Germany, Italy, and Japan. Six weeks prior to
his approval of "Rainbow 4," President Franklin D. Roosevelt,
on June 10, 1940, condemned Italy for its aggression against
France, and also pledged that "in our unity" the United States
would "extend to the opponents of force the material resources
of this nation" with "full speed ahead." In addition, he dedicated
American resources for "any emergency and every defense."[2]

With France blitzed into submission, Britain remained the
only significant "opponent of force" still in the field. American
army planners, including General George C. Marshall, considered Britain's plight hopeless. They believed England would
have to make peace or become the next Wehrmacht victim. It
also seemed possible that Japan would invade Indo-China, perhaps first attacking Hawaii or the Panama Canal and perhaps
allying herself with the Soviets. To army experts, "Rainbow 4"
and the projected defense build-up for it appeared vitally urgent. These officers cautioned Roosevelt to subordinate British
aid to United States rearmament.[3]

Meanwhile, on May 28, Roosevelt revived the Advisory Commission to the Council on National Defense, inactive since 1918,
which began the tremendous task of economic mobilization.
Congress voted funds to swell the size of the army and provide
seacoast defense, aircraft, and other items, so that by October
the entire scope of defense funds reached $17,500,000,000. By
the end of the summer United States authorities federalized the
organized reserve and the National Guard and instituted the first

[2] Department of State, *Peace and War: United States Foreign Policy 1931–
1941*, 548–49; for the substance of the "Pot of Gold" and "Rainbow 4" war
plans, see Leighton and Coakley, *Global Logistics*, 28.
[3] Mark Skinner Watson, *Chief of Staff: Prewar Plans and Preparations*, 108–11;
Leighton and Coakley, *Global Logistics*, 28.

peacetime draft in United States history. Roosevelt approved army plans for a 1,400,000 man force by July, 1941, and also the great Munitions Program of June 30, 1940, necessary to equip the projected army. With their Protective Mobilization Plan, the army envisioned a build-up of equipment and reserve supplies for 2,000,000 men by the end of 1941. Planners hoped the airplane industry would turn out 18,000 planes a year so that the air forces, by the spring of 1942, would be fifty-four combat groups (12,000 aircraft) strong. Beyond these immediate goals, strategists sought to create sufficient productive capacity to equip and support a future army of four million. To supplement the army and air forces, Congress, on July 19, 1940, proposed to build a two-ocean navy, roughly double its existing strength.[4]

This great mobilization activity existed, in 1940, largely on paper. In addition, it was not the all-out effort that the military had asked. Faced with political reality, the President held back regardless of personal feelings. He refused army requests to put the munitions industry to work on an accelerated basis (the army asked for longer hours and three shifts); he hesitated to begin complete mobilization; and he firmly insisted upon continuing all possible aid to Britain. In the face of Marshall's advice to the contrary, Roosevelt directed acceptance of British munitions orders even if they conflicted with the rearmament effort. The President's calculated risk proved correct in the long run. In July, Britain neutralized the bulk of the French navy (and with it any immediate Nazi hope of German naval expansion evaporated), and in mid-September the Royal Air Force wrested control of Britain's air space from the Luftwaffe (minimizing the immediate menace of German invasion). American army tacticians hastily revised their estimate of the situation and by the end of September came up with the cautious notion

---

[4] Civilian Production Administration, Bureau of Demobilization, *Minutes of the Advisory Commission to the Council of National Defense*, iii. Hereafter cited as *Minutes of the Advisory Commission*. Watson, *Chief of Staff*, 166–82; Leighton and Coakley, *Global Logistics*, 29.

that England might hold out for at least six months. Army experts conceded aid to Britain might possibly be considered as "a long-term investment in American security."[5]

When Britain and France first began to buy war supplies in America, the War and Navy departments designed procedures to co-ordinate their purchases. The President, however, desired to control the limited-aid program himself and established the President's Liaison Committee as the controlling body. The Treasury Department, in turn, influenced the committee, as Roosevelt knew it would. So it was by design that Treasury Secretary Henry L. Morgenthau, Jr., close personal friend of Arthur B. Purvis, the Canadian who headed the Anglo-French Purchasing Board, played a leading role in a foreign aid supply. If this represented a bypass of the War Department, Secretary of War Henry Woodring's outspoken isolationism was a cause.[6]

The President's Liaison Committee functioned in routine and unexciting fashion until the Blitzkrieg rocked Europe in the spring of 1940. Overnight the situation changed, and French and British aid appeals became frantic. When France fell, the British Purchasing Commission supplanted the Anglo-French Board and absorbed all French contracts. The greatly accelerated purchasing activity made new controls necessary. On June 28, 1940, Congress gave the President authority to establish priorities for army and navy orders above all others. On October 21, 1940, Roosevelt delegated this authority to a newly established priorities board within the Advisory Commission to the Council of National Defense. Thus in 1940 the British-aid question divided itself into two parts—what could be given immediately from United States army stocks and what could be planned on a long-term basis.[7]

---

[5] Watson, *Chief of Staff*, 110–13; Leighton and Coakley, *Global Logistics*, 29–30.

[6] Leighton and Coakley, *Global Logistics*, 30–31.

[7] Winston S. Churchill, *Their Finest Hour*, 23–25; Edward R. Stettinius, Jr., *Lend-Lease, Weapon for Victory*, 31–32; *Minutes of the Advisory Commission*, 104; Leighton and Coakley, *Global Logistics*, 32.

In March, 1940, army officials had drawn up what they considered a fairly extensive list of obsolescent stocks that could be turned over to Latin-American and European neutral nations without retarding rearmament. On March 12 the War and State secretaries agreed that the surplus could be sold directly to neutral governments, but not to an intermediary who would be in a position to resell to belligerents and hold the administration open to a charge of violating the neutrality laws. In May, Roosevelt reversed this policy in spite of Woodring's objections. On June 11, 1940, he invoked the provisions of a 1917 law and made possible the government sale of federal surplus equipment to the United States Steel Export Corporation, which on the same day and at the same price resold the material to Great Britain. The inventory included five times as many Enfield rifles as had been on the army's March list, three times as many 75-mm. guns plus mortars, revolvers, Browning automatic rifles, and ammunition for all. The object was to arm England's Home Guard and the troops extricated from Dunkirk. As a separate transaction the army traded ninety-three light bombers back to the manufacturer to deliver as part of a British contract; the navy followed suit with fifty dive bombers. The American armed services did not favor any further transfers, but Roosevelt kept the door open. On June 28, Congress provided the only check on the executive by requiring certification of materials as surplus by the chief of staff. Even so, the United States transferred more equipment to Great Britain. By February, 1941, the total number of rifles sent numbered over one million. American troops in training went short, but the deprivations were not considered serious.[8]

These army stocks obviously put the British in a stronger position to resist invasion. Also the trade, announced September 3, 1940, of fifty over-age but serviceable United States destroyers for Atlantic bases bolstered water communication, on which

[8] Watson, *Chief of Staff*, 309–12; Leighton and Coakley, *Global Logistics*, 33–34; Stettinius, *Lend-Lease*, 24–29.

British survival depended. Although these were not strictly neutral acts by the United States, the public accepted them as risks necessary to prevent the collapse of Great Britain. At the same time the public may not have realized the surplus transfers to be only stopgap measures, for Britain could hardly win the war or continue to fight indefinitely without continuing support from the United States. Thus the United States, while not moving to war, stretched its fabric of neutrality as far as possible without tearing it.

During the summer and fall of 1940 the presidential campaign competed with the European war and American mobilization for newspaper headlines. In June, Roosevelt appointed two leading Republicans to his cabinet, Frank Knox to the Navy post and Henry L. Stimson to the War post, to the chagrin of their party. In addition, the isolationist wing of the Republican party lost control of the convention, which nominated Wendell Willkie, an internationalist, for president. In July the Democrats called upon Roosevelt for a third term. Although the candidates differed sharply on domestic affairs, their foreign policy statements were quite similar. Both promised aid to those resisting aggression and pledged abstention from foreign wars. Willkie approved the destroyer-for-bases deal even though a sizable segment of his party did not. Willkie polled an impressive popular vote, but the nation gave an overwhelming electoral victory to Roosevelt. His office secure for another four years, Roosevelt proceeded with aid to Britain.

On August 2, 1940, Interior Secretary Harold Ickes wrote Roosevelt, "It seems to me that we Americans are like the householder who refuses to lend or sell his fire extinguishers to help put out the fire in the house that is right next door although that house is all ablaze." At a meeting with the Defense Advisory Commission in the late summer of 1940, Roosevelt suggested leasing ships to Great Britain for the duration of the war rather than selling such vessels outright. At a November 8 cabinet meeting after the election, Roosevelt repeated his idea in greater detail. He reported that British accounts were dangerously short of dollars, although they could still liquidate about $2,500,000,-000 in credit and property. The time would come, Roosevelt observed, when Britain would need loans or credit or both to continue to obtain war supplies. The United States could meet the situation by leasing supplies to England. "He thought that we could lease ships or any other property that was loanable, returnable, and insurable. It seemed to me," Ickes remarked, "that this was a very good suggestion."[9] By the end of 1940 the British financial situation had deteriorated rapidly. Something had to be done or the aid program would come to a halt. On December 8, Churchill, only too well aware of the dilemma, dispatched a lengthy memorandum to the President. The eloquent British war leader told Roosevelt that he did not believe the people of the United States wanted to see Britain "stripped to the bone." Setting down in detail a program of need, Churchill asked Roosevelt to consider his letter not an appeal but a "statement of minimum action necessary to achieve our common purpose."[10]

Roosevelt received Churchill's message on board the U.S.S. *Tuscaloosa*, as he relaxed and fished in the blue Caribbean. Lean and sickly Harry Hopkins, the only guest along outside of the President's immediate staff, revealed the profound effect of this letter on Roosevelt. Some time between December 12 and 16, Roosevelt came up with his Lend-Lease idea, although, Hopkins observed, he did not know how to accomplish it legally. While the *Tuscaloosa* cruised on its leisurely way, Edward R. Stettinius, Jr., William S. Knudsen, Donald Nelson, Knox, and Secretary of State Cordell Hull bustled to Stimson's Washington

[9] Stettinius, *Lend-Lease*, 62; Ickes also gave British aid a good deal of thought and may have been the source from which Roosevelt drew his Lend-Lease idea; see Roosevelt Library, President's Secretary's File II, Box 21, letter Ickes to Roosevelt, Aug. 2, 1940, and Harold L. Ickes, *The Lowering Clouds, 1939–1941* (Vol. III of *The Secret Diary of Harold L. Ickes.*), 367.

[10] Churchill, *Their Finest Hour*, 566–67. The full text of Churchill's letter may be found on 558–67.

home. The Secretary of War called the meeting to ask these officials for their help in mobilizing the thinking of the American people for a great production effort. To Stettinius, Knudsen, and Nelson went the important job of explaining both America's and Britain's needs to the business world. With W. Averell Harriman, William L. Batt, John Biggers, and other businessmen, they immediately set to work to arrange meetings with United States Chamber of Commerce officials and other business organizations. Independent of the President, a well-timed campaign began to emphasize the President's decision to broaden aid to Britain.[11]

Upon ending his vacation on December 17, rested and refreshed, with his old assurance returned, Roosevelt lunched at the White House with Morgenthau and some British guests. He told the assembled company that, so far as aid to England was concerned, "the thing to do is to get away from the dollar sign." He did not want to put help "in terms of dollars or loans." We ought to increase production, Roosevelt told them, with a wave of his long cigarette holder, and then say to England, "We will give you the guns and the ships you need, provided that when the war is over you will return to us in kind the guns and ships we have loaned to you."[12]

Shortly after, Roosevelt advised a White House press conference that America's best defense was Britain's success in defending herself. So, the President asked the reporters, why should we not do everything we can to help her? Why should the United States be bound by the traditional means of finance, such as loans? Why should we not lease supplies to Britain? "Now," drawled Roosevelt, "what I am trying to do is to eliminate the dollar sign. That is something brand new in the thoughts of everybody in this room, I think—get rid of the silly, foolish, old dollar sign." Then with the homely analogy of "suppose my

[11] Robert E. Sherwood, *Roosevelt and Hopkins: An Intimate History*, 222–24; Stettinius, *Lend-Lease*, 63.

[12] Morgenthau diary, reprinted in William L. Langer and S. Everett Gleason, *The Undeclared War, 1940–1941*, 238.

neighbor's home catches fire, and I have a length of garden hose," the President presented the case for Lend-Lease. Few Americans thought there could be very much danger in lending their garden hose to the British, who stood heroically alone. Probably very few thought they would ever get the hose back, but it seemed a simple solution. Robert E. Sherwood believed Roosevelt won the fight for Lend-Lease right then.[13]

While Stettinius and others brought home to American business the need to step up production and the public thought over the "garden hose" idea reported in their papers, Roosevelt readied himself to bring his case directly to the people. As American citizens gathered around their radios on December 29 to listen to another in the President's series of fireside chats, Londoners recoiled from one of the heaviest bombings of the war. It seemed that Hitler intended to punctuate the address for Roosevelt. The phrase "Arsenal of Democracy" had been used previously in a newspaper editorial, but the President made it famous that evening. The United States had to be the great Arsenal of Democracy. Roosevelt admitted it was risky, but the alternative was to submit docilely to an Axis victory and be attacked later on. From this arsenal, aid must flow abroad— aid in increasing amounts. Labor and capital would have to cooperate to boost defense production. On January 6, 1941, the President used the State of the Union message to put the matter before Congress. First to the press, then the people, then Congress, Roosevelt developed the role the United States must play. Americans became well aware of Britain's dollar exhaustion, the peril to her war effort and American security, and the need to turn British orders into American orders through the elimination of the dollar sign.[14]

By January, 1941, public opinion in the United States sup-

[13] Roosevelt Library, Press Conferences, Vol. 16, Box 236, 353–55; Sherwood, *Roosevelt and Hopkins*, 225.
[14] Sherwood, *Roosevelt and Hopkins*, 226, 228; Langer and Gleason, *The Undeclared War*, 249, 252–53; Raymond H. Dawson, *The Decision to Aid Russia, 1941*, 8.

13

ported aid to Great Britain even at the hazard of war, but it also opposed entry into war. On December 30, 1940, Senator Burton K. Wheeler, the noted isolationist, went on the air in an attempt to counteract the positive effect of the President's fireside address. Wheeler's reply was harsh and negative without producing a positive program. White House mail clearly supported the Greenville, Texas, man who advised Roosevelt to "put Wheeler behind bars as a Nazi agitator." Along with other extreme isolationist elements, Wheeler proved to be out of touch with grass-roots sentiment. What disturbed Wheeler and his friends was not only the dangerous aid program but also the notion that the President was thinking of a combined effort with other enemies of the Axis as well. The idea of an "Arsenal of Democracy" certainly implied more than just British aid. In the previous year Roosevelt had pledged aid to the "opponents of force." The United States had taken steps to become a not-so-very-neutral partner of the Allies.[15]

Even before the State of the Union address, Roosevelt assigned Treasury Department officials the task of writing a Lend-Lease bill, largely because of their thorough knowledge of Britain's financial position. On January 2, after a meeting with Morgenthau and representatives of the British Purchasing Commission, Edward H. Foley, Morgenthau's general counsel, and Foley's assistant, Oscar Cox, began work on the bill. The Secretary of the Treasury told his assistants to frame the bill to allow the President a free and open hand in the allocation of defense production. Roosevelt wanted to run the production machinery without always having to go through Congress, Morgenthau explained, and also the authority to determine compensation

---

[15] Roosevelt Library, President's Official File 4193, Box 5, Miscellaneous, telegram Harrison Stewart to Roosevelt, Dec. 31, 1940. Although the mail ran heavily in favor of Mr. Stewart's view, the other viewpoint is represented. From Kew Gardens, N. Y., Dec. 30, 1940, Mr. Lloyd Estenchied telegraphed, "Heed Senator Wheeler and stop plunging us toward war." See also Langer and Gleason, *The Undeclared War*, 250; Dawson, *The Decision*, 8.

for aid given. The idea was to make the Lend-Lease bill as broad as possible.[16]

Working feverishly, Foley and Cox finished one draft of the bill by midnight, January 2. On January 3 they conferred with War and State Department representatives, Speaker of the House Sam Rayburn, Justice Felix Frankfurter, and others. Frankfurter advised the writers not to delineate the President's powers and not to list the countries to be given aid. The Justice also proposed the title of the bill. At still another meeting on January 7, State Secretary Hull seconded Frankfurter on not specifying nations eligible for aid, "possibly having in mind the future problem of the Soviet Union." Final clearance came at the White House after a cabinet meeting on January 9. This was a strategy session as well, because besides the cabinet, various Senators and Representatives attended. They reached the unusual decision to have House and Senate majority leaders introduce the bill into Congress the next day. The bill dropped into the House hopper, by no coincidence whatever, in time to bear the dramatic number H.R. 1776.[17]

Sherwood, close to the administration, believed Roosevelt ran great political risk by asking Congress to pass such a revolutionary law. He, along with the administration up to this time, overestimated the influence of the isolationists. Senator Wheeler exemplified isolationist bitterness with his tasteless tart remark that Lend-Lease was Roosevelt's triple-A foreign policy, "it will plow under every fourth American boy." This stung the President, who castigated the statement as "the rottenest thing that has been said in public life in my generation." The customary tangle of Congressional hearings and debate followed for two months, but there was not much doubt of the bill's passage in the House. Debate centered largely on the sweeping powers

[16] Langer and Gleason, *The Undeclared War*, 254–55; Sherwood, *Roosevelt and Hopkins*, 228.

[17] Langer and Gleason, *The Undeclared War*, 256–58.

granted to the President and lack of restriction on eligibility for aid. Former presidential candidate Willkie urged only that Congress specify what nations might be aided. Although the possibility seemed remote at the time, debaters both in Congress and out expressed—in vain—a desire to exclude Soviet Russia from any benefits. In the end the act passed the House, 260–165, and the Senate, 60–31, in almost the form that the President asked. At ten minutes past four on the afternoon of March 11, 1941, Roosevelt put his signature on the document.[18]

According to Public Law 11, the Lend-Lease Act, in the interest of national security the President could authorize his agents to manufacture or procure any article for any nation whose defense he deemed vital to the defense of the United States. Defense items were broadly defined so that food and other non-military supplies could be included. The President could transfer such items on his own terms to the countries in need. The act, which would expire in two years, required the President to report quarterly to Congress on the operations of Lend-Lease. It was not to be construed as authorization for convoy of the supplies. Congress retained the right to withdraw the delegated powers by concurrent resolution. Transfer of defense articles under previous procurement acts could not be made under Lend-Lease in excess of $1,300,000,000, and such exchange had to be approved by either the chief of staff or the chief of naval operations or both. This "billion three" clause formed the basis for most of the aid in the first few months even though Congress appropriated $7,000,000,000 on March 27, 1941. Passage of the act could not provide instant aid; it would take time to convert good intentions into factories, ships, planes, tanks, and guns.[19]

After the act passed, the Republican minority closed ranks in

[18] *Ibid.*, 259, 275, 280, 283–84; Sherwood, *Roosevelt and Hopkins*, 264; Stettinius, *Lend-Lease*, 82.

[19] U.S. President, *First Report Under the Act of March 11, 1941* (*Lend-Lease*) 1–2, 19–23. Hereafter cited as *First Report on Lend-Lease, Second Report on Lend-Lease, Third Report on Lend-Lease*, etc.

support. Congressman Joseph Martin and Senator Arthur Vandenberg, who had fought against the act, spoke for most of the minority as they pledged their co-operation. "It is now our fixed foreign policy whether we like it or not," Vandenberg wrote on March 19. "We have no alternative except to go along unless . . . H.R. 1776 is used by the President in a fashion which is not short of war." Vandenberg's son commented that his father, in the spring of 1941, felt "only a miracle" would keep America at peace; therefore, "unity at home was essential in the face of world crisis." Only a few die-hards, led by Senators Wheeler and Gerald Nye, continued to fight. On March 14 at the annual White House correspondents' dinner, Roosevelt declared: "Yes, the decisions of our democracy may be slowly arrived at. But when that decision is made, it is proclaimed . . . with the voice of one hundred and thirty millions. . . . And the world is no longer left in doubt." Telegrams and letters in the White House mail confirmed Roosevelt's stand. To Churchill, amid exploding bombs in London, the passage of Lend-Lease came as a welcome relief. He later wrote, "This was at once a comfort and a spur. The stuff was coming."[20]

Within three hours after he signed the Lend-Lease Act, Roosevelt issued two directives to put the program into motion. The first came as no surprise. It declared the defense of Great Britain vital to the defense of the United States; the second accomplished the same thing for Greece. As if defiant of this American move, Hitler launched his spring offensive. Bulgaria joined the Axis on March 2; by April 6 the ruthless Nazis stormed into Yugoslavia, while their panzers rolled across the simmering sands of Libya to penetrate Egypt by April 14. On April 23 ancient Athens trembled under the boots of yet another con-

[20] Arthur H. Vandenberg, Jr. (ed.), *The Private Papers of Senator Vandenberg*, 11–12; Langer and Gleason, *The Undeclared War*, 284; Winston S. Churchill, *The Grand Alliance*, 128; Roosevelt Library, President's Official File 4193, Box 4, Miscellaneous, March 10, 1941. Calculation showed 935 letters in favor of Lend-Lease and 120 against, an unusually high proportion of favorable letters.

queror. In the West on March 25, Hitler extended the North Atlantic war zone to include Iceland and the entire ocean westward to the coast of Greenland. German battle cruisers, *Scharnhorst* and *Gneisenau*, slipped past the British Home Fleet and destroyed 115,000 tons of Allied shipping in less than two months. In addition, "wolf packs" of Nazi submarines preyed upon North Atlantic shipping, sending down record tonnages in April, May, and June. The total number of ships lost from January through the end of May reached 569 British and Allied, plus twenty-five neutral vessels, or a total of 594. Between April 1 and 10, Roosevelt met his military and civilian advisers daily. Roosevelt knew that Lend-Lease made sense only if it reached Britain; therefore, everything possible that the United States could do to insure delivery had to be done. Stimson advocated that the United States convoy Lend-Lease aid to Britain, but the President was unwilling to go that far. Out of these meetings came the decision announced April 7 to reinforce U.S. bases at Newfoundland, Bermuda, and Trinidad, and that on April 10 to put Greenland under our protection and to remove the Red Sea from the list of combat areas forbidden to our shipping. Also on April 10, Roosevelt decided to extend the Neutrality Zone eastward to longitude 25 west. "I want to tell you," Roosevelt cabled Churchill on April 11, ". . . [that] the United States Government proposes to extend the security zone and patrol area." The idea, Stimson remembered, was to "patrol and follow the convoys" and to "notify the British warships" of enemy movements. The country's resources and climate of opinion, the President felt, would allow him to go no further at that time.[21]

Although this did not provide for actual convoys, it became clear that Americans intended to implement Lend-Lease to the brink of war. If Roosevelt moved with relative speed to assure

[21] Stettinius, *Lend-Lease*, 89; Frederick C. Lane with Blanche D. Coll, Gerald J. Fischer and David B. Tyler, *Ships for Victory: A History of the Shipbuilding Under the U.S. Maritime Commission in World War II*, 65 & n.; Churchill, *The Grand Alliance*, 782; Langer and Gleason, *The Undeclared War*, 421–35.

delivery, he moved more slowly to set up effective administering and operating procedures. On March 27 the President designated Hopkins as his Lend-Lease adviser but did not confer a title, such as administrator, on him. Hopkins, however, performed that function throughout the war. "In one huge area of authority," his friend Sherwood wrote, Hopkins was "the *de facto* Deputy President." Certainly few men so close to the President had greater knowledge of the problems involved. Back in January, Hopkins had suppressed his fear of flight in order to visit the Prime Minister and report firsthand on conditions in England. Hopkins dined often with Churchill and spent several weekends (huddled in an overcoat against the cold) at Chequers, the Prime Minister's country estate. He absorbed much information about Britain's military situation and returned to the United States just after the Lend-Lease Act passed. With this new dimension added to Hopkins' administrative experience of the 1930's, his familiarity with government operation, and his unquestioned personal loyalty to the President, no wonder Roosevelt chose Hopkins for the Lend-Lease job.[22]

To maintain accounts and reports and to be a central clearing house of information and a channel for the agencies participating in the Lend-Lease program, Roosevelt, on May 2, 1941, established the Division of Defense Aid Reports in the Office of Emergency Management. Although innocuously tucked away within another agency and called a "report" division, this office took up where the President's Liaison Committee left off and directed the entire Lend-Lease program. Since no new procurement systems were set up, Lend-Lease operated through a va-

[22] Bureau of the Budget, *The United States at War*, 49; Sherwood, *Roosevelt and Hopkins*, 230–60, 267. Morgenthau, on February 20, suggested that the secretaries of war, navy, state, and treasury form an "All-Inclusive Defense Policy Board" to administer the Lend-Lease Act. On February 25, Roosevelt proposed to the secretaries involved that they act as an "advisory committee" under Hopkins' chairmanship. This group never actually functioned. See Roosevelt Library, President's Secretary's File, Box 32, Morgenthau to Roosevelt, Feb. 20, 1941, and Roosevelt to secretaries of war, navy, state, and treasury, February 25, 1941.

riety of agencies. The War and Navy departments purchased war material; the Maritime Commission built and repaired ships; the Department of Agriculture procured food and other agricultural products; the Treasury Department obtained raw materials and industrial equipment. As Stettinius remarked with considerable understatement, "The Lend-Lease program cut across the entire war effort. It was intimately involved with our foreign policy, our defense production, our military policy, our naval policy, and our food policy."[23]

Foreign governments eligible for Lend-Lease sent their agents to confer with the military and technical officers of the United States department or agency best qualified to deal with the specifics of their purchasing program. For its part, the War Department established the Division of Defense Aid in the Under Secretary of War's office and also the Defense Aid Requirements Committees, which included foreign officers. The Division received foreign requisitions and transmitted them to Hopkins' Division of Defense Aid Reports, which then forwarded them to the appropriate procurement agency for study. Items transferred from current stocks or contracts let before March 11 required presidential assent; purchasing agencies might let new defense contracts, but final disposition still needed Roosevelt's approval.[24]

On May 6, 1941, Roosevelt named Major General James H. Burns to the post of executive officer of the Division of Defense Aid Reports. Burns, "an . . . officer of vision and ability" had served on the President's Liaison Committee that handled aid problems prior to May 2. Burns brought with him the two Brigadier Generals Spalding, Sidney P. (chief of the production di-

---

[23] *First Report on Lend-Lease*, 26; Stettinius, *Lend-Lease*, 95.

[24] *First Report on Lend-Lease*, 15–16, 27–29. War Department responsibility later shifted to the International Division of the Army Service Forces. The navy created a Lend-Lease liaison office; the Treasury Department expanded its Procurement Division; the Department of Agriculture greatly enlarged the staff of the director of Food Distribution. Procedures did not differ as greatly for the others as for the War Department.

vision) and George R. (in charge of storage and shipping). Burns remained on the staff of Under Secretary of War Robert P. Patterson and thus remained in direct touch with the War Department's procurement program. Though titleless, presidential assistant Hopkins ran Lend-Lease with the help of Oscar Cox (counsel) and Philip Young (general improviser), whom he brought into the Division of Defense Aid Reports from the Treasury Department. The staff, housed in the Federal Reserve Building, remained small compared with other Washington agencies. Ordinarily careless and untidy, Hopkins now submitted himself and his staff to strict security regulations.[25]

The Division set to work to convert the $1,300,000,000 from previous appropriations and the $7,000,000,000 Lend-Lease fund into defense aid for foreign countries, primarily to Great Britain. Foreign missions attempted to conduct their business directly with Hopkins, which disturbed Hull's State Department. Greater friction occurred following the appointment of Harriman as expediter of Lend-Lease in London with the rank of minister. John G. Winant, as ambassador, outranked Harriman, but Harriman had the ear of Downing Street. This meant that Churchill, through Harriman and Hopkins, enjoyed a direct and secure communications line to the President that short-circuited Hull's office.[26] It quickly became apparent that Roosevelt intended to keep Lend-Lease aid in his hands as he had British aid through the President's Liaison Committee. Not only the State Department but also the War Department soon came to understand that basic Lend-Lease decisions could be arrived at only through Hopkins and Roosevelt.

Although Lend-Lease presented no overwhelming difficulties at first, Hopkins' responsibilities soon became greater than ever before and weighed all the more heavily on him since his health was very poor. He resumed rigorous treatments, including

[25] *First Report on Lend-Lease*, 26; Stettinius, *Lend-Lease*, 95–96; Sherwood, *Roosevelt and Hopkins*, 279.

[26] Stettinius, *Lend-Lease*, 96; Sherwood, *Roosevelt and Hopkins*, 269.

transfusions and injections, just to stay alive. He conducted much of his business from his White House bed. Isador Lubin, an economic advisor to the President, frequently acted as Hopkins' eyes and ears, a practice continued throughout the war years. Industry's effort essentially to meet wartime production demands and keep the illusion that the United States was still at peace provided the greatest trouble for Lend-Lease and Hopkins. Business hesitated to convert to war production on the necessary scale. A few isolationist industrialists such as Henry Ford refused to fill war orders for Britain. Other entrepreneurs felt the war would be over soon because of German victories. And for all businesses, sales and production boomed. In 1941 the automobile industry reached an all-time high in civilian manufactures. The government could not compel industrialists to convert their plants or convince them to do so with satisfactory long-term contract guarantees. American businessmen faced an unreal problem of providing material for unknown millions of men, an unknown number of nations, and a war as yet only potentially theirs. Stoppages or strikes, partly the result of Communist efforts to sabotage the "imperialist's war," added to the serious production difficulties.[27]

Hopkins used his bedside telephone as a weapon to cut through and expose bottlenecks. Admiral Emory S. Land, head of the Maritime Commission, nicknamed Hopkins "Generalissimo of the Needle Brigade" because of his prodding to get things done. Hopkins' staff, Cox, Young, Lubin, Leon Henderson (director of Price Administration and Civilian Supply), Sidney Hillman, Robert Nathan, and Stacy May (from the Office of Production Management) joined Hopkins in the prodding.

[27] Sherwood, *Roosevelt and Hopkins*, 280–81; *The United States at War*, 60–61. For a dramatic example of Lubin's pinch-hitting for Hopkins during the war, see the rosters of those present at War Production Board Meetings, January 1942–October 1945; Civilian Production Administration, *Minutes of the War Production Board*, hereafter cited as *W.P.B. Minutes*. On Communist strike activity, see, in addition to Sherwood, Richard J. Purcell, *Labor Policies of the National Defense Advisory Commission and the Office of Production Management, May 1940–April 1942*, 174–75.

They all believed that United States industry could achieve the impossible—a high level of war production necessary for the "Arsenal of Democracy." At the same time Hopkins needled Roosevelt for bold action to speed up and insure the arrival of aid to Britain.[28]

To the battle cruisers *Scharnhorst* and *Gneisenau* and the cruiser *Hipper,* poised at Brest, and to the active undersea fleet, Hitler, in mid-May, added a new and terrible threat to the Atlantic life line. The formidable battleship *Bismarck,* accompanied by the new cruiser *Prinz Eugen,* under cover of rain and overcast, slipped out of Norway's Bergen Fjord and ran through Denmark Strait into the North Atlantic. His Majesty's Navy gave chase, and lost the British battle cruiser *Hood* in the process. Obviously, until the turbulent Atlantic was cleared of the German navy above and below the water, help for Britain was only a gamble. Out of the warm Mediterranean skies above the island of Crete, hundreds of German paratroopers came to conquer, handing Britain another serious reverse. Jolted by mounting British losses, the sinking of the American freighter *Robin Moor,* and U-boat attacks on American destroyers, Roosevelt's cabinet joined Hopkins to urge the President to safeguard more effectively the Atlantic highway to Great Britain. America had cleared legal pathways to provide material help, but a determined belligerent stood astride the geographic pathways.[29]

The President hesitated to go any further. He postponed for thirteen days a radio address scheduled for Pan American Day, May 14. Perhaps Roosevelt delayed because of persistent isolationist attacks throughout the Spring that accused him of courting war in the Atlantic. On May 27 the *Bismarck* was finally sunk, but the *Prinz Eugen* escaped to Brest. Communist pickets, denouncing the imperialist war, plodded up and down in front of the White House, and the President went on the air at last.

---

[28] Sherwood, *Roosevelt and Hopkins,* 282, 287–88.

[29] Churchill, *The Grand Alliance,* 305–20; Langer and Gleason, *The Undeclared War,* 456.

Within the White House, Latin-American ambassadors, perspiring in black-tie attire, gingerly settled on the little gilded chairs in the East Room. Technicians fussed with the radio apparatus; newsreelmen and reporters closed in from around the sides of the room. Then Roosevelt, outwardly poised and serious, settled behind the desk and spoke to 85,000,000 radio listeners as well as the audience before him. For three-quarters of an hour America listened. "We shall give," he promised, "every possible assistance to Britain and to all who . . . are resisting Hitlerism . . . with force of arms. Our patrols are helping now to insure delivery of the needed supplies. . . . All additional measures necessary to deliver the goods will be taken. Any and all further methods, or combination of methods, which can or should be utilized, are being devised. . . ." And then, to emphasize the seriousness of the situation, the President informed his auditors, "I have tonight issued a proclamation that an unlimited national emergency exists and requires the strengthening of our defense to the extreme limit of our national power and authority." The public response was generally favorable, but when Roosevelt held a press conference the next day, he anticlimactically brushed aside the idea that the United States would convoy supplies to Great Britain. He had guaranteed the safety of the North Atlantic supply line, but over a month passed before he gave effective orders to that end. On July 11, Roosevelt quietly issued the order to convoy American and Icelandic shipping.[30]

On June 2, Adolf Hitler met his Axis partner Benito Mussolini in a conference at Brenner Pass. The world wondered, Sherwood observed, "what new terrors were being hatched." No invasion signs appeared along the Channel coast, but observers reported large German concentrations in eastern Poland. Early

[30] Sherwood, *Roosevelt and Hopkins*, 296–98; Langer and Gleason, *The Undeclared War*, 456–61; S. Shepard Jones and Denys P. Meyers (eds.), *Documents on American Foreign Relations*, Volume III, 55, 58, 765–75; Charles A. Beard, *President Roosevelt and the Coming of the War, 1941*, 106.

in June, Winant came home from Britain to report that the British could resist invasion, if it came, but "at the same time I . . . cannot see how the British Empire can defeat Germany without the help of God or Uncle Sam." Laurence Steinhardt, United States ambassador in Moscow, cabled that nearly all the wives of German and Italian diplomats had departed for home. Something big must be in the wind, Steinhardt implied, because one German official even sent home his inseparable companion, a pet dog, by special plane.[31]

The concentration of troops on the Russian border caused no surprise to British and American diplomats, or to the Kremlin, although Russia refused to admit any danger existed. The non-aggression pact between Germany and the Soviet Union contained no love, and other suitors for Russia's hand remained in the wings. Britain and Japan stood close by, and in the summer of 1940 the United States joined the group. All met with very little encouragement because the Kremlin believed that the capitalist world was divided—an advantageous situation that meant Soviet co-operation could be had only on Soviet terms. Britain and America wooed Russia because they recognized Nazi-Russian collaboration as only a temporary expediency, a factor relatively clear in their mutual distrust. On the other hand, only very chilly relations existed between the United States and Russia. The Nazi-Soviet accord, the Finnish war, the seizure of the Baltic states, and the generally unsatisfactory mutual relationship since 1917, superimposed upon the ideology of communism and world revolution, left Americans little reason to feel very warm toward the Soviets. In addition, under the terms of the Nazi-Soviet trade agreement, Russia supplied Germany with vitally needed commodities such as oil, which made it easier for Hitler to continue war against the Western powers. While some considered this as evidence of Russia's hostile intent, it was also true that the sooner such agreements could be termi-

[31] Sherwood, *Roosevelt and Hopkins*, 299–301.

nated, the greater relative advantage could be accrued to the Western world.[32]

So, without forgetting the nature of the Soviet Union or its distasteful course in Europe, diplomats moved to try *rapprochement* in order to neutralize Russia or even to ally her with the West. It seemed an uphill attempt at best, yet the harsh reality of the military situation in Europe in mid-1940 warranted the cautious step. The United States committed itself to the defeat of Hitler through physical aid to "opponents of aggression" as well as through aroused American and world public opinion. In this light Under Secretary of State Sumner Welles began a series of conversations with Soviet Ambassador Constantin Oumansky. But all did not go smoothly. Machine tools, worth $4,300,-000 and previously purchased by Amtorg (Soviet trading company in the United States), posed a stumbling block because the United States refused to release them for export. The American rearmament program required vital machine tools, but Oumansky suggested political discrimination against Russia as the real reason for export prohibition. With the talks stalled near the end of 1940, Welles and Hull tried another move. They decided to remove the moral embargo placed on the Soviet Union at the time of the Finnish war, hoping this might clear the diplomatic air. Roosevelt agreed to the action, provided it would be given no publicity. The gesture did not satisfy Oumansky, characterized by Hull as a very difficult diplomat who "had an infallible faculty for antagonizing those of us with whom he came in contact." Oumanky insisted on a public announcement and, in addition, strongly urged the United States to recognize Soviet absorption of the Baltic States. Welles could not concede on the Baltic issue but gave in on the matter of publicity. On January 9 he asked Roosevelt to permit a formal announcement of the embargo's removal, and the President reluctantly consented.[33]

[32] Langer and Gleason, *The Undeclared War*, 358; Dawson, *The Decision*, 15–16; Sumner Welles, *The Time for Decision*, 168–69.

[33] For full accounts of the conversations between Under Secretary of State Sumner Welles and Soviet Ambassador Constantin Oumansky (or Umansky) up

On January 10, 1941, Moscow negotiated a new trade agreement with Berlin but presumably attempted to offset this in Anglo-American circles with an Oumansky report of increased Soviet aid to China and a slap at Japanese expansion plans in Asia. In addition, the Kremlin announced, on January 12, its distress over German action in Bulgaria. Following these statements, Welles notified Russia on January 21 that the December, 1939, moral embargo on shipments of aircraft, aircraft-construction material, and aviation-gasoline patent processes to Russia had been cancelled. In practice the step meant little because the Munitions Control Board, established in November, 1939, and the Export Control Act of 1940 assumed regulation of the previously banned commodities. Hull claimed the end of the embargo to be a significant psychological step, but it had no visible effect on Oumansky. Welles tried unsuccessfully to secure a partial release of machine tools. In order to perpetuate the impasse, the Kremlin insisted upon United States recognition of the Sovietization of the Baltic States. Vyacheslav Molotov, Soviet commissar of foreign affairs, insisted upon such recognition, and Oumansky told Welles that it would continue as a factor in their conversations.[34]

Meanwhile Britain complained that American exports to Russia found their way to Germany, a charge Oumansky denied and used to accuse the United States of discriminating against Russia in Britain's favor. Welles applied to various defense agencies in the United States for the release of materials ordered by the Soviets. These agencies, however, also feared retransfer

to the time of the German attack on Russia, see *Foreign Relations of the United States, Diplomatic Papers, 1940*, Vol. III, 244–441, and *Foreign Relations of the United States, Diplomatic Papers, 1941*, Vol. I, 667–764, hereafter cited as *Foreign Relations*, with year and volume number. Dawson, *The Decision*, 16; on scarcity of machine tools in the U.S., see *Minutes of the Advisory Commission*, 89, 111–12; Roosevelt Library, President's Secretary's File, II, Box 21, bulletin to Roosevelt, July 7, 1941.

[34] *Foreign Relations, 1941*, I, 118–20 (see also reference for conversations in n. 33, above); Dawson, *The Decision*, 17; Murray Salisbury Stedman, Jr., *Federal Arms Exports Administration, 1935–1945*, 23, 139–40; *United States at War*, 32; Langer and Gleason, *The Undeclared War*, 338–39.

of the equipment to Germany. The Under Secretary's efforts to obtain priority for Amtorg's orders and to secure their release seemed to be in vain. The Welles-Oumansky talks continued on their stormy way even though they were roundly criticized in the United States. Secretaries Ickes and Morgenthau lacked confidence in Welles and believed he had not tried hard enough to make friends with Russia. "It is incomprehensible to me," Ickes said, "that we should not make every effort to be on as friendly terms as possible with Russia. This is especially so now. . . . At the rate we are going, if England should fall, the United States won't have a friend in the world." Other Americans believed Roosevelt's administration had gone too far. The Un-American Activities Committee branded Moscow as an enemy of freedom as ruthless as Germany and accused the Soviets of being a financial front for the Axis in the United States. Senators and Representatives alike denounced the removal of the moral embargo. Segments of the press agreed on the grounds that the policy was inconsistent with all aid to Britain. Since the moral embargo's end came just as the Lend-Lease Act was under discussion, it gave point to fears of Russia's inclusion.[35] Nevertheless, since the administration sought Soviet friendship, however expediently, a specific denial of aid to the Soviet Union in the pending Lend-Lease bill would only have further damaged the effort. Finally, on April 11, the State Department established a general policy to allow export of finished articles not needed in the defense program or by a government receiving Lend-Lease assistance. This neither solved Welles's problem nor smoothed his path with Oumansky.[36]

At the same time, rumors of an impending German attack on Russia circulated quite freely in Europe. If the Kremlin suspected something of the sort, it gave no hint. Moscow stepped up wheat deliveries to Germany and pushed Far Eastern rubber

[35] *Foreign Relations, 1941*, I, 713, 715; Langer and Gleason, *The Undeclared War*, 340–41; Dawson, *The Decision*, 19–21; Ickes, *The Lowering Clouds*, 340–41.

[36] *Foreign Relations, 1941*, I, 737–39.

over the Trans-Siberian railroad to Berlin. They even abandoned their pro-Yugoslav course in the face of Nazi displeasure. As early as February 6, 1941, the United States minister to Rumania concluded that evidence pointed to "an early war between Germany and Russia." Sam E. Woods, United States commercial attaché in Berlin, learned of Nazi discussions of an attack on the Soviets as early as the summer of 1940. In January, 1941, a friend inside the Nazi government passed to Woods, in the darkness of a German theater, a copy of Hitler's directive No. 21. This document described Hitler's preparations for "Operation Barbarossa," the invasion of Russia. Even while the Lend-Lease bill was under debate, American officials knew the Nazi-Soviet accord would crumble.[37]

Although authorized to do so on March 1, Steinhardt declined to pass this information to Foreign Commissar Molotov in Moscow. Steinhardt feared the Soviets would consider it an Anglo-American plot to pull Russia into the war on their side, or that it would cause Russian appeasement at the expense of Turkey or Finland or both or would throw Berlin and Moscow closer together. Welles, after consulting Roosevelt and Hull, told Oumansky of Hitler's plans on March 1 in Washington. "Mr. Oumansky turned very white," Welles observed. "He was silent for a moment." Then he thanked Welles and told him of Russia's gratitude. For a time it seemed as if the diplomatic scene would brighten. By the end of March, Oumansky indicated the Soviet apprehension of Germany to Welles, belittled the trade difficulties that plagued Russian-American conversations, and observed that the United States and the Soviet Union shared

---

[37] *Foreign Relations, 1941*, I, gives ample evidence of the war rumors. For example, from Finnish sources, 2–3; Swedish, 133–34; Rumanian, 129–30; and Germany, 134–35, 139–40, 148, 151; the same source also illustrates Soviet "all's well" attitude, 123–24, 135–36, 141, 147, 148–49. Nevertheless, there were evidences of some Russian preparedness for the German attack (same source), 133–34, 136; movement of Russian troops and equipment westward from the Far East, 145–46, 150–51. See also Molotov's statement to Hull, June 3, 1942, in *Foreign Relations, 1942*, III, 587; Cordell Hull, *The Memoirs of Cordell Hull*, 967–68; Langer and Gleason, *The Undeclared War*, 334, 336–37.

long-range policy aims. By April the wind from the Kremlin blew cool again, although Oumansky pressed for an economic agreement and foreign policy understandings. He let Welles know the basis would be recognition of the Baltic States as part of Russia. Then on April 13, Moscow concluded a neutrality pact with Japan; the Kremlin desired to avoid a two-front war.[38]

The American public, unaware of the pending Nazi invasion of Russia, reacted against the Japanese-Soviet pact. Many citizens interpreted this as a green light for Japan in Asia. Others, including some isolationist congressmen, saw in it a defeat for Hitler. But in the terms Steinhardt predicted, *Pravda* announced on April 20 that the treaty foiled an Anglo-American attempt to embroil Russia in war. In May, Soviet-American relations were set back further when American defense officials requisitioned additional industrial equipment bought and paid for by Amtorg. Oumansky accused the United States of hostile intentions. Britain too experienced difficulty in her attempt to woo Russia. Like the United States, London had warned Moscow of German intentions but had received no reply. In early June, Great Britain offered assistance to Russia in case of Nazi invasion. The Kremlin replied that the gesture would have been more welcome if preceded by Britain's recognition of the Baltic States' fate.[39] On this point at least, the Kremlin followed a consistent policy.

The American State Department was worried that Churchill, in his effort to reach an understanding with the Soviet Union, would modify his position on the Baltic States. The British as-

[38] *Foreign Relations, 1941*, I, 713–14; Dawson, *The Decision*, 48, 49, 50, 51; Welles, *Time for Decision*, 170–71; Langer and Gleason, *The Undeclared War*, 337, 354, 357.

[39] See references in n. 37, above, and Dawson, *The Decision*, 52–55; Langer and Gleason, *The Undeclared War*, 529; Churchill, *The Grand Alliance*, 360. Tass, the Soviet News Agency, reported on June 14, 1941, that the British and foreign press were responsible for false rumors of a pending German attack on the U.S.S.R. "Rumors that Germany intends to break the [non-aggression] pact and attack the U.S.S.R. have no grounds whatsoever." Quoted from *Pravda*, June 1941, p. 1.

sured American officials that they would hold firm, but at the same time appealed to the United States to adopt a policy of Soviet aid when the attack came. The State Department coolly replied, "We are making no approaches. . . . We treat them [Russia] with reserve. . . . We will not sacrifice any principles." On June 10, Hull requested Russia to recall two of their military attachés as *personae non grata,* but Oumansky successfully protested; on June 14 the United States froze all assets of Continental European powers, including the Soviet Union, to which Oumansky unsuccessfully objected. On June 21 the State Department's Division of European Affairs proclaimed that if Germany invaded Russia, the United States planned to relax Soviet export restrictions, but only so far as it would not imperil the defense program or aid to Great Britain. The policy statement continued with the observation that if Russia fought Germany, it would not mean they either defended or adhered to principles of international relations supported by the United States. In contrast to the aloofness of the State Department, the more flexible Roosevelt instructed Winant to inform Churchill that America would second any declaration of alliance with the Soviet Union that the Prime Minister might make if Russia were attacked. Thus, Anglo-American agreement over Russia existed only at the top. In Britain, Churchill answered a reporter's query of how an ardent anti-communist such as he could support Russia, with the terse statement that "if Hitler invaded Hell I would at least make a favorable reference to the Devil in the House of Commons."[40]

In Moscow on June 20, Steinhardt received a cable from Washington that advised him to evacuate all American citizens from Russia. On June 21 a United States diplomatic official traveling east to Vladivostok observed between 200 and 220 westbound trains, of twenty-five cars each, partially loaded with troops and

---

[40] *Foreign Relations, 1941,* I, 150, 621–22, 623–24, 629, 761, 764, 766–67; Dawson, *The Decision,* 59–61; Langer and Gleason, *The Undeclared War,* 530–31; *United States at War,* 66; Churchill, *The Grand Alliance,* 369.

army supplies. The same day, Nikita S. Khrushchev, Ukrainian Communist party leader, lifted the phone in his Kiev office to hear Stalin alert him that the Nazis might begin military operations against Russia the next day, June 22.[41]

In the waning hours of Saturday evening, June 21, American short-wave radios crackled with reports of the German attack. Halfway across the world in the gray dawn of June 22, Hitler's panzers pushed eastward into Russia from the Polish partition line. Simultaneously the Luftwaffe surprised and destroyed a large part of the Soviet air force before it could get in the air. At 5:30 A.M. Berlin summer time, Joseph Goebbels brayed Hitler's proclamation of the attacks to the German people to convince them that this new action countered the threat of a "Bolshevik Anglo-Saxon plot" of "Jewish Anglo-Saxon warmongers." As usual, the assault involved no declaration of war. In England the Prime Minister slept through the early news but made a broadcast over the B.B.C. that evening. In the United States on Sunday, Robert Sherwood attended a "Fight for Freedom" rally at the Golden Gate Ballroom in Harlem. As he entered the hall, he crossed the lines of Communist pickets whose placards condemned the Fight for Freedom warmongers as tools of Anglo-American imperialism. When he left an hour and a half later, the pickets were gone. Sherwood assumed the party line had changed, and the *Daily Worker* confirmed his opinion on Monday when it suddenly became pro-British, pro-Lend-Lease, pro-interventionist, and, for the first time in years, pro-Roosevelt.[42]

[41] *Foreign Relations, 1941*, 150–51; Milovan Djilas, *Conversations with Stalin*, 123. Khrushchev chose either to forget or dismiss this conversation when he addressed the Twentieth Congress of the Communist Party of the Soviet Union on February 25, 1956—see Columbia University, Russian Institute, *The Anti-Stalin Campaign and International Communism, A Selection of Documents*, 44–49.

[42] *Foreign Relations, 1941*, I, 151, 152, 154; Churchill, *The Grand Alliance*, 369–71; Sherwood, *Roosevelt and Hopkins*, 303.

CHAPTER TWO

Russia's Reverses and Lend-Lease

Berliners, at first shocked and apprehensive at Hitler's Napoleonic enterprise, nevertheless convinced themselves that victory in the East would be theirs within a reasonable time. Across the narrow, choppy Channel, embattled Englishmen gathered around their radios at nine o'clock on Sunday evening to hear the B.B.C. broadcast the Prime Minister's address. Churchill's deep growl greeted them with determination and hope. "We have but one aim. . . . We are resolved to destroy Hitler. . . . From this nothing will turn us," he reminded his people. "Any man or state who fights on against Nazidom will have our aid. . . . That is our policy. . . . It follows . . . that we shall give whatever help we can to Russia. . . . We shall appeal," Churchill emphasized, in a gesture aimed across the Atlantic, "to all our friends and allies . . . to take the same course. . . . The Russian danger is . . . our danger, and the danger of the United States. . . . Let us . . . strike with united strength."[1]

Also on Sunday, from New York to Los Angeles, excited newsmen broadcast the word of Hitler's latest venture to an astonished America. On Monday, June 23, Acting Secretary of State Welles gave the press a cool and reserved formal statement. "To the people of the United States . . . principles and doctrines of communist dictatorship are as intolerable . . . as are the principles . . . of Nazi dictatorship. Neither kind of imposed overlordship," the communique continued, "can have . . . any sup-

[1] *Foreign Relations, 1941*, I, 153; Churchill, *The Grand Alliance*, 372–73.

port . . . in the mode of life . . . of the American people." Nevertheless, in conclusion, it was "the opinion of this government . . . that any defense against Hitlerism . . . from whatever source . . . will . . . redound to the benefit of our own defense and security." Roosevelt had penciled the last line on the draft: "Hitler's armies are today the chief dangers of the Americas." It contained no clear promise of Russian aid but only reflected the State Department's policy announced two days earlier.[2]

Impatient with Roosevelt and the State Department for their caution, Ickes threw a bouquet to Churchill, who "did much to direct our own public opinion and policy so far as Russia was concerned." Ickes added, "If Churchill, the British Conservative . . . could say a kind word for Stalin and Russia at such a moment, surely we should not be over-critical." Hull, at home ill, phoned Roosevelt, Welles and State Department officials to tell them, "We must give Russia all aid to the hilt. We have repeatedly said we will give all the help we can to any nation resisting the Axis. There can be no doubt for a moment that Russia comes within that category." Stimson called the Nazi attack a "providential occurrence." He saw a chance to win the war in the Atlantic while the Germans diverted their strength eastward. Knox agreed that the Nazis provided the United States with an opportunity to "deliver a smashing blow," to "clear a path across the Atlantic," and to deliver the weapons manufactured for Britain.[3]

Stimson and Knox disagreed with Hull and Ickes on the question of aid. Along with the General Staff, they thought Russia would be unable to contain Hitler, although Russian resistance would provide a temporary breather in the West. Scarce and valuable equipment, hastily sent to the Soviet Union, might fall into Hitler's hands. Stimson and Knox argued instead for un-

---

[2] *Foreign Relations, 1941*, I, 767–68; Dawson, *The Decision*, 118–19.

[3] Roosevelt Library, President's Secretary's File, II, Box 21, Knox to Roosevelt, June 23, 1941; Ickes, *The Lowering Clouds*, 549; Hull, *Memoirs*, 967; Dawson, *The Decision*, 116; Sherwood, *Roosevelt and Hopkins*, 303–304; Langer and Gleason, *The Undeclared War*, 537–39.

restricted aid to Britain as the most effective method of helping Russia. Outside cabinet circles, opinion divided into isolationist and interventionist camps. Former President Herbert Hoover thought that the Nazi attack on Russia provided "one-half a dozen more reasons for the United States to stay out of the European war." Senator Wheeler told an America First rally that the new war was not an American one but the death struggle of nazism and communism. Although the isolationists wanted to remain aloof, many did sanction the British build-up as a defense measure. Interventionists disagreed over the extent of United States involvement but concurred with increased British support. The American public sympathized much less with the Soviet Union than with Britain but preferred a Russian victory to a Nazi one; Americans detested communism, but did not fear Soviet power. Germany remained the key threat.[4]

Tuesday, June 24, at a White House press conference reporters pressed Roosevelt to comment on Monday's formal statement. Flashing his old smile, the President indicated that the statement covered the situation. "Of course," he added with a grin, "we are going to give all the aid that we possibly can to Russia." He immediately qualified this with, "We have not yet received any specific list of things," and when we do, "it will probably be a list of such a character that you can't just go around to Mr. Garfinckel's and fill the order and take it away with you." Besides, he reminded the newsmen, Britain had priority on American arms production. When a reporter asked if the Russians would be included in Lend-Lease, Roosevelt replied that he did not know. He parried a question from another reporter who wanted to know if the defense of the Soviet Union was essential to the defense of the United States.[5]

Although the official statement contained no evidence that Roosevelt would keep his earlier pledge to Churchill, his re-

[4] Dawson, *The Decision*, 68–85, 100–101; Leighton and Coakley, *Global Logistics*, 97, 129.

[5] Roosevelt Library, President's Press Conferences, Box 237, Vol. 17, #750, June 24, 1941, 4:00 P.M., 408–10.

marks at the press conference made it clear he would. On Tuesday the President thawed recently frozen Soviet assets of $40,-000,000 and on Wednesday decided not to apply the provisions of the Neutrality Act to Russia. In addition to the cash-and-carry provisions of the act as amended in 1939, it was up to the President to "find" when a war existed. Since Germany had not formally bothered to declare war on Russia, the President used this legal loophole to allow United States shipping to continue to call at Russian ports not in previously defined European combat zones. In so doing Roosevelt kept Vladivostok open to American shipping. None of these actions committed the United States to anything specific but indicated at least a degree of American moral support. Along with the press conference statements, the gestures provided a test of American public reaction to Russian support. On June 26, Oumansky visited Welles, expressed Soviet satisfaction with American good will, and informed the Acting Secretary of State that as yet his government had not instructed him on the aid matter. On June 27, Oumansky, with Andrei Gromyko, then Soviet embassy counselor, called on Assistant Secretary of State Dean Acheson and reported Amtorg's distress with the slow processing of export permits. Acheson informed them that Charles Curtis, Jr., special assistant to the under secretary of state, headed a new purchasing organization to process their applications. Soviet military requests, Acheson explained, should be filed at Welles's office because they had to go through the President or his representatives. Oumansky, at least, should have felt that Soviet requests met with greater sympathy than before.[6]

On Sunday, June 29, one week after the Nazi war machine had rolled eastward, Steinhardt met Molotov in the Kremlin. The Commissar, smiling, assured Steinhardt that Russia under-

---

[6] Dawson, *The Decision*, 122; *Foreign Relations, 1941*, I, 768–73. The Curtis Committee, as of June 30, 1941, included representatives of the Division of Defense Aid Reports, the administrator of Export Control, the Office of Production Management, the Army and Navy Munitions Board, and when necessary, the Maritime Commission.

stood and appreciated the American attitude. Since Oumansky had reported that the United States was sympathetic, the Kremlin sent him their first schedule of requirements. As if to challenge Steinhardt, Molotov expressed skepticism that the United States could meet Russia's requests. On Monday, June 30, Oumansky delivered the Soviet order to Welles. It included anti-aircraft guns, fighter planes, short-range bombers, anti-tank guns, aircraft factory equipment, cracking plants for aviation gasoline, tire-manufacturing machinery, light-alloy rolling mills, and the like. Oumansky also expressed a desire for credit and not Lend-Lease. The State Department considered Russian emphasis on manufacturing equipment as a good omen. It appeared that the Soviets planned to fight on even if they lost industrial western Russia.[7]

Welles asked the Russians for a more complete analysis of their requests. During the following week the Soviets complied, and their program, as processed by Curtis' committee for the July 18 cabinet meeting, totaled $1,836,507,823. Most urgently needed were three thousand bombers and three thousand fighters, anti-aircraft guns, toluol, aviation gasoline, and lubricants. The remainder, raw materials, machinery, and industrial plants, comprised only slightly more than $80,000,000. The committee recommended $15,680,000 worth of equipment for immediate shipment and an additional $172,119,000 within the next year. But $1,648,708,116 worth of military items, outside the committee's jurisdiction, remained for Presidential decision. The government immediately issued export licenses for $9,000,-000 worth of items.[8]

As Russian-American relations cleared, Oumansky renewed the diplomatic offensive for recognition of the conquest of the Baltic States. He first pressured Loy Henderson, the State Department's assistant chief of the Division of European Affairs,

[7] *Foreign Relations, 1941*, I, 774–75, 779–81; Langer and Gleason, *The Undeclared War*, 545.

[8] *Foreign Relations, 1941*, I, 788; Dawson, *The Decision*, 128–29, 131; Langer and Gleason, *The Undeclared War*, 545.

but Henderson would not yield. Oumansky's persistence on the Baltic issue, combined with Soviet-Polish discussions and with Finland's renewed war on Russia on June 25 (in retaliation for Russian bombings), worried the State Department. Some of the State Department policy makers believed that the Soviet Union intended to establish a sphere of influence that included Finland, the Baltic States, Poland, Czechoslovakia, Yugoslavia, and perhaps also Rumania, Bulgaria, and Hungary. They supposed the Baltic States would remain incorporated within the Soviet Union, a puppet ruler would head Finland, and the Soviets would in some way dominate the others. The State Department seriously considered these possibilities, and by August 1, department members decided to support the independence of the various states and leave boundaries for post-war settlement. They also recommended that the United States take an active part in post-war European reconstruction.[9] This attitude prevailed throughout the war and nettled Oumansky and his successors. It initiated the United States policy of postponing political questions until the end of the war and emphasized United States determination not to use war aid as a political lever.

Along with his resumption of the Baltic States question, Oumansky, more stridently than ever, resumed his complaints about the small quantity of American goods actually exported to Russia. The Russians also troubled American officials with their policy of keeping United States military observers or reporters from visiting combat areas. Welles took this matter up with Oumansky on June 26 and June 30, as did Henderson during a dinner with the Russians on July 1. They got nowhere. Even Stimson's plea for front-line observation went unheeded. In another area, State Department officials complained of Russian espionage, basing their conclusion on the Soviet request for specific secrets. The State Department decided that Russian inspectors at American war plants should be given only normal

[9] *Foreign Relations, 1941*, I, 784–85, and 785n.; Dawson, *The Decision*, 134–37; Langer and Gleason, *The Undeclared War*, 556–57.

privileges and denied military secrets since United States observers were denied access to Russian war zones.[10]

Roosevelt was neither as alarmed by Russian political goals as State Department experts were, nor was he as convinced as his military advisers that the Nazis would blitz the Soviet Union out of the war. The President listened closely to Joseph E. Davies, former ambassador to Russia, who was, in July, 1941, the Soviet's best friend in America.

Davies believed that the Germans might swallow the Ukraine and march into Moscow, but he also felt that Russia was capable of fighting on from behind the Urals if necessary. Davies did, however, fear a separate peace. Russian participation in the war presented the United States and Great Britain with a great opportunity if she could be kept in, or a great danger if she could not. Few American military men shared Davies' confidence in the power of the Soviet army or people. Davies lunched with Welles on July 7, met Hopkins at the White House on July 8, received Oumansky on July 9 and again talked with him at the Soviet Embassy on July 12, saw Welles again on July 15, visited with the President on July 16, and sent Hopkins a lengthy "Memorandum Regarding the Russian Situation" on July 18. Davies placed himself at the disposal of the Soviet Embassy, with Welles' concurrence, as a sort of unofficial liaison man. Davies told Welles, "Russia should receive every possible aid from this country and as speedily as possible," and he thought the Nazi-Soviet fight was "possibly a turning point of the war." By July, Steinhardt, usually cautious, partially shared Davies' optimism, and he telegraphed from Moscow (July 1, 2, and 3) his opinion that Stalin would not make a separate peace. On July 10 the doors of the White House opened to Oumansky for the first time since 1939. The Soviet Ambassador conversed with Roosevelt and Welles for forty-five minutes. Roosevelt told Oumansky that if the Soviets could hold on until October 1, winter

[10] *Foreign Relations, 1941*, I, 771, 781, 782, 789–90, 795–99; Henry L. Stimson and McGeorge Bundy, *On Active Service in Peace and War*, 526.

weather would tie the Nazis down and valuable time would be gained. He emphasized that United States aid depended upon a joint Anglo-American decision. The time gained would not only be useful for completing aid shipments but also for overcoming domestic opposition to Russian aid on the premise that perhaps it was even less likely that the United States would have to enter the war.[11]

From the practical political standpoint, aid to Russia seemed impossible. In July, Congress considered legislation designed to exclude Russia from Lend-Lease and to compel the United States to apply the Neutrality Act to the Soviet Union. In addition, some members of Congress feared that any sort of overt activity on the part of the United States, such as a naval convoy in the Atlantic, might draw the country into war. Isolationists successfully headed off Neutrality Act amendments aimed at allowing the President to arm merchant ships and send them into war zones. Lawmakers seriously debated extending the periods of National Guard and draftee service, and a proposal to use conscriptees outside the hemisphere drew such a bitter attack that it was withdrawn. In other words, much of the preparedness program hung by a thread as Roosevelt sought to aid Russia. The President authorized the occupation of Iceland as planned but retracted convoy orders before they could be carried out. Until Congress solved the political problems of rearmament, Roosevelt soft-pedaled aid to Russia, urgent as it was.[12]

Along with Congressional difficulties, there existed the formidable physical problem of actually getting aid to Russia. Each of the three main available routes was long and hazardous, and the shortest of the three, to Murmansk, was exposed to German action. The Persian Gulf route, from a military and logistical standpoint, seemed preferable, but it was as yet undeveloped. Vladivostok was the longest and most tedious and in-

[11] Joseph E. Davies, *Mission to Moscow*, 487–98; Langer and Gleason, *The Undeclared War*, 545–46; Dawson, *The Decision*, 142–43.

[12] Dawson, *The Decision*, 146–47.

volved the use of Japanese waters. Roosevelt could not rely upon overloaded British resources or the tiny Russian merchant marine. The acute problem of finding supplies in the United States was compounded by the demands of the rearmament program and commitments to Great Britain (which could not be met even then), China, the Netherlands East Indies, and others. In addition, so long as the Russians remained outside the scope of Lend-Lease, questions of priorities, financing requirements, and legal procedures for transfer of war material further confused the situation. Although Roosevelt was aware of these problems, he was unsatisfied with progress toward their solution. He was particularly vexed by the negative attitude of the executive agencies involved. The President informed Welles on July 9 that he wanted all aid possible sent to Russia by October 1. Welles suggested creating an American-British-Soviet commission to survey needs and decide matters of allocation. On July 11, Hopkins notified General Burns, executive officer of the Division of Defense Aids Reports, to get ready to take care of Soviet supply at the President's request. Burns, Young, and Sid Spalding agreed to set up a special section for the task. Spalding asked the White House to transfer his former military academy classmate, Colonel Philip R. Faymonville, to the Division of Defense Aid Reports to handle the job. Faymonville arrived on the scene on July 13, recruited Professor John N. Hazard to assist him, and set to work establishing the necessary office.[13]

Transfer of Soviet assistance to the Division, which also oversaw Lend-Lease, did not mean extension of that program to Russia, but it did mean that Soviet help was put into sympathetic hands more easily controlled by Roosevelt. On July 21, Roosevelt directed Burns to review Russian requirements and within forty-eight hours to report what items could be shipped immediately for delivery before October 1. Secretaries Stimson and Knox, along with Director General William S. Knudsen of the Office of Production Management, were requested to co-

[13] *Ibid.*, 149–52; Langer and Gleason, *The Undeclared War*, 559.

operate fully. At five in the afternoon the following day, officials met to consider the Russian list. They approved about $60,-000,000 out of the total request, which had now grown to $1,-856,000,000, but only $22,000,000 for shipment before October 1, 1941. The equipment and facilities proposed for immediate export included oil industry items, automobile-tire apparatus and plants, machine tools, wool, aviation gasoline, toluol, and the like. The group took no action on aircraft and ordnance supplies, which constituted the bulk of Soviet orders, because these did not fall within their jurisdiction. Roosevelt assented to the committee's proposals on July 23 and turned the list over to his military aide, Edwin M. ("Pa") Watson, on July 25 to clear through the War, State, and Navy Departments "by tonight." Final clearance came promptly, and Oumansky received the authorized export list on July 27. Items originally requested but not yet cleared were turned over to the Office of Production Management for further study. The total value of supplies approved for Russian delivery grew to almost $250,000,000 by September 1, still excluding aircraft and ordnance material.[14]

Meanwhile, Faymonville greeted the Soviet military mission that arrived in the United States on July 26. Headed by Lieutenant General Filipp R. Golikov, the mission, along with Oumansky, visited American officials and pointed out the importance of the Soviet front, the urgent need for supplies, and the necessity of co-ordination with Great Britain and the United States. Golikov's confidence in Russian military ability and his "attractive personality" helped offset Oumansky's talent for irritation. Among other things, Oumansky complained loudly about the delay in providing aircraft, but when it came to aircraft, even fast friends such as Britain encountered delivery difficulties. The War Department held tenaciously to the view that it could provide no bombers for Russia and probably no

[14] Dawson, *The Decision*, 152–55; Langer and Gleason, *The Undeclared War*, 559; Civilian Production Administration, Bureau of Demobilization, *Industrial Mobilization for War: History of the War Production Board and Predecessor Agencies, 1940–1945*, 130–31.

more than fifty fighters, over and above any Britain might contribute from American production destined for her.[15]

In the entire month of July, exports to Russia totaled only $6,521,912 in value, and for the period to October 1, the estimate of actual shipments read only $29,000,000, no more than a token contribution to Soviet defense. Outraged, Morgenthau told Roosevelt that the Russians were getting a typical Washington "run around." The President thought so too, and, in a forty-five-minute lecture to his cabinet on August 1, he pointed this out. As Morgenthau observed, Roosevelt said "he didn't want to hear what was on order, he said he wanted to hear what was on the water." Ickes wrote that Roosevelt gave the "State Department and the War Department one of the most complete dressings down that I have witnessed. . . . The President insisted that things must move at once." Roosevelt admonished, Ickes recalled, that "we must not permit such a situation to exist as a result of which Ambassador Oumansky or the Russian Military Mission would be in a position to cable Stalin that they could get no help or encouragement here," especially since Hopkins had just left London for Moscow.[16]

Stimson found the President's lecture aggravating inasmuch as the army was short of equipment for training purposes and not able to meet the British orders. The week before, Stimson had agreed to release to Russia 150 fighters already shipped to Britain and another 50 still in the United States but on a British order. Stimson naturally stood by the War Department's view. Along with Marshall and the army he intended no further releases from army stocks. Ickes sided with Roosevelt. "My own view" of the aid situation, he wrote, "is that we ought to come pretty close to stripping ourselves, if necessary, to supply England and Russia, because if these two countries between them

[15] T. H. Vail Motter, *The Persian Corridor and Aid to Russia*, 22; Langer and Gleason, *The Undeclared War*, 559.

[16] Langer and Gleason, *The Undeclared War*, 560; Ickes, *The Lowering Clouds*, 592–93; Elliott Roosevelt (ed.), *F.D.R., His Personal Letters, 1928–1945*, II, 1195.

can defeat Hitler, we will save immeasurably in men and money." As Stimson knew, even if such a move was desired, it would be difficult to implement. National defense and Lend-Lease priorities absorbed the nation's armament production. As for munitions already manufactured, most were produced under specific contracts made before Lend-Lease. The Lend-Lease law itself permitted transfers from this category to Lend-Lease recipients, but only up to $1,300,000,000. A nation not under Lend-Lease could not use this device. Surplus or obsolescent military materials certified by the chief of staff as nonessential to national defense could be released, but no surplus existed. Everything in that category had been turned over to Great Britain. Even if there was a way out of this dilemma, the large number of agencies involved in the production and supply program further complicated any move. No wonder Stimson remarked that the President had "no system. He goes haphazard and scatters responsibility among a lot of unco-ordinated men and consequently things are never done."[17]

Roosevelt obviously disagreed about the locus of the blame, for, impatient and desirous to "get things moving," he appointed yet another official. Wayne S. Coy, special assistant to the President and liaison officer with the Office of Emergency Management (in which the Division of Defense Aid Reports was located), took on the task of expediter of Soviet aid. On August 2, Roosevelt asked Coy to "please, with my full authority, use a heavy hand—act as a burr under the saddle and get things moving!" At the same time Roosevelt took Welles's earlier suggestion and appointed Hopkins, Oumansky, and Arthur Purvis as an intergovernmental committee on Russian aid. They held their first (and final) meeting on August 2, with Burns substituting for Hopkins. Also on August 2, Welles and Oumansky exchanged diplomatic notes that committed the United States to a formal policy of aid, replacing the previous unilateral declar-

17 Dawson, *The Decision*, 157–59; Langer and Gleason, *The Undeclared War*, 560–61, and discussion on 736–37; Ickes, *The Lowering Clouds*, 595.

ations of support. The American note began, "The United States has decided to give all economic assistance practicable for the purpose of strengthening the Soviet Union in its struggle against armed aggression." The aggressor who attacked the Soviet Union also threatened the security of "all other nations," therefore strengthening Russia "is in the interest of the national defense of the United States." The United States was extending to urgent Soviet orders "priority assistance upon the principles applicable to the orders of countries struggling against aggression," and also the Department of State was "issuing unlimited [export] licenses," while at the same time considering requests for American shipping facilities to expedite export to Russia. The Soviet note replied, through Oumansky, "My Government has directed me to express . . . its gratitude for the friendly decision . . . and its confidence that the economic assistance . . . will be of such scope and carried out with such expedition as to correspond with the magnitude of the military operations."[18] At last Oumansky had an agreement, assurance of unlimited export licenses, and even assurance of all possible shipping.

The news of this commitment, published a few days later, caused little public excitement. As expected, isolationist critics charged that the United States had now become one of the "allies of Bolshevism." By August of 1941, in spite of isolationist sentiment and apparent lack of public enthusiasm, American opinion seemed to support sale of war materials to Russia.[19]

Three weeks prior to the August 2 agreement with Russia, a chain of events had begun that culminated in Hopkins' flight to Moscow and the eventual inclusion of the Soviet Union in the Lend-Lease program. Friday evening, July 11, 1941, Roosevelt and Hopkins had met in the President's study and discussed the complicated problem of aid to Britain and Russia. The President, criticized at this time for "making haste slowly,"

[18] *Foreign Relations, 1941*, I, 815–17; Roosevelt, *F.D.R., Personal Letters*, Vol. II, 1195; Dawson, *The Decision*, 159; Langer and Gleason, *The Undeclared War*, 561–62; Stettinius, *Lend-Lease*, 124.

[19] Langer and Gleason, *The Undeclared War*, 562.

45

wanted to know how Russian aid and British aid could fit to-gether. Russian supply involved extending the convoy routes, an assignment the British could not assume without relief else-where. Much of the help sent to Russia would have to come from British orders. Faced with this situation, Roosevelt had to know specifics of British requirements, naval situation, and strategic planning. This was in addition to discussions planned for the President and the Prime Minister when they met in August. Roosevelt decided to send Hopkins, who got on well with Churchill and who was the President's "other self" in Lend-Lease matters, to London personally to find the answers.[20]

Events moved quickly from that point. On Saturday morning Hopkins breakfasted with Sidney Hillman and discussed pro-duction problems; at lunch Welles briefed him on the Russian supply situation; in the afternoon he conferred with Admiral Howard L. Vickery of the Maritime Commission and Burns of the Division of Defense Aid Reports on shipping and supply. Saturday evening Hopkins dined with British Ambassador Lord Halifax (Edward F. L. Wood). Early Sunday morning, Hopkins, who detested air travel, flew via Montreal to Gander, New-foundland, where he caught a Lend-Lease B-24 bomber for Prest-wick, Scotland. Although the flight made Hopkins very ill, he sought out the Prime Minister immediately upon arrival.[21]

Hopkins also conferred with Harriman, whose return to Lon-don from a tour of the Middle East was almost simultaneous with Hopkins' appearance. Harriman and other American mis-sion officers criticized British Middle-Eastern organization, re-porting a heavy demand for American technicians and frowning on British plans for an offensive there. They reasoned that Amer-ican equipment required for British success in this area might better be used in Russia. If some military men viewed the Rus-sian situation with greater hope, it was because the Red army

---

[20] Sherwood, *Roosevelt and Hopkins*, 308; Langer and Gleason, *The Un-declared War*, 563.

[21] Sherwood, *Roosevelt and Hopkins*, 308.

had by then held out for nearly a month, more than the minimum that British planners had believed possible. It looked also as if the minimum set by American military forecasters would soon be passed, with the Red army, even though falling back, still very much in the war. It began to seem more likely that if the Soviets could keep fighting until October, winter weather might slow the Nazis down and allow time to ease the critical supply situation. In order for America and Britain to determine distribution of munitions from the Arsenal of Democracy, they would have to have detailed information about the Russian military situation. A British military mission in Moscow could gather nothing helpful. Hopkins felt Roosevelt and Churchill, in their forthcoming Atlantic meeting, ought to have a clear appreciation of Russia's needs and potentials in order to make that part of their conversations meaningful. Though still very ill, Hopkins cabled Roosevelt on July 25 for permission to go to Russia and see Stalin himself.[22]

Late Saturday evening, July 26, while spending the week end at Chequers, Hopkins received Roosevelt's permission to go to Russia, and the President wired Hopkins a message to take along and hand to Stalin. Roosevelt requested Stalin to "treat Mr. Hopkins with the identical confidence you would feel if you were talking directly to me." Arrangements for Hopkins' departure were made with dispatch. As Hopkins strolled with Churchill across the well-manicured Chequers lawn toward Harriman's car, the Prime Minister asked Harry to tell Stalin "that Britain has but one ambition today, but one desire—to crush Hitler. Tell him that he can depend on us." As Hopkins climbed in to the auto, Churchill added, "Good-by—God bless you, Harry."[23]

A lone Royal Air Force Coastal Command PBY Catalina rose from Invergordon and disappeared into the sky. In the tail gunner section, wearing one of Churchill's Homburgs, rode Hop-

<hr>

[22] *Ibid.*, 309–18; Langer and Gleason, *The Undeclared War*, 563–64.

[23] Sherwood, *Roosevelt and Hopkins*, 318, 321; Langer and Gleason, *The Undeclared War*, 564; *Foreign Relations, 1941*, I, 797–98.

kins. Two United States Air Force officers, in addition to the British crew, accompanied him. The PBY flew relatively low and close to the Norwegian coast, easy prey for any German fighter. The journey was not a comfortable one for the ailing Hopkins. Disembarking at Archangel, the cold and tired visitor from America was greeted by the usual reception committee—representatives of the United States and British embassies, Russian army, navy, and air force officers, local commissars, and the secret police. Hopkins sighed with relief at the news that they would not be able to fly on to Moscow that night, because he wanted a chance to rest. That opportunity vanished, however, when the Russian admiral invited him to dinner on his yacht. The party lasted four hours, Hopkins reported, and the dinner was "monumental." The vodka, he exclaimed, "has authority. It is nothing for the amateur to trifle with." Later, he managed to get two hours of sleep.[24]

A Russian Douglas transport carried Hopkins to Moscow in four hours. Another reception committee, Steinhardt included, greeted him. Hopkins remarked that he shook as many hands as if he "were running for office." At Spasso House, the American Embassy, Hopkins conferred with Steinhardt. The Ambassador poured out a tale of diplomatic frustration caused by suspicious Soviet authorities who maintained a heavy veil of secrecy. After a restful night and a day of sightseeing around Moscow, Steinhardt drove Hopkins to the Kremlin to meet Stalin at 6:30 P.M.[25]

The Soviet dictator and the American official presented a study in physical contrast. Hopkins, lean, sallow, obviously unwell, but with sharp eyes and an even sharper mind, confronted the "austere, rugged, determined figure in boots that shone like mirrors, stout baggy trousers, and a snug-fitting blouse." Stalin, Hopkins decided, resembled a "football coach's dream of a tackle." In the first conversation, Hopkins asked what "Rus-

24 Roosevelt Library, President's Personal File 4096, Harry Hopkins, Hopkins to Roosevelt (telegram), July 27, 1941; Sherwood, *Roosevelt and Hopkins*, 323–26.
25 Sherwood, *Roosevelt and Hopkins*, 326–27.

sia would most require that the United States could deliver immediately, and . . . what would be Russia's requirements on the basis of a long war?" In the first category Stalin asked for about 20,000 anti-aircraft guns of from 20 to 37 mm. because of their rapid fire and mobility. About 2,000 pursuit planes could then be transferred from defense to attack duties. He also needed large-size machine guns for the defense of his cities and, if possible, a million or more rifles. In the second category the Soviet Union required aviation gasoline, aluminum for aircraft construction, and the other items mentioned on the list then in Washington. Stalin requested that supplies be sent via Archangel since the capacity of the Iranian route was too small and the distance to Vladivostok too great. At the conclusion of the meeting Stalin informed Hopkins that he would be available for consultation from six to seven every evening. Hopkins arranged to meet Molotov the next day and left to talk with Russian technical experts. The conference at the lower level disappointed Hopkins since none of the experts could comment on anything that had not been cleared by Stalin.[26]

On Thursday morning, July 31, Hopkins called on Britain's ambassador in Moscow, Sir (Richard) Stafford Cripps. Primarily they discussed the coming Roosevelt-Churchill meeting in its relation to Russia. They agreed that the Prime Minister and the President should ask Stalin to participate in a supply conference and drafted a tentative proposal for the two leaders to send to Stalin. That afternoon Hopkins and Steinhardt visited Molotov as previously arranged. Their discussion centered about the Far East and Japan. Molotov believed the United States ought to take a firmer attitude toward Japan (as Churchill also thought) in order to prevent further Nipponese expansion in Asia. At 6:30 P.M., Hopkins returned to the Kremlin alone for a three-hour session with Stalin.[27] As he spoke, Stalin wrote down

[26] *Ibid.*, 327–30, text of Hopkins' memo also in *Foreign Relations, 1941*, I, 802–805.

[27] Sherwood, *Roosevelt and Hopkins*, 331–33.

the four basic Russian needs: light anti-aircraft guns, aluminum, 50-caliber machine guns, and 30-caliber rifles.[28]

Stale smoke hung in clouds in the conference room as the two men talked, chain-smoked, and sampled each other's cigarettes. Hopkins impressed upon Stalin that the United States and Great Britain would do everything they possibly could to get supplies to the Soviet Union, but that they could not work miracles. That which the two nations could send immediately would have to be material already manufactured, and Hopkins observed that even this probably could not get to Russia before winter. Hopkins suggested that the three governments concerned hold a supply conference. Stalin indicated he would welcome such a conference, and Hopkins proposed it be held between October 1 and 15. Stalin agreed and then expressed the hope that the United States would come into the war against Germany because Britain and Russia alone would have great difficulty crushing Hitler. The Soviet leader suggested that perhaps a declaration of war alone, perhaps without even a shot fired, would turn the trick.[29]

In two brief sessions with the Communist dictator, Hopkins learned more about the Russian situation than anyone else had since the Nazis attacked. As Hopkins reported, Stalin talked "straight and hard." The Russian wasted neither words nor gestures and knew what he wanted. He asked clear, concise, and direct questions, which led Hopkins to confess, "I found myself replying as tersely." The visit to Moscow both elated and depressed Hopkins. Elated him because he hoped, as did others, that this meeting marked a turning point in war-time relations between the three states and because supply calculations would no longer have to be clouded by having to envisage Soviet defeat as imminent. At the same time, the totalitarian atmosphere

28 Sherwood, *Roosevelt and Hopkins*, 338–40.

29 *Ibid.*, 341–43. Text of this Hopkins' memo also in *Foreign Relations, 1941*, I, 805–14.

of Moscow depressed him. The obvious fear and respect that high-ranking officers had for Stalin and the immense concentration of power in the one man awed the frail Hopkins.[30]

Hopkins cabled Washington his confidence that the Russians would not collapse. Even Steinhardt confessed to having changed his mind and added that he believed Hopkins' visit "will prove to have exercised a most beneficial effect upon Soviet-American relations" and also "greatly encouraged the Soviet war effort." Hopkins' return to Britain resembled a scene from an old melodrama. He forgot his medicines and fell desperately ill. An unidentified destroyer fired on his plane. The angry waters of Scapa Flow buffeted the PBY upon landing. Only a deftly handled boat hook kept Hopkins from the sea as he sprawled aboard the slippery deck of an admiral's launch.[31] Finally the President's trouble shooter joined Churchill on the HMS *Prince of Wales,* which weighed anchor for a secret rendezvous with Roosevelt.

Meanwhile, harried Washington officials faced the complicated problem of financing Russian aid. While the United States defrosted Soviet assets, Russia still lacked enough dollars to meet the demands of their initial purchase requests. On July 30, Oumansky proposed that the American government grant Russia a five-year credit for payment of the orders it placed in the United States, believing then that a limited loan was preferable to Lend-Lease. Just why the Soviets wished to remain outside Lend-Lease is a matter of speculation, but perhaps they wanted to conduct their own purchasing operations, which they could not do under Lend-Lease. However, the idea of a loan to the Soviets was no more palatable to the adminstration than covering them with Lend-Lease because either way would require Congressional approval. If Roosevelt could not risk Con-

---

[30] Sherwood, *Roosevelt and Hopkins,* 343–45.

[31] *Ibid.,* 346–48; Langer and Gleason, *The Undeclared War,* 567; *Foreign Relations, 1941,* I, 814–15.

gressional blessings for a Lend-Lease program that included Russia, neither could he risk it for credit. Either method would take time to accomplish, and time was in short supply.[32]

Roosevelt's government pursued different courses of action. Morgenthau, on August 2, agreed to buy Russian gold at the legal price of $35 an ounce for one calendar year. Welles sought to implement United States purchase of critical and strategic raw materials from the Soviet Union. Discussion of the raw-material purchase operation began as early as July 7, and by July 28 the State Department sent the Soviet Embassy a list of commodities the United States would buy. The Administration also directed Jesse H. Jones, secretary of commerce and federal loan administrator, to investigate a possible loan from the Reconstruction Finance Corporation or one of its subsidiaries. Jones was willing to make a loan, but the legal question of collateral provided a stumbling block. By August 21, Jones was still unable to work out an agreement. On August 15, Morgenthau temporarily came to the rescue with a $10,000,000 advance against gold shipments, a fact kept secret for over a month.[33]

Oumansky met with Roosevelt at the White House on September 11. He informed the President that Russia needed $140,000,000 just to finance outstanding orders, but Amtorg had no such balance. Roosevelt repeated the political difficulties in the way of large credits, but at the same time assured Oumansky that the Soviet's immediate need would be met through a barter agreement. The next day, acting on Hopkins' suggestion, the President directed Jones to purchase from Amtorg up to $100,000,000 worth of manganese, chromite, asbestos, platinum, and other materials and to advance Amtorg $50,000,000 against the purchase. This agreement was quickly reached and scrupulously observed by the Soviets. As it turned out, the Defense

32 Dawson, *The Decision*, 163–66, 169; *Foreign Relations, 1941*, I, 780–81.
33 Dawson, *The Decision*, 169–71, 241–42.

Supplies Corporation of the Reconstruction Finance Corporation actually profited in the long run.[34]

Aboard the *Prince of Wales* in the North Atlantic, Churchill sped to his first meeting with Roosevelt. Hopkins wrote the reports of his Moscow trip and played backgammon with the Prime Minister during the uneventful journey. On Saturday, August 9, the British battleship arrived at its Argentia, Newfoundland, rendezvous with the USS *Augusta* and its distinguished passenger, the President. At dinner on the *Augusta*, Roosevelt, Welles, Harriman, Hopkins, and leading American military men discussed with Churchill and his staff Japanese aggression and the proposed joint declaration, later named the Atlantic Charter. The Americans, more interested in Lend-Lease priorities and production schedules as affected by the Russian front, disappointed the British, who hoped to talk strategy. However, Hopkins' news of Russia interested everyone. Churchill advocated a conference in Moscow for the rebuilding of the Russian armies, very much along the lines that Hopkins had discussed with Stalin. Churchill decided to name Lord Beaverbrook (William M. Artken), a famous journalist and minister of aircraft production, as his representative and assumed Hopkins would return to Moscow for Roosevelt. Lord Beaverbrook arrived at Argentia on Monday, August 11. Thanks to the Hopkins reports, there was virtually no Anglo-American disagreement on Russian aid. Therefore, the Hopkins-Cripps proposal for a conference was, with slight modification, delivered to Stalin by the American and British ambassadors on August 15.[35]

---

[34] *Ibid.*, 244–46; Roosevelt Library, President's Secretary's File, Russia, Box 14, memo, Hopkins to Roosevelt, September 5, 1941; Jesse H. Jones with Edward Angly, *Fifty Billion Dollars, My Thirteen Years with the RFC*, 381–83. A very important difficulty in Soviet-American relations was the religious problem, which, among other things, Roosevelt discussed with Oumansky on September 11. This was not the first time the U.S. advocated a softening of the Soviet attitude toward worship in the U.S.S.R. Dawson surveys this subject in detail: *The Decision*, 147–49, 230–38.

[35] Sherwood, *Roosevelt and Hopkins*, 349–59.

In effect, this joint message from the Anglo-American leaders pointed out to Stalin that the time had come to think of other things, if not actually ships and shoes and sealing-wax, at least a longer-term policy of aid. Roosevelt and Churchill asked Stalin "for a meeting to be held at Moscow, to . . . discuss these matters directly with you." The statement contained a pledge of American resources to a common three-power pool for the avowed purpose of Germany's defeat. It was the first joint declaration on Russian aid and the broadest American statement up to that time.[36]

Promises of aid appeared to pile up faster than aid itself. If finance presented such thorny problems for temporary patchwork short-term assistance, obviously only Lend-Lease could solve the long-term riddle. As the time drew near to ask Congress for a second Lend-Lease appropriation, it was not at all clear that such a bill would pass if Russia were included; in fact, the whole program might be imperiled. The isolationists in Congress remained opposed to Russian aid, but also there were "objections or hesitations" even among some New Dealers. If the Soviet Union were to be included in Lend-Lease, it would have to await the proper psychological moment. On July 8, 1941, Welles denied that Lend-Lease to Russia had been discussed; he repeated this statement on July 26; on July 30 he denied Hopkins' trip to Moscow had anything to do with Lend-Lease. Roosevelt, on August 1, told reporters that Russia was not a part of the Lend-Lease program. Concurrently with their technically correct denials, the government carefully fostered the impression that the Russians capably financed their own program, but it did not make public the true nature of that program.[37]

During July and August many Americans rejoiced that Hitler's blitz had been slowed down. The press played up Russia's heroic defense. Conservatives, then including *The New York Times*, argued that America's aid ought to be restricted to proven

[36] *Foreign Relations, 1941*, I, 822–23.
[37] *Ibid.*, 163–64, 167, 168.

friends such as Great Britain and China. At the same time others thought the Russian front might be America's salvation; if Russia remained in the war, the United States might not have to enter it. In late July and August, Congress debated this subject. While isolationists insisted that aid to Russia was aid to communism even in this country, their attack was not a concentrated one. Russian survival furnished them an excuse to work against American involvement, and their attention focused on the extension of the draft act. It seemed to them that the emergency receded with Russia in contention. This strategy nearly worked, for the House extended selective service by only one vote. The vote in the House came on August 12, the day the Atlantic Conference ended. British reaction mixed astonishment with wonder: "Americans are curious people. . . . One day they're announcing they'll guarantee freedom and fair play for everybody everywhere in the world. The next day they're deciding by only one vote that they'll go on having an army."[38]

Public opinion poll figures, though not an accurate measure, at least operated as a barometer of sorts. In July the Gallup poll indicated that 54 per cent of the American public opposed Russian aid, but by September those opposed registered only 44 per cent and those who favored Russian help rose to 49 per cent. As Hopkins wrote Brendan Bracken, British minister of information, shortly after Labor Day, "The American people don't take aid to Russia easily." Administration leaders were acutely aware of this; they knew the American public would probably come around to full support in time, but they were also aware that they did not have much time if Russia was to be kept in the war. Thus the administration's strategy was to keep the Russian aid program entirely separate from Lend-Lease. Roosevelt submitted a bill to Congress on September 18 for a second Lend-Lease appropriation of over $5,900,000,000. The day before, the government announced the $100,000,000 barter agreement with Russia, and also on September 18 the Treasury

[38] *Ibid.*, 185–92; Sherwood, *Roosevelt and Hopkins*, 367.

Department released news of the $10,000,000 advance against Soviet gold deliveries. Almost simultaneously Roosevelt clearly stated in the second report on Lend-Lease operations, "The Soviet Government's purchases here are being made with its own funds through its regular purchasing agency." Obviously, during the debates on the second Lend-Lease appropriation, the government intended the evidence to point to separate financing of Russian aid. They did not want Lend-Lease jeopardized by any assumption of Soviet inclusion.[39]

Beginning in August, Oumansky complained about the paucity of American assistance. With Golikov, Oumansky visited Ickes at his office on Wednesday afternoon, August 6, "commented sarcastically" on the limited amount of help made available. On the other hand, Office of Production Management Director Knudsen protested the release of 1,200 tons of aluminum and aircraft industry machine tools on the grounds that American bomber production would suffer. Oumansky's churlish disposition and chronic complaints coupled with United States production difficulties only served to impede the trickle to Russia. Roosevelt sent a memorandum on August 30 to both Stimson and Knox that outlined the result of Hopkins' Kremlin visit and informed the secretaries of the planned Moscow conference. "I deem it of paramount importance," Roosevelt wrote, "for the safety and security of America that all reasonable munitions help be provided for Russia . . . as long as she continues to fight the Axis powers effectively." Early assistance, the President noted, must come from production already provided for. With this in mind, he directed Stimson and Knox to submit within ten days a list of supplies that could be committed to Russia for delivery by June 30, 1942, so that British and American representatives could come to specific conclusions on the nature and scope of Soviet aid when they met with the Russians in Moscow.[40]

[39] Dawson, *The Decision*, 227–28; Sherwood, *Roosevelt and Hopkins*, 372; *Second Report on Lend-Lease*, iv.

This order to Stimson and Knox upset current War Department planning. By early July planners arrived at a figure of 20 per cent of monthly production for defense aid transfer, with 80 per cent reserved for a United States build-up until basic war plan requirements were filled. The War Department had informed Great Britain and China what they would receive up to June 30, 1942. The new Presidential directive required remaking defense aid schedules. The army proceeded to draft a new minimum requirements policy, largely at the expense of United States troops in training. Along with a reduction of scheduled deliveries to Great Britain, substantial allocation of materials to the Soviet Union became possible. Roosevelt received the new estimate list, which provided the basis for discussion at Moscow, on September 12. In a memorandum to Roosevelt, Stimson gave his opinion that Russia would have to be brought under Lend-Lease to facilitate transfer of the items on the billion-dollar estimate list. The administration was well aware of this stark reality as it tried to convince Congress that Russian aid was financed separately from Lend-Lease.[41]

As the summer sun shone on perspiring American leaders in Washington, bleak gray clouds hovered over Eastern Europe, and Nazi columns scored new successes. Soviet forces in the South withdrew across the Dnieper River in mid-August; farther north, German tanks rumbled through Smolensk on the way toward Moscow. Soviet armies remained intact, if in retreat, but Russian industrial potential shrunk nearly in half. The Anglo-American fear of the Russo-German negotiated peace, perhaps as a result of Communist political collapse brought about by continued Nazi success, again loomed as an awesome specter. From Moscow, Steinhardt urged increased Anglo-American sup-

[40] Roosevelt Library, President's Secretary's File, II, Box 21, Roosevelt memo to Stimson, August 30, 1941; Ickes, *The Lowering Clouds*, 595; Roosevelt, *F.D.R., Personal Letters*, II, 1201–1203; *Foreign Relations, 1941*, I, 826–27; Dawson, *The Decision*, 201–204.

[41] *Foreign Relations, 1941*, I, note 14, 848; Leighton and Coakley, *Global Logistics*, 92–99; Dawson, *The Decision*, 206–12, 217.

port to keep Russia in the war. On September 3, Stalin cabled Churchill a bleak picture of industrial losses, pleaded for a second front in the Balkans or France, and asked for aluminum, planes, and tanks. To reassure the West, Stalin told Cripps that Russia would not make a separate peace, and Steinhardt relayed this message to Hull on September 13. Kiev fell on September 20, and with it the Soviets lost immense stores and half a million men. This victory, Hitler announced boastfully, followed "the greatest battle in world history." In the south the Nazis sped toward Kharkov and Rostov, although in the north the Red army clung stubbornly and heroically to Leningrad and Moscow. But Steinhardt warned that military valor was not enough. The great material losses would have to be replaced or Russia might have to give up the struggle anyway. He believed it urgent to complete long-term military supply arrangements quickly, partly in order to boost sagging morale.[42]

On September 3 the White House announced that Harriman would head the supply mission to Moscow. General Burns and Colonel Faymonville of Lend-Lease, Major General George H. Brett, chief of the air corps (replaced at the last moment by Lieutenant General Stanley D. Embrick, retired), Admiral William H. Standley, former production management official, and William L. Batt, deputy director of the Office of Production Management's production division, completed the United States delegation. Hopkins cabled Churchill on September 9 to set up preliminary British-American talks that would open in London on September 15. In London, Lord Beaverbrook headed the British group. To simplify matters, he recommended that the United States make over-all allocations to Great Britain and let the

42 *Foreign Relations, 1941,* I, 825, 828–29, 829–30, 831–32, 834, 836; Dawson, *The Decision,* 195–96; Ministry of Foreign Affairs of the U.S.S.R., *Correspondence Between the Chairman of the Council of Ministers of the U.S.S.R. and the Presidents of the U.S.A. and the Prime Ministers of Great Britain During the Great Patriotic War of 1941–1945,* I, 20–21; hereafter cited as *U.S.S.R. Correspondence;* see also Churchill, *The Grand Alliance,* 455–57 [wording in the Soviet volume differs slightly from that in Churchill]; Langer and Gleason, *The Undeclared War,* 788, 811.

British sub-allocate to the Soviet Union. Harriman refused; he observed that the United States would make its own commitments in addition to those the British made. He reminded Beaverbrook that the purpose of the conference was to agree on specific offers of help from each nation and present those offers to Stalin as definite pledges. The American aid proposals jolted the British because of the tremendous cutbacks these meant for them. The conference deadlocked over tank allocations, which Roosevelt solved by ordering tank production doubled. The British successfully protested release of heavy bombers to Russia because, under the schedules, it meant a 75 per cent reduction in deliveries to Great Britain. Again Roosevelt came to the rescue; no heavy bombers were sent to Russia, but allocation of aircraft in other categories was increased. The tank problem subsequently meant that United States Army quotas were reduced; the army delayed equipping five armored divisions and postponed activation of a sixth. If the conference ended in harmony, it was because of high-level, common agreement that Russia must be kept fighting.[43]

Before the conference at London was concluded, Harriman cabled Roosevelt to ask how the United States intended to finance the Russian program, something he, Roosevelt, Morgenthau, Jones, and Hopkins had been unable to work out before he went to England. Replying for Roosevelt, Hopkins dodged the issue by commenting that the President could not give definite financial instructions at that time. Hopkins urged Roosevelt to bring Russia under Lend-Lease, but Roosevelt still held back. So, without knowing how the program would be financed, the American mission proceeded to Moscow.[44]

[43] Roosevelt Library, President's Official File 220, Box 2, press releases, September 3, 1941; Dawson, *The Decision*, 212–16; Sherwood, *Roosevelt and Hopkins*, 385.

[44] Roosevelt Library, President's Official File 220, Box 2, memo, Hopkins to General Watson, September 5, 1941; President's Personal File 4096, Harry Hopkins, Harriman to Roosevelt, September 19, 1941; Langer and Gleason, *The Undeclared War*, 811.

Harriman and Standley, with Beaverbrook and his mission, embarked on the HMS *London*, a heavy cruiser, at Scapa Flow, for Archangel on September 21. The trip lasted seven days and was a rough one until almost at the end. The British mission, Sherwood commented, could not forget that Lord Kitchener (Horatio Herbert) had met death on a torpedoed British cruiser en route to Archangel in 1916. The junior members of the American group, now including Major General James E. Chaney, ranking United States Air Force officer in London, flew to Russia on September 22 in two army B-24's. Newscaster Quentin Reynolds, who hitch-hiked along, recommended Distinguished Flying Crosses for the pilots because of their "amazing flight under terrific conditions." This was the first United States Army Air Corps mission over Luftwaffe territory.[45]

The Moscow supply conference convened on September 28. Harriman and Beaverbrook met with Stalin three times, on the evenings of September 28, 29, and 30, for a total of nine hours. Subcommittees of army, navy, air force, raw materials, and medical supplies met during the days. One of Standley's friends described the subcommittee meetings as "exercises in frustration." At the time, Standley thought his Russian counterparts were indecisive and lacked information, but later he reflected that they were "evading the issue. As usual in Soviet Russia, nothing of real importance could be decided below the highest level of government," something Hopkins had concluded two months earlier.[46]

The first meeting with Stalin was cordial. He discussed the military situation as frankly as he had with Hopkins. He pegged Germany's superiority in the air at three to two, in tanks as four to one, and in army divisions as eight to seven. Stalin discounted

---

[45] Sherwood, *Roosevelt and Hopkins*, 385–86; William H. Standley and Arthur A. Ageton, *Admiral Ambassador to Russia*, 62–63; Langer and Gleason, *The Undeclared War*, 811.

[46] *Foreign Relations, 1941*, I, 837–38; Dawson, *The Decision*, 249–50; Sherwood, *Roosevelt and Hopkins*, 387; Standley and Ageton, *Admiral Ambassador*, 67.

the satellite divisions, such as the Italian, that fought alongside their German masters. He discussed military items that he needed, with tanks heading the list, followed by anti-tank guns, medium bombers, anti-aircraft guns, armor plate, fighter and reconnaissance planes, and barbed wire. He mentioned again the need for a second front in Europe. He asked for British forces to fight in the Ukraine. Harriman suggested delivery of United States aircraft to Russia via Alaska and Siberia, but Stalin demurred when Harriman suggested the planes be brought with American crews. Harriman thought Stalin wished to avoid provoking Japan. Stalin brought up the question of peace objectives, which Beaverbrook and Harriman avoided, observing "we must win the war first." Harriman brought up the subject of religion in Russia and mentioned Roosevelt's concern for American public opinion on this issue, but Stalin did not seem to attach importance to this.[47]

The second meeting was less friendly. Stalin, apparently under a great strain, paced up and down in a constant cloud of smoke from his many cigarettes and, as Harriman noted, "rode us pretty hard." The only real agreement was to hold another meeting the next evening. Standley described the mood of Harriman and Beaverbrook afterwards as "indigo blue."[48]

The next day, Goebbels, the master German propagandist, sneered at the Moscow meeting with the comment that the British and Americans could never find common ground with the "Bolshevists." The conference at six o'clock that evening contrasted pleasantly with the previous one. "It is up to the three of us," Standley quoted Stalin, "to prove Goebbels a liar." Beaverbrook read a long memorandum that listed everything the Soviets asked for, commenting on which could not be provided immediately, which could, and what extras the Anglo-Americans could add. The list pleased Stalin, and, as Beaverbrook recorded,

[47] *Foreign Relations, 1941,* I, 839; Sherwood, *Roosevelt and Hopkins,* 387–88; Standley and Ageton, *Admiral Ambassador,* 66; Dawson, *The Decision,* 250.

[48] Sherwood, *Roosevelt and Hopkins,* 388–89; Standley and Ageton, *Admiral Ambassador,* 67.

interpreter Litvinov bounded out of his seat to exclaim "now we shall win the war." Stalin again emphasized the need for jeeps and American trucks. The nation that produced the most gasoline engines would win the war, he observed. In general the British-American negotiators did their best to convince Russia of their good faith and to offer her every encouragement. Burns, Faymonville, and Batt enthusiastically supported Harriman. Except for religious freedom, the Americans scrupulously avoided any intimation that they sought concessions in return. The third meeting broke up with Stalin enthusiastically inviting Harriman and Beaverbrook to dinner the next evening, an invitation they accepted.[49]

At three o'clock Wednesday afternoon, October 1, 1941, Molotov presided over the final meeting of the three delegations. He announced that complete agreement had been reached, and he, with Harriman and Beaverbrook, signed the First, or Moscow, Protocol. As he closed the conference, Molotov remarked, "During these days we were completely able to convince ourselves of the degree in which the decisive, vital interests and common aspirations of our great . . . countries have brought them together and have led them into close co-operation. . . . A combination of states has at last been formed against Hitlerism." Harriman, overly optimistic, wrote that if "personal relations were retained with Stalin, the suspicion that has existed" between Russia and Britain, and America "might well be eradicated." Certainly the United States, for a country not at war, had taken giant, unprecedented steps to supply Great Britain and Soviet Russia in their struggle with Germany.[50]

After the signing, Standley, Batt, and probably others of the two missions, toured industrial facilities in the Moscow area. But the farewell highlight was the dinner at the Kremlin on

[49] Sherwood, *Roosevelt and Hopkins*, 389–91; Standley and Ageton, *Admiral Ambassador*, 68; Dawson, *The Decision*, 250–51.
[50] Sherwood, *Roosevelt and Hopkins*, 391, 394–95; Standley and Ageton, *Admiral Ambassador*, 69; Stettinius, *Lend-Lease*, 205; Langer and Gleason, *The Undeclared War*, 814.

October 1. They banqueted in the white marble, glass and gold Catherine-the-Great Room of the Kremlin. Standley counted thirty-one toasts that interrupted the repast. Coffee and liqueurs followed in an anteroom, and Stalin moved from group to group talking with all. The guests then watched two Russian movies, a propaganda film of 1935 vintage and a lively musical. Champagne was served with the movies. Standley heard that this was the first time since the Revolution that such an elaborate ceremony had been staged in the Kremlin. On October 2 the group made diplomatic calls and said farewells; on October 3 they worked on their reports, and Steinhardt gave a dinner to repay the hosts. Steinhardt's party lasted "far into the morning of October 4th," the day the mission was scheduled to depart Moscow. Faymonville, at Hopkins' request, remained in Moscow as Lend-Lease representative. This appointment kept Russian aid in the hands of the White House, since Hopkins thought the United States military attaché, Major Ivan Yeaton, unsuitable.[51]

The United States signed this First (Moscow) Protocol, promising the Russians about 1,500,000 tons of supplies through June 30, 1942, without any financial provisions. Hence, the United States depended upon the catch-as-catch-can financing for Russia at least until Congress co-operated with funds and public opinion supported Russia's inclusion in Lend-Lease. Roosevelt ordered Stimson to give October shipments to Russia priority over those to all other countries; Hopkins instructed Lend-Lease officials to put the Russian aid programs through without delay. Harriman and Batt appeared in person before the Supply, Priorities, and Allocations Board on October 29 and, along with Hopkins (a member), rammed the Russian program through. Office of Production Management Administrator Leon Henderson figured the program would create "problems of civilian supply" but approved the list, "subject to . . . minor adjustments" after discussion. New Soviet estimates revealed that

[51] *Foreign Relations, 1941*, I, 840; Standley and Ageton, *Admiral Ambassador*, 71–75; Dawson, *The Decision*, 256; Sherwood, *Roosevelt and Hopkins*, 395.

Russia would need $150,000,000 by the end of October. By that date, with Morgenthau's and Jones's co-operation, the Soviets had received cash advances totalling $90,000,000—$40,000,000 from the Treasury on gold pledges and the remainder from the Defense Supplies Corporation against future raw material delivery. Still there was not enough to pay for the Russian program even through the end of the year, as Roosevelt apparently had hoped. American officials, especially those of the Division of Defense Aid Reports and the War Department, with Jesse Jones as well, advocated Lend-Lease as the only solution.[52]

At the same time, Roosevelt worked to bring his strategy, politically and legally, to fruition. "Harry the Hop," as the President called his aide with affection, remained quite ill in the late summer of 1941, giving Roosevelt an excuse to take some of the Lend-Lease burden from his shoulders. On August 28, 1941, Hopkins summoned Stettinius to his busy bedside and told him that Roosevelt wanted him to take over Lend-Lease. A few days later Roosevelt appointed Stettinius a special Presidential assistant, at $10,000 a year, "to act as Administrator of the Lend-Lease program." Ickes believed that this appointment marked part of the President's strategy to get the second Lend-Lease money bill through Congress. Ickes thought Hopkins' "standing on the hill" insufficient, but Stettinius, "who can be depended upon to do whatever Harry tells him," could "front" for Hopkins very well. On Capitol Hill, Congress vigorously debated the second Lend-Lease appropriation. In spite of administrative efforts to keep Russia out of the debates, Russophobes in Congress tried unsuccessfully to amend the bill to exclude specifically the Soviet Union. But the $5,985,000,000 act passed easily, and Roosevelt signed it on October 28. That day he created the Office of Lend-Lease Administration and granted Stettinius nearly full powers. The President reserved only the right to

<hr/>

[52] Roosevelt Library, President's Secretary's File, Russia, Box 14, memo, Hopkins to Roosevelt, September 5, 1941; Civilian Production Administration, Bureau of Demobilization, *Minutes of the Supply Priorities and Allocation Board*, 21–22, hereafter cited as *S.P.A.B. Minutes*; Dawson, *The Decision*, 254, 270–74.

designate Lend-Lease countries and negotiate master agreements. Hopkins was relieved of the routine of Lend-Lease business, and although he was not the administrator, he still oversaw the program.[53]

Working out a supply agreement was one thing, procuring and financing the program another, and delivering the goods still a third, not so easily solved. By mid-July the United States Navy was escorting American and Icelandic shipping as far as Iceland. The Atlantic Conference and the attack on the destroyer, USS *Greer*, prompted the President's often-delayed decision, on September 11, to convoy other than American shipping to Iceland, which meant in effect that the United States began a shooting war in the Atlantic. This freed forty British destroyers and corvettes for use elsewhere. In the Middle East, Britain and Russia sought to establish a route to Russia and to secure their flanks by jointly occupying Iran. The United States also moved into Iran on the basis of a September 13 Presidential directive, with Lend-Lease aid for Britain and Russia under army supervision. Colonel Raymond A. Wheeler, a rail and highway specialist, became chief of the United States military mission to Iran on September 27. So deeply involved had the United States become that revision of the Neutrality Act now was anti-climactic. By September of 1941 many lawmakers favored repeal of the entire act. Roosevelt and Hull wanted only those sections that excluded American shipping from combat areas and forbade arming of merchantmen repealed because these were illogical obstacles to the aid program as it was developing. Finally, on October 9, Roosevelt laid before Congress the proposal to repeal Section VI of the act, which would allow merchant ships to be armed, but the President let it be known that authority to enter combat zones and carry supplies

[53] *Third Report on Lend-Lease*, 42–45; Roosevelt Library, President's Official File 4559, press releases, August 28, 1941, and letters, Roosevelt to Stettinius, and Stettinius to Roosevelt, September 16, 1961; also Roosevelt to Stettinius, September 18, 1941; Stettinius, *Lend-Lease*, 105–106; Sherwood, *Roosevelt and Hopkins*, 376–77; Ickes, *The Lowering Clouds*, 616; Dawson, *The Decision*, 274–82.

The War at a Glance, 1941[*]

Within two months after the June, 1941, attack on the U.S.S.R., the Nazis swept through Pskov in the north and Smolensk in the center. Kiev was encircled by the middle of September. The pace of the German army slowed because of the long supply lines and the weather, but by December the army was within thirty miles of Leningrad and Moscow. The Russian army then launched a counterattack on the Moscow front. Although seriously hurt by the swift Nazi attack, the Red army was not destroyed. Hitler, disappointed, shook up the Nazi high command. No new offensives could be launched during the winter.

[*] See the Chronology in Appendix C.

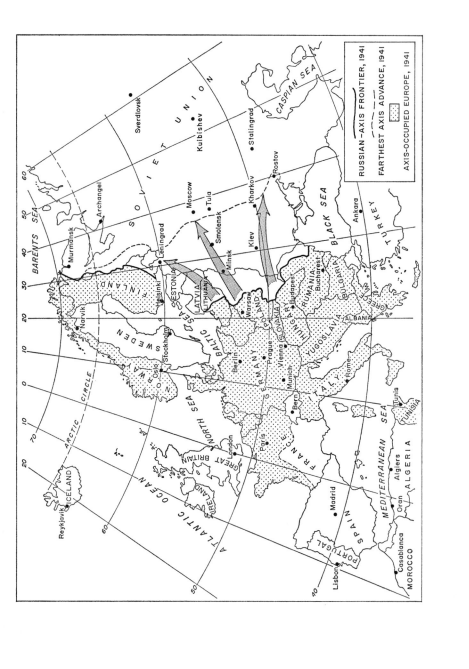

RUSSIAN–AXIS FRONTIER, 1941

FARTHEST AXIS ADVANCE, 1941

AXIS-OCCUPIED EUROPE, 1941

to friendly ports was also at issue. The torpedoing of the USS *Kearney* on the eve of the House vote may have been influential, but the repeal passed the House on October 17. The Senate gave its assent on November 7.[54]

When the struggle in the Soviet Union had reached a desperate phase on October 30, with fierce fighting around Leningrad and Moscow and near collapse on the southern front, Stalin went on the air to appeal for a supreme effort to save the fatherland. On the same day, Roosevelt cabled Stalin to report that he had examined the record of the Moscow conference and had approved all the munitions items and raw materials requested and that he had directed deliveries to "commence immediately" and in "the largest possible amounts." He added:

> In an effort to obviate any financial difficulties immediate arrangements are to be made so that supplies up to one billion dollars in value may be effected under the Lend-Lease Act . . . I propose that the indebtedness thus incurred be subject to no interest and the payments of the U.S.S.R. do not commence until five years after the war's conclusion and be completed over a ten-year period thereafter.

Payments, Roosevelt concluded, would be in raw materials and other commodities.

Stalin replied on November 4:

> Your decision . . . to grant the Soviet Union an interest-free loan to the value of $1,000,000,000 . . . is accepted by the Soviet Government with heartfelt gratitude as vital aid to the Soviet Union in its tremendous and onerous struggle against our common enemy.

He went on to "express complete agreement with your terms." With the Soviet acceptance, Russia at last came under Lend-

[54] Langer and Gleason, *The Undeclared War*, 742–57; Samuel Eliot Morison, *The Battle of the Atlantic*, 78–79; Motter, *Persian Corridor*, 16, 17; for the complete story of the occupation in Iran, see Motter, Ch. I–V.

Lease. The exchange of telegrams was made public on November 6, and on November 7, Roosevelt declared the defense of the Soviet Union vital to the defense of the United States, completing the legal requirement. After four months of political and financial maneuvering, Lend-Lease benefits were extended to Russia.[55]

[55] *Foreign Relations, 1941,* I, 851; Stettinius, *Lend-Lease,* 129–30; *U.S.S.R. Correspondence,* II, 15; *Third Report on Lend-Lease,* 33–34, Hopkins drafted Roosevelt's cable, see Sherwood, *Roosevelt and Hopkins,* 396–97.

CHAPTER THREE

Moscow Protocol to Master Agreement

IT IS RIDICULOUS," proclaimed the *Chicago Tribune* on October 17, 1941, "that sane men should have the slightest faith that Stalin, who brought on the war by selling out the democracies, will not sell them out again and make another deal with Hitler."[1] Sane or not, American leaders already had drafted the Protocol of aid and awaited only the right political moment to add Russia to the Lend-Lease list.

Stettinius observed that the supply Protocol with Russia constituted "a binding promise by this Government [the United States] to make specific quantities of supplies available for shipment to Russia by a specific date." The United States had pledged 1,500,000 tons of supplies for the Soviets by June 30, 1942. First monetary estimates hovered around $1,000,000,000, but within four months the two nations completed arrangements for a second $1,000,000,000.[2] The dollar sign, which Lend-Lease presumed to omit, remained as a ghostly quantitative measure. United States production facilities had scarcely begun to approach the necessary capacity, with billions of dollars and over a million tons of war supplies committed to Russia, an even larger quantity guaranteed Great Britian, and a still greater amount contracted for American rearmament.

The tardy United States industrial mobilization dumbfounded General Golikov and his colleagues of the Soviet military mission

[1] Quoted in Langer and Gleason, *The Undeclared War*, 819.
[2] Stettinius, *Lend-Lease*, 126, 205; *U.S.S.R. Correspondence, II,* 19–21, and also *Foreign Relations, 1942,* Vol. III, 690–92.

to the United States. Production goals and capacity trailed Arsenal of Democracy commitments, hampered by the very peace they sought to preserve. In February, 1941, Knudsen told the Office of Production Management Council, especially the war and navy secretaries, that he aimed to outline a comprehensive program for production of all material required by current and future military authorizations, as well as anticipated Lend-Lease needs. The Army, Navy, Maritime Commission, and Great Britain co-operated, and by early April a few fairly reliable estimates of productive capacity emerged. The results indicated that "the Nation would have to shift from its 'business as usual' lethargy to an all-out effort in order to realize production goals. On the basis of actual appropriations and contract authorizations for fiscal 1941, including the Lend-Lease program, the estimates totaled $48,700,000,000. According to the Production Planning Board's report, production would have to be stepped up greatly, labor would have to be absorbed and trained more rapidly than ever within the next six months, raw material shortages would have to be met, and curtailment of consumer income or production or both would be necessary. Five times, from April 3 to June 18, the Production Planning Board begged Roosevelt to prepare a program to establish "the munitions objective of a general strategic plan" of over-all requirements and put such a plan into effect.[3]

Various officials also urged the President to appoint a production "czar" to rule over industry. Roosevelt declined. On June 3 the secretaries of war and navy, perhaps impressed with a predicted deficit of 1,400,000 tons of steel (vis-a-vis requirements) for the calendar year 1941, proposed to treble the existing production program. Knudsen and the Office of Production Management agreed to undertake the increase for the military, and on July 9, Roosevelt asked Hopkins and the war and navy secretaries to explore the over-all production requirements. Shortly thereafter the Russian list arrived in Washington, and on July 21

[3] *Industrial Mobilization for War*, 134–36; Stettinius, *Lend-Lease*, 123–24.

the President instructed the army, navy, and the Office of Production Management to find out what could be sent to Russia in the immediate future. The Secretary of War advocated creation of an over-all strategy board so that conflicting requirements might be avoided. The Bureau of Research and Statistics worked in July and August to compile a consolidated requirements sheet. Meanwhile, on August 28, Roosevelt created another office instead of appointing a production chief.[4]

The new set of initials added to the growing alphabet agency lexicon, S.P.A.B., stood for the Supply, Priorities, and Allocations Board. The Office of Production Management's priorities board lacked sufficient authority to establish and maintain war production goals, a condition not true of this latest concoction. To Knudsen, Hillman, Stimson, and Knox of the old group, Roosevelt added Vice-President Henry Wallace (chairman), Donald Nelson (director), Leon Henderson, and of course Harry Hopkins. On September 17, Nelson asked the Army, Navy, Maritime Commission, and Lend-Lease Administration for their estimated requirements for the next two years. The War Department and the Lend-Lease Administration compiled as best they could, but the navy and the Maritime Commission refused to submit programs until after the country was actually at war. The Office of Production Management staff made its own estimates of the needs of the two nonco-operating departments and, in addition, studied Russian requirements as outlined in the First Protocol. Partly in response to Hopkins' needling in S.P.A.B. sessions and elsewhere, the Office of Production Management worked out a program for essential civilian production to co-ordinate with the military program. The combined new estimate was called the Victory Program. The final report on the feasibility of the Victory Program in terms of national industrial potential was made on December 4, 1941.[5]

[4] *Industrial Mobilization for War*, 137–39; Roosevelt Library, President's Secretary's File, II, Navy Department, Box 21, Roosevelt to Knox, July 9, 1941.

[5] *Industrial Mobilization for War*, 139–40; *S.P.A.B. Minutes*, 19; Langer and Gleason, *The Undeclared War*, 736.

The Victory Program feasibility report noted that the production schedule as it then existed would have to be doubled if the goals outlined in the Victory Program were to be achieved by September 30, 1943. The output of durable consumer goods would have to be severely curtailed. The labor force was adequate if better use could be made of the old and young and of women, and if more skilled workers could be trained. The Victory Program was workable, but only under a wartime economy. The Japanese solved that problem only three days later at Pearl Harbor. However, as parts of the Victory Program emerged in September and October, their magnitude astonished and appalled official Washington. For the first time since Hitler's rampage began, the United States had systematically analyzed its objectives and requirements for the ultimate defeat of the Nazis. It is significant that the United States arrived at this stage of planning, not production, after the attack on the Soviet Union, nearly concurrently with the first Soviet supply schedule, and only shortly before the sneak attack on Pearl Harbor.[6]

Since the United States came so late to comprehensive production planning, it should not be surprising that the Lend-Lease Administration itself grew slowly in its own measurement of progress. Philip Young, acting deputy administrator, told a Lend-Lease "clinic" on June 2, 1942, about the "changing basis

[6] *Industrial Mobilization for War*, 140; Langer and Gleason, *The Undeclared War*, 741. Langer and Gleason have a good brief summary of the general development of the Victory Program, 738–41. What the Victory Program meant to the army is told in the army histories: Maurice Matloff and Edwin M. Snell, *Strategic Planning for Coalition Warfare, 1941–1942*, 58–62; Leighton and Coakley, *Global Logistics*, 126–29; Ray S. Cline, *Washington Command Post: The Operations Division*, 60–61; and R. Elberton Smith, *The Army and Economic Mobilization*, 133–39. The Chicago Tribune released details of this "secret plan," says Smith, on December 4, 1941, "to 'scoop' the new Chicago Sun . . . on the day of its launching." On this "scoop" see also Watson, *Chief of Staff*, 359. See also the administration's reaction, in Ickes, *The Lowering Clouds*, 659–60, and Roosevelt Library, President's Secretary's File, War Department, Box 27, press release, December 5, 1941. Roosevelt accused the *Chicago Tribune* of securing a copy of the Victory Program "surreptitiously" and, by publishing it, of violating "one of the most fundamental obligations of citizenship."

of the Lend-Lease organization." Lend-Lease operations began, Young commented, with "considerable money appropriated to us. We used this to get goods in production so we could supply our foreign Lend-Lease constituents. All the emphasis . . . was fiscal. We had to get the contracts made," put money in the hands of the procurement agencies, and make "reports on obligations, on allocations, on disbursements, and on expenditures." All Lend-Lease measurement of progress before December 7, 1941, "was fiscal in nature. That was true because it took so long to make anything. We couldn't get any planes . . . tanks . . . shells or guns, anything that really counted in this war, to go out and shoot somebody with, made in less than six, eight, ten months." By June of 1942, though, "the whole emphasis . . . shifted from dollar figures to unit figures . . . how many planes, how many tanks . . . how many eggs."[7]

When Japanese bombs fell on Pearl Harbor, the Nazis had been fighting in Russia for less than six months, the First Protocol was only nine weeks old, and Lend-Lease to Russia was one month old to the day. On the other hand, Great Britain had been fighting for over two years, and, through the President's Liaison Committee and Lend-Lease, the British aid program had been under way for a year and a half. Lend-Lease to Russia shared not only the disadvantage of relative unpopularity in America, but also that of another war program in a nation not ready for full war production. No huge fleets of aircraft or battalions of tanks or stacks of weapons or stockpiles of raw materials existed to re-equip the hard-pressed Red army. Materials shipped under the First Protocol and under the Russian purchase programs came from the small stocks on hand or from stocks originally intended to rebuild shattered British and infant American armies. United

---

[7] *Lend-Lease Clinic,* 4. The army also streamlined its organization with respect to Lend-Lease. Stimson delegated his functions to Assistant Secretary John J. McCloy, and by October 1, 1941, along with the army's Defense Aid director, Colonel Henry S. Aurand, the two ran nearly all army aspects of Lend-Lease: see Leighton and Coakley, *Global Logistics,* 79–80.

States Army reluctance to release material necessary for the United States build-up and British disappointment with their diminished share existed as evidence that even the trickle of possible aid pained the democracies, although they sent it off without regret. They did not undervalue the military significance of the Soviet battlefront.[8]

The United States finally came around to a full, staggering realization of what the defeat of Hitler required so far as production was concerned, and at the same time it opened its scanty military cupboard to the Soviets without any strings attached. Uncle Sam charged Uncle Joe no interest on the first billion-dollar Lend-Lease credit and postponed repayment—in raw materials and other commodities—until five years after the war ended. Although later agreements modified this first one, it nonetheless shoved the dollar sign into the background. Not only were virtually no financial ties connected to the aid, but also the United States sought no political concessions, according to previously established policy. In early December, 1941, British Foreign Secretary Anthony Eden packed for Russia to discuss "some kind of political agreement" and "certain postwar problems." The United States made it quite clear to Great Britain that the former would consider it "unfortunate for any of these three governments . . . to enter into commitments regarding specific terms of the postwar settlement. Above all, there must be no secret accords." To convince the Soviet Union of its good faith, the United States carefully followed the policy of aid, unencumbered by any conditions, especially political.[9]

The First (Moscow) Protocol committed Great Britain and

---

[8] Langer and Gleason, *The Undeclared War*, 735–36; Leighton and Coakley, *Global Logistics*, 97. See also letter of William A. Batt to Joseph Davies, October 27, 1941: "The Russians . . . know how to use the materials and equipment we have promised . . . and as long as they are fighting, the war will stay forever away from our shores. That is why I say deliver . . . the goods . . . at whatever sacrifices are necessary." Quoted in Davies, *Mission to Moscow*, 509.

[9] *Third Report on Lend-Lease*, 33–34; *Fourth Report on Lend-Lease*, 34; Sherwood, *Roosevelt and Hopkins*, 401–402; see also Chapter II above.

the United States to make available at their "centres of production" the supplies listed, as well as to "give aid to the transportation of these materials . . . and . . . help with the delivery." Aircraft headed the list. The Soviets asked for 400 planes a month, made up of 300 short-range bombers and 100 fighters. The United States agreed to provide 100 bombers and 100 fighters a month, and Great Britain agreed to supply 200 fighters. Tanks occupied second place, with 1,100 small or medium ones requested monthly, but only 500 monthly promised. Anti-aircraft guns, anti-tank guns, scout cars (2,000 monthly requested, 5,000 total promised), trucks (10,000, 1½- to 3-ton size, requested each month, but no specific commitment made by the United States), aluminum (4,000 tons a month requested, 2,000 tons a month from Canada promised and *perhaps* 2,000 tons a month from the United States), barbed wire (4,000 tons a month), toluol (4,000 tons a month requested, 1,250 tons promised monthly, and 10,000 tons of TNT to be shipped over nine months, in addition), petroleum products (gasolines, components, oils, greases—20,000 tons monthly asked, but no firm promise made), wheat (200,000 tons monthly from Canada), sugar (70,000 tons from the Philippines and Dutch East Indies), and cocoa beans (1,500 tons from Great Britain) stood out as major items on the list of seventy. In addition, a naval annex called for an Anglo-American "enquiry" into a Soviet "Program of Requirements," in which the Soviet Union asked for eight destroyers, nine minesweepers, and various types of naval armament with the emphasis on anti-aircraft guns. Also requested were 490 marine diesel motors and 150 marine diesel generators. A medical request listed instruments and supplies that the Anglo-Americans promised to look into, while the American Red Cross "already agreed to give some of the items." This list included eighty-three items, from cocainhydrochloricum, novocain, and xeroform to scalpels, nippers, amputation saws, and Richardsons balls.[10]

[10] Department of State, *Soviet Supply Protocols*, 3–11. Others items on the

Moscow promised to consider an additional annex, titled "Supplies Which Great Britain Desires to Obtain from the Soviet Union." Britain marked items such as chrome ore, pine tar, and platinum as urgent. Other stocks from beeswax to canned salmon followed. No such annex existed for the United States because of the raw material agreement concluded with the Soviets prior to Lend-Lease. Although the United States committed itself to provide certain quantities of the supplies, the Protocol did not indicate the actual extent of delivery. First, by request of the United States, the Soviets selected items from the Protocol list to fit available shipping space. Also, urgent Russian requests often were met by addition to the Protocol or by substitution for listed items, and war risks such as shipping failures intervened. Shipment in excess of commitment became another factor in later protocols.[11]

Second in size to the British aid program, this Soviet package presented a gigantic challenge to the infant United States war industry in addition to the tremendous problem of delivery and the annoying factor of surliness on the part of Soviet Union itself. With British, Chinese, Soviet, Dutch, and Latin American demands placed on American production, no wonder United States Army men found themselves scrapping for planes, tanks, and weapons produced under their own contracts. Ever since 1940, to take one example, the fifty-four-group program of the United States Army Air Force had been sidelined in favor of British orders. United States planes came on United States contracts and British planes came on their own and Lend-Lease contracts prior to the Soviet agreements. Soviet orders forced a

---

list included: field telephone apparatus and wire, tin, lead, nickel, molybdenum, cobalt, copper electrolytic, brass, magnesium alloys, zinc armor plate, hard alloys and cutting tools, silver-steel, various other types of steel, steel wire, steel rope, nickel chrome wire, nitroglycerin powder, phenol, other chemicals, metal-cutting machine tools, electric furnaces, forging and press equipment, diamonds, abrasives, graphite, rubber, jute, shellac, sole leather, wool, army boots, and army cloth. Some of the commitments were quite vague. See, for example, *W.P.B. Minutes*, p. 34.

[11] *Soviet Supply Protocols*, iv, 12.

reappraisal of the entire aircraft program, so that out of planned production through June 30, 1942, Great Britain would receive 6,634 tactical airplanes, the United States, 4,189, the Soviet Union, 1,835, China, 407, and others, 109. About 68 per cent of American tactical production would go abroad, with Britain receiving about 75 per cent of the exports. The U.S. Army Air Force had to take a back seat, and total production figures remained absurdly low when placed against the ambitious estimates of the 1940 plans. "The problem of allocation," two War Department historians somewhat sarcastically remarked, "remained one of dividing a deficiency."[12]

Ground equipment problems in allocations proved just as difficult. In response to heavy White House pressure, in September, 1941, Marshall approved an allocations formula that would clearly retard "the pace of rearmanent" and divert "the lion's share of American production to lend-lease" as quickly as possible. By October, Colonel Henry S. Aurand, the army's defense aid director, operated from a release schedule based on the new formula. Not only did the advent of the Russian Lend-Lease program cut deeply into American military build-up efforts, but it slashed into the British war effort as well. Great Britain, shipping large numbers of tanks to Russia, nearly stripped her own Middle East command. In November, Britain feared a Nazi attack through the Caucasus and urgently appealed to the United States for tanks. As they came off United States production lines in November, December, and January, 350 medium tanks, very nearly the entire United States medium tank production, were sped to bolster weakened Middle East defenses. American armored forces had to use light tanks as substitutes in training.[13]

China, chronically unsatisfied with unfulfilled arms promises, feared further cutbacks in view of the Russian program. Chiang

[12] Leighton and Coakley, *Global Logistics*, 103–104.

[13] *Ibid.*, 104–105; Roosevelt Library, President's Secretary's File, War Department, Box 27, letter, Stimson to Roosevelt, November 12, 1941.

Kai-Shek and Dr. T. V. Soong both appealed directly to Roosevelt in October, 1941, for accelerated shipments, without any success. In November, the Dutch East Indies were attempting to ready themselves for an anticipated Japanese invasion and clamored for anti-aircraft guns, light artillery, small arms, and ammunition, with about as much success as the Chinese. On the other hand, on December 3 the Army War Plans Division proposed increased, first-priority aid to the Soviet Union wherever possible, even above the Protocol, with an equal division of material between Russia and Great Britain in categories where other countries had no claims. In practice this could have resulted in reduction of Protocol schedules in some short-supply items such as tanks. Since the Protocol was a political agreement, the army could not change it. Marshall had to reject the logical War Plans Division proposal. The facts showed that the Russian Lend-Lease program slowed United States military build-up and caused serious repercussions in the military status of Britain, China, The Netherlands East Indies, and other of the thirty-three Lend-Lease nations.[14]

Since the first promises of help in June, 1941, a total of fifty-seven ships, carrying 342,680 tons of supplies, had departed from the United States for Russia. Twenty-eight of these, with about 137,760 tons of cargo, sailed in October and November for North Russian and Soviet Far Eastern ports. One of these ships cleared, in November, for the Persian Gulf, and two vessels were lost at sea. At this point, with war production planning just commencing, the kinks in war material allocation just beginning to be smoothed out, and the Russian aid program just slipping into gear, the Japanese dropped a wrench into the machinery.[15]

[14] Leighton and Coakley, *Global Logistics*, 105–107; *Third Report on Lend-Lease*, 16; Sherwood, *Roosevelt and Hopkins*, 406–409.

[15] Report on War Aid Furnished by the United States to the U.S.S.R., 14–15, hereafter cited as Report on War Aid; Motter, *Persian Corridor*, 481; Stettinius, *Lend-Lease*, 203. All tonnage figures in the text are short tons (2000 pounds) even where sources are in long (2240 pounds) or metric (2024.622 pounds) tons, for consistency.

On December 7, 1941, 360 Japanese war planes launched an attack against the United States naval base at Pearl Harbor and other nearby military installations. Shock immediately rippled through the entire foreign aid program when news that the major portion of the Pacific Fleet was destroyed reached the United States. The army arbitrarily stopped the flow of all supplies abroad. Ironically, war came to America not because of its aid to Britain and Russia and its determination to end the menace of Hitlerism, but because Japan had to destroy the United States Pacific Fleet in order to continue its Far Eastern expansion.[16]

From the first inkling of the sneak attack at 1:40 P.M. (Eastern Standard Time) until the President retired at 12:30 A.M., the White House was the scene of bustling activity. The switchboard hummed with calls to cabinet members and with navy news of the disaster. Churchill telephoned, and Roosevelt told him they now were in the same boat. The President conferred with Stimson, Knox, and Marshall. Executive orders were hurriedly typed. Conferences with both the cabinet and legislative leaders were held. Roosevelt told them all he planned to go to Congress on Monday for a declaration of war. Hull recalled that at the cabinet meeting they "early agreed that the outbreak of the war should not interfere with the flow of supplies to Britain and Russia." That decision, as important as any other made that Sunday evening, assured the Lend-Lease program continued life. The Nazis and Fascists joined Japan in the war on the United States—three days later.[17]

During the remainder of December, the army gave top priority to its own needs. Axis propagandists claimed that American entry into the war meant the end of aid for Britain and Russia, and apparently even the British were momentarily alarmed. Roosevelt sought to sweep away any doubts and countered the propaganda by announcing that U. S. entry into the war meant

[16] Watson, *Chief of Staff*, 515–18.
[17] Sherwood, *Roosevelt and Hopkins*, 430–34; Hull, *Memoirs*, 1099.

increased Lend-Lease aid. Churchill and his entourage arrived in Washington on December 22 for the series of conferences code-named *ARCADIA*. An Allied declaration reaffirmed the Atlantic Charter, making Russia a subscriber to it, and the first military objective emerged as Europe. This meant Lend-Lease to Britain and Russia would have to be increased. So far as Russian aid was concerned, paragraph 15 of the strategic planning memorandum read: "In 1942 the main methods of wearing down Germany's resistance will be . . . assistance to Russia's offensive *by all available means.*" This remained high on the Allies' priority list, and Roosevelt and Hopkins reaffirmed it several times from February through April. Protocol deliveries fell behind schedule, not for lack of determination or faulty high-level priority planning, but because physical difficulties and administrative problems caused the failure.[18]

After studying the Victory Program in light of the attack on Pearl Harbor, Roosevelt asked Donald Nelson to prepare a production-objective schedule for specific items. The Supply, Priorities, and Allocations Board approved Nelson's proposals on January 1, 1942, and Nelson sent them to Hopkins for the President. Nelson outlined a bold program that called for annual aircraft manufacture of eighty thousand units and annual tank building of sixty thousand. Nelson's aggressive goals resulted from Beaverbrook's estimates of the war needs of all the Allied powers compared with Axis production. Beaverbrook's optimistic estimates of American industrial potential rubbed off on Roosevelt as well, and Roosevelt proposed goals that surpassed Nelson's. In his January 6 message to Congress the President spoke of 125,000 planes, 75,000 tanks, and 10,000 tons of merchant shipping to be sent annually by 1943. As the nation and government officials gasped at Roosevelt's challenging figures, the President finally acted to centralize control of American indus-

[18] Roosevelt Library, President's Official File 4193, Box 1, press release, December 8, 1941, and Press Conference Statement, December 12, 1941; Leighton and Coakley, *Global Logistics,* 247; Sherwood, *Roosevelt and Hopkins,* 440, 459, 502, 510, 519, 526; Stettinius, *Lend-Lease,* 204.

try. Beaverbrook had recommended that Hopkins head a committee of production, but Roosevelt created a War Production Board headed by Nelson, in whom he vested full administrative authority. When the new agency began to function on January 16, the Supply, Priorities, and Allocations Board expired, although its personnel lived on with the War Production Board.[19]

War Production Board officials doubted that the President's goals could actually be met. Roosevelt and Hopkins both refused to back down as long as any possibility of attaining their objectives existed, thus causing constant reappraisal of various phases of the production program. On May 1, Roosevelt swept away any doubts about basic production aims by listing them for Nelson and the War Production Board. The War Production Board then set 1943 industrial goals, in general, above the President's figures. Merchant shipping, for example, grew to an anticipated fifteen million tons.[20]

Military and industrial strategy established at the *ARCADIA* conference set the direction for United States participation in the Allied war effort. The strategy of "get Hitler first" would have been impossible without Soviet engagement of the bulk of the German Army, a fact that military planners recognized. Anglo-American strategists also knew that Russia could not survive with determination alone. Their choice focused on two courses of action: establish a second front to relieve pressure on the Red army or, failing that, build up Soviet forces by shipment of supplies. Stalin's request for a second front could not be complied with immediately; therefore, shipment of supplies be-

19 *Industrial Mobilization for War*, 207, 277–78. Members of the W.P.B.: Nelson (chairman), War Secretary Stimson, Navy Secretary Knox, Jesse Jones, the Federal Loan administrator, Knudsen and Hillman of the O.P.M., Leon Henderson of the O.P.A., Vice-President Wallace, chairman of the Board of Economic Warfare, and Hopkins (special assistant to the President supervising defense-aid [Lend-Lease] programs). Churchill, in *The Grand Alliance*, 689, misquotes Nelson's memorandum of the meeting with Beaverbrook.

20 *Industrial Mobilization for War*, 279–83; see also *W.P.B. Minutes*, 7, 13, 17, 33, 44. Effect of production and shipping goals on the army is explored in detail in Leighton and Coakley, *Global Logistics*, 197–212.

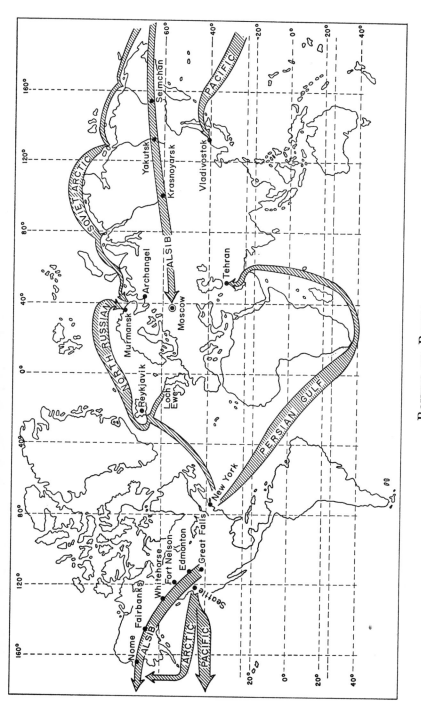

ROUTES TO RUSSIA

came an urgent matter. Since Protocol aid with the Soviet Union reflected top-level diplomatic commitment, military leaders in America could do little but accept its terms. Even agencies of such a high echelon as the Munitions Assignments Board could not control the Protocol except in matters of detail. The military had to recognize the strategic value of Russian aid, for Roosevelt was unwilling to violate the Protocol agreement in any way, except when "sheer physical difficulty made delivery impossible or when it interfered directly with a major Allied project such as the invasion of North Africa." So the effort to supply Russia became a fixed determinant in an equation of many variables.[21]

The five main Soviet supply routes were the Soviet Arctic, the Black Sea, the North Russian, the Persian Gulf, and the Soviet Far East. Of these, Soviet Arctic ports, iced in except during the summer months, remained the least important. Only 506,240 tons of supplies found their way to Russia over that route throughout the war. The Black Sea route, the last to be opened, operated for only five months of 1945, and during that time 762,720 tons of goods floated in. Murmansk, with Archangel as an alternate port, prevailed as the shortest route from the United States to Russia (4,500 miles), and from October, 1941, through April, 1942, it served as the main artery of supply. Axis attack rendered it unreliable after that until mid-1944, by which time other routes had been opened. Even so, Anglo-American vessels carried 4,439,680 tons of material to the North Russian ports. The safest all-year route through the Persian Gulf was also the longest in mileage and ship turn-around time, but it nevertheless remained a military necessity because of the safety factor. Distant or not, 4,659,200 tons of cargo journeyed to the Soviet Union via the Gulf. The busiest route to Russia extended from American West Coast ports to Soviet eastern Siberian ports, through Japanese waters. The tremendous total of 9,233,280 tons of sup-

---

[21] Matloff and Snell, *Strategic Planning*, 101–102; Leighton and Coakley, *Global Logistics*, 551; Sherwood, *Roosevelt and Hopkins*, 459.

plies, in Russian ships or ships leased to Russia, arrived in the Soviet Union via this potentially dangerous sea lane. Technically, only non-military supplies were carried as "Japan winked at the traffic to her ally's enemy." Forty-seven per cent of all Russian aid supplies from the Western Hemisphere skirted Japan.[22]

Although the American Lend-Lease officials made every effort, under repeated Presidential command, to deliver Russian goods on schedule, they fell far behind in the last part of 1941 and the first part of 1942. There were several difficulties. Russian and American authorities disagreed on the capacity of ports such as Murmansk and Archangel; American suppliers, unfamiliar with Russian specifications, had difficulty satisfying the Soviets; material prepared for shipment in haste arrived incomplete, defective, or damaged. All these problems "made a very bad impression on the Russians" and served to increase their protests over American delay and inadequacy. The War Department had planned to catch up with the schedule in December, 1941, only to be interrupted by Pearl Harbor. At that time, suspension of Lend-Lease shipments and diversion of material and shipping provided a further set-back. Marshall and Stimson both advocated a revision of the Protocol because of greatly increased United States military needs, although they favored continuing Russian aid. But Roosevelt, on December 28, 1941, directed that the Russian aid program be resumed by January 1 and deficits be wiped out by April 1, 1942.[23]

[22] Report on War Aid, 15; Motter, *Persian Gulf*, 432–33. Tonnage figures in text are short tons converted from long tons in the sources.

[23] Leighton and Coakley, *Global Logistics*, 112–16, 552; Stettinius, *Lend-Lease*, 203–205. One example of how Pearl Harbor affected foreign aid production: On December 11, 1941, an air force major attached to the Aircraft Scheduling Unit telegraphed the Reynolds company that "any aluminum sheet already produced or now in process for Russia or for any other foreign country" must be used to fill past due orders for the U.S. Armed Forces. It took a week for the S.P.A.B. to hear of this irregular order and countermand it on December 19. The loss of a week's production resulted. Failing this, the military protested to the S.P.A.B., which ended the controversy when the President's December 28 order came through. For this story see: Charles M. Wiltse (C.P.A. *Historical Reports*), *Aluminum Policies of the War Production Board and Predecessor Agencies, May 1940 to November 1945*, 124–25.

On December 30, Stimson sent Roosevelt a new schedule of deliveries that did not agree with the Protocol in all cases. For example, the tank, truck, and aircraft deliveries could not be met on schedule by April 1, although Stimson thought all could be made available by June 1. The quantity of ammunition shipped would be limited, and certain chemicals, including explosives would be delayed until August. Some of the anti-aircraft and anti-tank guns promised could not be sent off until March. Stimson warned Roosevelt that it was dangerous to make and expect the country to honor "absolute commitments" in wartime. Roosevelt accepted Stimson's recommendations as minimum schedules, but insisted the goal of April 1 remain for the Protocol schedule. Perhaps Britain's better record of delivery embarrassed the President. Harriman reported on December 24, 1941, "that Britain was 100 per cent on schedule," while the United States was 75 per cent behind.[24]

Additional problems, linked with the difficulties over specifications, arose because the Soviets signed the First Protocol before they knew all their own needs. That, added to discovery of other American production items which they desired, led to a series of requests for supplies in addition to those on the Protocol. In early 1942, Russia requested tractors, transport planes, radar, radio equipment, rubber floats, pyroxylin smokeless powder, and Sten submachine guns. Russian representatives also demanded extraordinary American efforts to meet their needs and blamed almost all failures on the War Department. Even so, tanks, trucks, and planes became available in almost the quantity Stimson had scheduled for June 30, 1942. Out of 1,800 aircraft, 1,311 actually were exported, but not all of them reached Russia—some were immobilized in England, awaiting convoy;

[24] Leighton and Coakley, *Global Logistics*, 115, 552–53. The British record is strikingly reflected in the correspondence between Churchill and Stalin: See *U.S.S.R. Correspondence, I*, 15, 16, 17, 19, 20–21, 22–23, 24, 26–27, 30, 31–32; and Churchill, *The Grand Alliance*, 387, 454, 455–57, 459, 463, 465–67, 471, 528. Russian versions differ slightly in wording, containing a few items not in Churchill.

others went to the bottom with their carriers. In tanks, 2,010 out of 4,500 were sent off to Russia. Of 90,000 cargo trucks requested, 36,881 were shipped. Supplies were made available at "British and U.S.A. centres of production" in accordance with the terms of the Protocol. Lend-Lease goods actually became Russian property as soon as the finished item received assignment to their quota.[25]

In order to meet First Protocol schedules, the army requisitioned all gasoline-powered light tanks from American tankmen in March and cancelled Britain's April quota. All of the field telephone wire produced in the United States in January, 1942, plus 90 per cent of the production for the next two months, went to Russia. The United States exported all 2,421 rubber floats asked for, 81,287 of the 98,220 submachine guns, 400 of the 624 scout cars, and other items from the special request list. With the backing of the Combined Chiefs of Staff, Marshall refused to allow export of transport planes, the only special request he turned down. These planes represented so critical a commodity that even the White House pressure could not shake them loose. The Soviet military mission in Washington demanded another special request: factory inspection privileges for their agents, to prevent shipment of defective equipment. Stimson granted this privilege, "very carefully circumscribed," in February, 1942. The War Department also tightened its inspection and shipment procedures, and Soviet packaging complaints decreased. Other procedural changes that occurred as American production shifted into war gear relieved problems concerning spare parts, ammunition quotas, and defective equipment. None of these irritations disappeared entirely, and new ones appeared, but a higher degree of Soviet-American co-operation eased the difficulties. The relative smoothness that characterized Anglo-American industrial relations never applied to similar Soviet-

[25] *Soviet Supply Protocols,* 3; Report on War Aid, 2. Conflicts with letter from Secretary of War to President, cited by Leighton and Coakley, *Global Logistics,* 559.

American affairs. Of course the Soviets did not object when they discovered the jeep more practical than the motorcycle side-cars they ordered or when the army substituted standard .45-caliber Thompson submachine guns for the Sten requested.[26]

Tremendous activity took place in the complicated business of contracting for Russian supplies. The Russian section of the Lend-Lease office reported the first billion-dollar credit exhausted by the end of January, 1941. In February, 1942, Roosevelt cabled Stalin his proposal that "a second billion dollars be placed at the disposal of your Government upon the same conditions as . . . the first." Stalin's reply on February 18 accepted Roosevelt's decision with "sincere gratitude." However, Stalin could not pass up the opportunity to complain about the scarcity of shipping and to advocate greater use of the Murmansk route. In decrying the lack of shipping, Stalin touched a tender nerve.[27]

With American participation in the war, United States flag shipping had to be spread around the world, the loss of Allied merchant ships mounted, and Allied shippers found frustrating any attempt at foresighted planning. For example, on January 12, 1942, the Combined Chiefs of Staff took their problem to the White House. To maintain two large convoys, "Magnet-Indigo" (northern Ireland-Iceland) and "Poppy" (New Caledonia), they would have to cut either Lend-Lease shipments of tanks, vehicles, and aircraft to the Middle East or Russian aid. They recommended the cut in Russian aid. As Marshall posed the problem, the reduction would have been 30 per cent, or seven freighters. Roosevelt observed that he liked the program, "if only some means could be found to take care of the Russians." After more discussion, Roosevelt turned to Hopkins and asked if he could "get enough ships" to continue the Russian run and still not impair the army convoys. Hopkins thought he could if Admiral Land of the Maritime Commission knew the need.

[26] Leighton and Coakley, *Global Logistics*, 553–55; Stettinius, *Lend-Lease*, 209.

[27] *Foreign Relations*, 1942, III, 690–92; also Russian version, *U.S.S.R. Correspondence*, II, 19–21; Stettinius, *Lend-Lease*, 205.

After a good deal more discussion, Roosevelt approved Marshall's plans and remarked, "We will make . . . Hopkins find ships." But if results were the measure, Hopkins was not very successful. Russian deliveries fell off until March 17 when Roosevelt directed Stettinius, Nelson, and Land to act. Give Russia "a first priority in shipping," the President demanded of Admiral Land. Curtly he ordered Nelson to get the Protocol promises translated into delivery "regardless of the effect . . . on any other part of our war program." It was very difficult to get the shrunken blanket of shipping to cover the whole bed.[28]

Hopkins found it impossible to round up the fifty vessels that the Lend-Lease Administration estimated were necessary to move scheduled January, 1941, cargo. Even the Presidential directive of December 28 could not be effective against ineffective shipping control or ships useless in war zones because they were not as yet degaussed (demagnetized) or equipped with anti-aircraft guns. Thus only twenty ships sailed for Murmansk in January and four for Vladivostok. Roosevelt was upset and complained to Land, but five fewer ships sailed to Soviet ports in February. In March, forty-three ships embarked on the Russian run, but because of earlier failures and fourteen sinkings in these three months, the schedule lagged as badly as ever. On March 17 came Roosevelt's strongest directive to the Maritime Commission and Hopkins' candid remark to Harriman and Faymonville that "the Russian protocol must be completed in preference to any other phase of our war program." In April, 79 merchantmen set out for Russia and 19 of them died at sea. Roosevelt proposed a regularly scheduled North Russian run of fifty ships between March and November, and half that in the

[28] Roosevelt Library, President's Official File 220, Box 2, Stimson to Roosevelt, February 17, 1942; Motter, *Persian Corridor*, 36; Leighton and Coakley, *Global Logistics*, 156–58; Sherwood, *Roosevelt and Hopkins*, 461–65; Stettinius, *Lend-Lease*, 205; *W.P.B. Minutes*, 34. Even the pre-Pearl Harbor shipbuilding policies of the navy and the Maritime Commission were severely criticized by the War Production Board. See: William Chaikin and Charles H. Coleman (C.P.A. *Historical Reports*), *Ship-building Policies of the War Production Board, January 1942–November 1945*, 1–11.

winter months. The War Shipping Administration calculated that it would take 260 vessels for this one route. Nevertheless, they tried to work their plans into the President's objective. Since only sixty-four ships put out for Russian ports in May and June combined, the program still had a long way to go.[29]

Yet another of the many complicated problems faced by Russian Lend-Lease was the port shell game. Was the Lend-Lease-for-Russia material located at New York, or Boston, or Philadelphia, or Baltimore? With no central agency to oversee Soviet shipments, it often was not clear. To handle this problem, a Russian shipping board, made up of representatives from the Maritime Commission, the Army's Defense Aid section, the Lend-Lease Administration, and Soviet officials, met weekly in the Commercial Traffic Branch of the Office of the Quartermaster General. Philadelphia became the Russian port, and improvement in the shipping situation became apparent in April, as clearances rose.[30]

Molotov, dubbed "Mr. Brown" for security's sake, arrived in Washington late Friday afternoon, May 29. He had come from a series of London conferences with Churchill and had flown routinely to Washington via Iceland and Labrador. The only excitement apparently occurred when his plane blew a tire on land-

[29] Report on War Aid, 14; Leighton and Coakley, *Global Logistics*, 556; Stettinius, *Lend-Lease*, 205. Roosevelt directed Admiral Land of the Maritime Commission to give Russian Protocol shipping first priority and to take ships from Latin-American and Caribbean runs if necessary. At the same time he directed Donald Nelson to release all material promised under the Russian program regardless of the effect on any other part of the war program. Roosevelt ordered Stettinius to submit definite schedules of material availability and shipping. Similar directives went to the War and Navy departments. Stettinius observed, "It was the only way we could possibly hope to make real progress on the Protocol shipments." On February 7, 1942, Roosevelt created the War Shipping Administration with Admiral Emory S. Land as administrator, thus transferring ship allocation and operation activities into the President's executive office and presumably into his control. Land also continued with the Maritime Commission, and the two offices remained tied closely together; Roosevelt Library, President's Official File 173-B, Attorney General Francis Biddle to Roosevelt, February 7, 1942.

[30] Leighton and Coakley, *Global Logistics*, 557, Stettinius, *Lend-Lease*, 205.

ing. A cable from Churchill revealed that Molotov seemed primarily interested in a second front, and the British leader had discussed the *BOLERO* (United States build-up in the United Kingdom for a cross-channel attack), *SLEDGEHAMMER* (plan for a limited 1942 cross-channel attack), and *ROUNDUP* (plan for a major Anglo-American cross-channel attack in 1943) schemes with his guest.[31]

Molotov, Litvinov, and two interpreters met immediately with Roosevelt, Hull, and Hopkins at the White House. There followed some discussion of tangental matters, such as the unsuccessful effort to get Russia to adhere to the Prisoner of War (Geneva) Convention of 1929. Hopkins later remarked, "You don't have to know very much about Russia . . . to know there isn't a snowball's chance in hell for either Russia or Germany to permit the International Red Cross really to inspect any prison camps." At this first meeting discussion of the inspection question, Japanese matters, and the use of poison gas by Germany led nowhere, so Hopkins broke it up by suggesting that Molotov take a rest.[32]

Although Roosevelt felt the business of talking through interpreters and to a person such as Molotov cramped his style, he accepted it as a challenge. Saturday morning the talks resumed without Hull, but with Marshall and Admiral Ernest J. King, chief of naval operations. Roosevelt told the military men that Molotov had come to discuss a second front, and that "we [Roosevelt, Hull, and Hopkins] regarded it as our obligation to help the Soviets to the best of our ability." Because of strategic and logistical difficulties, the President played down the second front possibility. Molotov, however, put forth the Soviet arguments quite persuasively. Roosevelt then asked Marshall if "developments were clear enough so that we could say to Mr. Stalin that we are preparing a second front." Marshall's answer

[31] Sherwood, *Roosevelt and Hopkins*, 556–57, 568.

[32] Sherwood, *Roosevelt and Hopkins*, 559–60; *Foreign Relations*, 1942, III, 566–68, 572.

was affirmative, and the President then instructed Molotov to tell Stalin, "We expect the formation of a second front this year." One of the problems in the way of such an operation, both Marshall and King agreed, was that of Soviet supply. It absorbed so much transport and cover service that only a very tenuous margin remained with which to send our army to England. If the Soviets would provide better convoy protection on the Murmansk run, such as bombing Nazi air and naval bases in Norway, and open the Alaska-Siberia route for flight delivery of aircraft, to save cargo space, they would facilitate Allied supply problems. Molotov objected to the ALSIB idea as impractical.[33]

Saturday's lunch was held with an expanded group, including the Vice-President, Senator Tom Connally of the Foreign Relations Committee, Congressman Sol Bloom of the Foreign Affairs Committee, Under Secretary of the Navy James Forrestal, Soviet and American military and naval aides, and the like. Roosevelt returned to his study afterward and handed Molotov a draft copy of the Second Protocol. This included 8,000,000 tons of material that the United States proposed to produce for Russia between July 1, 1942, and June 30, 1943. The President made it clear that only about 4,100,000 tons could actually be shipped.[34]

Sunday afternoon Roosevelt and Hopkins met with the Joint Chiefs of Staff. The President wanted to give Molotov a more specific statement in regard to the second front. He proposed that *BOLERO* (the build-up for the invasion) begin during the summer and last as long as the weather permitted. A cross-channel invasion would mean that Russian-aid shipping would have to be reduced in order to free vessels for the build-up. Hopkins

[33] Sherwood, *Roosevelt and Hopkins*, 562–65; *Foreign Relations*, 1942, III, 575–78; General John R. Deane, in a comment to the author, observed that the second front promise at that time, so far as Marshall's office was concerned, "was a pious hope surrounded by a myriad of 'ifs' and was realistically overoptimistic. To the Russians it was a commitment—the first of several such promises—made and broken—which made our relations with the U.S.S.R. in Lendlease as well as other matters much more difficult."

[34] Sherwood, *Roosevelt and Hopkins*, 568.

believed that so long as the Soviets received "those munitions which they could actually use in battle this year," with assurances of the invasion sometime in 1942, they would not object to shipping cutbacks. King observed that reduction in northern route shipping would provide more vessels for the build-up, "very substantially relieve the pressure" on the British navy, and free destroyers for Atlantic convoy. Roosevelt cabled Churchill that American combined staffs "are now working on proposals to increase the shipping for *BOLERO* use by making large reductions of materials for Russia which we could not manufacture in any case before 1943." The President wrote on a memorandum how he planned to cut the total number of tons of Russian aid down in order to free ships for *BOLERO*. Hopkins observed, "The President is very insistent, however, that all of the tough items of supply go through." Essentially Roosevelt proposed to allow shipment of all 1,800,000 tons of planes, tanks, and guns, but reduce the 2,300,000 tons of "General Supplies" to 700,000. That added up to a saving of 1,600,000 tons of shipping, or a total of 2,500,000 tons rather than the 4,100,000 then promised.[35] In other words, Roosevelt would substitute the second front build-up for 1,600,000 tons of supplies.

On Monday morning, June 1, at 10:30 A.M., Litvinov, "Mr. Brown," and an interpreter arrived at the White House to confer again with Roosevelt, Hopkins, and their interpreter. They discussed the creation of the Alaska-Siberia air ferry, among other matters, but Molotov only replied that he did not know what decision the Kremlin had reached. Finally the conversation came around to the draft of the Second Protocol, and Roosevelt advanced his idea for a cutback from 4,100,000 to 2,500,000 tons, to "speed up the establishment of that [second] front." Hopkins assured Molotov that there "would be no cut in the volume of tanks and ammunition." Molotov, doubtless taken by surprise, stammered that he would "report this suggestion at home." He expressed concern for such non-military items "as metals and rail-

[35] *Ibid.*, 568–70.

road material," electrical plants, machinery production, and other vital supplies that would affect the Russian rear. Roosevelt reflected that "ships could not be in two places at once." Molotov retorted that "the second front would be stronger if the first front still stood fast" and sarcastically asked what would happen if the Russians cut down their demands and no second front materialized? More insistently, he asked, "What is the President's answer with respect to the second front?" Roosevelt answered that the United States "expected" to establish one and that it would be possible sooner if the Soviet government would allow the United States to "put more ships into the English service." In spite of this excited exchange, Molotov departed cordially. Molotov released the press announcement after his return to Moscow. Hopkins and Marshall felt that the statement, "full understanding was reached with regard to the urgent task of creating a second front in Europe in 1942," was too strong, but Roosevelt wished to have it included. Molotov's statement added that "measures for increasing and speeding up the supplies of . . . war material from the United States" to Russia were also discussed.[36]

One more diplomatic item concluded the period of State Department activity during the First Protocol period, and that was the conclusion of the Lend-Lease Master Agreement with Russia. On March 18, 1942, Harry C. Hawkins, chief of the State Department's Division of Commercial Policy and Agreements, advocated conclusion of a Lend-Lease Master Agreement with Russia similar to the one concluded with the United Kingdom on February 23. The argument for such an understanding ran, in part, as follows: First, as matters then stood, Russia owed two billion dollars under the terms of the two previous agreements. In comparison with British terms, this represented "a clear discrimination against the U.S.S.R." If removed, the effect should be to avoid "Soviet resentment and of greatly strengthening our relations with the U.S.S.R. in the war effort." Second,

[36] *Foreign Relations, 1942*, III, 578–83, 593–94.

repayment of "even one billion . . . would constitute a very heavy war debt in terms of Russia's capacity to pay. . . . Even if they [Russia] could squeeze out enough goods and gold to meet their payments, it would not be in our interest to have them do so since the goods and gold sent here would provide no purchasing power for American exports during the ten-year repayment period," the result being that American exports to Russia would dwindle to nothing. It also would strain commercial relations between Russia and other countries. An agreement along the lines of the United Kingdom agreement "would avoid a settlement which would severely burden commerce if lived up to, and set the stage for repudiation, with all that would mean in terms of bitterness and recriminations." Third, the Soviet Union probably would welcome such an agreement, which would not preclude "cash payment if later deemed advisable." And, finally, it *would commit the Soviet government to co-operate* in regard to current and future economic action in line with principles advocated by us [the U.S.]."[37]

The idea, clearly stated, re-emphasized the original Lend-Lease concept as Roosevelt first phrased it, to "eliminate the silly, foolish, old dollar sign." Important in the formulation of the entire Master Agreement idea, was also the notion to trade a post-war debt situation for post-war economic co-operation. Hull hoped Molotov, as commissar of foreign affairs, would be able to conclude the agreement while he stayed at the White House. Litvinov, however, had to send it to the Foreign Office, and the agreement was not signed until June 11. Even this was nearly record time for a Soviet-American accord. Perhaps Molotov's visit and the promise of a second front had something to do with the speed. The Master Agreement with the Soviet Union differed from that with Britain in emphasis on Russian subscription to the principles of the Atlantic Charter, but in no other significant way. "Final determination of the terms . . . upon which the [U.S.S.R.] . . . receives such aid . . . should

[37] *Ibid.*, 699–700.

be deferred until the extent of the defense aid is known" and until the future discloses what mutual "conditions and benefits" will serve to "promote the establishment and maintenance of world peace."[38]

Article V of the agreement provided for a return, after the emergency, of defense articles not destroyed, lost, or consumed "as shall be determined by the President" to be useful in U. S. defense "or to be otherwise of use to the United States of America." But the State Department believed that Article VII was important. The Soviet Union, the United States, and "all other countries of like mind," shall, by "appropriate international and domestic measures," take steps to eliminate "all forms of discriminatory treatment in international commerce," all trade barriers, and work for the "attainment of all the economic objectives set forth in the" Atlantic Charter. This article provided a rosy dream for a post-war world free of conflicting economic nationalism.[39]

[38] *Ibid.*, 705, 708; Edward R. Stettinius, Jr., *Report to the 78th Congress on Lend-Lease Operations* (bound with *President's Reports on Lend-Lease Operations*), 70–74.

[39] Soviet Master Agreement also printed in *Eighth Report on Lend-Lease*, 50–54. On the importance of Article VII, see George M. Fennemore, The Role of the Department of State in Connection with the Lend-Lease Program, 249.

CHAPTER FOUR

Icebergs and Submarines

L END-LEASE FOLLOWED THE EXAMPLE of the iceberg by largely slipping from public view. After the debates surrounding the passage of the act died down, only certain obvious administrative activities, and very few operational ones, remained visible to the public eye. Roosevelt had helped this situation along by giving control of the operation to Hopkins and keeping it there throughout the war. As special assistant to the President, Hopkins answered only to Roosevelt. The Division of Defense Aid Reports, created by Roosevelt, had remained properly obscure in the beginning, as the President had intended. The Office of Lend-Lease Administration and its impeccable administrator provided, thereafter, a convenient organization to deal with congressmen and handle routine affairs.

Roosevelt and Hopkins ruled on over-all policy matters, as might be expected of the executive, and quite often such policy was not public. For example, a broad cloak of military secrecy covered the purchase and distribution of war material. In this area, the Lend-Lease Administration bowed to policy decisions of the Munitions Assignment Board, headed by Hopkins and responsible to Roosevelt, Churchill, and the Combined Chiefs of Staff. Lend-Lease Administrator Stettinius represented the most visible part of the iceberg. He held press conferences, appeared before Congressional committees, and in general explained, interpreted, and implemented policy.

Throughout and even after the war, the image of Lend-Lease

to Russia never clearly revealed itself to the American public, although citizens learned a great deal more than their Soviet counterparts. In 1942, *The New York Times* reported a $26,494,-265,474 navy appropriation bill signed by Roosevelt, with funds transferable to Lend-Lease. Further information concerning Lend-Lease was also presented:

1. Lend-Lease aid neared $30,000,000,000.
2. A new Soviet "loan" was likely even though the United States remained behind in monthly quota deliveries.
3. Pearl Harbor threw the Russian schedule off, but Roosevelt expected the United States would catch up by March 1.
4. Britain exported over 9,000 planes and 3,000 tanks to all theaters including Russia.
5. Roosevelt signed a $32,762,737,900 appropriation bill, the largest in history, as additional money for the army, Lend-Lease, and maritime administration.
6. Roosevelt used his authority as commander-in-chief to order the War and Navy departments to fulfill the Soviet Protocol schedules.
7. The new Lend-Lease agreement [Master agreement] included a section on post-war international trade freedom.
8. When the United States and Russia signed the Master Agreement, they agreed to create a second front in 1942, and a new and better world after the war.
9. The United States, Britain, and Russia signed a new protocol that called for delivery of $3,000,000,000 worth of equipment to Russia.
10. The Ford Motor Company, at the request of the United States, sold Russia an entire tire factory.
11. The United States bought the Douglas Oil Refinery near Los Angeles for shipment to Russia under Lend-Lease.[1]

---

[1] Because the war news remained largely confidential, it was not possible for Americans to know in detail how Lend-Lease to Russia (or anywhere else) actually operated. Americans did learn a great deal from their newspapers about non-sensitive occurrences. *The New York Times* is used here as representative of the American press even though they excelled most other newspapers in the scope of their coverage. The alert reader will note a number of inaccuracies of

It appeared that the United States appropriated and spent vast sums of money, that she made agreements with Russia to deliver substantial amounts of equipment, and that equipment delivery fell far enough behind schedule to cause Roosevelt to command the War and Navy departments to catch up. In October, 1942, *Fortune* noted that "U.S. officials generally admit that we are delivering less than we planned." They added that "U.S. aid to Russia was 'less than marginal,' " and (*Fortune* quoting *The New York Times*) "it would appear that despite Russia's pleas . . . Britain and the U.S. cannot do more than a fraction of what they would like to do for the Soviets." It became clear that Lend-Lease money was more easily committed than transformed into munitions and delivered.[2]

Some vessels traveled unobstructed over the Soviet's favorite delivery route, the North Russian run to Murmansk, but Hitler, severe ice conditions, and the long, pale Arctic day combined to impede the trip. The German dictator, fearing a British attack on Norway and determined to obstruct the Russian run, shifted the strength of his navy to Norwegian fiords. The *Tirpitz* ran to Trondheim in January, the pocket battleship *Scheer* joined her in February, the heavy cruiser *Hipper* followed in March, and the pocket battleship *Luetzow* appeared in May—all with their complements of destroyers. The battle cruisers *Scharnhorst* and *Gneisenau* and the cruiser *Prinz Eugen* all suffered damage on the dash from Brest through the English Channel in February. The *Scharnhorst* and *Gneisenau*, damaged by mines (and the *Gneisenau* put out of action for the remainder of the war by air attack during repair at Kiel), never made it to Norway. The *Prinz Eugen* was torpedoed by the British submarine *Trident*, and limped to Trondheim. From there the cruis-

fact, which do not reflect upon the news media, but on the conditions under which all operated during the war. *The New York Times*, 1942: February 10, p. 3; February 11, p. 5; February 17, p. 8; February 18, p. 5; February 22, p. 6; March 7, p. 7; March 28, p. 3; May 27, pp. 1, 4; June 12, p. 1; October 7, p. 1; October 30, p. 8; October 31, p. 6; November 3, p. 22; November 24, p. 2.

2 "Lend-Lease to Date," *Fortune*, 108f.

er escaped to Germany for repair. A portion of the Nazi under-sea fleet was ordered from the Atlantic stations to reinforce the other elements of the German navy in Norway. Luftwaffe squadrons established bases in northern Norway and Finland. German naval and air forces recognized a tremendous opportunity not only to raid convoys, but also to fight, pretty much on their own terms, the Anglo-American covering forces. Except for the submarines, however, the German navy "seldom rose to the occasion."[3]

The "P.Q.'s" (convoys that assembled at Hval Fjord, Reykjavik, Iceland, or Loch Ewe, Scotland, from October, 1941, through October, 1942) worried more about the U-boats in their coats of polar white paint, the reconnaissance planes, and the torpedo planes and screaming dive bombers than they did about the German surface fleet. In addition, to the Nazi-made hazards, the gray-cold, heavy Arctic seas, floating ice, flying snow, and drifting fog took their toll. An uncontested passage was unpleasant; a fighting passage, hell. Murmansk proved no haven for those who safely ran the gauntlet, with German aircraft based only a few minutes flying time away. Archangel, miles farther, provided greater port safety but remained ice-locked from November to early summer. The Allies could not depend upon Soviet naval and air support; there existed no Russian naval air force, and the army air force flew reluctantly over water. Soviet submarines maintained a regular patrol off the Norwegian coast, but there were not enough of them to give much trouble to Hitler's navy. The burden of convoy protection

[3] Winston S. Churchill, *The Hinge of Fate*, 256–57; Morison, *Battle of the Atlantic*, 160–61; Leighton and Coakley, *Global Logistics*, 557. One should not imply that the only difficulty with Hitler's navy was a result of its efforts to contest the northern route. Lend-Lease vessels still had quite a distance to cover before assembling at Hval Fjord or Loch Ewe, and some did not make it. One example of this hazard is the case of the SS *Kolkhoznik*, carrying a cargo of "planes, tractor tanks, barbed wire, and nitro cellulose," that was torpedoed on January 17, 1942, in Canadian waters off Halifax, Nova Scotia, en route from Boston to Archangel. See Truman Library, President's Official File, 356, Box 1038, memo, Charles M. Irelan to Charles S. Murphey, September 14, 1957.

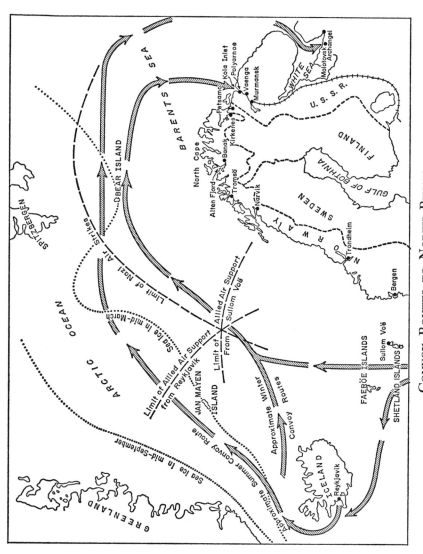

CONVOY ROUTES TO NORTH RUSSIA

fell primarily to the Royal Navy, until an American task force, including the new battleship *Washington,* the heavy cruisers *Wichita* and *Tuscaloosa,* the carrier *Wasp,* and Destroyer Squadron 8, arrived in Scapa Flow on April 3, 1942. Minus the *Wasp,* they joined convoy protection on April 28.[4]

Beginning with P.Q. 12 that sailed from Iceland on March 1, 1942, the Nazis undertook to wipe out each of the vital supply movements. Nazi Vice-Admiral Otto Ciliax, commander of the *Tirpitz* attack force, lost an opportunity to score and allowed the P.Q. 12, with sixteen merchantmen, to make it safely to Murmansk. He wasted so much fuel oil that it took the German navy until July 1 to supply enough for another run. The *Tirpitz* outmaneuvered a dozen British torpedo planes on its return journey. On March 20, P.Q. 13, with nineteen merchantmen, steamed out of Reykjavik into foul weather and a German welcome. In gale winds, recurrent snow-squalls, and rough seas the convoy fought German submarines, destroyers, and Luftwaffe high- and low-level attacks. The United States merchantman *Effingham* and one British and two Panamanian vessels were sunk. Although the British cruiser *Trinidad* was damaged it sank the German destroyer Z-26. The remainder of the convoy arrived in Murmansk, after a narrow escape from pursuing submarines, only to be greeted by Luftwaffe bombs.[5]

P.Q. 14, with twenty-four ships, left Iceland on April 8 and reached Murmansk on April 19 with only seven merchantmen. One of the ships was sunk by a German U-boat and sixteen others turned back because of heavy seas and ice. Two vessels of United States registry accompanied the remaining five, mainly British, into Murmansk harbor. P.Q. 15, with twenty-five ships, departed Reykjavik on April 26. Only three of the vessels were American freighters, and one of them, the *Expositor,* carried five thousand cases of TNT. After successfully avoiding a float-

---

[4] Morison, *Battle of the Atlantic,* 161, 162–63, 168, 176–77.

[5] Stephen Wentworth Roskill, *The War at Sea, 1939–1945,* Vol. III, part II, 432; Morison, *Battle of the Atlantic,* 165, 166, 178–79.

ing mine field, the convoy spent forty-eight hours under constant air or submarine attack. Luftwaffe torpedoes sank three vessels, and a munitions ship, the British *Cape Corso,* blew up in a spectacular pyrotechnic display. The remaining twenty-two cargo ships docked at Murmansk on May 5.[6]

The return run from Murmansk to Iceland seldom offered the mariners much respite from Nazi attack. Convoys moving in this direction carried the designation "Q.P." Returning merchantmen hauled lighter and less dangerous cargo such as chrome, potassium chloride, magnesite, furs, skins, wood products, and similar items. Nevertheless, these ships provided a target for the Nazi war machine too, especially since Q.P.'s and and P.Q.'s usually crossed at sea, making possible one heavy cover force for both.

Westbound Q.P. 10, with sixteen ships, and eastbound P.Q. 14 ran into the destroyer-submarine-aircraft attack common to the eastbound convoys. This group lost four ships, two to U-boats and two to aircraft. Q.P. 11, with thirteen cargo vessels (two American), the British cruiser *Edinburgh,* eight destroyers, some corvettes, and an armed trawler, ran into heavy Nazi attack, as did P.Q. 15, moving in the other direction. Submarines damaged the *Edinburgh.* The German destroyer *Schoemann* finished it off with a torpedo, but not until the *Schoemann* itself took a fatal salvo from the cruiser. The German destroyers also shelled the convoy itself, sinking a straggler. Twelve merchantmen made it safely to port.[7]

In April, the quantity of American Lend-Lease shipments increased because of administration pressure, and the number of cargo ships in each convoy swelled to over thirty. At the same

[6] Roskill, *The War at Sea,* Vol. III, part II, 432; Morison, *Battle of the Atlantic,* 167, 169, 170.

[7] Roskill, *The War at Sea,* Vol. III, part II, 432–34; Morison, *Battle of the Atlantic,* 161, 168–69. Convoys P.Q. 12 and Q.P. 8 crossed, as did P.Q. 13 and Q.P. 9, P.Q. 14 and Q.P. 10, P.Q. 15 and Q.P. 11, P.Q. 16 crossed Q.P. 12, and P.Q 17 crossed Q.P. 13. Items in the return cargoes were not "reverse Lend-Lease" but deliveries under the $100,000,000 Defense Supplies Corporation contract with Amtorg.

time, the Arctic day lasted for twenty-four hours, and Hitler strengthened his Luftwaffe in Norway. P.Q. 16 left Iceland on May 21 with thirty-five merchantmen and a strong naval escort of cruisers (four), destroyers, flak ships, armed trawlers, and submarines. The convoy apprehensively approached Bear Island in Denmark Strait and ran into a cloud of Nazi aircraft, so great in number that for the next five days it must have seemed as if the entire Luftwaffe were involved. One American freighter, *City of Joliet,* experienced eight torpedo attacks and eighteen dive bomber attacks on the first day. The freighter saw little action on the second day, but the next day she received ten separate air attacks, although no direct hits, and was so badly damaged that she had to be abandoned. The *City of Joliet,* three other American ships, and three British ships went to the bottom. Six of the losses were caused by air attack and one by submarine attack. Some 32,400 tons of cargo out of a total of 125,000 tons slid beneath the waves with these ships.

Westbound Q.P. 13, with thirty-five vessels (nine American), experienced submarine alarms and was followed by Nazi aircraft, but the convoy found shelter in fog through most of their voyage. The shelter proved not as effective for navigation, however, as the convoy wandered into a defensive mine field at the entrance to Denmark Strait. British mines blew five ships, two American, into wrecks.[8]

With more Nazi aircraft searching out and attacking north-run ships than ever before, and with the strong German surface fleet suspiciously quiet since the first of May, it seemed that the Arctic sea war would soon come to a head. The loss of seven ships in P.Q. 16 brought the total sunk to sixteen in the east-bound convoys, and the five merchantmen of Q.P. 13, lost in the British mine field, brought the westbound loss to eleven.

[8] Roskill, *The War at Sea,* Vol. II, 132 (P.Q. 16 lost 147 tanks out of 468, 77 aircraft out of 201, 770 vehicles out of 3,277), and Vol. III, part II, 432, 434; Morison, *Battle of the Atlantic,* 171–73, 178.

Determined virtually to wipe out the next eastbound convoy, the Nazis hatched operations *KNIGHT'S GAMBIT* (*Rösselsprung*). Planned as a combined operation below, on, and above the water, Hitler's admirals assigned the *Tirpitz*, the *Scheer*, the *Hipper*, and seven destroyers to the surface fleet. Apparently the German navy also had excellent intelligence concerning the departure and make-up of P.Q. 17. The twenty-two American cargo carriers composed a majority among the thirty-six merchantmen, and for such a large movement the escort was increased and supplemented by an impressive covering force. The merchantmen left Iceland June 27 and ran into such heavy fog and ice floes in Denmark Strait that two cargo ships put back to Iceland. On July 1 the escort shot down a reconnaissance plane, and on July 2 six U-boats delivered an unsuccessful attack. The Nazis then hesitated, apparently confused by their own reports. Q.P. 13, in nearly the same area but moving in the other direction, acted as one jumbling factor; also Nazi pilots mistakenly reported two cruisers as aircraft carriers and a third as a battleship. Although the German command did not really know what the Allies had on the sea, they decided to act on July 2.[9]

Twenty-six Luftwaffe planes bombed the convoy on July 3, with little success because of poor visibility. Meanwhile the British Admiralty pondered its intelligence reports that the *Tirpitz* had left Trondheim on July 3 and moved with an attack force toward P.Q. 17. The British admiral in charge of the escort force had been ordered not to tangle with any enemy surface units that he could not handle; if the *Tirpitz* showed up, she was to be fought by the heavy cover force that included two battleships and the carrier *Victorious*. These heavy vessels steamed far to the west as they also had to cover Q.P. 13. When the British decided the *Tirpitz* force had sailed to intercept

[9] Roskill, *The War at Sea*, Vol. III, part II, 433, 434; Morison, *Battle of the Atlantic*, 179–81; Churchill, *The Hinge of Fate*, 262–63.

the convoy, they ordered the escort force to withdraw (9:11 P.M., July 4) and the convoy to disperse (9:23 P.M., and 9:35 P.M., July 4).[10]

British naval intelligence proved no better than the German. The *Tirpitz, Scheer, Hipper,* seven destroyers, and three torpedo boats sped out of Norway; but Luftwaffe reports so confused them, that the Nazi admiral, determined to preserve the great *Tirpitz,* steamed east of the North Cape for a few miles, then turned around, and returned to port without making contact. The British learned of this German failure too late to reassemble the convoy. Meanwhile the scattered merchantmen, with a third of the journey ahead (destination—Archangel), remained as ducks in a pond for German aircraft and U-boats. Caught singly or in small groups, thirteen were sunk by air attack and ten by submarine action. Seven of the eleven merchant ships that limped into Archangel between July 11 and 25, 1942, were American. P.Q. 17 managed to deliver 896 vehicles out of 4,246, 164 tanks out of 594, 87 aircraft of 297, and 57,176 tons of other cargo out of 156,492 tons originally loaded. Hitler had succeeded in breaking up the North Russian Lend-Lease convoys. Another P.Q. did not sail until September, and it was attacked so fiercely (thirteen of forty ships lost) that the next convoy sailed under cover of the Arctic night in mid-December.[11]

American merchantmen on the North Russian run carried poor armament to protect them from aircraft or submarines. The first American cargo vessel bound for Murmansk with an armed

[10] Churchill, *The Hinge of Fate,* 263–64.

[11] Roskill, *The War at Sea,* Vol. II, 143; Morison, *Battle of the Atlantic,* 158–92, chapter titled "The North Russia Run," is by far the most exciting account. However, Morison wrote right after the war (published 1947) before careful compilation of statistics was possible. Therefore the statistics in the account are from Roskill (published 1960) wherever possible. Discrepancies in Morison occasionally make his figures difficult. For example, P.Q. 17 included 22 American merchantmen (p. 179), but "21 American merchantmen carrying Naval Armed Guards" (p. 191). Morison lists the names of the 15 American merchantmen sunk. He also observes that 33 ships in the convoy (Roskill, 36: two turned back, leaving 34) originally carried 188,000 tons of cargo and lost 123,000 tons of cargo on the 22 sunk (Roskill, 23 sunk).

guard of navy gunners mounted one four-inch gun and eight .30-caliber machine guns. Just how an ensign and his crew of eight could operate all of them is not clear. A later crosser, the *Expositor*, equipped with a four-inch gun and four .30-caliber machine guns, added two 20-mm. Oerlikon and one twin-mount Hotchkiss machine guns, in Scotland. But .30- and .50-caliber machine guns, though useful, seldom knocked down Junkers, or kept them a respectful distance away. Frequently the ammunition allowance for the merchantmen would be exhausted by the time the ship completed the outward run, and at least once American naval officials in North Russia begged .50-caliber ammunition from the Soviets so vessels could defend themselves on the return journey. In another instance an ensign of the armed guard put the 37-mm. guns of two tanks carried as deck cargo in readiness and used ammunition from the hold—"one of the rare instances in naval history when barratry has been rewarded by a decoration." On August 4, 1942, 581 American survivors (and over 700 of other nationalities), merchant seamen whose ships sank under them, waited in North Russia for transportation back home. Though it provided no comfort to the shipwrecked sailors, the navy finally began to equip ships on this route with 20-mm., three-inch, and even five-inch guns and to increase the size of the naval crews aboard.[12]

With a total of 343,504 tons of cargo lost at sea during the First Protocol period, mostly on the North Russian run (131,716 tons lost from P.Q.'s 16 and 17 alone), planners diverted American shipping to other routes. Twenty-one of the forty-three ships that sailed to the Persian Gulf between October 1, 1941, and June 30, 1942, did so in May and June, 1942. Twenty-six of the seventy-seven ships that sailed to the Soviet Far East departed in April, May, and June, and in June they sought out Soviet Arctic ports other than the North Russian. In the same period twenty-two vessels unloaded Russia-bound cargoes in the United Kingdom to await transshipment rather than tie up

[12] Morison, *Battle of the Atlantic*, 160, 169, 172, 180, 191–92.

shipping for indeterminate periods as they awaited convoy. Great Britain could not organize and defend convoys as fast as United States shipping arrived in Iceland and Scotland, largely because of the successful German challenge in far northern waters. Hopkins unsuccessfully tried to push Churchill into unstopping the shipping bottleneck in April. Roosevelt told the Prime Minister that the situation "greatly disturbed" him and he was "anxious that ships should not be unloaded" in the United Kingdom. Churchill bluntly replied, "What you suggest is beyond our power . . . we are absolutely extended." Roosevelt reluctantly agreed to the British limit on convoy movements (three convoys every two months) but pressed them to maintain a thirty-five-ship size. Stalin, aware of the bottleneck, cabled Churchill "to take all possible measures" to expedite dispatch of Lend-Lease supplies. The Prime Minister summed up the situation in a communication to his chief of staff, Major General Sir Hastings Ismay, on May 17, 1942:

> Not only Premier Stalin but President Roosevelt will object very much to our desisting from running the convoys now. The Russians are in heavy action, and will expect us to run the risk and pay the price entailed by our contribution. The United States ships are queueing up. . . . The operation is justified if a half gets through. Failure on our part to make the attempt would weaken our influence with both our major Allies.[13]

With the P.Q. 17 disaster and P.Q. 18's departure postponed, Churchill sent a lengthy explanation to Stalin. "The President and I," he wrote, "are ceaselessly searching for means to overcome the extraordinary difficulties which geography, salt-water, and the enemy's air-power interpose." Stalin curtly replied, "According to our naval experts, the arguments of British naval ex-

[13] Report on War Aid, 2, 14; in the same nine months Great Britain lost 565 merchantmen (see *Statistical Digest of the War*, table 158) from enemy action. Churchill, *The Hinge of Fate*, 258–61; *Foreign Relations*, 1942, III, 552, 553–54. Also Hopkins needled Lewis Douglas of the War Shipping Administration, Sherwood, *Roosevelt and Hopkins*, 546–47.

perts on the necessity of stopping the delivery of war supplies to the northern harbors of the U.S.S.R. are untenable. . . . No major task can be carried out in wartime without risk or losses. . . . Deliveries via Persian ports can in no way make up for the loss." Churchill never answered Stalin specifically, for, "after all," he explained, "Russian armies were suffering fearfully." The German naval commander-in-chief gloated, "Our submarines and aircraft, which totally destroyed the last convoy, have forced the enemy to give up this route temporarily." Northern convoy cutbacks caused a rapid remaking of shipping plans in Washington. Hopkins and Lewis Douglas (of the War Shipping Administration) blocked berthing of ships scheduled for the North Russian route, detoured as many as possible to the Persian Gulf, and diverted released shipping to the army. The fact emerged that even though at last the Protocol goods could be made available, they could not be shipped, and backlogs swelled warehouses in the United States.[14]

Because the Soviets assigned higher priorities to shipment of munitions than to trucks, and because they shipped standard United States Army trucks before the nonstandard vehicles specially ordered for them, an especially important backlog in trucks grew. By April 1, 1941, 28,000 trucks appeared on the April assignment schedule. Since the nonstandard vehicles shipped out last, they were useless to the United States Army and could not be transferred to them. Other backlogs cropped up also and further illustrated that by the time the availability problem ended, the shipping problem loomed ever larger. The only great failures to furnish Protocol materials were in anti-aircraft and anti-tank weapons. The United States always furnished greater amounts than available shipping could handle in other instances of Protocol deficits.[15]

Diversion of vessels to the Persian Gulf proved no solution

[14] *U.S.S.R. Correspondence*, I, 52–54, 56; Churchill, *The Hinge of Fate*, 267–70, 270–71, 272; Leighton and Coakley, *Global Logistics*, 557–58.
[15] Leighton and Coakley, *Global Logistics*, 558–59.

to the shipping bottleneck in the spring of 1942. After the joint Anglo-Soviet occupation of Iran in August, 1941, the Russians attempted to handle supplies north of Teheran, while the British managed the larger task of sending goods into the Gulf, unloading them, and getting them across the full length of Iran to the Russian zone. The country, difficult and primitive, impeded the flow of supplies. Nevertheless, a steady trickle began before the end of 1941. Britain was unable to build the facilities necessary, and depended upon United States Lend-Lease. In September and October, 1941, American engineers planned port expansion projects, and in September, 1941, Colonel Wheeler arrived in Iran as chief of the United States Military Iranian Mission. At Khorramshahr, northwest of Abadan on the Tigris River, Americans built wharves, piers, and jetties, and dredged channels, erected cranes, built roads, put up truck and aircraft assembly plants, and laid out an air field. A flight of B-25's from Miami via North Africa arrived in Iran in March, 1942, headed for Russia, and by June 30 seventy-two planes had made the long air journey. A-20's and P-40's had arrived previously by water. In addition, forty-three ships with full cargoes and twenty-eight with partial cargoes brought 264,320 tons of supplies for Russia before June 30.[16]

Even so, more equipment poured into the Persian Gulf ports in the spring of 1942 than the Americans could handle. Admiral William H. Standley arrived in Basra, Iraq, on March 29, on his way to Moscow as the new United States ambassador. The next day he inspected waterfront facilities from a "fast motor boat," presumably having zipped down the Tigris to Khorramshahr and Abadan. He found a lamentable shortage of dockside space and unloading apparatus. He also discovered that some ships were forced to idle at anchor for "two or three weeks to be unloaded," and that many other vessels were diverted to Karachi, India.

[16] Report on War Aid, 2, 14–15; Stettinius, *Lend-Lease*, 215–16; Motter, *Persian Corridor*, 15–18 (survey of aircraft assembly problems in the Persian Gulf area, 125–36, survey of truck assembly problems, 140–50).

Later, from Moscow, Standley strongly recommended that heavy power machinery be sent to the Persian Gulf to speed unloading. The Admiral also reported "hundreds of P-40 fighters and Aircobras sitting there in the shifting winds, sanding up." He scored the Russians for their delay in taking delivery and then complaining of improper assembly and testing when they found sand in the engines. Unlike the B-25's, the P-39's and P-40's arrived disassembled in crates, and an air corps assembly plant put them together. The truck assembly plant had just begun to nibble on the thousand crated trucks on hand at the time of Standley's visit. As in the United States, the Allies at Basra, Iraq, and Khorramshahr, Iran, found the Soviet inspectors overcritical and rigidly exacting, rejecting a high percentage of both aircraft and trucks. And also as in the United States, the situation improved with time and understanding.[17]

Standley's DC-3 Pan American Airways plane landed on the snow-blanketed military airfield near Kuibyshev on April 7. Kuibyshev became the alternate Soviet capital when the Nazis knocked on Moscow's doors. Not until April 23 did Stalin receive the Admiral, although Standley flew to Moscow nearly two weeks earlier. After the opening pleasantries, Standley remarked that part of his job was to see that no "obstacles to the free flow of supplies" existed, and observed that Roosevelt took firm steps to expedite Russian Lend-Lease deliveries, a fact Stalin already knew from his correspondence with the President. Standley then pressed for better communications between Moscow, Kuibyshev, and Washington and suggested an Alaska-Siberian air route. Stalin asked if Standley had considered an airlift via Canada-Iceland,-Murmansk to Moscow, but Standley continued to argue for Alaska-Siberia. Stalin commented, "I'm afraid our *friends*, the Japanese, won't like the Alaskan-Siberian route." He then proceeded to give his opinion of American Lend-Lease. "Your contractors," he admonished Standley, "don't want

[17] Standley, *Admiral Ambassador*, 104–105; Motter, *Persian Corridor*, 73, 74–75.

111

to accept Russian orders. . . . In America . . . we have come to feel that the contractors just don't want Russian orders. The second cause [for delay in delivery] is the lack of shipping and heavy loss of ships because ships from America are not convoyed." Standley, "being a Navy man . . . was considerably annoyed at this criticism" but tried not to show it. Stalin did not seem very well informed on American naval activities or ship losses. Up to then (before heavy Nazi concentration in Norway) American losses had been light.[18]

Establishment of an Alaskan ferry route for aircraft had appealed to War Department planners ever since August, 1941, but received only a Soviet cold shoulder. Persistently the army prompted the Harriman mission and finally the State Department to try to accomplish something, and Standley carried the point as strongly as possible to Stalin. In May, Hopkins discussed the Alaska-Siberian delivery route with an army tactician, Brigadier General Dwight D. Eisenhower, and the War Department followed up with a practical and simple delivery plan. The Soviets agreed "in principle" to the plan but took no action. Maxim Litvinov, now ambassador to the United States, visited Hopkins on June 9 and informed him that Russia agreed to the use of that route. Roosevelt cabled Stalin on June 17 and again on June 23 to request the establishment of the route and, with Stalin's affirmative answer, suggested Russian pilots fly the aircraft. Stalin agreed to a meeting of Soviet-American officials in Moscow to work out the details. Nevertheless the ALSIB route did not open in time to ease deliveries under the First Protocol. It finally became a reality in August, 1942.[19]

The greatest and steadiest volume of cargo carried to the

18 Standley, *Admiral Ambassador*, 153, 154, 156; *U.S.S.R. Correspondence*, II, 19; see also *Foreign Relations, 1942*, III, 690.

19 Matloff and Snell, *Strategic Planning*, discuss early air-ferry planning, 142–45; Sherwood, *Roosevelt and Hopkins*, 551–52, 584; *U.S.S.R. Correspondence*, II, 25–28; *Foreign Relations, 1942*, III, 597, 599–600, 603–604; Wesley Frank Craven and James Lea Cate (eds.), *Services Around the World* (Vol. VII of *The Army Air Forces in World War II*), 154–55.

Soviet Union with the least risk left the United States West
Coast for the Soviet Far Eastern ports, uncomfortably close to
Japan. After Pearl Harbor, obviously, only Soviet ships made
the journey. Japan winked at this traffic because it desired to
keep Russia out of their part of the war. Russia carried 412,160
tons of supplies in seventy-six ships safely across the Pacific
between June 22, 1941, and June 30, 1942. The disadvantage,
as Sherwood put it, was that "any bullet sent by that route
had to travel halfway around the world before it could be
fired at a German." With the great Nazi offensive against the
North Russian route, the Pacific sea lanes as well as the Persian
Gulf took on a new importance despite the great distances involved. The United States transferred fifty-three cargo vessels
and six tankers to Soviet registry to supplement Russian merchant marine on the North Pacific run.[20]

[20] Report on War Aid, 3, 14–15; Sherwood, *Roosevelt and Hopkins*, 545.

CHAPTER FIVE

The Washington Protocol

S MILING UNDER HIS MUSTACHE, Vyacheslav Molotov tucked his autographed picture of Franklin D. Roosevelt under his arm and left the White House for New York on June 1, 1942. If he beamed with satisfaction, it was because he had the President's promise of a second front and a tentative Second Protocol, which he had already sped on its way to Moscow.[1]

As Molotov knew, this proposed Second Protocol had been several months in the drafting by the Office of Lend-Lease Administration and other agencies. Coincidentally, but conveniently, on March 2, 1942, Russia established a "Purchasing Commission of the Soviet Union," headed in the United States by Belyaev, "to function . . . in exactly the same way as the British commission." Significantly, Konstantin I. Lukashev, Amtorg's president and board chairman became vice-chairman of this new commission because "he was so fully familiar with the questions involved." Eleven days later, Hopkins notified Faymonville in Moscow that the time had come "to provide for the continuance of supply after June." Faymonville agreed and suggested a conference with Russian and British officials in Washton to work out a new arrangement. Advised by both the military and Hopkins to continue Russian aid, Roosevelt asked the War Department, the War Production Board, and other agencies for tentative monthly schedules of material for Russia, for the period July 1, 1942–June 30, 1943, to be handed him by April 6.

[1] Sherwood, *Roosevelt and Hopkins*, 574–75.

Hopkins acted for Roosevelt as the co-ordinator of the new proposed Protocol and combined an early April Russian request list with a schedule of available items submitted by the co-operating departments. By May 7 the proposed Second Protocol emerged from the committee, won Roosevelt's approval, and circulated among the agencies involved for their comments.[2]

A subcommittee of the Joint Chiefs of Staff doubted the feasibility of the proposed Second Protocol, but Hopkins, as head of the Munitions Assignment Board, assured them that the Board had considered all United States Army and Navy needs prior to arriving at the specifications. The draft Protocol, and later the final document, contained an escape clause that mollified War Department planners. "It is to be understood," read paragraph 5 of the Protocol, that "this programme is subject to variations to meet unforeseen developments in the progress of the war." Although this qualification was "much more sweeping" than any included in the First (Moscow) Protocol, King and Marshall, meeting with Roosevelt on May 31, warned him that the allocation of over four million tons for Russia would mean reducing some other part of the war effort, such as *BOLERO*. Roosevelt subsequently met with Molotov but failed to get the Russian to agree to any curtailment. In fact, Molotov wanted to add four conditions of his own. The President did not press the reduction any further, and the Joint Chiefs of Staff remained faced with what they considered an impossible shipping situation.[3]

As Molotov went off to New York City, Roosevelt and Hopkins departed for Hyde Park and the more relaxed atmosphere of the stucco and brick home on its hill above the Hudson. Hopkins received a memo from Burns when they arrived, describing Molotov's four requests. Hopkins directed Burns to ans-

[2] Fennemore, Role of the Department of State, 216; *Foreign Relations, 1942,* III, 696, 697, 709; Matloff and Snell, *Strategic Planning,* 229; Leighton and Coakley, *Global Logistics,* 560–63; *Industrial Mobilization for War,* 350.

[3] Matloff and Snell, *Strategic Planning.* 230; Leighton and Coakley, *Global Logistics,* 560–63.

wer Molotov for Roosevelt, and Burns did so orally during the evening of June 3. Molotov had asked first that the United States send one escorted convoy to Archangel each month. The only assurance Molotov obtained was the United States and the United Kingdom would make every effort to get supplies to Russia. The Soviets, Burns observed, could exert "very important influence" on the quantity delivered to North Russia by providing effective air cover for the convoys. Molotov next requested flight delivery of fifty B-25's via Africa to Basra or Teheran. To this Burns noted that the proposed new Protocol provided for twelve B-25's monthly through October, at least, and those would be delivered as requested. The heavy European air offensive requirements made any change after October unlikely, but the subject would be considered further and decided in "due course." Molotov also solicited 150 Boston-3 bombers to be delivered to and assembled at Persian Gulf ports. The Boston-3 bombers, however, were no longer being manufactured, and Burns replied that Russia would instead get one hundred A-20's monthly through October, delivered as requested. Beyond that, the same conditions applied to A-20's as to B-25's. Molotov also wanted three thousand trucks each month transferred at the Persian Gulf, and to this Burns agreed. Burns observed that this response disappointed Molotov but that he remained "very friendly and very appreciative." The Soviet envoy told Burns that "all munitions supplied to the U.S.S.R. would be put to work against the Germans as promptly and effectively as possible, and that Russia could be relied upon to continue the war until victory is won." Shortly thereafter, the mysterious "Mr. Brown" departed for Britain on the first leg of his return trip to Moscow.[4]

A week later, Thomas B. McCabe, acting Lend-Lease administrator, telegraphed Faymonville in Moscow that the proposed Second Protocol had been turned over to Molotov on May 29. It included 1,800,000 tons of "machinery, materials, and indus-

[4] *Foreign Relations, 1942*, III, 707–708; Sherwood, *Roosevelt and Hopkins*, 568, 576–77.

trial equipment," 1,100,000 tons of munitions, and 4,300,000 tons of food from the United States. In view of limited shipping facilities, McCabe observed, the Soviets had been requested to select 4,400,000 tons from the joint United States–United Kingdom offering. Non-protocol items, as well as anything from the First Protocol not shipped by June 30, automatically would be included in the new agreement, and the Second Protocol offering would be reduced accordingly. McCabe emphasized that every effort would be made to get all First Protocol material shipped by June 30. He instructed Faymonville to urge the Russians to make their selections as quickly as possible. In the meantime, Belyaev prepared a priority list for July. Again, on June 25, McCabe repeated to Faymonville that all cargoes loaded in June would be credited to the First Protocol, those of July 1 and after to the Second.[5]

On July 7, Litvinov handed Hull a formal note of conditional acceptance of the Second Protocol. Although the Soviets accepted the document "with satisfaction," they wanted to include statements that the monthly delivery of aircraft from the United States after October, 1942, would be increased to the possible limit; that Great Britain would not decrease her aircraft delivery or the transfer of aluminum ingots; that the United States would provide cobalt at the old schedule; and that the United States and the United Kingdom would supply nickel to Russia at the rate of four hundred tons a month over what was necessary for the production of manufactured goods offered in the Second Protocol. At the same time, Moscow took the big step of putting its own Washington Purchasing Commission in charge of "adjustment and clarification" of the new agreement. Litvinov reminded Hull that he had the authority to sign the agreement, but the conditional acceptance actually delayed the signing.[6]

Six weeks later, with the Second Protocol as yet unsigned,

[5] *Foreign Relations, 1942*, III, 709–10. The 4,400,000 ton figure did not include Russian tonnage in the Pacific and was not the same figure that Roosevelt and Molotov discussed (see above Chapter III).

[6] *Ibid.*, 712–13, 722.

Burns, Sid Spalding (Burns's assistant), Arthur Van Buskirk (a Lend-Lease Administration lawyer), and G. Frederick Reinhardt (of the State Department's European Affairs Division) met to discuss the problem. Besides Litvinov's "conditions," Burns indicated that the changed supply situation loomed as the major factor in the delay. Convoy difficulties in the North Atlantic prompted a proposed shipping schedule readjustment along with similar production schedule changes, both necessary to avoid large accumulations of unshipped stocks. On July 29 the Soviet Purchasing Commission "energetically opposed" the production schedule changes. To meet Soviet objections, Burns's office agreed not to modify production schedules but rather to divert products when necessary to avoid accumulation of stocks. The Russians did not reply, which Burns took for agreement. Burns proposed that Lend-Lease officials make an abridged draft of the Protocol, affirm that it had been in effect since July 1, and then notify the Soviets that their conditions would be met if at all possible. Van Buskirk accepted the task of drafting this document. Then the British balked at the Russian conditions. By October 2 most of the scheduling difficulties had been worked out, and Hopkins sent Belyaev a report on the production program, which became a part of the protocol. Rather than any decrease because of shipping or any other difficulties, the Hopkins schedule represented an increase of 500,000 tons. On October 6, 1942, in Washington, Welles, Litvinov, and Sir Ronald I. Campbell signed the Second Protocol for the United States, the Soviet Union, and the United Kingdom.[7]

The Second (Washington) Protocol aggregated seven million tons of supplies, valued at $3,000,000,000. Munitions accounted for two-thirds of the valuation, while industrial equipment ($400,000,000) and foodstuffs ($600,000,000) shared the remainder. Of this total the United States and United Kingdom still asked the Soviets to select 4,400,000 tons for shipment to the northern and Persian Gulf ports. Anything over the 4,400,000

[7] *Ibid.*, 722–23, 723–24; *Soviet Supply Protocols*, 16, 35–36.

figure would have to be shipped by the Soviets themselves on the Pacific route. A sample of Russian requests and Anglo-American responses in important categories as they appeared in the Protocol is shown in the following table:

Item	Request	Response
Aircraft	4,200	212 a month, July through October with the "progress of the war" determining future delivery
Tanks	5,250	7,500
Hand machine guns, .38- and .45-caliber	247,878	240,000 Thompson .45-caliber
Scout cars	24,000	6,000 plus 18,000 jeeps
Trucks	120,000	120,000
Motorcycles	36,000	10,500
Aluminum ingots	48,000 tons	26,880 tons
Duraluminum	18,999 tons	6,720 tons
Cold-drawn carbon and alloy steels	188,160 tons	144,480 tons
Hot-rolled steel	168,000 tons	107,520 tons
Rails	268,800 tons	241,920 tons
Toluol and TNT	60,000 tons	48,000 tons
Radio sets	12,000	11,500
Generators	10,000	10,000
Petroleum products	240,000 tons	240,000 tons
Army cloth	18,000,000 yards	18,000,000 yards
G.I. Boots	4,800,000 pair	2,400,000 pair
Wheat and flour	2,400,000 tons	2,400,000 tons
Meat	180,000 tons	180,000 tons

NOTE: All tonnages here and in the text are converted to short tons.

For the United States schedule alone there were seven categories of supplies, with thirty-four items in the first group, eighty-four in the second, and seven in the fourth, the other categories not lending themselves to similar breakdowns. The British–Russian aid section was, necessarily, quite brief.[8]

On October 2, Roosevelt directed Stimson, Knox, Morgenthau, Stettinius, and Admiral Land (head of the War Shipping Administration) to effect all necessary arrangements, including production priorities to fulfill the protocol commitments. Availability of materials had presented serious difficulties with regard to the First Protocol, but the President's mandate proved an important factor in reducing that problem. Shipping remained the major bottleneck, although Roosevelt's October 2 order specified that every effort should be made to fill the United States quota in convoys to North Russia and to float all cargo that could be cleared through the Persian corridor.[9]

Roosevelt received monthly reports on Russian aid from various officials, including the Secretary of War, the chairman of the War Production Board, and the Lend-Lease administrator. Faced with direction of the entire war effort, it did not seem logical for the President to act as co-ordinator of just one phase. Besides, the informal committee headed by Hopkins to draft the Second Protocol had worked well. So on October 30, 1942, it became the nucleus of the President's Soviet Protocol Committee. The President's order establishing the group made it "responsible for the over-all co-ordination of the Russian Protocol through action by appropriate existing agencies and in conformity with policies approved by me." Hopkins became chairman, of course, and Burns became the executive officer. Therefore, on the military side, it had "an interlocking directorate with the M.A.B." (Munitions Assignment Board). A State Department official counted Litvinov and seven other Russians plus eighteen Americans (including Stettinius and Acheson) at a September meeting of the committee-to-be. The committee held

[8] *Soviet Supply Protocols,* 17–34.
[9] *Industrial Mobilization for War,* 352; Leighton and Coakley, *Global Logistics,* 592.

only one other meeting in 1942, although various sub-committees functioned toward the end of the year. The Protocol Committee also received non-protocol Russian requests; despite its title, it operated over the full range of Soviet aid.[10]

Unlike the discouraging production and availability reports that hampered the First Protocol, more optimistic reports on the Second were received by the President. On January 14, 1943, Donald Nelson reported favorably on the supply of critical materials. Those most urgently needed by Russia exceeded amounts called for in the protocol schedules through December. Of the nearly one hundred major items definitely committed in groups II (industrial equipment) and III (material for specific industries), only nineteen lagged 30 per cent or more behind the required schedules. Of the nineteen, either the commitments had been made late or else they were items, like carbon steel, of which the Russians already had accumulated large, unshipped stocks.[11]

Those concerned with the Soviet program also ultimately agreed to alter production schedules to take advantage of the limited shipping available. Thus increased emphasis was placed on selection, with the object of insuring delivery of those items of greatest strategic importance. A new policy of supplying maximum aid possible under existing conditions replaced the old policy of exact adherence to the letter of the protocol agreement.[12] In July the Soviets had suspiciously opposed production schedule changes and had won a 500,000-ton increase in commitments before signing the Protocol. Nevertheless, they finally accepted the American position of scheduling manufacture of items that stood a reasonable chance of being shipped.

[10] *Industrial Mobilization for War*, 352; Leighton and Coakley, *Global Logistics*, 560; *Foreign Relations, 1942*, III, 753.

[11] *Industrial Mobilization for War*, 353–54. The materials designated as most urgent by Russia were: nonferrous metals, alloy steel, tin plate, various types of steel wire, wire rope, and barbed wire. All the metal items, Nelson observed, were either on schedule or up to 150 per cent ahead of schedule.

[12] *Ibid.*, 354.

As the record shows, Soviet fear of production cutbacks proved groundless.

The total shipping available was only a little more than half that anticipated during the last half of 1942, and factory deliveries continued to outstrip the means to move them. More shipping than was expected followed the Pacific route, under Russia's flag, where munitions could not be carried. Consequently Russia shifted her priorities from munitions to food and oil products. Only planes, trucks, and communications equipment continued in the highest priority. As a result, trucks, carbon steels, chemicals, and other items piled up in warehouses. To reduce the backlog of unshipped goods, General Brehon B. Somervell, commander of the Army Service Forces, and long-time friend and W.P.A. associate of Hopkins, recommended that Russian goods not be allowed to accumulate over one and one-half times the monthly protocol figure. In mid-November the President's Soviet Protocol Committee, to which Somervell belonged, accepted his report as a policy but only in certain cases such as trucks. Somervell also asked that diverted material not be subject to replacement, but the Soviet Protocol Committee flatly turned this request down since it would have given the War Department power to reduce the Protocol in the unshipped categories.[13]

The Russian representatives co-operated by occasionally cancelling items that they no longer needed. By the end of April they either completely or partly set aside their orders for tanks, anti-tank guns (57 mm.), anti-aircraft guns (both 37 mm. and 90 mm.), and Thompson submachine guns. The effect of the victory at Stalingrad reflected the shift in Soviet needs. The War Department heaved a sigh of relief at the troublesome tank

[13] Leighton and Coakley, *Global Logistics*, 593–94. John D. Millett, *The Organization and Role of the Army Service Forces*, 52, hereafter cited as *The Army Service Forces*. The Soviets became more co-operative on the matter of selection of supplies to accord with available shipping. When this same problem confronted them in the Third Protocol, they quickly agreed without any protest. *Foreign Relations of the United States, 1943*, III, 776.

category, for cancellation meant that the backlog (2,583 tanks in February, 1943) went into hard-pressed American and British armor programs. Reduction of gun orders also meant that less American ammunition had to be shipped, and the reduction of heavy orders, such as the tanks, made shipping space available for trucks.[14]

Tight shipping schedules provided only one reason why Russia shifted certain priorities in order to put greater emphasis on food shipments over the Pacific route. The loss of much fine agricultural land in the Ukraine and North Caucasus regions and the failure to produce enough elsewhere to compensate for the losses partially prompted the shift. Very strict rationing had been in effect in Russia from the beginning, with war workers permitted a ration that Americans estimated to be not more than two-thirds of the United States minimum for good health. Soviet requests emphasized canned meats, fats, dried peas and beans, and dehydrated fruits and vegetables. Such requests resulted in rapid expansion of American dehydrating facilities, and dehydration itself proved a tremendous space-saver. Stettinius remarked, "When we can send ten shiploads of potatoes in one ship by dehydrating them, when we can send seven shiploads of eggs in one ship . . . the amount of extra food we can supply to Russia and the amount of space on ships and trains and trucks that become available . . . is very great."[15]

"Tushonka," a canned pork product prepared from a Russian formula and put up by several Midwestern packers, provided Soviet soldiers with a familiar food that was edible either hot or cold. The Red soldier also became used to items such as "two-inch-square packages no bigger than a box of safety matches" that carried powdered soups, including borsch. Russian fat shortages continued to be serious even though large amounts of lard, edible linseed and peanut oils, and margarine were shipped through Lend-Lease. Prior to June 30, 1943, only a small

---

[14] Leighton and Coakley, *Global Logistics*, 595.
[15] Stettinius, *Lend-Lease*, 226–27.

amount of butter (12,000 tons—less than 1 per cent of United States production) appeared on the Lend-Lease account. This represented the only foreign Lend-Lease shipments of butter; none went elsewhere. The Soviets claimed to use it only in military hospitals. Although food shipments reached one-third of the total tonnage shipped under the Second Protocol, they met only a small part of the Red army's calorie requirements (by United States standards), and little remained for civilians.[16]

Dehydration and increased Pacific route food shipments could only palliate the unsolved shipping problem. Even while P.Q. 17, at the mercy of Nazi air and undersea attack, groped for Archangel, American and British officials sought to increase the amounts going by the Persian Gulf route. At 4 A.M. on July 8, McCabe cabled Faymonville that Hopkins had directed Sid Spalding to survey the Persian Gulf supply route. Hopkins wanted to know, McCabe said, if "everything possible is being done to improve transport facilities and to make certain that material to be delivered under the Second Protocol will be forwarded as promptly and as efficiently as possible." Hopkins also ordered Spalding to confer with Russian officials in Iran and inspect their part of the route as well. Faymonville, McCabe suggested, could meet Spalding in Teheran to find out the results of the survey.[17]

At the same time the War Department considered a proposal, first made by Churchill, then by Wheeler, and most recently by Harriman, that the United States take over the Iranian railroad. As Harriman's suggestion came before the decision to suspend northern route convoys, he observed that only a few more convoys could make the run before winter closed in and that there was little time to lose in order to ready the Persian Gulf for additional winter traffic. In a memo to Hopkins, Marshall and King agreed with Harriman that all trucks shipped in July should go

[16] *Ibid.*, 227–28.
[17] Matloff and Snell, *Strategic Planning*, 337; *Foreign Relations, 1942*, III, 713–14.

over the Persian route and all bombers delivered after July should be flown. In addition to Nazi action, the demands of *TORCH* (invasion of North Africa) restricted the number of ships available for northern route convoys, especially warships necessary for cover. Both Roosevelt and Churchill worried about the tight shipping situation; this was one reason for Harriman's visit to Iran in mid-August, 1942, after his return from the Moscow conference. Harriman caught up with Churchill in Cairo, where the two decided to request United States operation of the British section of the Iranian railway as well as the ports the railroad served. General Spalding concurred, as did General Russell L. Maxwell, commander of U.S.A.F.I.M.E. (United States Army Forces in the Middle East) since mid-June. On August 25, Roosevelt ordered the Joint Chiefs of Staff to prepare a plan, and within ten days the Services of Supply drafted a detailed operations and development scheme for Iranian transportation facilities. United States take-over in Iran presented "one possible means . . . of directly strengthening the Soviet hand in 1942."[18]

During the summer of 1942 for week ends when he could not travel as far as Hyde Park, Roosevelt established a hideaway called Shangri-la in the Maryland hills about sixty miles north of the capital in the woods overlooking the Catoctin Valley, actually in the middle of a marine training camp. There Roosevelt and Hopkins often concluded state business while sitting on the small screened porch or inside the living room that served as an office. Sometimes, very pressing matters required a visitor to report. One was Harriman, who arrived to break the quiet of Sunday, August 30. He reported on his meeting with Churchill and Stalin in Moscow two weeks earlier.[19]

Churchill, who felt he carried "a large lump of ice to the North Pole," told Stalin that there would be no second front in 1942.

[18] Matloff and Snell, *Strategic Planning*, 337. For the full story of Persian Gulf development, see Motter, *Persian Corridor*, especially pp. 33–43, 61–92, 101–104, 113–14, 123, 139, 148–55; the S.O.S. plan, 174–98.

[19] Sherwood, *Roosevelt and Hopkins*, 626–27.

Churchill also tried to explain the effectiveness and necessity of *TORCH*. Churchill remembered that the first two hours of the Moscow meeting "were bleak and sombre." Stalin, "glum" and "unconvinced" by the abandonment of the second front, nevertheless appeared "intensely interested" as Churchill explained *TORCH*. Yet Standley observed that on the next day Stalin spoke "some plain facts positively and bluntly. The Kremlin did not like *TORCH*. The Western Allies had failed miserably to deliver Lend-Lease aid as promised. Meanwhile, the Russians were taking the whole weight of the German army with terrific casualties." As if to underscore the Lend-Lease accusation, Churchill got word of the P.Q. 17 disaster that same day. Harriman reported that the Red army was capable of preventing a breakthrough at Stalingrad, which would keep the Nazis from Caucasian oil fields and, in fact, from the Middle East and Iran. Harriman also discussed the Persian Gulf situation and reported that certain British officers viewed the proposed American take-over with alarm, telling Churchill it meant "foreigners" would be in control of an essential Empire communications line. Churchill replied, "And in what *better* hands could it be?"[20]

Harriman had scarcely returned from his journey when Wendell Willkie embarked on a more elaborate, if less important, one. With Joseph Barnes, linguist and former foreign editor of the *New York Herald-Tribune* and currently deputy director of the Office of War Information, Willkie secured Roosevelt's blessing and took off for Iran, Iraq, Syria, Saudi Arabia, Egypt, Chungking, and Moscow in an army B-24 bomber named *Gulliver*. Standley, who did not get along with Willkie, considered Willkie's trip to Russia "a sincere but misguided effort to help the United States and Russia get on with the war." Standley also believed that Willkie used the time for his own political enhancement. At any rate, Willkie listened to Kremlin accusa-

[20] Churchill, *The Hinge of Fate*, 475, 478, 481; Standley and Ageton, *Admiral Ambassador*, 212; Sherwood. *Roosevelt and Hopkins*, 627.

tions that Britain was stealing Lend-Lease material assigned to Russia (this, Sherwood observed, referred to unloading of Russia-bound vessels in the United Kingdom). This touched Hopkins, who had consented to unloading and diversion of the vessels. Hopkins had once made a "slurring remark" about Willkie, in Roosevelt's hearing, only to be surprised when Roosevelt stung Hopkins with a pointed reproof. "You of all people ought to know that we might not have had Lend-Lease . . . or a lot of other things if it hadn't been for Wendell Willkie. He was a godsend to this country when we needed him most."[21]

Willkie's internationalist foreign policy views had helped back in 1940. But soon Willkie's statements, especially those concerning the "failure" to open the second front, stung Roosevelt enough for him to use a press conference to call Willkie a "typewriter strategist" and imitate Willkie's pronunciation so that correspondents would have no doubt of the reference. Sherwood noted that Willkie "ended his mission of good will in a fury of rage at the President." Perhaps Willkie realized, or perhaps not, that Stalin had used him to transmit gibes aimed at the United States and Britain such as the one about stolen Lend-Lease and another about diverted Aircobras. With the northern route problems (P.Q. 18 arrived in Murmansk with great difficulty on September 17, and the decision to close the route followed shortly thereafter), the poor performance of the Persian Corridor route, the arguments over ALSIB, the requests for more vessels for the Soviets to use on the Pacific run, the slow start on Second Protocol deliveries, and the poor performance on the First Protocol, it is obvious that Stalin felt he had enough disappointments to vent on the West through Willkie.[22]

While the President made a swing around the country in late September, largely because of the approaching Congressional elections, Hopkins cabled him to "give full consideration" to a

[21] Sherwood, *Roosevelt and Hopkins*, 627, 634, 636; Standley and Ageton, *Admiral Ambassador*, 265, 269, 291.

[22] Sherwood, *Roosevelt and Hopkins*, 635; Standley and Ageton, *Admiral Ambassador*, 287–88.

proposal for a joint Allied air force to be established in the Caucasus. "If we must now tell Stalin that the convoys on the northern route must be discontinued," Hopkins wrote, "then it seems to me that it is almost imperative that we make a direct . . . offer to place our armed forces at his side. . . . The only armed force which we can get there is our air force." Marshall calculated that it would be quite possible to establish a heavy bomber group in the Caucasus by the end of 1942. However, by late November it became clear that the Soviets had no intention of accepting this substitute for Lend-Lease delivery. Even so, negotiation dragged on for another month before Stalin squelched the idea altogether.[23]

Meanwhile, Standley, who was unhappy in Moscow, decided to return to the United States. Standley reckoned that the Willkie journey had hurt his prestige as ambassador. In a sense it bypassed the embassy since Willkie carried a message for Stalin and had an audience at which Standley was not present. Standley also felt his prestige had diminished in Soviet eyes because their foreign office "countenanced and facilitated" the bypass. So Standley, to protest such activities, packed to fly home. But another reason, representing yet another bypass, compounded his decision to visit Washington. Faymonville and his nearly autonomous control of Lend-Lease matters annoyed Standley. As Lend-Lease representative in the Soviet Union, Standley "was given to understand" that his authority as ambassador "did not extend to Philip Faymonville." Standley complained that Faymonville allowed the Russians to obtain "not only material covered by the Protocol, but much American and British military information, which could never under any circumstance be considered Lend-Lease material."[24]

With a military man's respect for channels, it disturbed Standley to be the chief United States officer in Russia and yet not

23 Sherwood, *Roosevelt and Hopkins*, 636–38; Matloff and Snell, *Strategic Planning*, 333–36.

24 Standley and Ageton, *Admiral Ambassador*, 237–38, 295.

entirely so. Standley did not object to the extra-curricular Lend-Lease communications channel as such, but insisted that Faymonville allow the embassy's military and naval attachés to control all military information. But it was not quite so simple. Standley recalled that Faymonville had told him: "As . . . representative of Lend-Lease, I'm only a communication agent. If the Russian authorities request information either military or commercial, I have to pass that request on to the Lend-Lease Administration. If they obtain the information and send it back to me to deliver to the Russians, I have just got to deliver it." Standley remained unconvinced. He told Faymonville, "If I were captain of a ship . . . again and you were one of my officers, I'd know what to do. I'd say, 'Damn it all, Faymonville, do what you're told or else.'" The more Standley thought about the situation, the more he became convinced that every American representative in the Soviet Union ought to be brought under his command.[25]

Shortly before his departure from Russia, *Pravda* published Stalin's reply to Associated Press correspondent Henry Cassidy's question, "How effective is the assistance from the Allies to the Soviet Union and what would it be possible to do in order to expand and improve this assistance? Reply: In comparison with the assistance which the Soviet Union, drawing off the main forces of the German fascist troops is rendering to its allies, the assistance from the Allies to the Soviet Union is meanwhile of little effect. To expand and improve this assistance only one thing is required: complete and timely fulfillment by Allies of their obligations." As Standley remarked, "Of course, we all realized that Mr. Stalin would not have answered this letter of Mr. Cassidy's so promptly . . . unless Henry had happened to ask some questions on which Mr. Stalin wished to propagandize." As Stalin used Willkie in mid-September, so he used Cassidy on October 3.[26]

[25] *Ibid.*, 238, 246–47.
[26] *Ibid.*, 296, 298; *Foreign Relations, 1942*, III, 461.

By October 10, Standley, carrying a message from Stalin for Roosevelt, had collected his military and naval aides and also the second secretary, and they took off for Teheran and the United States in Major General Follett Bradley's bomber. Although Standley knew why he chose to fly home, no one in the United States seemed to know why. Hopkins cabled Harriman that "none of us knows exactly" why the Ambassador wanted to return. Roosevelt "awaited with some apprehension" both Standley's return and the personal message from Stalin which he carried. Standley arrived in Washington before dawn on Tuesday, October 20, and checked in at the Mayflower Hotel. At noon he took his wife to lunch at the Army and Navy Club, where they ran into Burns along with another Lend-Lease official. Burns asked about Lend-Lease in Russia, but Standley buried him under a barrage almost before the conversation began. He asked Burns why the Second Protocol wasn't signed (it had been on October 6) and what Burns intended to do about Faymonville. "I can't have him running wild around Moscow the way he has been." Burns and his friend suddenly remembered another appointment.[27]

On Wednesday morning Standley reported to Hull, who could give him only a few moments. Standley complained about Willkie's "junket" and left. The State Department assigned him an office in their building. Later in the afternoon he learned that he would lunch with the President on Thursday. Standley's visits to State Department division and section heads for briefing included in each case a complaint about the Willkie trip and "Special Representatives" of any kind. "They listened with comforting sympathy," Standley lamented, "but I knew that, as in Moscow with Premier Stalin and his bureaucrats, the decision rested higher up—with the Boss."[28]

Standley reached the East Wing entrance to the White House

---

[27] Standley and Ageton, *Admiral Ambassador*, 303, 304, 305; Sherwood, *Roosevelt and Hopkins*, 640.

[28] Standley and Ageton, *Admiral Ambassador*, 305–306.

at precisely 12:30 P.M., Thursday, October 22. If Roosevelt and Hopkins had not learned in two days' time what bothered Standley, it had not been the Admiral's fault. Roosevelt, seated behind his memento-covered desk, reached out and took Standley's hand. The Roosevelt smile flashing, he said cordially, "Hello, Bill. What brings you home?" Standley observed how well the President looked, how "ruddy" compared to Hopkins' sallow appearance, and answered, "Trouble, Chief. Plenty of trouble." Standley exchanged greetings with Hopkins, who sprawled in an armchair behind the President. Roosevelt asked for the Stalin letter and apparently was relieved to find nothing new; Willkie had carried substantially the same message to the President.[29]

As Roosevelt settled back more easily into his wheel chair, a waiter brought in plate lunches. Roosevelt inquired about the military situation and also asked about Stalin as a person, "his attitudes, whims, eccentricities." As dessert arrived, the discussion turned to Lend-Lease, and Hopkins participated for the first time. Standley advocated that the United States "stop acting like a Santa Claus . . . and get something from Stalin in return." He also complained about Faymonville's independence and Willkie's trip, both examples that made it look as if the Ambassador did not "enjoy the confidence" of his own government. When Roosevelt asked what could be done to change the situation, Standley listed as one condition that Faymonville be put firmly "under my administrative direction and control." Hopkins said nothing to this, but Roosevelt's warm smile reassured Standley. "We'll see what we can do, Bill," the President advised.[30]

Standley enjoyed the fine fall weather, spending much of it on the golf courses such as Burning Tree with men like Frank Knox for companions. Standley waited a long time before Hopkins and Lend-Lease made up their minds about Faymonville. But if it consoled him any, he learned that Stalin's reply to

[29] *Ibid.*, 306–307; Sherwood, *Roosevelt and Hopkins*, 640.
[30] Standley and Ageton, *Admiral Ambassador*, 308–10.

Roosevelt's acknowledgment of Stalin's Standley-carried message followed the Litvinov-Hopkins route and bypassed the State Department. Hull often shared the same frustrations as Standley. Although Standley spent much time in conference with Lend-Lease officials, not until December 12—nearly two months later —did he get Faymonville ordered to report to him, and it took the direct intercession of Hopkins to accomplish that. Exactly one week later, on December 19, Standley and party climbed aboard a converted B-19, the *Kay Bird,* at Bolling Field and took off into a gray sky on his return to the Soviet Union.[31]

The Congressional elections of November 3 nearly turned out disastrously for Roosevelt. The Republicans came within nine seats of a majority in the House and gained ten senators. Roosevelt, however, had little time to worry about the narrow victory. The preparations for the *TORCH* operation landings on November 8 involved considerable work on Roosevelt's part, as did diplomatic difficulties afterward. Not only *TORCH,* but also the British reconquest of Northeast Africa and the great battles at Stalingrad on the Russian front were under way. Negotiations between Stalin, Churchill, and Roosevelt for a top-level conference began in early December. In the end Stalin did not attend, but preparations continued for a meeting of Churchill and Roosevelt. At the annual White House New Year's Eve affair for family and friends, Roosevelt showed the Humphrey Bogart–Ingrid Bergman film, "Casablanca," which, unknown to most, was Roosevelt's destination in mid-January.[32]

In January, 1943, Roosevelt again hammered at "the necessity of meeting Soviet needs . . . a matter of paramount importance." In letters to Stimson and the Joint Chiefs of Staff he observed that Second Protocol shipments reached only 55 per cent of schedule at year's end. Roosevelt's desire that the schedule be met embarrassed the army as much then as it had a year before. A restudy of the available shipping disclosed that 156

[31] *Ibid.,* 310–17.
[32] Sherwood, *Roosevelt and Hopkins,* 644–65.

more ships could be utilized, but only at the cost of reducing the number of troops and equipment destined for Europe. At that time the army fixed European Theater troop goals in terms of *ROUNDUP*, a plan for a cross-channel attack in 1943. More ships for the Russian runs meant, the army calculated, 375,000 fewer United States troops transported to England.[33]

In mid-January, Roosevelt, Hopkins, and the military chiefs flew to meet Churchill and his military staff at Casablanca. After passing over African desert, which Hopkins called "hardly worth fighting for," their aircraft "suddenly came upon the fertile fields of N. Africa—looking like the Garden of Eden should look and probably doesn't." Roosevelt and Hopkins stayed in what Hopkins claimed to be a California-type bungalow, and Churchill, who had already arrived, was in another close by. For ten days Roosevelt, Churchill, Hopkins, and the Combined Chiefs of Staff discussed the war situation. The Russian aid program provided them with one of their major problems. Soviet aid, granted a priority second only to the anti-submarine campaign and operation *HUSKY* (the invasion of Sicily), reduced any possibility of a cross-channel invasion in 1943. Shipping could not be stretched to include *ROUNDUP*. The Combined Chiefs of Staff worked out a schedule of Lend-Lease shipments to Russia which they reported to Roosevelt and Churchill on January 23. In conclusion they observed, "It will be possible to meet full commitments [for the Second Protocol] by the end of the calendar year 1943." On January 25, Churchill, in "his ever flaming bathrobe, bed-room slippers and the inevitable cigar," whacking with his cane at the cameras of newsmen who tried to photograph him in this weird costume, saw Roosevelt and Hopkins off at the air field. Churchill spoke about the hard road facing the Allies, but radiated confidence. Roosevelt, coughing, appeared very tired. Churchill promised to send the two a painting of the Atlas Mountains, which he intended to paint from the tower in his villa. As a good omen, Roosevelt learned of the Russian

[33] Leighton and Coakley, *Global Logistics*, 587.

victory at Stalingrad when his plane touched down in the United States.[34]

Although the War Shipping Administration and the Joint Chiefs of Staff quarreled over the shipping schedule set up at Casablanca, they had little choice except to attempt to maintain it. Much depended upon Allied ability to maintain the North Russian route to Murmansk and Archangel. But on March 18, Churchill informed Roosevelt that the renewed concentration of the Nazi navy at Narvik made sending convoys over the Northern route too risky. On March 30, Churchill told Stalin of this decision, and Stalin, of course, sharply criticized his Western allies. With north-route convoys postponed, any hope of keeping the Casablanca schedule for spring and summer evaporated. Meanwhile congestion in the Persian Gulf, despite steadily improving performance, prevented fulfillment of that section of the schedule. With the addition of fifty-three ships and six tankers in the Pacific, the Soviets managed to surpass the Casablanca schedule, but not by enough to make up for deficiencies on the other routes. The Casablanca schedule, although not strictly kept, was in no sense chimerical. By June both the Persian Gulf and the Pacific could carry the necessary loads or more, and the loss rate, estimated at 2.4 per cent a month, fell considerably below that figure. The Casablanca schedule aimed at meeting all Protocol stipulations by December, 1943, and at least that goal was reached.[35]

Generally unfavorable war news blanketed February with the chill of a seasonal snowstorm. United States forces in North Africa took a pounding from Rommel at Kasserine Pass and lost some hard-won ground. In Russia the Soviets wound up their winter offensive, and the Nazis turned around and recaptured Kharkov. Stalin, morose, pressed Roosevelt and Churchill for a Continental second front and questioned the value of the whole

[34] Sherwood, *Roosevelt and Hopkins*, 673, 690, 694–95; Leighton and Coakley, *Global Logistics*, 587–89.

[35] Leighton and Coakley, *Global Logistics*, 589–92.

African operation. Tension characterized British-American relations with the Kremlin. Back in Moscow, "the apparent ingratitude of Soviet Government officials for the aid which . . . the American people were extending to Russia" troubled Standley. Standley searched for evidence of American aid in the places he visited and in Soviet newspapers and magazines; he also questioned Soviet citizens. As the Ambassador later wrote, "My efforts met with scant success." Rebuffed in his efforts to get a public acknowledgment of Lend-Lease aid from Molotov or any other top Russian official, Standley lashed out in anger at the Soviets during a March 8 press conference.[36]

The press conference got off to a slow start in the Spaso House library, with correspondents making no notes. Then apparently one correspondent asked about the status of Lend-Lease. "You know, boys," Standley remarked, "ever since I've been here I've been looking for evidence that the Russians have been getting a lot of material help from the British and us." Standley paused, mentioned Congress' helpfulness and big-heartedness, and continued. "I have also tried to obtain evidence that our military supplies are in use by the Russians. I haven't succeeded. The Russian authorities seem to want to cover up the fact that they are receiving outside help. Apparently they want their people to believe that the Red Army is fighting this war alone." When asked if this was off the record, Standley urged the newsmen to use it. As Standley later confided to his diary, the statement "stirred up a mare's nest at home." The State Department promptly asked for reasons for the statement, but Standley had already dispatched them. Molotov asked Standley to come to the Kremlin. In a warm transfer of opinion on March 10, Molotov and Standley argued the case, but they parted cordially.[37]

[36] Sherwood, *Roosevelt and Hopkins*, 704–705; Standley and Ageton, *Admiral Ambassador*, 331–32, 340–41.

[37] Standley and Ageton, *Admiral Ambassador*, 341–48; Sherwood, *Roosevelt and Hopkins*, 705–706. Standley, in his book, confuses the extension of the Lend-Lease Act, then before Congress, with the Second Protocol. The Soviet press had indeed "cooled off" toward their allies; see Ch. VII.

In the United States, the reaction was mixed. Standley's statement, newsmen agreed on March 9, hit Washington like a "bombshell." Reporters feared that sensitive congressmen might withhold the extension of Lend-Lease, then under debate. Acting Secretary of State Welles promptly announced that Standley spoke on his own, although when pressed by reporters, Welles would not repudiate Standley's stand. Various congressmen either deplored or expressed amazement at Standley, while former presidential candidate Willkie lashed out at the Ambassador. Nazi propagandists chortled over this rupture of Allied unity. Moscow correspondents of American papers warned their readers that the cold Russians were not given to expressions of gratitude for Allied acts so obviously in the Allied interest. From London, Harriman reported that Standley's statement secretly pleased many in government circles. Standley later wrote that the Moscow press remained silent for three days and then broke out in a "veritable rash of statements about American aid to Russia."[38]

Standley, who had had enough of special emissaries, soon found yet another headed toward Moscow. A telegram received on April 8 announced the approaching visit of General James H. Burns, the most important figure in Lend-Lease next to Hopkins. The situation for Standley was not especially pleasant because he believed Burns was after his "Ambassadorial scalp." Standley showed Burns every courtesy, but Burns apparently busied himself with Faymonville and spent little time with the Ambassador. Meanwhile Roosevelt attempted to persuade former Ambassador Davies to return to the ambassadorial post in Moscow, feeling that Standley, after his sharp criticism of Soviet gratitude, could be of little more help. Davies was in poor health and could not return, but suggested that Hopkins take over the task. Roosevelt vetoed that idea. So Davies accepted Roose-

[38] *The New York Times,* March 9, pp. 1, 5 and March 10, pp. 1, 5; Standley and Ageton, *Admiral Ambassador,* 347–48; Sherwood, *Roosevelt and Hopkins,* 705–706.

velt's compromise that he, Davies, go to Russia to ask Stalin to meet with the President to work out their mutual problems. When Standley discovered that still another "special emissary" was on the way, he observed that "the position of Ambassador here is impossible" and on May 3 sent his resignation to Roosevelt.[39]

The Standley affair gave official Washington a discussion topic for March. In addition, Anthony Eden visited the capital to discuss postwar affairs and settlements, although he spent at least some of his time considering the endless shipping problems. Churchill tried to set up another meeting in North Africa to talk over the proposed Sicilian campaign, but Roosevelt wanted to wait until the Tunisian affair ended. On May 7, United States and British forces broke into Bizerte and Tunis, bringing that campaign near a close. Four days later the *Queen Mary* docked in New York, loaded with thousands of German and Italian prisoners of war as well as Winston Churchill with his chiefs of staff and a party of almost one hundred. The two weeks of conferences, code-named *TRIDENT*, produced definite plans for the invasion of Normandy and set the date as May 1, 1944. Besides Roosevelt, Stimson, Knox, Hopkins, Harriman, and Stettinius, at least six admirals and ten generals attended the conferences on the American side. American and British affairs seemed to be moving nicely: an Allied food conference met at Hot Springs, Virginia; the United States and United Kingdom abandoned the idea of "extra-territorial rights" in China and the Soviet Union dissolved the Comintern; and Churchill and Marshall flew to North Africa and succeeded in setting up the unified French Provisional Government-in-Exile. But relations between the two Anglo-Saxon nations and the Soviets continued to deteriorate.[40]

Davies arrived in Moscow on May 19. Litvinov, returning from Washington, arrived in Moscow only a day or so after

[39] Standley and Ageton, *Admiral Ambassador*, 350, 351, 358; Sherwood, *Roosevelt and Hopkins*, 733.

[40] Sherwood, *Roosevelt and Hopkins*, 727–33.

Davies. On May 20, Davies spent eleven hours with Stalin and convinced him that the proposed meeting between Roosevelt and himself had no purpose except to cement their friendship. They set a date for July 15. Davies and Burns flew back to the United States together on May 29 over the ALSIB route. Soon after Davies' departure, Standley delivered the *TRIDENT* conference plans to Stalin. By the end of June, Stalin replied to Churchill with an accusation of Allied bad faith for postponing the second front again, this time until 1944. Churchill, without consulting Roosevelt, retorted with a heated denial of Stalin's charges. Anglo-American–Soviet relations, already poor, suffered another shock. Russia's two ambassadors to the West returned to Moscow. A new wave of fear that the Russians might seek a separate peace swept Washington. Positive that the Soviets would not stop fighting so long as Germans remained in Russia, Standley tried "to play this down," and certainly could report no Moscow sign of Soviet intentions to break relations. It appeared that although Russia felt her Allies were timid, she intended—since there was no other realistic course—to continue the uncertain partnership.[41]

In spite of all of the difficulties of the 1942–43 Second Protocol period, Russia received Lend-Lease from the United States amounting to 3,816 aircraft (including a large segment of the United Kingdom commitment delivered by the United States), 1,206 tanks, 16,158 jeeps, 77,555 trucks, 10,200 motorcycles, 59,249 short tons of explosives, 62,292 submachine guns, and 1,117,517 tons of food (that accounted for one-third of the total tonnage sent Russia under the Second Protocol). The 3,420,815 tons of supplies delivered represented 76 per cent of the planned amounts, a sizable piece of aid to help the Red army stop the Nazi advance at Stalingrad.[42]

[41] Standley and Ageton, *Admiral Ambassador*, 364, 368–69, 380–81; Sherwood, *Roosevelt and Hopkins*, 734.
[42] Report on War Aid, 3; see Stalingrad calculations in Chapter VI.

CHAPTER SIX

No Easy Road to Russia

O N OCTOBER 1, 1942, Chief of Staff George Marshall directed General Donald H. Connolly to assume leadership of the Persian Gulf Service Command. Connolly's job, Marshall noted, was to "insure the uninterrupted flow of an expanded volume of supplies to Russia." Although he operated under the auspices of the Commander of the United States Armed Forces in the Middle East until December 10, 1943, Connolly exercised a great deal of independent authority, even to the extent of reporting administrative matters directly to Marshall. Perhaps it was a coincidence, but Connolly, C.W.A. administrator in Los Angeles in 1934 and subsequently administrator of the W.P.A. in Los Angeles (1935–1939), knew Hopkins well.[1] Like Faymonville, even though he wore an army uniform, Connolly became an important part of Hopkins' Russian Lend-Lease team.

Specific recommendations that emerged in the Services of Supply plan came from the Cairo meeting. In a memo, Spalding reckoned that a minimum of 200,000 tons of Soviet aid each month should be established as a Persian Gulf route goal. Spalding implied that this would be a difficult target since it was twice the May estimate. To accomplish this goal, he proposed that the United States operate Iranian railways south of Teheran and the docks at Bandar Shahpur, Khorramshahr, Tanuma, and Bushire, as well as set up its own trucking or-

---

[1] Matloff and Snell, *Strategic Planning*, 338; Motter, *Persian Corridor*, 206–207.

ganization. If the British continued to run Basra in Iraq and Abadan and Ahwaz (later added to the United States list) in Iran and continued their own trucking operation, it might be possible to meet the estimated 200,000 tons a month. This American operation ultimately required 28,584 troops: port battalions, railway-operating battalions, truck regiments, engineer battalions, and road maintenance groups. In addition, the project required 75 steam locomotives, 2,200 twenty-ton freight cars (or their equivalent in heavier cars), and 7,200 trucks (averaging seven tons capacity) for the truck fleet. Although it would not be easy to find the necessary men and equipment quickly, Burns did not flinch at the requirements Spalding had set down.[2]

Most service troops required for the expanded Persian Gulf operation had been previously allotted to *BOLERO* or were designated for *TORCH*. Heavy transportation equipment, in limited production in the United States, had been largely destined for Great Britain. The army eventually transferred nearly 9,000 men from *BOLERO* assignments, requisitioned another 8,000 from other units (many of which were not at full strength, and some of which had not yet completed their training), and raised 1,500 more in newly activated groups. At former railroader Harriman's suggestion, 57 high-powered diesel locomotives from American service replaced the 75 steam locomotives in the plan. The Army diverted 1,650 twenty- and forty-ton freight cars from *BOLERO*. In late September, the Munitions Assignment Committee (Ground) assigned 150 ten-ton trucks, 656 two-and-one-half-ton tractors with seven-ton trailers, and 2,600 two-and-one-half-ton cargo trucks to the Persian Gulf Service Command; the heavy trucks were obtained through repossession from Great Britain. By mid-October supplies or reasonable substitutes were available if they could be shipped.[3]

[2] Leighton and Coakley, *Global Logistics*, 575–80; Matloff and Snell, *Strategic Planning*, 339.
[3] Leighton and Coakley, *Global Logistics*, 579; Matloff and Snell, *Strategic Planning*, 339.

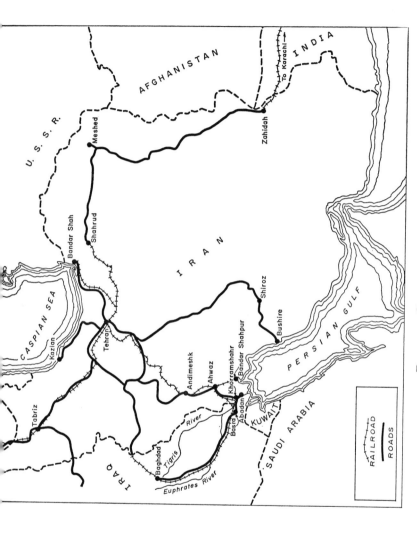

PERSIAN GULF ROUTES TO RUSSIA

The *West Point* departed from New York on November 1 with 5,500 troops and landed them at Khorramshahr in December. The *Ile de France* sailed from San Francisco in December, and the *Mauretania* sailed in January, both with contingents of troops for India as well as the Persian Gulf. By mid-March, 1943, when the *Mauretania* arrived, the total number of troops in United States Persian Gulf operations tallied about 17,500. The Persian Gulf Service Command finally reached its 28,000-man figure in August, 1943. The problem of shipping the materials for road, railroad, and port building loomed as a more serious threat to the operation than the disappointingly slow build-up men. Although planners scheduled five ships a month, only eight sailed in the four months from October through January. Partly because of sinkings and partly because of expanded North African and Pacific operations, Admiral Land's War Shipping Administration found very few ships available. In addition, over-crowded Persian Gulf port facilities, crammed with vessels loaded with Soviet aid, provided another reason why fewer ships were sent—more ships would only add to the obstruction and confusion. The June, 1943, target date estimated by British and American transportation experts would clearly be required for a 200,000-tons-a-month operation, and it proved much more realistic than the February, 1943, deadline that Spalding and Harriman had recommended.[4]

Between January and May, 1943, the United States Army assumed step-by-step control, generally having full responsibility by May 1. From July through December, 1942, fifty ships sailed from the Western Hemisphere for the Persian Gulf with aid for Russia, while another thirty-one departed with partial cargoes, bringing the supply tonnage to 540,960. From January through June, 1943, seventy-five ships embarked for the Persian Gulf ports, and an additional fifteen followed with partial cargoes, the two groups carrying a total of 619,360 tons of freight. In

[4] Leighton and Coakley, *Global Logistics*, 579, 580.

terms of tonnage delivered, 44,800 tons passed through the corridor in September, 1942, 57,120 in January, 1943, 113,120 in April, and by September the total reached 222,880 tons. The Iranian State Railway, which hauled 40,320 tons in August, 1942, hauled 122,080 tons in June, 1943.[5]

Poor planning both in Washington and in the Persian Gulf caused the congestion and subsequent waste of shipping in the Gulf. Many more ships arrived than facilities could handle, with the ridiculous result that in mid-January thirty-two vessels rode idle at anchor awaiting their turn to discharge their cargo. Unloading time in January, 1943, averaged fifty-five days a ship. A War Shipping Administration report noted that one vessel remained in port for 124 days, although most cleared in from twenty to sixty days. By December, 1943, turnaround time fell to eighteen days, a considerable improvement but too late to affect Second Protocol deliveries.[6]

During the last six months of 1942, when the Persian Gulf proved so disappointing as an alternate route, Hitler contested the north route as sharply as before. In order to aid his heavy warships, the *Tirpitz*, *Scheer*, and *Hipper*, now based at Narvik rather than Trondheim, he sent the light cruiser *Koln*. Also, by the end of August, the United States withdrew its task force from Arctic waters. Refitted, the *King George V* reunited with the British battle fleet while the new battleship *Anson* trained its crew on a shakedown cruise prior to joining the fleet also. Even without the American ships, the British group, including the *Duke of York* and *Renown*, was capable of delivering a considerable punch if it should have the opportunity to engage the Narvik-based Nazi nuisance fleet.[7]

[5] *Ibid.*, 583; Report on War Aid, 14, 15; Motter, *Persian Corridor*, 488, 490. All tonnage figures in text converted from long to short tons for the sake of consistency.

[6] Motter, *Persian Corridor*, 407–408; Leighton and Coakley, *Global Logistics*, 583.

[7] Roskill, *The War at Sea*, II, 277–78.

Meanwhile, on August 12, the heavy cruiser U.S.S. *Tusca-loosa* docked in Scotland and loaded three hundred tons of cargo for Russia, primarily munitions. The United States destroyers, the *Emmons* and the *Rodman*, took on twenty tons of Royal Air Force provisions and nineteen tons of general supplies each. En route they picked up an additional screen of three British destroyers, and the six sped for Kola Inlet, gateway to Murmansk. On August 20, seven days out, a Nazi search plane sighted the group, but the vessels lost their discoverer in a fog. Outside Kola Inlet, three destroyers, two British and one Soviet, waited to escort the group into Murmansk. Supplies were unloaded quickly, over five hundred convoy survivors and four Russian diplomats were taken aboard, and the flotilla departed the next morning. The mission arrived safely in Iceland on August 28. The only other ships that left for Arctic ports in August were two Russian freighters, which left Iceland independently, and after a very long voyage arrived intact.[8]

The run of cargo-carrying American warships to Russia reflected advance planning for the next merchant convoy, P.Q. 18. The American ships took in replacement stores for Allied vessels then in North Russia, especially anti-aircraft ammunition and the like which had been lost with P.Q. 17. They also carried men and equipment for British air squadrons to be stationed in North Russia. British naval planners agreed that the most important duty of their North Russia air groups would be to keep an eye on the northern Nazi naval force. By the first week in September, British airmen established themselves at Vaenga, near Murmansk.[9]

As the *Tuscaloosa* group churned to Murmansk, the *Scheer* left Narvik to intercept Soviet shipping believed to be using the North Siberian route, but found only one ice-breaker and returned to Narvik by August 30. Meanwhile, having laid mines at the entrance to the White Sea, the Nazi minelayer *Ulm* ran

8 Morison,, *Battle of the Atlantic*, 360–61; Roskill, *The War at Sea*, II, 278.
9 Roskill, *The War at Sea*, II, 278–79.

afoul of the British destroyers escorting the *Tuscaloosa* on the return and went down southeast of Bear Island. Other German vessels, including submarines, destroyers, and an auxiliary mine-layer, journeyed to the White Sea entrance and also laid mines in what they believed to be the path of the next convoy. This Nazi mine-laying activity continued in late September and early November with the *Hipper* and destroyers dropping mines along the Barents Sea lanes. For all their hard work, they bagged only one Russian tanker. Thus the Germans with mines and the British and Americans with aircraft maneuvered for advantage before the next convoy.[10]

Admiral Sir John Tovey, commander-in-chief of Britain's Home Fleet, decided that a "fighting destroyer escort" of twelve to sixteen ships should deter Hitler's navy from using surface ships against a convoy. Besides, Tovey opposed sending a heavy battle fleet into the Barents Sea with all the long-range destroyers it would take to screen it; he much preferred to use the destroyers as the actual escort. Thus Rear Admiral R. L. Burnett, commander of the escort, flew his flag from the destroyer *Scylla*. The *Scylla*, along with sixteen other destroyers divided into two squadrons, accompanied the eastward- and westward-bound convoys (P.Q. 18 and Q.P. 14) during the dangerous parts of their prospective journeys. An escort carrier, the *Avenger*, with a two-destroyer screen of her own, joined the group, marking one of the first such uses of escort carriers. Intermediate and distant cover forces, fuel ships, and the like (thirty-six warships in all, cruisers to submarines) also put to sea. These included the brand new battleship *Anson*, the *Duke of York*, and the cruiser *Jamaica*. The convoy itself composed thirty-nine merchantmen, a rescue ship, an oiler, three minesweepers bound for Russia, and two fleet oilers. Admiral Tovey ran the entire operation from Scapa Fow aboard the *King George V*.[11]

On Wednesday, September 2, eastbound convoy P.Q. 18

[10] *Ibid.*, 279–80.
[11] *Ibid.*, 280–81.

sailed from Loch Ewe as scheduled. On September 8 a Luftwaffe reconnaissance plane spotted the Allied ships north of Ireland. The German navy scattered twelve U-boats in three groups along the anticipated course. On September 10 the *Scheer, Hipper,* and *Koln,* with a few destroyers, moved from Narvik north to Alta Fjord as if in preparation to intercept. Hitler warned his admiral, Erich Raeder, not to risk his fleet in battle except in the defense of Norway, so the vessels remained idle. The Luftwaffe, on the other hand, made a determined effort against the convoy. The escort carrier became the main target of Hitler's Norway-based air force. Fog, rain, and snow, along with the heavy Arctic seas, shielded the convoy from air attack until Sunday, September 13. That morning U-boats torpedoed two ships, but alert destroyers and air patrol spoiled further U-boat successes. In the afternoon, 450 miles from Nazi shore bases, the air raid began. A few Junker 88's dropped some bombs ineffectively from a high level. An hour later, about forty German torpedo planes, painted black with orange and green wing tips, swept into a thousand-gun anti-aircraft barrage. The unusually warm welcome surprised the Nazi pilots, for it was the first time a north-route convoy had carried really adequate armament. Darting up, down, and around, to confuse the gunners, a few intrepid Nazis actually came within forty feet of selected targets before dropping their torpedoes. For seven or eight hectic minutes, that seemed like as many hours to the sailors, planes zoomed about as the rattle of anti-aircraft and machine guns drowned out the slap of the ocean and the howl of the wind. Then suddenly the skies emptied, and the guns fell silent. Survivors from eight sunken or sinking ships fought the bitter cold sea along with the crews of five torpedo bombers, but the frigid waters gave up few survivors. Late in the evening the convoy beat off two more attacks.[12]

Meanwhile, on September 12 an escort ship sank the U-88,

[12] *Ibid.,* 282–83; Morison, *Battle of the Atlantic,* 360–61; *U.S.S.R. Correspondence,* I, 57, 64–65.

and on the fourteenth a Swordfish from the *Avenger* teamed up with a destroyer to blast the U-589. Also on Monday a submarine fatally damaged one of the convoy's oilers. British intelligence had lost the *Tirpitz*, which caused the Vaenga-based torpedo-bombers to make an offensive sweep, but they found nothing. Not until September 18 did the *Tirpitz*, "exercising" in a fiord, return to her anchorage. For four days she kept the British navy skittish. During this time the Nazis launched another air torpedo attack against the convoy on Tuesday, September 14. Again they concentrated on the *Avenger* and the anti-aircraft ship, *Ulster Queen*, which was with her. These two vessels crossed in front of the convoy to gain room to maneuver. The naval escort and the convoy put up such intense fire that the attackers dropped their torpedoes at long range. Gunners aboard the S.S. *Nathaniel Greene* enjoyed a fine day. Their three-inch gun scored a direct hit on the lead plane, and before the day's action ended, they had downed five Nazi attackers. In this one attack the defenders destroyed thirteen torpedo-bombers and lost no ships. Later another wave of Luftwaffe swept in only to be accorded a general reception no less warm than earlier. Nine of the enemy fell from the skies, as did three of the *Avenger's* Hurricanes that flew through the convoy's air barrage. One ship, the U.S. *Mary Luckenbach*, blew up with a tremendous flash, causing considerable damage to others nearby.[13]

Tuesday, September 15, remained relatively quiet except for recurring submarine alarms. A high-level bombing attack failed. A dozen submarines unsuccessfully tried to decoy the screen from the convoy. On Wednesday, marking the second week out from Loch Ewe, a destroyer sank the U-457. That afternoon the main escort left P.Q. 18 (about fifteen warships remained: two destroyers, two anti-aircraft ships, four corvettes, three minesweepers, and four trawlers) to pick up the westbound Q.P. 14,

[13] Roskill, *The War at Sea*, II, 283–84; Morison, *Battle of the Atlantic*, 261–63.

The War at a Glance, 1942[*]

Unable to destroy the Russian armies in 1941, the Nazis next planned to capture the vast resources of the Ukraine and the Caucasus. The Germans launched their attacks in May, took Sevastopol in July, and pushed deep into the Caucasus in the summer. They reached Stalingrad in September. A victory there would have allowed the Nazis to isolate Moscow as they had Leningrad and, in such strategic positions and with vast economic resources available, perhaps bring the war in Russia to a successful conclusion in 1943. Stiff Soviet defense and heavy counterattacks prevented the fall of Stalingrad and cost the Nazis the German Sixth Army as well as the strategic advantages of the position. The Nazis never again gained the initiative to any great extent in the south.

[*] See the Chronology in Appendix C.

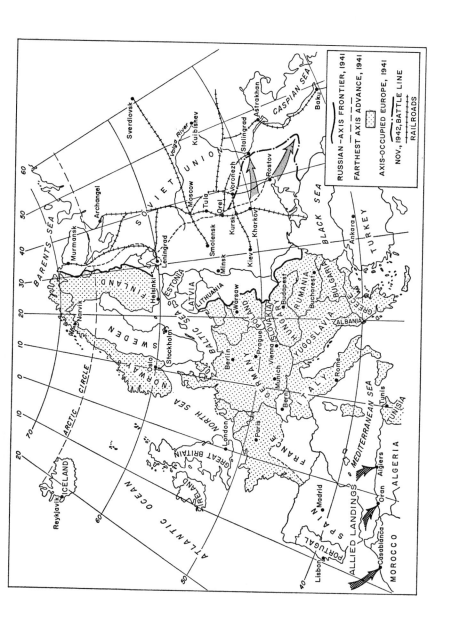

and four Russian destroyers appeared as added escort for P.Q. 18. As the convoy entered the White Sea on Friday, they again underwent attack from bombers and torpedo planes. The black-painted Nazi planes sank another freighter at a cost of four aircraft. The Luftwaffe returned again on Saturday and Sunday but without success. Urged on by Marshal Hermann Göring, the German air force lost nearly forty planes and failed to break up the convoy. P.Q. 18, on the other hand, lost ten ships to air attack and three to U-boat action.[14]

The fifteen ships of westbound Q.P. 14 left Archangel on September 13 under the command of Commodore J. C. K. Dowding, who had also commanded the ill-fated P.Q. 17. On September 17 the convoy picked up Burnett's destroyer force. After a quiet few days, the mine-sweeper *Leda* blew up when struck by a torpedo, and later in the day another U-boat got the *Silver Sword*, a survivor of P.Q. 17. With his convoy now out of air-attack range, Admiral Burnett sent the *Avenger* home with four destroyers as escort. The convoy soon felt the absence of the carrier planes as U-boats began to make successful hits. A submarine torpedoed the destroyer *Somali*. On Tuesday, September 22, the U-435 sank three ships in a matter of minutes, including the *Bellingham*, another P.Q. 17 survivor, and a fleet oiler. On Wednesday a Catalina long-range air escort appeared and sank the U-253, and other submarine attacks ceased. Twelve of the original fifteen freighters of Q.P. 14 steamed into Loch Ewe on Saturday, September 26.[15]

Hitler lost four submarines, thirty-three torpedo planes, six long-range bombers, and two search planes in his unsuccessful attempt to break up the north route convoys. September's two convoys cost the Allies sixteen merchantmen and three naval craft and immobilized many escort vessels needed elsewhere. In the meantime, Roosevelt and Churchill agreed, on Septem-

---

14 Roskill, *The War at Sea*, II, 284–85; Morison, *Battle of the Atlantic*, 364–65. The thirteen ships sunk included eight American.

15 Roskill, *The War at Sea*, II, 286–87; Morison, *Battle of the Atlantic*, 365. The *Silver Sword* and *Bellingham* were American.

ber 5, to carry out the invasion of North Africa (operation *TORCH*). Anglo-American tacticians had forty ships loaded for Russia and ready for another convoy at the end of September. British naval planners decided not to launch P.Q. 19, partly because *TORCH* would have to be postponed for at least three weeks and partly because of the hazardous passage even a heavily armed convoy faced. The "no convoy" decision came at a time when it seemed that no satisfactory route for munitions to Russia existed. In place of convoys, the "trickle" method, or independent sailings, occupied the "moonless period" between October and a new convoy series in December. From Reykjavik, thirteen vessels departed for North Russia; three turned back, four sank, one foundered, and five arrived safely. Of the twenty-three that trickled westward, one was sunk by a U-boat and twenty-two arrived unharmed in Iceland. In November westbound Q.P. 15 sailed from Archangel in order to return some of the many Allied vessels anchored in Arctic ports. The twenty-eight ships and the small escort fought gale winds almost all the way, were unable to stay in any formation, and lost two of their number to U-boats, but otherwise they managed to make it to Iceland. This ended the P.Q.-Q.P. convoy series.[16]

Hitler's orders restricting the use of his fleet to the defense of Norway remained in force. Some minor fleet movements took place, such as the return of the *Scheer* to Germany and her replacement by the *Nürnberg*. The *Luetzow* came from the Baltic to Alta Fjord, which led Admiral Tovey to re-establish the Denmark Strait patrol lest this ship escape into the Atlantic. The Admiralty also decided to resume convoys in December. Not only would they bear new code numbers (J.W. for eastbound and R.A. for westbound), but they would also be smaller than the summer convoys had been in order to take better advantage of the Arctic night and to be more maneuverable in the rough winter seas.[17]

[16] Roskill, *The War at Sea*, II, 287–89, and III, part II, 432–34; Matloff and Snell, *Strategic Planning*, 306; *U.S.S.R. Correspondence*, I, 71–72.
[17] Roskill, *The War at Sea*, II, 289–90.

Convoy JW-51A, with fifteen freighters and an oiler escorted by seven destroyers and five smaller ships, sailed from Loch Ewe on December 15, 1942. It remained unsighted, even though it passed south of Bear Island, and arrived as a Christmas present, on Christmas Day, in Kola Inlet. JW-51B, with fourteen merchantmen, six destroyers, and five smaller escort ships, departed Loch Ewe a week after the other convoy. Struck by a gale, five freighters and two escort vessels lost touch with the convoy. A radar-equipped minesweeper, detached to find the strays, found the *Hipper* instead and was sunk. Meanwhile four of the merchantmen and one of the escorts managed to rejoin the convoy. The remaining freighter and the other lost escort made it to Kola Inlet safely but not in convoy. Admiral Burnett, who had taken the *Sheffield* and *Jamaica* and two destroyers to Murmansk along with JW-51A, now swept out to look for the German fleet and cover JW-51B. Along with the *Hipper*, the *Luetzow* and six destroyers had put to sea to intercept JW-51B, which had been reported by a U-boat. The Nazi navy did not know that Burnett's fleet was at sea, or they would not have been there because of orders not to risk battle with equal or superior forces.[18]

On New Year's Eve there were only a few feeble flickers of a pale sun that never rose above the horizon, and an uncertain overcast of gray clouds shaded into the gray sea to make the gray-painted destroyers difficult to distinguish. The weather was further complicated by intermittent but fierce snow squalls, and a spray froze hard on the decks of the warships, causing destroyers difficulty in using their forward guns. At this point the Nazi naval squadron engaged the convoy. For a time they fought cruisers as well; the entire operation became a comic-opera battle of appearance and disappearance, confusion, and missed opportunities. In the end the escort held off the German cruisers but at a cost of a destroyer and a minesweeper. However, the *Hipper* received damage and a Nazi destroyer sank, balancing the losses. The *Luetzow*, ordered to break into the Atlantic after

[18] *Ibid.*, 291–92.

this sortie, did not go; the *Hipper,* though repaired, never saw active service again. JW–51B entered Koln Inlet on January 3, 1943, unscathed.[19]

Convoy JW–52, which departed Loch Ewe on January 17, brought thirteen vessels into Murmansk safely out of fourteen that began the journey (one turned back to Loch Ewe because of heavy weather). Convoy JW–53 departed Loch Ewe on February 15 and, except for six ships that could not take the pounding of heavy seas, arrived safely at Murmansk. Of the westbounds, RA–51 departed Kola Inlet on December 30 and arrived at Loch Ewe safely on January 11; a U-boat got one of the RA–52's merchantmen early in February; and in March RA–53 had considerable trouble, with three vessels sunk by submarines and one foundered from a sea damage. In all, the three RA's brought back fifty ships and lost only four by enemy action.[20]

Meanwhile a variety of factors again led the Allies to suspend convoys to North Russia. First of all, Admiral Karl Doenitz replaced Raeder as the head of the Nazi navy, and Doenitz concentrated his U-boat strength in the Atlantic sea lanes. As a result, escort vessels normally needed for the North Russia run had to be diverted to the Atlantic. Doenitz also moved the *Scharnhorst,* the *Tirpitz,* and the *Luetzow* to Alta Fjord in March—a threat that meant battle fleets would have to cover convoys even into Barents Sea, which Tovey would not risk. And, equally important, the Russians "started a new campaign of obstruction against our [British] officers in North Russia" by ordering two of the four British radio stations in the North closed in February and refusing to allow R.A.F. ground staff to operate, both of which the Royal Navy deemed necessary to any operation of summer convoys. British radio and R.A.F. stations would not have been so vital if the Soviets had kept their September, 1942, promise to station "48 long-range bombers, 10 torpedo

---

[19] *Ibid.,* 293–98; Morison, *Battle of the Atlantic,* 366–67.

[20] Roskill, *The War at Sea,* III, part II, 432–34. Of six Russian ships that sailed independently, the Nazis got two, and four arrived safely in Russia.

bombers, and 200 fighters, including 47 long-range fighters" in North Russia to assist P.Q. 18 and other convoys. Apparently "a few squadrons arrived, stayed for a short time, and left," but not enough even to deter German bombing of Murmansk. In April, 1943, rumors circulated among correspondents that no convoys would sail the North Russian route "until the question of protection had been settled."[21]

From July, 1942, through March, 1943, 441,400 tons of cargo departed from the Western Hemisphere for the North Russian route, 90,720 tons were lost during the same period, and 239,680 tons were unloaded in the United Kingdom to be reshipped later. Roughly 112,000 tons from the Western Hemisphere arrived at North Russian destinations aboard the sixteen United States ships that arrived safely (fifty-six sailed from Western Hemisphere ports, eleven were lost and thirty were unloaded in the United Kingdom).[22]

Stalin informed Roosevelt on October 7, 1942, that in order to help relieve the tight shipping situation he would agree to curtail some war material orders, especially tanks, artillery, and certain munitions, if the Americans paid greater attention to planes, trucks, aluminum, and grain. Protocol foodstuffs could all be shipped to Vladivostok provided the United States transferred twenty to thirty ships to Russia for Pacific service. Stalin emphasized that everything except aircraft already made up a part of the Second Protocol. Army planners resisted sending more airplanes than scheduled, and this time Roosevelt backed them up; instead they offered Stalin an American base in the Caucasus (which Stalin turned down) and two hundred, perhaps three hundred, transport planes before the end of 1943. Another

21 Roskill, *The War at Sea*, II, 397–401; Morison, *The Atlantic Battle Won*, 229.Transfer of escorts to North Atlantic service helped tip the scales against the U-boat in April and May, 1943, when fifty-six Nazi submarines were destroyed, thus ending the most serious U-boat campaign of the war. See also Roskill, *The War at Sea*, II, 371–79; *U.S.S.R. Correspondence*, I, 66; Walter Kerr, *The Russian Army: Its Men, its Leaders, and its Battles*, 230.

22 Report on War Aid, 14, 15. Tonnage figures in the text have been converted from long tons to short tons for consistency.

offer, more reasonable but quite difficult to fulfill, was to furnish Russia with twenty cargo ships at the rate of five a month beginning on November 1, 1942. Belyaev wanted all twenty transferred at once, but total shipping demands remained so heavy that Hopkins, who tried to find all twenty, had to admit it could not be done. Under great pressure from the White House, the ship transfers took place ahead of the original schedule. In addition to the twenty serviceable old steamers, the United States also delivered five new Liberty ships. In all, through June 30, 1942, fifty-three United States merchant vessels and six tankers were transferred to Russia.[23]

The shipping capacity increase in the Pacific did not reflect an equal increase in cargo carried. Soviet-controlled Pacific vessels took a longer turnaround time than estimated and often failed to meet shipment schedules. Nevertheless, between July, 1942, and June, 1943, under Russia's flag, 319 ships with full cargoes and another fifteen with partial cargoes carried 1,733,-760 tons to the Persian Gulf. Since only 112,000 tons traveled over the North Russian route, the Pacific route carried most of the material. Including a few tons to the Soviet Arctic ports in July and August, 1942, and May and June, 1943, the total tonnage shipped from the Western Hemisphere for the Second Protocol period, less losses, reached 3,420,816 tons, or 76 per cent of the 4,500,720 tons scheduled.[24]

Still this did not tell the story of all Second Protocol deliveries to Russia. Flight shipment of aircraft from Alaska to Siberia, a project dear to army air planners and one that had been off-again, on-again in negotiations with the Soviets, began on September 3, 1942. On Tuesday, September 1, a flight of five A-20 light bombers lifted off from Gore Field at Great Falls, Montana, and going via Edmonton, Alberta, Fort Nelson, British Co-

[23] Leighton and Coakley, *Global Logistics*, 584–86; Sherwood, *Roosevelt and Hopkins*, 639–40; Report on War Aid, 3; *U.S.S.R. Correspondence*, II, 35, 36–37. See also *Foreign Relations, 1942*, III, 730–35.

[24] Report on War Aid, 3, 14, 15. Tonnage figures in the text have been converted from long tons to short tons for consistency.

lumbia, and Whitehorse, Yukon Territory, they hopped to Fairbanks, Alaska, touching down on September 3. Nine more A-20's, thirty P-40's, and six C-47's were turned over to Russian pilots at Fairbanks during the rest of September.[25]

Colonel Joseph Michela, Ambassador Standley's aide, and Standley himself, on July 3 and July 4, 1942, notified both Roosevelt and Hull that Stalin had finally accepted the Alaska-Siberia (ALSIB) air ferry route proposal. The army selected Major General Follett Bradley to work out the details and sent him immediately to Washington to confer with Belyaev. On July 18, Bradley suggested that the transfer point be Fairbanks; that Soviet ferry pilots be trained there; that a United States Air Force survey party fly the Russian section of the route; and that within ten days the United States would have at Fairbanks, ready for transfer, fifty A-20's and twelve B-25's. In addition, Bradley noted, within three weeks forty-three P-40's and fifty P-39's would be delivered. Bradley took these proposals to Moscow on July 20, and Colonel Alva L. Harvey surveyed the proposed route in a Soviet bomber. Belyaev accepted Bradley's proposal for Russia on August 3. There remained one condition. The Soviet Union needed, said Belyaev, forty-three transport planes in order to move the ferry crews to Fairbanks. Air Force Chief Henry H. Arnold replied that the United States could not spare as scarce an item as military transports, especially since the United States did not have enough for its own service. Belyaev also told Burns of the need for transports, and Burns and Hopkins decided, even with air force scarcity, to supply the Soviets with ten transports. Russia protested that they needed more and on August 25 informed the United States that without a greater number of transports, the undertaking would be too small to be worth the effort and would be, as of that date, abandoned.

[25] Edwin R. Carr, "Great Falls to Nome: The Inland Air Route to Alaska, 1940–45," an unpublished doctoral dissertation, 52, 192. Carr's dissertation, with minor changes, originally was prepared as the official air force history, "History of the Northwest Air Route to Alaska, 1942–45."

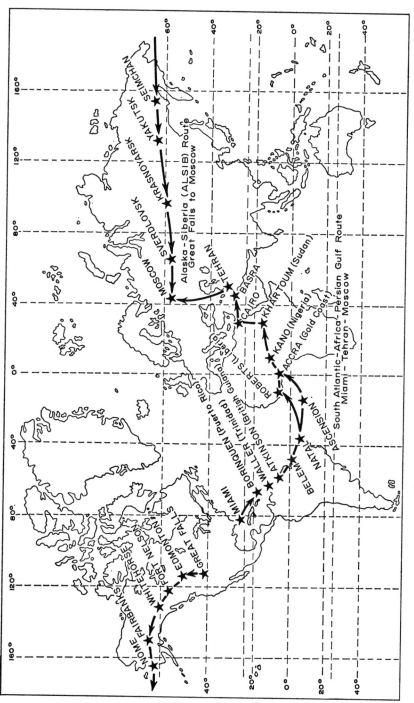

FLIGHT DELIVERY OF AIRCRAFT TO RUSSIA

General Arnold replied that the United States would therefore take over the entire responsibility for the ALSIB air ferry; Belyaev answered quickly, on August 26, that after reconsideration the Soviet Union would proceed with the operation.[26]

Air force planners decided on August 29 to send 143 planes over the route in September and 272 in October (the figures included some deliveries from the British account). Belyaev reported that the Soviet section of the route could not accommodate such numbers. Under a reduced schedule, the air force decided to send off 142 planes each month until Russia could take more. By this time twenty bombers and thirty fighters had been flown to Russia. Then suddenly, on September 19, Arnold received a letter from Belyaev indicating that the Soviet government had decided to discontinue using the route. Air force officials, given only the explanation "for various reasons," froze all delivery and internal procedures connected with ALSIB. On September 19 the air force orders to ready fighter aircraft for water delivery and bombers for flight delivery via Brazil and Africa. Almost as abruptly, a smiling Belyaev strode into Arnold's office and notified the astonished General that Russia had changed her mind, and by October 6 the project was on again.[27]

During the remainder of 1942 the ALSIB project moved very slowly. The first aircraft landed at Fairbanks on September 3, but the first Russian ferry pilots did not arrive until September 24 and did not depart for Nome with the first planes until September 29. By the end of October only ninety-three planes had reached Fairbanks, representing only two-thirds of the 142 scheduled. In November the United States delivered only forty-

[26] Carr, "Great Falls to Nome," 63–64; Matloff and Snell, *Strategic Planning*, 343–44. The Soviet Siberia route, west to east, included Moscow, Krasnoyarsk, Yakutsk, and Seimchan. Roosevelt cabled Stalin on January 9, 1943, concerning the matter of transports and indicated that two hundred, perhaps three hundred, C-47's would be shipped to Russia (*U.S.S.R. Correspondence*, II, 50).

[27] Carr, "Great Falls to Nome," 65–66; Matloff and Snell, *Strategic Planning*, 344.

eight aircraft, in December, only seven. But by April, 1943, ALSIB operators finally achieved the monthly goal and in June easily surpassed it with 329 planes, two-thirds of which were A-20's. The one thousandth plane delivered over ALSIB took off for Russia on June 24.[28]

A variety of factors prevented prompt fulfillment of air force schedules over ALSIB, many of which could not be traced to conditions under air force control. Backlogs occurred all the way from the factory to Gore Field. For example, on January 21, 1943, 239 aircraft remained stacked up at various points. Of seventy-two B-25's and P-39's scheduled for October only twenty-four reached Fairbanks by January 1. Not one of the ninety-two allotted for November arrived. Harry Hopkins, responsible for the movement of protocol goods, sent Arnold a sharp memorandum on February 2 in which he reminded Arnold of the President's October directive that aircraft for Russia should "be delivered in accordance with protocol schedules." Arnold attempted to speed up modification procedures, find adequate manpower and tools, and eliminate such time-wasters as the winterizing of thirty-four A-20's and then sending them off over the African route. Mechanics and inspectors trained on the job as did Air Transport Command office personnel. Thus routine procedures slowly worked themselves out. The Air Force could not control bad weather, another factor in delay, but they maintained inadequate weather reporting, forecasting, and communications facilities. Even so, by June 30, 1943, 1,107 aircraft arrived at Fairbanks on the Russian account, or an average of slightly less than 111 planes a month since September, 1942. Although the Air Force had few transport planes to spare and American authorities originally promised only ten, ninety-five reached Fairbanks for Russia by the end of June. The delivered aircraft reached 92 per cent of the total Second Protocol allot-

[28] Carr, "Great Falls to Nome," 67, 178–80.

ment. The entire commitment had been met at the factory, but 325 aircraft still awaited movement by land or water.[29]

Not only did American and Russian pilots ferry the aircraft to Fairbanks and then to the Soviet Union, but these aircraft also often carried cargo. The monthly Great Falls Air Base Intelligence Activities reports noted that such freight consisted of "airplane parts and accessories, books, magazines, drills, nails and bolts, newspapers, drawings and blueprints, drugs, and diplomatic mail." Passengers made up another sort of cargo. Joseph Davies returned from a trip to Moscow in June, 1943, via the ALSIB route. Minor Russian officials, minor diplomats, service officers, writers, and correspondents also traveled the same route.[30]

As operations of the ALSIB route smoothed out in 1943, the American press called Lend-Lease functions to the public's attention with greater frequency throughout the year than it had seemed to do previously. In mid-January, 1943, *The New York Times* reported that Congress, hearing complaints from China and Russia that Lend-Lease goods were piled up in ports because of transportation shortages, intended to inquire into Lend-Lease and take another look at the broad powers given to the President. The *Times* speculated that if a serious investigation of Lend-Lease ensued, the target would be Harry Hopkins of the Munitions Assignment Board, who had the real power, not Administrator Stettinius. The next day the same paper carried an article about the establishment of the President's Soviet Protocol Committee with Hopkins as chairman. Hopkins, observed the reporter, was the firmest supporter of Russian aid in top government councils. The supply problems of the previous summer had been overcome, and the United States could then send more to the Soviet Union than its port facilities could handle. A week later the press reported a Stettinius statement that aid to Rus-

29 *Ibid.*, 181–90, 192, 194. Mr. Carr's table on page 192 shows incorrect totals, but the arithmetic is easily corrected, and the text figure is correct.

30 *Ibid.*, 170–71.

sia, in arms, currently surpassed even similar aid to the United Kingdom. Stettinius released some figures—2,600 planes, 3,000 tanks, and 31,000 vehicles—as evidence of this aid.[31]

Also in January, 1943, the Gallup poll (American Institute of Public Opinion) announced that 82 per cent of the American people favored Lend-Lease, 29 per cent believed that recipients of this aid would repay it in money or goods, and 58 per cent thought they would not. Nearly three-fourths, 72 per cent, of those questioned believed that beneficiary nations *should* repay the United States for Lend-Lease materials. This public attitude reflected in the Gallup poll worried some observers of the Lend-Lease scene. It appeared that Lend-Lease settlements were regarded too casually by the government, which augured ill for the future. One commentator pointed out that no recipient could know how much it would owe the United States at war's end and advocated that the President wipe out "in advance . . . the possibility that any international obligation will flow from lend-lease, regardless of who is the creditor and who is the debtor when the war is over." Otherwise this growth of sentiment for repayment might result in a United States economic policy that would be dangerous to postwar relations. In June, Senator Walter F. George, of Georgia, refused to worry about accounting, remarking to the press that he "was not interested in the bookkeeping if the funds would only shorten the war and prevent the spilling of American blood."[32]

Time magazine remarked that Lend-Lease was misnamed. The President's eleventh quarterly report made it clear to *Time's* editors that the United States neither lent nor leased the material but intended to write it off as part of the "U.S. contribution to the war." They quoted a *New York Times* writer who suggested that the name be changed to the more precise Cana-

---

[31] *The New York Times*, 1943: January 10, pt. IV, p. 3; January 11, p. 2; January 12, p. 22; January 21, p. 1.

[32] *The New York Times*, 1943: January 27, p. 18, and June 4, p. 35. William Diebold Jr., "Implications of Lend-Lease: Political Dangers in the Settlement," *Foreign Affairs*, Vol. 21 (April, 1943), p. 511.

dian "Mutual Aid Plan." In an article titled the "Cash-Register Spirit," the *Nation* attacked Senators Gerald P. Nye, Burton K. Wheeler, Allen J. Ellender, and Hugh Butler for their irrelevant and confused criticism of Lend-Lease. "Their basic assumption," said the writer, "is that this war is not our war but a struggle we are waging solely for the sake of foreign nations who are certain to prove ungrateful." Isn't it time, the *Nation* asked, "that this picture of Uncle Sam as a noble and naive philanthropist turning out his pockets for the sake of swindling bums was scrapped?" *Time*, unhappy with the program's name, at least conceded that Lend-Lease was a two-way street.[33]

Peering at Lend-Lease from the world trade point of view, yet another writer lashed out at the program because it cut no new trade channels for the future, but rather weakened pre-war marketing organization so that it languished and shriveled to the point where it would be difficult to restore after the war. "The fact that Lend-Lease is a substitute for the laborious breaking down of trade barriers, an avoidance of troublesome political controversies by a temporary war expedient, is likely to consolidate the barriers and weaken the organization of world trade." Here arose another serious charge for Americans to consider. Otherwise, news in 1943 centered around the Standley episode and the reorganization of the administrative agencies, new United States appropriations, and the extension of Lend-Lease. Unruffled by the Standley episode, the House, by a vote of 407-6 on March 11, and the Senate, 82-0 on March 12, extended Lend-Lease for another year.[34]

Americans were also informed that the Soviets continued to ask for a second front and had hastily broadcast the most recent public accounts of Lend-Lease; that Japan continued to allow

[33] "Lend-Lease," *Time*, Vol. 42 (September 6, 1943), p. 25; *Ibid.*, (November 22, 1943), pp. 18–19; "Cash Register Spirit," *Nation*, Vol. 157 (October 30, 1943), pp. 487–88.

[34] J. B. Condliffe, "Implication of Lend-Lease: Economic Problems in the Settlement," *Foreign Affairs*, Vol. 21 (April, 1943), pp. 499–500; *The New York Times*, March 12, 1943, pp. 1, 4.

Russian ships to ply from the Pacific to Vladivostok; and that the United States sent Russia 130,000 submachine guns, 98,000,000 pounds of TNT, and 188,000,000 pounds of copper and brass in addition to planes, tanks, and trucks (two-thirds of all supplies now sent to Russia traveled in American ships). Notice of Lend-Lease assistance continued to appear in the Moscow press, and American papers took careful note of it. Readers in the United States discovered that an American train carried supplies from the Persian Gulf to Teheran, one of the first to do so, and that all American truck convoys also operated on the same route. Americans also discovered that Soviet motion picture producers turned out a movie titled "Iran," which portrayed the assembly and delivery of Russian-bound United States and British materials in the Persian Gulf, as well as other Soviet newsreels about the battles on the Atlantic supply routes.[35]

In May, 1943, during the construction of a new protocol, the news appeared that Canada, in the future, would join the United States and Great Britain in the agreement. *The New York Times* reported that Moscow radio extended its usual news broadcast by twelve minutes to devote the time to Roosevelt's latest message to Congress on Lend-Lease operations. Early in June more Lend-Lease funds were appropriated, bringing total funds to nearly $25,000,000,000. That they appeared to be well-spent seemed patent from a series of articles on Soviet military progress and success that always included mention of United States material alongside the Russian. The plywood Yak fighter flew alongside the P-39; United States M-3 tanks rumbled along next to Russian T-34's; United States and Soviet artillery shot up the same battlefields. The cheering news that the new protocol represented an increase in promised aid reached the streets in company with the unhappy news that lack of shipping and limited port facilities overseas caused delivery under the last protocol

[35] *The New York Times*, 1943: March 12, pp. 4, 16; March 13, p. 4; March 14, p. 3; March 15, p. 4; March 16, p. 5; March 31, p. 6; April 16, p. 7; April 22, p. 4.

to fall below expectations. But, the news media announced optimistically, many of the obstacles had been or were about to be overcome, and, in addition, the vast amount of material already sent to Russia, such as 750,000 tons of steel and steel products, had made itself felt. In July, 1943, Stettinius revealed that the total Lend-Lease bill had reached nearly $13,000,000,000 by June, and in his August quarterly report (echoed by the Soviet Press) Roosevelt observed that the amount spent on Russia totaled $2,444,000,000.[36]

In early September newsmen learned that the executive offices of Economic Warfare, Lend-Lease, and Relief and Rehabilitation would be reorganized, probably under State Department co-ordination. On September 25, Roosevelt announced the creation of the Foreign Economic Administration, and the selection of Leo T. Crowley to head it. Crowley, *The New York Times* reported, "will draw together all of the economic threads which formerly branched out . . . from scores of Washington offices." In October, Andrei A. Gromyko bowed in as the new Soviet ambassador and praised American aid. Donald Nelson, War Production Board head, left for a tour of Russia. The United States military mission in Moscow was being revamped, and Faymonville came home. In November, Nelson returned, impressed by his visit. Just before the Pearl Harbor anniversary, news came from Teheran that Stalin had boasted victory with the statement that "without American machines, the United Nations never could have won the war."[37]

[36] *The New York Times,* 1943: May 12, p. 6; May 29, p. 7; June 4, p. 35; June 10, p. 2; June 11, p. 3; June 13, p. 9; June 15, pp. 3, 13; June 19, p. 5; July 21, p. 6; August 26, pp. 1, 11; August 27, p. 16; August 30, p. 9.

[37] *The New York Times,* 1943: September 3, p. 1; September 26, pp. 1, 14; October 5, p. 8; October 9, p. 7; October 10, p. 38; October 12, p. 5; October 19, p. 3; November 11, p. 4; December 7, p. 1.

CHAPTER SEVEN

The Last Two Protocols

JULY, 1943, the first month of the Third Protocol, saw increasing Allied pressure on Europe. Allied bombs rained on German cities in ever increasing tonnages; the Red army moved forward on the Orel front, two hundred miles southeast of Moscow; Anglo-American troops landed on Sicily; and in Rome, Mussolini resigned only to be arrested and replaced by Marshal Pietro Badoglio. So important did the Italian situation appear to Roosevelt and Churchill in August that they arranged *QUADRANT*, a meeting at the citadel of Quebec.

At *QUADRANT* the Allied leaders directed a successful effort to obtain Italy's unconditional military surrender and persuade her to switch sides. Roosevelt and Churchill reaffirmed *OVERLORD* (the invasion of Northern France, set for May 1, 1944) and decided to supplement that operation with another in southern France, at first called *ANVIL* and later *DRAGOON*. Stalin, kept completely informed of the meeting, also learned that the Allies had obtained the military use of the Azores from Portugal, which was very important for the war against the U-boat in the Atlantic. Stalin also agreed to a meeting of the foreign secretaries in Moscow, news that excited Roosevelt and Churchill for it appeared to mean the beginning of three-way planning and doubtless also would ease East-West tensions. The *QUADRANT* conferees reaffirmed Russia's importance in the European war and on the post-war scene as well. Hopkins carried a high-level military memorandum which noted that after the

Nazi defeat no military power in Europe would match Russia's. At Quebec the Western Allies agreed to make every effort to secure Soviet friendship; she would have to be given every assistance in the prosecution of the war as one step toward that end.[1]

The Third and Fourth Protocols went a long way toward fulfilling the *QUADRANT* policy of "every assistance." The United States promised the Soviets 5,100,000 tons of stores under the Third Protocol but sent off 6,435,209 tons, an increase of nearly 30 per cent over commitments. Under Fourth Protocol terms, the United States agreed to make available 5,944,000 tons of supplies for Russia through June 30, 1945. The Fourth Protocol was reappraised and revised following the defeat of Germany in May, 1945, and again in September after the defeat of Japan. Even so, beginning on July 1, 1944, the United States shipped 7,867,392 tons of materials to Russia before Lend-Lease closed on September 20, 1945, or almost a third more than contracted.[2] The overages partly compensated for failures to meet scheduled quantities under the first two protocols, and were partly intended to convince Russia of America's sincerity, determination, and good will.

Food products stood as the largest single item of the Third Protocol (30 per cent of the total tonnage), and under the Fourth Protocol (at 21 per cent of the total), it nosed out metals by a few tons. Metals made up the second largest tonnage percentages under the Third Protocol (18 per cent) and challenged foodstuffs in the Fourth with 20 per cent. Trucks and other vehicles accounted for 13 per cent of the tonnage shipped during the Third Protocol period and 12 per cent during the Fourth. To fuel the planes and trucks shipped to Russia, petroleum products comprised an ever growing tonnage percentage, coming into third place with 13 per cent under the Fourth Protocol.

[1] Sherwood, *Roosevelt and Hopkins*, 744–48; *U.S.S.R. Correspondence*, II, 82.
[2] *Soviet Supply Protocols*, 53, 93; Report on War Aid, 4, 5, 6, 7.

Requests, offers, and actual shipments of selected munitions items can be noted from the following table.[3]

	Third Protocol			Fourth Protocol		
Item	Request	Offered	Rec'd	Request	Offered	Rec'd
Planes	8,160	3,462	4,003	4,190	3,020	3,549*
Tanks	0	2,000	1,770	3,173	3,173	2,070*
Trucks	144,000	132,000	121,947	149,755	139,996	147,709†
TNT (tons)	26,880	26,880	64,431	65,000	60,000	48,049*
Subchasers	12	0	70	72	40	35†
Marine engines	2,562	606	3,175	5,747	5,472	2,650‡

* Because of the revisions of the Fourth Protocol comparisons are not easily made; these items are listed through September 2, 1945.
† Through September 20, 1945.
‡ Through May 12, 1945.

Drafting of the Third and Fourth Protocols proceeded as it had with the Second. Beginning in the early spring of 1943 the President's Soviet Protocol Committee held discussions with the government agencies involved and brought forth a draft protocol for the period from July 1, 1943, to June 30, 1944. A similar procedure worked for the Fourth, which covered the period from July 1, 1944, to June 30, 1945 (although it was twice revised). American military men expressed their irritations with Russian Lend-Lease to Hopkins and to the Protocol Committee in March and April, 1943. They echoed Standley's charge that Russia gave "the United Nations little credit for the munitions we could ill afford to spare" and added that "lend-lease was designed to keep our Allies fighting until . . . we . . . built up our own armed forces," which had been accomplished. Now the United States should move its forces into combat and reduce aid to Russia, "using this equipment . . . for establishing

[3] *Soviet Supply Protocols*, 56, 57, 58, 61, 62, 96, 97, 98, 100, 105, 106; Report on War Aid, 4–7. All tonnage figures in text converted to short tons for consistency.

a second front." Also, America should be strong enough at the peace table "to cause our demands to be respected." Therefore, the United States should "give only such equipment to our Allies that they can put to better and quicker use than we can."[4]

In addition, army and navy support existed for designing the Third Protocol to give United States military and naval attachés and observers the same rights of battlefield visit and access to military information in the Soviet Union as their Soviet counterparts enjoyed in the United States. Marshall told the Joint Chiefs of Staff on May 22 that he did not favor such a stipulation, that political decisions to the contrary already prevailed. Military attempts to restrict Russian relief and to obtain reciprocal exchange of data was blocked again "by the White House policy that lend-lease to the USSR was not to be used as a basis for bargaining." Neither the Third Protocol, signed in London on October 19, 1943, nor the Fourth Protocol, which the participants concluded in Ottawa, Canada, on April 17, 1945, contained any such limiting provisions. The Russians delayed signing the Fourth Protocol until their request for long-range industrial equipment could be worked out. The Fourth Protocol contained the proviso that financial arrangements for the transfer of industrial materials with possible postwar uses would accord with the Master Agreement (signed June 11, 1942) "and with the terms and conditions of any amendment to said agreement which may hereafter be concluded by mutual agreement," or else the Soviet Union "may elect to purchase from the United States schedules of supplies for cash." These future financial arrangements never reached fruition, however, and production on the bulk of this industrial equipment never began.[5]

[4] Maurice Matloff, *Strategic Planning for Coalition Warfare, 1943–1944,* 282, hereafter cited as Matloff, *Strategic Planning II.* Actually, planning for the Third Protocol began much earlier. On January 7, 1943, for example, Stettinius asked Faymonville to discover the Russian needs in categories similar to those of the Second Protocol. *Foreign Relations of the United States, 1943,* III, 737–38.

[5] Report on War Aid, 5; *Soviet Supply Protocols,* 90; Matloff, *Strategic*

As Third Protocol deliveries began in July, 1943, as the might and military success of Allied arms in the air over Europe and in the Mediterranean increased, and as Anglo-American planning neared the final stages at *QUADRANT*, the necessity for cementing Soviet co-operation pressed more immediately on the the Western allies. For some months Secretary of State Hull had tried to set up top-level meetings between the Anglo-Americans and the Soviets. The dissolution of the Comintern (Third International) in May, 1943, seemed to Hull to be a slick of oil on the otherwise choppy sea of Russian-American relations, and although Stalin turned down an invitation to *QUADRANT*, he had agreed to a foreign ministers' meeting in Moscow in October. Roosevelt originally picked Welles for the Moscow mission, but Hull, at odds with Welles for a variety of reasons, soon decided to go himself. He surprised Roosevelt, who thought him too fragile for such a long journey. Hull admitted he was unwell, too old (nearly seventy-two), and had never been in a plane, but "just as an officer has to take his unit into battle whether he wants to or not," he exercised his resolution to go.[6]

Hull's decision to supplant Under Secretary Welles at Moscow marked the climax of a long dispute between the two men. Since Roosevelt agreed with Hull, Welles had neither the confidence of the President nor of the Secretary. Roosevelt reluctantly accepted Welles's resignation in order to bring a measure of peace to the State Department. On September 25, the President appointed Stettinius to the vacancy, a move quite acceptable to

Planning II, 282–83. In a comment to the author, General Deane noted that "there are two types of information which the United States might have sought from the U.S.S.R. The first is the information that our *established* intelligence agencies are continually seeking in order to round out their dossiers on foreign countries. This sort of intelligence had no direct relation to Lend-Lease. The second is information as to the need for and the use of munitions being sent to the U.S.S.R. under Lend-Lease. Such information would have benefitted all of the Allies by helping to insure that munitions were allotted to that nation that could put them to the best use in the war effort. President Roosevelt directed that the lend-lease program *not* be used to obtain *any* information that the Russians were not inclined to give us."

[6] Hull, *Memoirs*, II, 1247–56.

Hull, who regarded Stettinius highly. The promotion for Stettinius heralded a reorganization of the Lend-Lease apparatus. On September 25, Roosevelt created the Foreign Economic Administration within the Office for Emergency Management of the President's Executive Office. The Foreign Economic Administration included the Office of Lend-Lease Administration, the Office of Foreign Relief and Rehabilitation Operations, the Office of Economic Warfare, and most of the Office of Foreign Economic Co-ordination. Roosevelt named Leo T. Crowley, former director of the Office of Economic Warfare and, in that capacity, member of the War Production Board, to head the Foreign Economic Administration.[7]

On October 7, a beautiful, warm fall day, Hull boarded a new C-54 transport for the first leg of the trip to Russia. Included in his party were a group of State Department advisers, War Department liaison officers, a doctor, a naval officer to handle the plane's oxygen, and a Secret Service man. At Puerto Rico the group boarded the cruiser *Phoenix* for a relatively uneventful run to Casablanca. From there Hull's party boarded a C-54 and flew to Algiers. Hull dined with General Dwight D. Eisenhower and conversed with Free French General Charles de Gaulle. From Algiers the group flew to Cairo where young King Faruk of Egypt, King George II of Greece, and the youthful King Peter II of Yugoslavia called on Hull. The next hop took them to Teheran. There the new ambassador to the Soviet Union, W. Averell Harriman, and Major General John R. Deane, who was to be Hull's military adviser at the conference, joined the company. Standley, who had resigned, had returned to the United States a little over a week before Hull and his party departed. Hull had spent three days in briefing sessions with Standley, and Standley had been on hand to see Hull off on

[7] *Ibid.*, II, 1256; Sherwood, *Roosevelt and Hopkins*, 756; *Thirteenth Report on Lend-Lease*, 69–70; *The New York Times*, Sept. 26, 1943, 1; *Industrial Mobilization for War*, 577–78.

October 7. Harriman had spent one evening with Standley in Washington.

On a very cold October 18 in Moscow, the American C-54 touched down at the airport. To greet Hull and the new ambassador, Molotov, Litvinov, Andrei Vishinsky, and Ivan Maisky, the top Russian Foreign Office officials, stood smiling in front of an honor guard of ramrod-erect Red army men whose bayonets reflected the setting sun.[8]

The Moscow conference began that same evening. The three foreign ministers, Anthony Eden, Molotov, and Hull, met in a cordial and businesslike atmosphere. The meetings continued until October 30 and included a very wide range of diplomatic and economic discussions, many directed toward postwar aims. The achievements of the conference included a four-nation (United States, United Kingdom, Soviet Union, and China) pledge to establish a new organization for world peace after the war, an unsolicited pledge from Stalin that after the defeat of Germany he would join his allies against Japan, and a proposed meeting of Roosevelt, Churchill, and Stalin for the following month in Teheran.[9] The conference did not concern Lend-Lease specifically, but a direct connection existed; Harriman headed a reorganized Moscow apparatus that included General Deane, Hull's adviser at the Moscow talks.

In the fall of 1943 the Lend-Lease structure changed not only in Washington but also in Moscow. The old friction between Faymonville on the one hand and Standley and his attachés of the military services on the other had resulted in unhappy situations for all concerned, something Harriman remedied. In September conversations with Marshall, Harriman decided that the military mission in the Soviet Union would be clearly under the direction of the ambassador. Deane, secretary of the Joint

[8] Hull, *Memoirs*, II, 1274–77; Standley and Ageton, *Admiral Ambassador*, 489–99; John R. Deane, *The Strange Alliance*, 3.

[9] Hull, *Memoirs*, II, 1278–1313; for full discussion of military talks see Matloff, *Strategic Planning II*, 291–306.

Chiefs of Staff and United States secretary of the Combined Chiefs of Staff, was familiar with high-level strategic planning and joined Harriman as chief of the United States military mission in Moscow. Deane's staff included General Sidney P. Spalding, who had been associated with Lend-Lease from the beginning and who would be responsible for Lend-Lease affairs in Russia subject to Lend-Lease Administration policy. Rear Admiral Clarence E. Olsen and General Hoyt S. Vandenberg, U.S.A.A.F., completed the staff, although Vandenberg's appointment was temporary. As head of the American team in Moscow, Harriman proved a wise choice. He had been intimately connected with Lend-Lease for Russia since the beginning, was well acquainted with the leaders of the nations involved, and enjoyed his President's full confidence and also Russian admiration.[10]

Marshall and Harriman decided to appoint no military attaché or any representative of G-2 (army intelligence), who would be bound to conflict with Spalding as Faymonville had with Michela. If it became necessary to obtain military information from the Soviets, such would be obtained through the British or, if it could be done without disturbing the mission's objective, directly from the Russians. Deane's orders read that the new military mission must "promote the closest possible coordination of the military efforts of the United States and the U.S.S.R." Deane could discuss with Red army leaders any United

[10] Deane, *The Strange Alliance*, 10–11; Matloff, *Strategic Planning II*, 289–90. Subsequently, Deane's mission included, besides Spalding of the Supply (Lend-Lease) Division, Brig. Gen. William E. Crist, Rear Admiral Clarence E. Olsen, and, later, Rear Admiral Houston L. Maples. After Vandenberg's departure, the Air Division was headed by a succession of air officers, the first of whom was Maj. Gen. R. L. Walsh. At the peak of its activity the military mission included 135 United States service personnel. Harriman had a bad moment early in November when Mikoyan told him that Hopkins and Lukashev had already held discussions on Russian postwar reconstruction, which Harriman believed he was initiating. He indignantly protested to the State Department that they did not inform him of such conversations before he left the States. But when queried about the alleged conversations, Hopkins claimed he knew "of no discussions" on the subject. *Foreign Relations of the United States, 1943*, III, 781–87.

States strategy, plans, and the like that in his judgment were appropriate. By following these lines, Harriman explained to Marshall, the United States hoped to overcome Soviet suspicion. Ultimately the United States aimed to learn more about Russia's military plans in order to establish closer co-operation of East and West against Germany. The Americans also desired to obtain Soviet participation in the Pacific war. Russian officials agreed to the establishment of the new military mission on October 3, and upon the conclusion of the Moscow conference on November 1, it began to function.[11]

The United States military mission in Moscow experienced greater success than the previous organization. In April, 1944, the mission leased a small hotel (with the consent of the Moscow Soviet) to consolidate their living space. Deane broke out of the net that the Soviet Foreign Military Liaison Office (O.V.S.) kept around all foreign military officers when, as head of a military mission, he insisted upon direct contact with the Red army's general staff. He frequently saw Marshal Kliment Voroshilov, and the Soviets assigned Lieutenant General N. V. Slavin as Deane's constant contact with the Russian general staff. Deane felt that the mandate not to seek Russian military information made the task of the military mission easier and accounted for at least some of its success. Deane "studiously refrained" from seeking information about Red army equipment, weapons, and tactics, except in specific cases where such knowledge clearly aided the Western Allies in their fight against Germany. He noted, however, the contrast between United States operations in Russia and Russian operations in the United States. Soviet representatives visited United States manufacturing plants, schools, and testing facilities. Russian military men ac-

---

[11] Deane, *The Strange Alliance*, 11; Matloff, *Strategic Planning II*, 290–91. Harriman had not been in Moscow long before he began to worry that equipment the Russians asked for under Lend-Lease was not really for the war but for "post-war" purposes. Postwar arrangements would come under different financing. He wrote Hopkins to this effect on November 9, 1943. *Foreign Relations of the United States, 1943*, III, 786–87.

companied American headquarters in the field and witnessed United States military operations. New American inventions, especially in electronics, became available to the Russians once the United States Armed Forces used such gear and had exploited its surprise value. "We never lost an opportunity," claimed Deane, "to give the Russians equipment, weapons, or information which we thought might help our combined war effort." The Soviets, he felt, "never reciprocated" this attitude.[12]

On November 27, British, American, and Russian heads of state converged on picturesque Teheran, an operation codenamed *EUREKA*. This was in fact a meeting of East and West as surely as Teheran was a crossroads of the old and new. The burro that plodded before a grimy driver or carried his master's burden now shared the ancient streets with Lend-Lease trucks. The upshot of military discussions was the decision to launch a simultaneous invasion of Southern France to coincide with *OVERLORD*. Russian and American planners agreed to this strategy to the chagrin of Churchill and his delegation, who wanted further Mediterranean activity. Somervell, a member of the American group, learned directly from Stalin of Stalin's general pleasure with the work of the Persian Gulf supply operation, and Stalin made his famous statement at the closing dinner on November 30, 1943, that without the miracle of American production the war would have been lost. These two acts proved to be the Lend-Lease high spots of the first Big Three meeting.[13]

As Deane and Harriman, and Stalin and Molotov, returned to Moscow, Roosevelt and Churchill journeyed to Cairo to hammer out the details of Anglo-American military matters unsolved at their earlier meeting in Cairo. No other major diplomatic meeting materialized for nine months until Roosevelt and Churchill conferred at Quebec in September, 1944. Hopkins fell desperately ill on New Year's Day and remained out of things for seven

[12] Deane, *The Strange Alliance*, 28, 29, 30, 32–34, 49–50.

[13] Matloff, *Strategic Planning II*, 356, 367; Sherwood, *Roosevelt and Hopkins*, 793; Millett, *The Army Service Forces*, 80.

months, but this would not have prevented further conferences, just as it did not disturb the conclusion of the Third Protocol and the beginning of the Fourth. For the most part, Lend-Lease affairs fell into a well-oiled groove that required less of Hopkins' direct supervision. The President's Soviet Protocol Committee and the Munitions Assignment Board fixed policy for Crowley's Foreign Economic Administration and its Office of Lend-Lease Administration.[14]

Through the remainder of 1943 and into 1944, the United States military planners became ever more alert to the possibility of politico-economic bargaining but continued to be faced with the constant policy, still handed down from the White House, that no political strings could be attached to Lend-Lease. In February, 1944, Harriman suggested from Moscow that it should be the function of Deane's military mission to review Soviet Lend-Lease requests since crisis conditions no longer prevailed in Russia. Stettinius reported to Harriman on February 25 that the President's Soviet Protocol Committee would not agree, and Russian Lend-Lease priorities remained high.[15]

On March 31 Marshall informed Roosevelt that Lend-Lease food and transport played a vital role in Red army successes, as did combat aircraft. If Russia suddenly lost Lend-Lease, Marshall commented, the Nazis "could probably still defeat" her. "Lend-Lease is our trump card in dealing with the U.S.S.R.," Marshall pointed out, "and its control is possibly the most effective means we have to keep the Soviets on the offensive in connection with the second front." Marshall thus observed that the positive bargaining power of Lend-Lease was unnecessary, that the mere possibility of curtailment loomed as a tacit threat, thus preserving Soviet co-operation.[16]

The Joint Chiefs of Staff endeavored in early May to establish a policy of limited Lend-Lease aid to Russia after the collapse

[14] Matloff, *Strategic Planning II*, 369–73.
[15] *Ibid.*, 497.
[16] *Ibid.*, 497–98.

of Germany. The idea they proposed simply would continue aid to all of the Allies fighting Japan, and to no others. Marshall put the case to Roosevelt, who did not reply until September. He then told Marshall that on such matters of national policy he would make the decisions; no instructions came from Roosevelt's office, however. Hopkins, who had been very ill since New Year's Day, 1944, was not available to assist Roosevelt in matters such as Lend-Lease policy decision until August, 1944. Finally, the policy proposal made by the Joint Chiefs of Staff received approval on July 6, 1945, by another President, Harry S Truman.[17]

In April, 1944, Deane recommended that the United States approve Russian requests for heavy bombers if the Soviets would provide bases for United States air strikes against Japan. However, the War Department refused to send heavy bombers to the Soviet Union because, as the air force reminded Deane, Russia could not build up and train such a force prior to the spring of 1945. In addition, United States production schedules did not include bombers for the Soviets, and certain special equipment for the big birds continued in such short supply that they were scarce even for America. On the other hand, General Arnold had long wanted to set up United States air bases in Russia for shuttle bombing that would enable our bombing mission from England and Italy to strike targets in eastern Germany and Poland, land in Russia to rearm and refuel, and repeat the bombings on the way home. Harriman and Deane succeeded in getting Soviet permission to set up three shuttle bombing bases in the Ukraine, and they were operational in June. The air force flew seven missions during the summer; the last was a September 18 air drop to Poles in Warsaw, who rose up against the Nazis too soon to be successful. By the fall of 1944 the air forces no longer needed their new Russian bases since there was little Nazi territory they could not reach from elsewhere.[18]

[17] *Ibid.*, 498; Sherwood, *Roosevelt and Hopkins*, 804–809.
[18] Matloff, *Strategic Planning II*, 498–500.

Harriman, Deane, and the military mission in Moscow attempted in the summer of 1944 to put pressure on their Kremlin counterparts in order to get Russian approval for United States–Soviet air collaboration in the Far East against Japan. Not that the Siberian bases long desired by the U.S.A.A.F. would be indispensable, but because in July army planners had decided upon actual invasion of the Japanese home islands, and they wanted to begin active planning with Red army leaders for the day when Russia would join in the Pacific affair. Soviet authorities kept negotiations in the air, however, and seemed clearly determined to do nothing to excite Japanese fears until the European theater closed down. They allowed United States officers to inspect Siberian ports in June, but dressed as civilians. With negotiations inconclusive, Harriman wanted to use the threat of ending Lend-Lease to bring about a Siberian air base agreement, and, as in the case of all previous petitions of this sort, the White House disapproved the idea because it conflicted with established Lend-Lease policy.[19]

The Roosevelt administration faced another election in 1944, another reason why top-level diplomatic conferences, especially any that would take the President out of the country, were not held. Governor Thomas E. Dewey, the Republican candidate, energetically stormed up and down the country making speech after speech to bring the Republicans to the polls, but he avoided creating any major issues. Dewey disappointed Axis propagandists with his support of Roosevelt's foreign policy. Dewey also disappointed the powerful right wing of his own party by not attacking the New Deal's social objectives. Instead, he concentrated on the administration's domestic squabbles (Charles E. Wilson's resignation from the War Production Board, for instance) and emphasized that young men could finish the war and make the peace better than the tired old men who began the affair. Other Republicans attacked Roosevelt for having "lied us into a war" rather than having led us into it,

[19] *Ibid.*, 500–501.

or for allegedly sending a destroyer to rescue his dog, Fala, from an Aleutian Island (at a cost of millions of dollars). The Republicans refrained from any attack on Lend-Lease to Russia; that did not figure at all in the campaign.[20]

The Democrats, stressing the adage that it is unwise to change horses in the middle of the stream, chose "tired old" Roosevelt to run again. Sherwood, who returned from liberated Paris to write speeches, "was shocked" by Roosevelt's appearance. The President's face looked "almost ravaged," although "he seemed to be more full of good humor and fight than ever." Hopkins and "Pa" Watson had called Sherwood home because they were worried about the campaign, not because of Dewey but because of the President, who, Watson claimed, "just doesn't seem to give a damn." Hopkins and Watson wanted Sherwood to help get Roosevelt down from his lofty commander-in-chief perch and "into the dusty political arena." Along with Lubin (who sent Roosevelt a silly poem from the *Philadelphia Record*: "It may rain in New York, It may be foggy in San Francisco, But it will never be Dewey in Washington"), they succeeded. Roosevelt took the Fala story and turned it into an advantage. "The Republican leaders have not been content to make personal attacks upon me—or my wife—or my sons—they now include my little dog, Fala." The American people, someone claimed, would consider it a contest between Dewey and Fala. In the same speech Roosevelt replied to the "tired old men" charge that he was "actually four years older—which seems to annoy some people." Suddenly there was excitement in the campaign, sparked not by former prosecutor Dewey with his "gentlemen of the jury" speeches but by Roosevelt himself. There was Democratic noise to the effect that a winning team leaves the effective quarterback in until the game is won. Roosevelt scheduled five campaign speeches between October 21 and November 7, a far easier schedule than in 1940. While Roosevelt's margin was not

[20] Sherwood, *Roosevelt and Hopkins*, 819–21; *The New York Times*, October 14, 1944, p. 9.

as wide as in previous years, he carried thirty-six states with 432 electoral votes and gathered 25,600,000 popular votes to Dewey's 22,000,000.[21]

On Sunday, October 1, Hull visited the White House and informed the President that because of ill health, he (Hull) must resign. "The President," wrote Hull, "did not seem to want to believe me." Although disappointed himself, Hull said that he "had been overexerting . . . [himself] for some time and now found . . . [himself] in such physical condition that . . . [he] should have to resign." Hull, thereafter, spent nearly three weeks in bed at his apartment trying to recover and then another seven months at the Naval Medical Center at Bethesda, Maryland. Roosevelt visited Hull in the naval hospital to talk him out of resigning but succeeded only in getting Hull's promise not to quit until after the election. On November 21, two weeks after the election, Hull sent a formal letter of resignation to Roosevelt, who reluctantly accepted it. The names of James F. Byrnes and Sumner Welles came up as possible replacements for Hull, but Hopkins engineered another promotion for Stettinius. Meanwhile, Stimson, who wondered if at seventy-seven he ranked as one of the "tired old men" attacked by the Republicans, asked Hopkins if the President wanted him to resign. Although in better shape than Hull, he nevertheless worked limited hours. Hopkins told Stimson emphatically that the President did not want him to resign.[22]

While the presidential campaign in the United States droned into its last month, Churchill set up a meeting with Stalin in Moscow. Red army troops rolled into Poland, the Baltic States, Hungary, and Yugoslavia and pulled up at Turkish and Greek frontiers. The British army returned to Greece. Southeastern Europe presented urgent problems of military control that required top-level talks, and even American electors could not

[21] Sherwood, *Roosevelt and Hopkins*, 819–30; Roosevelt Library, President's Official File 4729, memo, Lubin to Roosevelt, October 31, 1944.

[22] Hull, *Memoirs*, II, 1714–17; Sherwood, *Roosevelt and Hopkins*, 834–35.

delay them. Under the circumstances, Roosevelt could not attend, but arranged with Churchill that during the talks, when matters pertaining to the Pacific area were discussed, Harriman would cover United States policy and political considerations and General Deane would cover the military situation. The President insisted on this arrangement because of the United States' paramount interest and responsibility in carrying on the Pacific war. As a result of these discussions, Stalin agreed that joint American–Soviet planning should commence against Japan, and at a meeting not attended by the British, Stalin presented a list of Soviet requirements for a supply build-up in Siberia. These constituted the basis of the so-called *MILEPOST* program. Stalin observed that deliveries would have to be completed by June 30, 1945. Harriman received instructions to tell Stalin that Roosevelt considered the Churchill–Stalin Moscow meeting as the "preliminary to a conference of the three of us." The three of them met later at Yalta, in the Crimea, on February 4, 1945. The Yalta location had been Hopkins' suggestion because Hopkins had warned Roosevelt that "there was not a chance of getting Stalin out of Russia at this time." Hopkins' view proved correct.[23]

Roosevelt arrived at Malta aboard the USS *Quincy* on February 2, met Hopkins, who flew into Malta via London and Rome, and, along with a large entourage, a bevy of army transport planes flew them to the Crimea, 1,375 miles away. Both Roosevelt and Churchill arrived at Yalta on Saturday, February 3, Stalin arrived on Sunday, and the first plenary session convened on Sunday at 5:00 P.M. The meetings, code-named *ARGONAUT*, turned out to have considerable significance for the future United Nations organization and for political and military affairs in both Europe and the Far East. In addition to the Big Three, the foreign ministers and the chiefs of staff of the three nations met in numerous sessions. The eight days

[23] Sherwood, *Roosevelt and Hopkins*, 832–34, 843–45; Deane, *The Strange Alliance*, 243–48, and personal comment to the author.

of meetings produced few references to Lend-Lease, the most notable exception occurring at Stalin's dinner on February 8. Proposing a toast to the President, the mustached Russian leader mentioned Lend-Lease "as one of the President's most remarkable and vital achievements in the formation of the Anti-Hitler combination and in keeping the Allies in the field against Hitler."[24]

Even though in the wings at Yalta, Lend-Lease remained quite vital. The participants knew that although the Fourth Protocol was in operation, it remained unsigned. Russia requested inclusion of industrial equipment which would very probably be of postwar use, but which, equally likely, could not be produced, shipped, and installed in time to be of any use in the war. United States officials balked at including expensive industrial equipment under the vague terms of Lend-Lease, and it also did not seem proper to divert energy into the production of items that could not contribute directly to the conclusion of the war. But the United States, in May, 1944, attempted to offer Russia an amended Master Agreement that included a financial arrangement for the industrial facilities at 2⅜ per cent interest. Such an agreement became possible under the terms of Section 3-C of the Lend-Lease Act as amended. If Russia did not enter into a formal agreement, all Lend-Lease would stop as of June 30, 1945, also according to section 3-C of the Act. If the Soviets did conclude the agreement tendered them by the United States, delivery could continue, if necessary, until July 1, 1948.[25]

Russia did not conclude the agreement as proposed by the Foreign Economic Administration's Lend-Lease officials. Instead, the Soviets countered with a proposal of their own that tied Lend-Lease with a long-term ($6,000,000,000) loan. The Soviet Union wanted this loan, Gromyko pointed out, for "the

---

[24] *Ibid.*, 849, 868–69; *Foreign Relations of the United States, The Conferences at Malta and Yalta, 1945*, 549–948, *passim*, hereafter cited at *Foreign Relations, Malta and Yalta.*

[25] *Foreign Relations, Malta and Yalta*, 316–17; *Eighteenth Report on Lend-Lease*, 56–57.

postwar and transition period," and sought to include railroad rolling stock and other railway equipment, trucks, and industrial plants ordered under Lend-Lease but not delivered by war's end. The Russians did not appear to understand that credit to Russia could be extended only under the Lend-Lease act by an agreement such as already tendered by United States officials. Otherwise, because of legal barriers which only Congress could remove, postwar credits could not be extended to the Soviet Union.[26]

Because Gromyko's $6,000,000,000 postwar credit request came shortly before the scheduled Yalta meeting, both Harriman and Stettinius believed the subject would come up at the conference. Harriman thought it was in the interest of the United States to "assist in the development of the economy of the Soviet Union," but "the Russians should be given to understand" that postwar co-operation in this respect "will depend upon their behavior in international matters." Harriman was convinced that the question of long-term, postwar credits "should be wholly divorced" from Lend-Lease negotiations. The State and Treasury departments and the Foreign Economic Administration all agreed with Harriman. He received instructions to proceed with the Fourth Protocol and continue to try to conclude "the 3-C agreement" (mentioned above) with Russia but presumably not at Yalta.[27]

At the Crimea, Roosevelt neglected, except in a rather perfunctory way, to heed a briefing request that he discuss Article VII of the Lend-Lease act with Britain and Russia. This article provided for the reduction of trade barriers to bring about less economic friction and maintain high levels of employment in the postwar world. In response to a prod from Stettinius, Roosevelt addressed a letter on the subject to Churchill, but not to

[26] *Foreign Relations, Malta and Yalta,* 310–11, 316–17, 319, 320–21. A detailed discussion of Russia and postwar reconstruction feelers may be found in Herbert Feis, *Churchill–Roosevelt–Stalin: The War They Waged and the Peace They Sought,* 642–48.

[27] *Foreign Relations, Malta and Yalta,* 321–24.

Stalin, on the next to the last day of the meetings. The chiefs of staff, attempting to co-ordinate military policy, worked out in considerable detail the Red army's needs for operation *MILE-POST*, that is, the stockpiling of Soviet supplies in Siberia for use against Japan following the conclusion of hostilities in Europe, when Russia promised to enter that theater. A joint logistics committee sent the schedule of supplies and equipment, which the Soviet military wanted the United States to furnish, to the President's Soviet Protocol Committee for action.[28]

Roosevelt returned from Yalta certain that the first positive steps had been taken for a better postwar world. As Hopkins noted, "The Russians had proved they could be reasonable," and he calculated that the United States "could live with them and get along with them peacefully." Hopkins had but one reservation: the future might well be uncertain if "anything should happen to Stalin." Stalin, however, survived Roosevelt.

As the warming Georgia sunshine coaxed blossoms from the forsythia, magnolia, and even the fruit trees, Roosevelt, resting at Warm Springs, complained of a terrific headache and died at 4:35 P.M. on April 12, 1945. Hopkins, who "looked like death" himself, flew to Washington from a bed in the Mayo Clinic to attend the funeral. Harry S Truman, vice-president and former Missouri senator, suddenly found himself at the head of the tremendous administrative apparatus that Roosevelt had personally overseen. Hopkins, "at the end of his physical rope," intended to resign and believed the entire cabinet, except Stimson and Navy Secretary James Forrestal, who took over when Knox died a year earlier, should do likewise. "Truman has got to have his own people around him, not Roosevelt's," Hopkins said.[29]

Roosevelt did not live to see the fruits, bitter and otherwise, of many of his policies that had been calculated to bring about a firm peace, including a friendly and understanding Russia.

[28] *Ibid.*, 325, 688, 962–63, 984.
[29] Sherwood, *Roosevelt and Hopkins*, 880–82.

His disillusionment, however, was pretty well established at the time of his death. Lend-Lease, with no political strings attached, was not the least of these policies. Five days after Roosevelt's death, representatives of the United States, Great Britain, Russia, and Canada formally signed the Fourth Protocol in Ottawa. When the war ended in Europe with the Nazi surrender on May 8, 1945, two months ahead of the Combined Chiefs of Staff schedule, the Fourth Protocol automatically came under review. After a cabinet meeting on May 8, Crowley and Joseph C. Grew, acting secretary of state, appeared in Truman's office with an order that Roosevelt had approved but not signed, authorizing the Foreign Economic Administration and State Department to cut back Lend-Lease upon Germany's surrender. "I reached for my pen," Truman remembered, "and, without reading the document, I signed it."[30]

As if he turned off a faucet, Crowley stopped Lend-Lease to Europe, and in fact, the Fourth Protocol came to an end on May 12. "The storm broke almost at once," Truman wrote, and "the Russians complained about our unfriendly attitude." Truman rescinded the cancellation order and explained that Lend-Lease was not being cancelled, but was gradually being readjusted. "I also made it clear," the new President remarked, "that all allocations provided for by treaty or protocol would be delivered." Actually, deliveries to Russian Europe, except for what remained "in the pipeline" (on the way), were curtailed, while shipment shifted to Siberia and operation *MILEPOST*. Russia was stirred up over the apparent cancellation of Lend-Lease and, with the United Nations organizational conference at San Francisco headed for the rocks, required special handling. Charles E. Bohlen, an officer of the State Department, and Harriman proposed that Hopkins be brought out of his new retirement to go to Russia in order to smooth things over and reassure Stalin

---

[30] *Foreign Relations, Malta and Yalta*, 830; Harry S Truman, *Year of Decisions* (*Memoirs*, Vol. I), 227–28; Herbert Feis, *Between War and Peace: The Potsdam Conference*, 27–28.

of United States friendship. Truman warmed to the idea, so Hopkins got up from his sick bed like the "traditional old fire horse at the sound of the alarm" and flew to Russia on May 23.[31]

Stalin, frank as always with Hopkins, told Hopkins on May 27 that the Soviet government felt that American attitudes toward the Soviet Union "had perceptibly cooled once it became obvious that Germany was defeated." Stalin gave several examples, the fourth one being curtailment of Lend-Lease. "The manner in which it had been done had been," in Russian opinion, "unfortunate and even brutal." Stalin saw the cutback as an attempt to "pressure" Russia into making concessions. Hopkins replied that he "thought it had been clear to the Soviet Union that the end of the war with Germany would necessitate a reconsideration of the old program of Lend-Lease to the Soviet Union." That, Stalin agreed, "was entirely understandable." Hopkins referred to Annex III of the Fourth Protocol (sent to the Russians on April 26, 1945), which involved delivery of supplies for the Far East, and told Stalin that the United States intended to carry out its commitment. Hopkins reminded Stalin that "he had seen no tendency on the part of those responsible for American policy to handle the question of future Lend-Lease to the Soviet Union in an arbitrary fashion." There had been, Hopkins admitted, "considerable confusion" in the United States concerning the status of Lend-Lease to Russia, but the incident of one ship being unloaded "did not have any fundamental policy significance." Stalin replied that he "fully understood the right of the United States to curtail Lend-Lease shipments," but he felt that the way in which "an agreement between the two Governments had been ended" had been "scornful and abrupt." Had there been proper warning, the Soviet government would have

---

[31] Truman, *Year of Decisions*, 228–29; Sherwood, *Roosevelt and Hopkins*, 885–87. On May 11, Truman allowed issuance of munitions to Russia under Lend-Lease when the Joint Chiefs of Staff considered them for use in the war against Japan. *Foreign Relations of the United States, The Conference of Berlin (Potsdam) 1945*, 1185. For a capsule view of American policy at this time see Feis, *Between War and Peace*, "Supplementary Note 2," 329–30.

had no feeling of resentment, and such warning was important "since their economy was based on plans." Stalin added that Russia had intended to "make a suitable expression of gratitude to the United States for the Lend-Lease assistance during the war but the way in which this program had been halted now made that impossible to do."[32]

Hopkins, snuffing out another cigarette, looked at Stalin and remarked that Stalin should know the United States would not use Lend-Lease "as a means of showing our displeasure." Although Hopkins did not say it, he implied that all throughout the war there had not been any attempt to use Lend-Lease in that way. "There was no attempt or desire on the part of the United States," Hopkins firmly stated, "to use it [Lend-Lease] as a pressure weapon." Stalin accepted Hopkins' explanation but asked Hopkins to consider "how it had looked from their side." Hopkins concluded the Lend-Lease discussion by remarking that it would be "a great tragedy if the greatest achievement in co-operation which the Soviet Union and the United States had on the whole worked out together on the basis of Lend-Lease were to end on an unsatisfactory note." Hopkins added "that we had never believed that our Lend-Lease help had been the chief factor in the Soviet defeat of Hitler on the eastern front," but next to the "heroism and blood of the Russian Army," Hopkins implied that it had indeed been important. Many other matters such as the composition of the Polish government, reparations policy, occupation of Germany, and the like composed their busy agenda. Hopkins discovered that the Russians intended to attack Japan in Manchuria in early August and that Stalin would accept the United States position on voting procedure in the Council of the United Nations, which meant that the San Francisco Conference had been "saved." So Hopkins not only presented the Lend-Lease case to Stalin but also managed to solve, temporarily, several other knotty problems.[33]

[32] Sherwood, *Roosevelt and Hopkins*, 893–96; *Soviet Supply Protocols*, 141.
[33] Sherwood, *Roosevelt and Hopkins*, 896–912.

Except for his membership on the President's Soviet Protocol Committee, this proved to be Hopkins' last public service. The work of the President's Soviet Protocol Committee virtually ended with Japan's surrender on August 14, and Hopkins sent Truman his resignation from that group on August 18. Three days later Truman announced that the Foreign Economic Administration had been directed to take appropriate steps to discontinue Lend-Lease operations. Crowley notified Russia of Lend-Lease's end on September 2 but allowed an additional eighteen days for the pipeline to empty, a "period of termination." Thus all Lend-Lease to the Soviet Union ended on September 20, 1945. On that same day the President's Soviet Protocol Committee dissolved. On September 27, by Presidential order, the State Department assumed Foreign Economic Administration function. One of Crowley's final acts was to ask foreign governments to compile an inventory of Lend-Lease items which they had on hand as of V-J Day, August 14. On October 15, 1945, the United States and the Soviet Union agreed that the United States would sell, and Russia would accept, certain items remaining in the Lend-Lease "pipeline" of value up to $3,000,000,000. Truman had planned to take up the matter of Lend-Lease settlement with the Soviets at Potsdam, "but there was no opportunity except for some preliminary talks about it."[34]

[34] *Ibid.*, 918; Truman, *Year of Decisions*, 476–77; *Twenty-First Report on Lend-Lease*, 5–8, 48–53.

CHAPTER EIGHT

The Arctic, Allah, and ALSIB

FAR FROM THE FIELD OF DIPLOMACY, military planning, and politics, the practical problems of concluding the war and meeting the protocol commitments continued to occupy the Western allies. By mid-1943 the shipping bottleneck relaxed somewhat, allowing the prospects for increased activity on the roads to Russia to brighten. Ship construction far outgained losses by enemy action in both tanker and non-tanker categories, making the previous Casablanca estimates seem unduly pessimistic. The submarine problem remained unsolved, however, because convoys still required large numbers of warships and escort vessels for safety's sake. Convoys still sailed slower, less direct routes. Turnaround time continued to be annoyingly lengthy as vessels waited at anchor for convoys to be organized. The pressures of *HUSKY* (the invasion of Sicily) and Nazi naval and air concentrations caused Britain to suspend north-route convoy operations in March, 1943. On the other hand, the British ran a convoy from Gibraltar to Alexandria in May, 1943, the first through the Mediterranean since 1941. The saving in shipping through the Mediterranean proved considerable since it shortened both distance and time to areas such as the Persian Gulf.[1]

The Nazis stationed the *Tirpitz*, *Scharnhorst*, and *Luetzow* in Norway and the British could not constantly keep a strong fleet of capital ships ready to force convoys past this Nazi dan-

[1] Matloff, *Strategic Planning*, II, 44–47; W. K. Hancock and M. M. Gowing, *British War Economy*, 415.

ger. The demands of Mediterranean operations reduced the number of men-of-war it was possible to hold in home waters. To help make up the deficiency, the United States Navy detached the *South Dakota,* the *Alabama,* and five destroyers from their Argentia, Newfoundland, station to strengthen Admiral Sir Bruce Fraser's Home Fleet (Admiral Fraser became commander-in-chief in June, 1943, replacing Admiral Sir John Tovey). In August the American battleships left for the Pacific, but two heavy cruisers, the *Tuscaloosa,* to which northern waters were nothing new, and the *Augusta,* plus the light carrier *Ranger,* arrived as replacements. The situation in northern Norway had changed somewhat since convoys had been stopped in March, a factor that caused Fraser to review the possibility of restarting convoys in September. Hitler had found other uses for a large part of his northern air force, although reconnaissance continued as effective as ever. The U-boat forces also had been reduced, but enough remained to be quite troublesome, and the Nazi surface force seemed more powerful than ever before.[2]

Fraser regarded the northern route to Russia as unimportant. He believed it unjustifiable to run a convoy unless the route proved absolutely essential for "the successful prosecution of the war"; therefore, no convoys moved in September, 1943, over Arctic Sea routes. The *Tirpitz, Scharnhorst,* and ten destroyers made sorties out of Alta Fjord on September 6 to bombard Allied shore installations on Spitzbergen and fled back into the safety of their rocky haven before the British fleet could be brought to play. Fraser and the British naval staff, however, had under consideration a daring plan to eliminate the heavy German fleet units that guarded the north-route passage. Brave Englishmen manned midget submarines and managed to get three of them into Alta Fjord to attack the *Tirpitz* on September 22. The main turbines, all three sets, were so badly damaged by the charges placed under the mighty Nazi ship that she was completely immobilized. The following day the *Luetzow* left

[2] Roskill, *The War at Sea,* III, Part I, 57–59.

The War at a Glance, 1943[*]

Although the Soviets had mounted counterattacks that had hurt the German army at important moments, such as at Stalingrad, the Russians were finally ready in the spring of 1943 to begin a series of full strength offensives and throw the Nazis on the defensive. With only a few setbacks, this effort continued until it reached Berlin in the spring of 1945. In 1943 the Soviets began a summer attack against the Germans in the southern sector. Orel, Kharkov, and Kiev had been recaptured by fall, Leningrad was freed in the winter, and the Nazis were driven from the Crimea in the spring of 1944. Odessa fell in April, and the Red army was in a position to strike into the Danube Valley.

[*] See the Chronology in Appendix C.

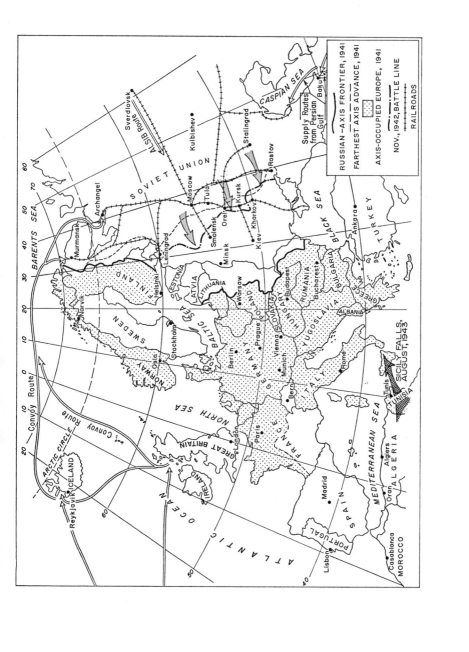

RUSSIAN–AXIS FRONTIER, 1941

FARTHEST AXIS ADVANCE, 1941

AXIS-OCCUPIED EUROPE, 1941

Supply Routes from Persian Gulf

NOV., 1942, BATTLE LINE

RAILROADS

SOVIET UNION

Sverdlovsk

ALSIB Route

Kuibishev

Stalingrad

Rostov

Archangel

Moscow

Tula

Kursk

Murmansk

Smolensk

Orel

Kharkov

Leningrad

Minsk

Kiev

CASPIAN SEA

Baku

BLACK SEA

TURKEY

Ankara

BARENTS SEA

FINLAND

ESTONIA

LATVIA

LITHUANIA

Warsaw

POLAND

Helsinki

SWEDEN

NORWAY

Stockholm

BALTIC SEA

Prague

SLOVAKIA

Vienna

HUNGARY

Budapest

RUMANIA

Bucharest

BULGARIA

YUGOSLAVIA

ALBANIA

GREECE

Narvik

Oslo

Berlin

G E R M A N Y

Munich

Bern

ITALY

Rome

NORTH SEA

GREAT BRITAIN

London

IRELAND

Paris

F R A N C E

SICILY FALLS, AUGUST, 1943

Tunis

TUNISIA

MEDITERRANEAN SEA

ARCTIC CIRCLE

Convoy Route

ICELAND

Reykjavik

Convoy Route

A T L A N T I C   O C E A N

SPAIN

PORTUGAL

Madrid

Lisbon

Casablanca

MOROCCO

Oran

Algiers

ALGERIA

Alta Fjord and managed to escape British attempts to attack her. She arrived safely in the Baltic to refit, returned to active service in 1944, but only in the Baltic, and then was destroyed on April 16, 1945, at Swinemünde in a heavy air raid. The United States fleet, now no longer needed with two of the three German heavy vessels out of the way, returned to the United States toward the end of November, 1943.[3]

The British Admiralty then decided to resume convoys to Murmansk. They planned to send a convoy of forty ships each month, but Fraser, like Tovey, believed this to be far too many ships in one convoy in the winter when the ships were likely to be scattered by gales and fall prey to U-boats and air attack. Fraser decided to run two smaller convoys through under strong escort with a cover force of cruisers for the most hazardous portion of the journey. This time the Russians stalled preparations for convoy resumption. Soviet bureaucrats refused visas for additional British personnel in North Russia, even for men destined to replace those whose North Russian tours were over. Churchill, on October 1, bluntly told Stalin, "If we are to resume convoys we shall have to reinforce our establishments in North Russia." Stalin replied on October 13 in language equally terse. The Russian leader claimed that British personnel "there now are not being used properly and have for months been doomed to idleness." Also, they had misbehaved, and "in a number of cases resorted to corruption in their efforts to recruit certain Soviet citizens for intelligence purposes." Churchill, thereupon, also told Stalin that any convoy promises over the north route did not constitute a contract or bargain, to which Stalin replied that it "cannot be treated other than as an obligation assumed by the British Government." Failure to carry through deliveries to Russia by halting Murmansk convoys, as the British government had done, Stalin angrily commented, could only be regarded "in the nature of a threat to the U.S.S.R."[4]

[3] *Ibid.,* 59–72.

Churchill complained to Roosevelt on October 16 that he "received a telegram from Uncle Joe [Stalin] which I think you will feel is not exactly all one might hope for from a gentleman." Actually Britain had begun to load cargoes for a convoy scheduled to leave on November 12 and did not let hot words from the heads of state interfere. Churchill, however, returned Stalin's message to the Soviet ambassador and remarked that he would not receive it. Eden, in Moscow for the Foreign Minister's Conference, managed to smooth the affair over in conversations with Stalin and Molotov. The new convoy cycle began on November 1 when RA–54A, thirteen empty ships from Archangel, returned safely to Iceland.[5]

The first convoy on the eastbound cycle, JW–54A, with eighteen merchantmen, sailed from Loch Ewe on November 15, three days behind schedule, and convoy JW–54B, with fourteen ships, sailed a week later. Though reported by Nazi aircraft, both arrived without incident. In mid-December, JW–55A, with nineteen ships, safely traveled to Murmansk, escorted all the way by Fraser himself and the *Duke of York*. This easy passage proved too much for the Nazi navy, and Admiral Doenitz told Hitler on December 19 that in company with a destroyer escort, the *Scharnhorst* would attack the next Arctic convoy if conditions appeared favorable. On December 20, 1943, JW–55B, with nineteen ships, weighed anchor at Loch Ewe, and on December 23, RA–55A, with twenty-two ships, steamed out of Kola Inlet. Each had an escort of ten destroyers and a few smaller vessels. Vice-Admiral Burnett, with three cruisers from the Home Fleet, provided the close cover for JW–55B, as Admiral Fraser aboard the *Duke of York*, with the *Jamaica* and four destroyers, sailed from Iceland to provide distant cover for both convoys. The Nazis picked up the eastbound convoy from air reconnaissance

[4] *Ibid.*, 76; Winston S. Churchill, *Closing the Ring*, 261–69; *U.S.S.R. Correspondence*, I, 166–67, 171–73.

[5] Churchill, *Closing the Ring*, 271–74; Roskill, *The War at Sea*, III, Part I, 77.

quickly enough but did not detect the westbound one or either cruiser cover force. Five Luftwaffe bombers attacked the eastbound convoy on December 23; two were shot down, and three driven off. A year earlier the air attacks would have been intensified on the following day, but no attack came on Christmas Eve.[6]

Early on Christmas Day, Fraser ordered four destroyers of westbound RA-55A detached to cover eastbound JW-55B, which increased its destroyer cover to fourteen. At 7:00 P.M. on Christmas Day the *Scharnhorst* put to sea with a screen of five destroyers. Early in the morning of December 26 the Admiralty learned that the *Scharnhorst* had sailed. As it happened, the *Scharnhorst*, unknown to her Nazi commander, headed into the midst of the British fleet. The ship steamed north toward the convoy (protected by fourteen destroyers), and Burnett and his cruiser force sailed on an intercept course from the northeast. Fraser, with the *Duke of York* and the *Jamaica*, hastened to cut off the escape, speeding in from the southwest. Burnett's cruiser force made radar contact with the *Scharnhorst* at 8:40 A.M. on the twenty-sixth and promptly engaged her. The *Scharnhorst* turned southward, directly toward Fraser's squadron. The Nazi destroyers, meanwhile, had been sent to find the convoy, missed it, and returned to Norway. At 4:17 P.M. the *Duke of York's* radar picked up the *Scharnhorst*, and when she opened fire thirty-three minutes later, she took the *Scharnhorst* by complete surprise. A turn to the north again brought fire from Burnett's cruisers, and British destroyers scrambled for position to launch torpedoes. The *Scharnhorst*, trapped, became a running target for the British navy, which pumped salvo after salvo at her. British destroyers nearly stalled the German vessel with torpedo attacks, and by 6:20 P.M. the *Scharnhorst's* main armament had been silenced. At 7:00 P.M. the German commander radioed Hitler that he would fight to the last shell, and at 7:28 P.M., after having loosed her seventy-seventh salvo, the *Duke of York*

[6] Roskill, *The War at Sea*, III, Part I, 77–80; Morison, *The Atlantic Battle Won*, 236–37.

ceased fire to let the destroyers finish the job. Altogether British destroyers launched fifty-five torpedoes; the last three probably finished the job. Through the darkness of the Arctic night only the flashes from the guns illuminated the scene; in addition to the darkness, dense smoke obscured the *Scharnhorst*, through which glowed faintly the fires aboard her. About 7:45 P.M. the British fleet heard a heavy explosion, and the *Scharnhorst* sank. The cruiser *Belfast*, first on the spot, rescued thirty-six sailors, but no officer survived. Some 1,980 Nazi sailors perished.[7]

Gleefully, Churchill reported to Stalin that Admiral Fraser had sunk the *Scharnhorst*. Stalin called the blow "masterly," and to Admiral Fraser remarked, "I firmly shake your hand." The danger of surface attack on Arctic convoys appeared non-existent with the *Tirpitz* damaged, the *Scharnhorst* sunk, the *Luetzow* refitting, the *Scheer* and the *Nürnberg* in the Baltic, and the *Hipper* in dock at Kiel. Now only the U-boat force, about two dozen, remained to patrol the north route. In January, JW–56A lost three ships, two American, to the U-boats. Later in the same month the Nazis lost a submarine in an attack on JW–56B but sank a British destroyer. In February, 1944, escorts of JW–57 got two U-boats but lost another destroyer. Eastbound RA–57 sank three U-boats and lost only one merchantman. The British navy ascribed the success of February, 1944, convoys partly to the use of escort carriers. The Nazis lacked enough Luftwaffe strength to increase northern air power; with the surface threat gone and U-boats in trouble, it seemed that Hitler had lost all chance to contest seriously the north route.[8]

Admiral Doenitz transferred more U-boats to Arctic waters in order to bring the Nazi squadron there up to twenty-eight in strength. This was just in time to fight JW–58, with forty-nine ships and the United States cruiser *Milwaukee*, being transferred to Russia as part of the Italian fleet settlement (an ar-

[7] Roskill, *The War at Sea*, III, Part I, 80–88; Morison, *The Atlantic Battle Won*, 238–43.

[8] *U.S.S.R. Correspondence*, I, 180; Roskill, *The War at Sea*, III, Part I, 89, 267–71; Morison, *The Atlantic Battle Won*, 305–308.

rangement between the Allies whereby Britain and the United States sent ships to the Soviet Union in lieu of Italian ships which had become available by virtue of Italy's surrender). The escort included twenty destroyers plus a variety of smaller craft and two escort carriers. The Luftwaffe lost six reconnaissance planes to the escort's fighters, which caused the local commander to cease daylight patrols. The submarine force lost four U-boats and also decided to discontinue daylight operations. Still the U-boats provided some trouble and in the westbound RA's managed to sink two of 122 merchantmen in March and April, 1944.

Repairs on the *Tirpitz* neared completion by the first of April, 1944, so the R.A.F. staged a heavy raid on her on April 3. Heavily damaged, she was out of action for another three months. As April turned to May, the British dispatched the last convoys they had agreed to run in the spring. Also, the merchant ship and warship build-up for *OVERLORD* would have made it difficult to provide north-route convoyed shipping. Churchill reported to Stalin since the fall of 1943, 191 ships (49 British dry-cargo ships, 118 United States dry-cargo ships, a crane ship, and others) had carried 232,000 tons of British and 830,000 tons of American Lend-Lease supplies for Russia, not including 171,000 tons of petroleum products and another 25,000 tons of "United States Army stores," presumably for the shuttle-bombing bases. "We . . . succeeded beyond our hopes," Churchill noted. Stalin beamed so much that he decorated Oliver Lyttelton, British minister of production, who had charge of Arctic supplies.[9]

After the invasion of northern France had been successfully launched, the British Admiralty again undertook to convoy merchant ships on the North Russian run. In July the British carried out an unsuccessful air raid on the *Tripitz*, seeking to destroy her. In July also, an experienced R.A.F. Coastal Command Group conducted a methodical campaign against Nazi submarines, sinking at least four and damaging a number of others. On

[9] Roskill, *The War at Sea*, III, Part I, 271–81; Morison, *The Atlantic Battle Won*, 309; *U.S.S.R. Correspondence*, I, 215–18.

August 15, JW–59 sailed from Loch Ewe with thirty-three cargo ships, a rescue ship, and eleven Lend-Lease submarine chasers for the Russian navy to use off Kola Inlet. The escort force included the cruiser *Jamaica*, two escort carriers, and eighteen smaller warships. Also the former British warship *Royal Sovereign*, transferred to Russia as the *Arkhangelsk*, made the run with the convoy and rendezvoused at sea with eight Russian destroyers, all of which likewise had been transferred by the British to Russia. They were from among the group originally given to Britain by the United States in the destroyers-for-bases deal of 1940. The convoy itself experienced an uneventful passage, the escort carrier planes keeping the U-boats at a distance. The U–344 sank one of the convoying sloops, the *Kite*, and the U–354 sank a convoying frigate, the *Bickerton*, but in turn both U-boats were sunk by aircraft of the convoy escort. RA–59A safely traveled the return route and cost the Nazis one U-boat.[10]

The next convoy pair, JW–60 and RA–60, departed Loch Ewe and Kola Inlet on September 15 and 18 respectively, and in spite of seventeen submarines deployed against them, lost only two merchantmen. The Nazi navy lost at least one U-boat to the escort carrier group. Also on September 15 a squadron of British Lancaster bombers, operating from North Russia, attacked the *Tirpitz* in Alta Fjord with twelve-thousand-pound bombs and damaged her so badly that she could not be repaired at anchor. The German naval command then transferred her to Tromsö for use as a floating coast defense battery and thus removed her from her threatening position on the north-run flank. In addition, the Royal Navy stepped up its campaign against Nazi submarines and surface shipping along the Norwegian coast with considerable success. Convoys JW–61 and RA–61 sailed from Loch Ewe and Kola Inlet on October 20 and 30 respectively, and both made it through without loss. The next outward convoy, JW–61A, carried eleven thousand Red army men, released by the

[10] Roskill, *The War at Sea*, III, Part II, 155–61; *U.S.S.R. Correspondence*, I, 220, 221, 229, 230, 240–41.

The War at a Glance, 1945[*]

In the summer and fall of 1944 the Soviets advanced rapidly toward Budapest and Vienna. In the north they pressed the Finns back to Viborg and concluded an armistice with them in September. The Baltic States fell like dominoes, and the Red army stormed into East Prussia and Poland. The Russians reached the Oder River in March, 1945, shortly before the allies on Germany's western front crossed the Rhine River at Remagen. Vienna was captured in early April, and on April 25, Soviet and American troops met at Torgau on the Elbe River. On April 29 the German armies in Italy surrendered. On April 30, Hitler committed suicide. On May 7 the surrender was arranged at Reims, France, May 8 was celebrated as V–E Day, and on May 9 a final act of capitulation was ratified in Berlin between the Russians and German armed forces commanders before representatives of the other allies. The Soviets entered the war in the Far East two days after the first atomic bomb was dropped on Hiroshima and began their sweep across Manchuria. After a second atomic bomb blasted Nagasaki, the Japanese accepted Allied surrender terms on August 14 and formally signed them on September 2.

[*] See the Chronology in Appendix C.

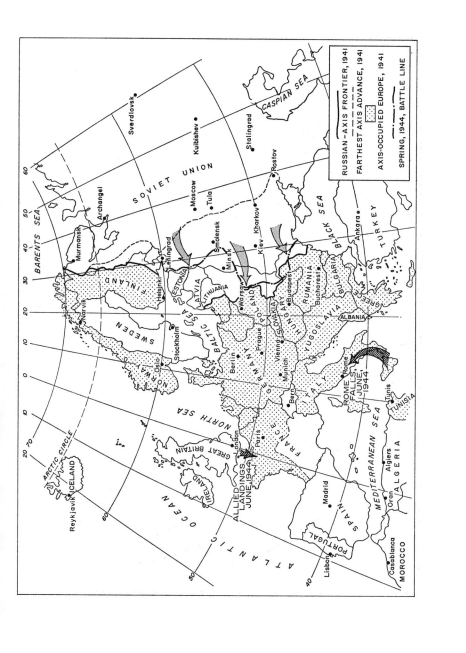

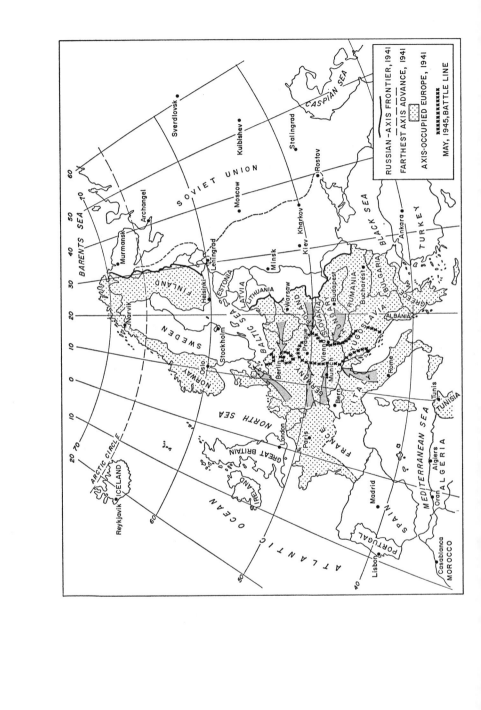

Allies from German prisons, back to Russia. On November 12, thirty-two Lancaster bombers caught the *Tirpitz* in her new anchorage near Tromsö and utterly battered the Nazi vessel, capsizing her completely. The *Tirpitz* could no longer, in anyone's imagination, be a threat.[11]

Convoys JW–62 and RA–62, sailing in late November and early December, experienced air attack once again as Junkers-88 torpedo planes, now useless in northern France, appeared in the Arctic. They did no damage to either convoy, nor did the submarines, which lost two more of their number. By New Year's Day, 1945, the Nazis had ceased to challenge north-route convoys with much effect. From August through December, 124 merchantmen sailed east and 102 sailed west, with a total loss of two sunk. The opening of 1945 saw no let-up in Nazi pressure, however, as the enemy continued to contest the passage of the next five convoys. U-boats sank two merchantmen of JW–65 and one of RA–64. Another cargo ship of RA–64 fell victim to air attack. During the same period four escort vessels went to the bottom. Approximately ten U-boats fell prey to escort or air patrol action in areas of north-route convoy activity.[12]

The record of the north-run convoys was, observed Captain Stephen W. Roskill, R.N., "as a whole . . . amazingly successful." Forty convoys made up of 811 cargo ships put to sea, thirty-three of which turned back for various reasons and eighty-five went to the bottom. The successful cargo carriers hauled 4,439,-680 tons of supplies, including 5,000 tanks, over 7,000 British and American aircraft, and large quantities of ammunition. "In almost every respect," noted Admiral (and historian) Samuel E. Morison, "North Russia convoys were exceptional." Only occasionally did Hitler hurl larger U-boat concentrations against convoys elsewhere, and never did the pressure let up on the northern convoys. Either British or American sailors took their

[11] Roskill, *The War at Sea*, III, Part II, 161–69; Morison, *The Atlantic Battle Won*, 310.

[12] Roskill, *The War at Sea*, III, Part II, 251–62, 432–35, 466–69; Morison, *The Atlantic Battle Won*, 310.

ships through the always heavy, often gale-driven, ice-strewn seas of the Arctic night, or through the equally tempestuous waters and reconnaissance dangers of perpetual daylight. "The faint hope," commented Morison, "that these efforts on Russia's behalf would produce a change of attitude on the part of the Soviet Government was not destined to be realized, even in the first flush of victory."[13]

On the record sheet, 218,520 more tons of cargo passed over the Persian Gulf route than through the Arctic seas to North Russia. Most of the cargo that was flown, carried, or pulled over the winding road and railroad from Khorramshahr to Teheran made the tortuous trip between July, 1943, and early 1945. The United States Army took over the motor transport system from the United Kingdom Commercial Corporation on March 1, 1943, although the army operated some trucks beginning in late February. Because the section of the road from Andimeshk south remained unfinished until nearly the end of 1943, the majority of the early United States truck convoys wound through deep gorges and rugged mountains, through Avej Pass (7,776 feet above sea level), up grades of 10 to 12 per cent, and through heavy, drifting snow and -25° F. temperatures in the winter. When the temporary road from Khorramshahr (euphemistically named in translation, "City of Delight") to Andimeshk became passable in 1943, drivers fought their way across a windy, dry, hot (temperatures 120° F. in the shade) plain characterized by dust storms in summer and heavy rains in winter. A member of the Persian Gulf command observed that truck drivers "were chilblained by snow, parboiled by sun, strangled by dust, and fired on by bandits." Clearly the men of the Motor Transport Service found the Persian Gulf anything but a resort.[14]

[13] Roskill, The War at Sea, III, Part II, 261–62; Morison, The Atlantic Battle Won, 313–15; Report on War Aid, 15. Tonnage figures converted to short tons for convenience.

[14] Motter, Persian Corridor, 310–16; Joel Sayre, Persian Gulf Command, 79–80, 92, 102.

The Americans soon discovered that running the trucking operation required them to control the highway, over which Russian, British, and Iranian traffic also moved. It proved easier to accomplish that than to train native drivers, reduce accident rates, stop stealing, overcome shortages of men and machines, and keep everything in good working order. The Motor Transport Service set up schools to train natives as mechanics, drivers, and interpreters. The obstacles to using native labor proved great, but the natives worked fairly well, considering the handicaps. Most of the Iranians had never ridden in a truck or in any other motor vehicle. They did not speak much, if any, English, yet they were instructed in that language. On the road, native Moslem fatalism provided an unexpected hazard. The native drivers "accepted the crash that followed rounding a sharp curve on the wrong side of the road as the will of Allah," or else they dealt with failing brakes "by leaping from the cab and letting the burdened truck careen to its destruction and the endangerment of all else on the road." A historian of the area also reported, with incredible understatement, that "there were . . . the handicaps imposed by widespread opium addiction." Although the Motor Transport Service schools graduated 7,546 drivers by the end of July, 1944, the largest number ever employed was 3,155. Graduates found they could work for the British or Russians as well, and many did. Yet most of those who drove for the Motor Transport Service proved, in spite of problems such as the ones mentioned above, to be skilled and competent.[15]

Military police, besides policing the traffic on the road, faced security problems. Native bandits took advantage of every kink in the road that forced drivers to slow down, enabling the bandits to clamber aboard a truck, "slit tarpaulins, and throw off items like tires, ammunition, sugar, flour, beans, and cloth." Occasionally a native driver would pull off the road and unload his cargo for confederates. Improved security stopped wholesale pilferage, but thieving continued as a problem until

[15] Motter, *Persian Corridor*, 316–25.

operations ended. Another problem, at least until the road was completely hard-surfaced, was the toll of men and machines taken by washboard roads that "shook the trucks to pieces . . . and pounded men's kidneys to jelly." One-third of those hospitalized in the Persian Gulf Service Command were truck drivers, although these accounted for only one-tenth of the command's manpower.[16]

Another natural hazard on the road included competition with occasional herds of livestock. In one instance Iranian nomads drove fifty thousand head of mixed livestock north through a gorge along the truck route and met a truck convoy headed south. The ensuing melee inspired a witness to observe: "A couple of M.P.'s who tried to direct traffic nearly went crazy. It was the lambing season and hundreds of baby lambs spilled off the road, paused in bewilderment under the trucks . . . and . . . began to bleat. The din was terrific—a monstrous scramble of kid bleats, ram baas, donkey brays like the screeking of an old pump, cow moos, horse whinnies, truck backfires, whistle trills . . . and, every once in a while, a blast of music from a tribal piper or drummer, all bouncing off the canyon walls." In spite of all the hazards, traffic continued on the truck route until December, 1943, which emerged as the peak month for truck freight hauled over Persian Gulf roads. The drivers moved 58,400 tons of Russian freight. The total of all Russian aid supplies carried by the Motor Transport Service during its period of operation reached 457,475 tons. This tonnage, while not great in itself, still "would have required a line of standard U.S. Army 2½ ton 6 x 6 cargo trucks standing bumper to bumper all the way from Baltimore to Chicago." According to the original plan, as soon as the railway proved capable of carrying Russia's cargo inland by itself, Motor Transport Service would be closed out. Accordingly, army planners discontinued Motor Transport on November 30, 1944.[17]

[16] *Ibid.*, 325–27.
[17] Sayre, *Persian Gulf Command*, 26–27; Motter, *Persian Corridor*, 328–29.

The Iranian State Railway, which linked Russia's battlefront to Western Hemisphere supply sources, provided the main reason for the joint British-Russian occupation of Iran. Before the Allies arrived, the railway could carry 200 tons a day; while the British operated it, their daily haul of Russian-aid freight averaged 740 tons; the daily average for American operation (April, 1943–May, 1945) reached 3,804 tons of cargo. Brigadier General Paul F. Yount, a relatively young West Pointer who had been specially trained for the task by a major American railroad, was primarily responsible for this achievement. The 865 miles of railway stretched from Bandar Shahpur on the Persian Gulf to Bandar Shah on the shore of the Caspian Sea. As the trains crossed the rugged Zagros Mountains, they roared through hundreds of unventilated tunnels (135 in one stretch of 165 miles) that filled with steam and smoke, and they emerged time and again on the edge of deep, sometimes spectacular, canyons. This operation so impressed James Thurber that he wrote about the fictional replacement officer reporting to "Captain Flagg of World War II shortly after the invasion of Normandy: 'I been railroadin' with the P.G.C., sir,' says the officer. 'Some of the guys in Iran think I was yellow to get myself transferred here.'" American trainmen shepherded trains as far as Teheran, while Soviet trainmen operated the road north to the Caspian and through the Elburz Mountains.[18]

Soviet and American railroad officials argued about tonnage targets and turnaround time, and, to simplify matters, Americans lent freight and gondola cars as well as locomotives to the Russians and repaired those worn out or damaged. The English and Americans quarreled about car allocations and various degrees of authority but managed to settle their differences speedily. It was not so easy with the Russians, who wanted tonnages increased but refused to recognize the American right to allocate

[18] Thurber quotation from preface to Sayre, *Persian Gulf Command*, xi, 120; Motter, *Persian Corridor*, 331, 347; comment by General Deane to the author. Tonnage figures in short tons.

cars. The Soviets asked for increased shipments and then, when they got them, proved unable to haul them away from Teheran without the loan of more American equipment. Besides administrative problems, others of security and safety plagued the Iranian State Railway. Pilferage became so bad that Russian guards rode the trains from Andimeshk to Teheran. Measures to curb theft in the yards and to control black-market activities became serious operations in themselves. The accident prevention record responded to strict mechanical safety measures. Rigid inspection, installation of air-brakes, and careful dispatching procedures headed the list.[19]

As it became clear that the war in Europe was nearing victory, the army tried to bring the Iranian railway and its physical equipment to prime condition for postwar Iranian operation. State Department officials, worried about the postwar Iranian economy, were partly responsible for this development. In the long run, the railroad wound up with enough rolling stock to pull fifty thousand tons a month. The peak month for freight haulage of Russian supplies on this line was September, 1944, when 190,512 tons were handled. Altogether, under both British and American operation, the Iranian railway carried 3,347,768 tons of Soviet-bound supplies, making it a major factor in the shipment of Lend-Lease to Russia. Greater tonnage moved to Russia on the Iranian State Railway than moved by ship over the Black Sea or Soviet Arctic routes.[20]

Neither the Motor Transport Service nor the Iranian State Railway could handle goods any faster than it could be unloaded from ships in port and reloaded aboard the inland carriers. Since ship turnaround time had been notoriously long, the improvement in 1943–44 was bound to attract attention. American operational control of the ports became complete on April 1, 1943, and in that month ship turnaround time averaged fifty-one days.

[19] Motter, *Persian Corridor*, 356–63.
[20] *Ibid.*, 377, 490–91; Report on War Aid, 15. Tonnage figures converted to short tons.

By Christmas, 1943, the average fell to eighteen and then to about eight days in September, 1944. The troops that handled cargo worked under difficult physical conditions, with temperatures ranging up to 140° F. from May through October, "accentuated by spells of high humidity and severe periodical dust storms." Temperatures often ranged from 104°–105° F. in hospital wards, making accurate reading of fever thermometers difficult. "When the sun was operating wide open," wrote an observer, "hardly anybody in the P.G.C. discussed the heat; you needed all your breath to fight it." October and November usually were pleasant by contrast, but from December through March the nights were cold and the days characterized by driving, torrential rains. In spite of these handicaps, the troops improved existing dock facilities, constructed new ones, built camps and barracks, and continued to unload supplies.[21]

Scheduling of shipping by any route continued to be a top-level decision throughout the war. When it seemed that Washington planners intended to reduce shipping through the Persian Gulf for the Third Protocol period, the Soviets naturally protested, claiming the Persian Gulf route was inefficient and demanding increased shipments especially over the north route. The improvement in discharge rate belied the Soviet charge. By December, Khorramshahr unloaded more than 173,600 tons. Throughout December, 1943, and the rest of the winter and early spring, port troops and native workers set record after record of daily discharge, the peak being 5,012 tons on May 15 from a ship at Bandar Shahpur. The peak month for the Persian Gulf ports proved to be July, 1944, when 2,956 Port troops plus native labor discharged 215,892 tons of cargo at Khorramshahr. By the end of 1944 the Persian Gulf ports were operating below capacity, as shipping began to be rerouted into the Black Sea, shortening the supply line considerably. The United States Army turned the port of Bandar Shahpur back to the British in

[21] Motter, *Persian Corridor*, 381, 392–95, 408, 484–85; Sayre, *Persian Gulf Command*, 79–81.

January, 1945; while Kohorramshahr closed as a Russian-aid port on June 1, 1945.[22]

Operations in the Persian Gulf were not restricted to reception, transfer, and haulage of cargo. Some of the cargo, such as aircraft, had to be assembled before Soviet representatives would accept delivery. At first, Douglas Aircraft Company representatives assembled planes at Abadan, averaging about seventy-five planes a month. The army took over from Douglas on April 1, 1943, and continued the assembly operation until January 31, 1945, when Abadan operations came to an end. During the Third Protocol period, the air force delivered 2,902 planes to Russian pilots, for an average monthly rate of 251.6 aircraft. The assembly operation proceeded with considerable dispatch in spite of variables such as the fluctuating rate of shipping, personnel, or the weather. During the Fourth Protocol period, Abadan operatives assembled only 482 aircraft for Russia. Large-scale operations ended in August, 1944, when deliveries fell to ninety; by December, only twenty-one planes flew out, and the Russians received only eight during the next five months.[23]

Persian Gulf servicemen built not only airplanes but also trucks. As early as 1938, General Motors' Overseas Division foresaw the need to locate emergency assembly plants at strategic sites the world over. In May of 1941 the British carried through parts of the General Motors plan when they ordered four emergency assembly units for the Middle East. When the United States Iranian mission moved into the Middle East, General Motors became a civilian contractor for them, building 29,751 vehicles in two assembly plants at Andimeshk and Khorramshahr before the army took over the operation on July 1, 1943. The United Kingdom Commercial Corporation ran another assembly plant at Bushire, and the British operated yet another at Rafadiyah. From March, 1942, through April, 1945, Persian Gulf truck assemblies numbered 184,112 for Russia, with an-

---

22 Motter, *Persian Corridor*, 408–13. Tonnage figures converted to short tons.
23 *Ibid.*, 264–70, 498.

other 7,000 turned out for the United States and British armies, Iran, and the United Kingdom Commercial Corporation. Truck assembly plant II at Khorramshahr produced over 28,000 trucks in 1943, over 40,000 in 1944, and over 14,000 in four months of 1945, all Russia bound. Truck assembly plant I at Andimeshk produced over 33,000 trucks in 1943 and another 36,000 in 1944. The truck assembly plants employed over 5,000 natives, who, a reporter noticed, "were so shiftless and unteachable that they could do no better than learn how to turn out trucks at the rate of one every five minutes." By the autumn of 1944, Russian battle lines had moved farther and farther from Persian Gulf ports of entry, the Royal Navy had opened the Mediterranean, and Allied planners looked for the Black Sea route to replace the Persian Gulf. On November 28, 1944, Hopkins' Munitions Assignment Board recommended that the two United States truck assembly plants be turned over to Russia for use in the Black Sea area. The plant at Andimeshk was dismantled beginning in December, 1944, and put aboard the Iranian railway for transfer to Russia. By April 24, 1945, the other plant at Khorramshahr had been boxed and loaded on railway cars for Russia. Actually the truck assembly operation moved along much more smoothly than any other Persian Gulf route activity.[24]

As Britain and the United States stepped up naval bombardment and air-raids on Japanese-held islands in the South Pacific, and Allied ground forces stormed ashore at Kiska (in the Aleutians) and Vella Lavella (in the Solomons) in July and August, 1943, Japan continued to permit Soviet shipping to ply between the United States and the major Soviet Far Eastern port of Vladivostok. In this manner Japan permitted the reinforcement of her ally's enemy (Russia) and continued to do so until that ally existed no more as a military force. Officially the Soviets did nothing to disturb this perilous neutrality with Japan. Japan even winked at the fact that 125 of the rusty-gray ships that

[24] *Ibid.*, 140–41, 155, 274–75, 281–83, 494–97; Sayre, *Persian Gulf Command*, 127.

regularly nosed between the Japanese-held Kuril Islands and La Pérouse Straits (dividing Japanese Southern Sakhalin from Japanese Hokkaido) for Russian ports were vessels lend-leased to Russia to exploit the unreal Russo–Japanese neutrality. Over 940 Soviet and Soviet-leased ships cleared American West Coast ports for Vladivostok from July, 1943, to September, 1945. They carried 2,769,760 tons through Japanese waters during the Third Protocol period and another 4,317,600 tons in the Fourth Protocol period and after, for a total of 7,087,360 tons in the last two years of the war.[25]

In December, 1944, with the Nazis in Italy bending under Allied military pressure, the United States First Army temporarily stunned by Hitler's last fling in the Ardennes, and the Red army fighting into Budapest, Hitler's Europe no longer had the strength to dispute the Mediterranean. Allied shipping slipped through the Bosphorus into the Black Sea, opening a new Lend-Lease supply route to Russia. Seven ships arrived in January, 1945, and through April the total number increased to twenty. After the victory in Europe in May, the number decreased as the United States decided to continue Lend-Lease only for the purpose of supplying Russian Far Eastern armies against Japan. In all, from January through September, 1945, seventy-eight ships docked at Black Sea ports with 762,720 tons of Russian aid supplies.[26]

Other Soviet-bound ships used the summer months of June through September to venture into the Arctic Ocean by way of the Bering Straits and into the East Siberian, Laptev, and Kara Seas. They went to Arctic ports such as Ambarchik at the mouth of the Kolyma River, dropping off petroleum to be taken hundreds of miles upstream to Seimchan on the ALSIB air route or to the mouth of the mighty Lena River. Cargoes were then delivered hundreds of miles south to Yakutsk, an

[25] Motter, *Persian Corridor*, 419; Report on War Aid, 14, 15; tonnage figures converted to short tons.
[26] Report on War Aid, 14, 15.

important central Siberian city also on the ALSIB route. Some Arctic route freight found its way to Igarka, a port far up the Yenisei River, to be transported much further inland to Krasnoyarsk's air facilities. Twenty-three ships plied these Arctic waters with much less difficulty than did the convoys moving from the west to Murmansk and Archangel, in 1942; thirty-two made the Arctic journey in 1943, thirty-four in 1944, and thirty-one in 1945. These vessels brought a total of 506,240 tons of goods to Russia, primarily to supply the ALSIB route.[27]

By the summer of 1943 and the beginning of the Third Protocol in July, some of the traffic over the ALSIB route was still fulfilling Second Protocol promises. To hasten completion of backlog deliveries, two hundred fighters were shipped over the southern route (South Atlantic–Africa) in November and December at Soviet request. Third Protocol deliveries responded more easily to demand as shortages of men, especially mechanics, eased; hangar building reached such a stage that mechanics no longer had to work outdoors and planes were sheltered so that extreme measures were no longer required to start them. Warehouses to hold supplies facilitated inventory control and prevented loss by exposure, greatly relieving the supply situation.[28]

Although the Third Protocol clearly stated that aircraft supply during the second half of the period would be reviewed in November, 1943, Harry Hopkins reminded General Arnold, on September 30, that Roosevelt had promised Stalin in June that aircraft shipments would certainly not be decreased in the first half of 1944. Hopkins urged Arnold to increase the offering and certainly not to decrease it. The air force decided to allocate the same number of planes for January–June, 1944, as had been allocated for July–December, 1943, but in different categories. As a result, the air force sent 1,703 planes through Siberia in the first

[27] *Ibid.*, 14, 15; Henry A. Wallace and Andrew J. Steiger, *Soviet Asia Mission*, 71.

[28] Carr, "Great Falls to Nome," 194–97.

half of the Third Protocol period and 1,576 via ALSIB during the second half. Part of the reason for the smaller figure grew from Russian insistence on having fighters shipped by the southern route during the winter months. The first twenty-six P-63 (Bell Aircraft's King Cobra) fighters flew off to the Soviet Union in June and gradually replaced the P-39's during 1944.[29]

ALSIB operations reached their peak during the Fourth Protocol period. On June 5, 1944, General Leonid G. Rudenko, new chairman of the Soviet Purchasing Commission, asked to have all aircraft delivered by way of Alaska. Thus ALSIB commitments under the Fourth Protocol reached 2,940 planes. The air force sent fifty pursuit planes from North Africa to Russia, and the thirty flying boats called for that could not be delivered over ALSIB. Additional allotments and Third Protocol leftovers made a total of 3,597 aircraft to be delivered through Great Falls and Fairbanks. The delivery from July, 1944, through August, 1945, included 3,587 planes, twenty of which were returned as Lend-Lease ended. Actually the war's end in Europe in May, 1945, interrupted Fifth Protocol discussions and brought about a reappraisal of the remainder of Fourth Protocol promises. Air force planners reduced allocation of AT-6 trainers but continued the remainder of Fourth Protocol shipments. Monthly "Aircraft Status Reports" indicated that by the end of July, 1945, with the exception of five planes, ALSIB deliveries completed the Protocol. During the entire period of its operation, the Soviets accepted delivery of 7,925 airplanes over the Alaska-Siberia route. The ultimate importance of the ALSIB passage is demonstrated by comparing aircraft deliveries to Russia over ALSIB with deliveries over the other routes. Flight delivery across the South Atlantic and Africa to Abadan accounted for 993 planes, aircraft crated and sent by ship for assembly at Abadan in the Persian Corridor totaled another 3,868, while those boxed and shipped to North Russia reached 1,232. The total of all aircraft accepted by Russia reached 14,203 (including 185 PBN

29 *Soviet Supply Protocols*, 56; Carr, "Great Falls to Nome," 194, 199–200.

and PBY patrol planes) by July, 1945. Another 780 planes went to the bottom of the sea, crashed in the United States, Canada, Africa, or Russia, or were rejected before reaching their destinations because of mechanical difficulties.[30]

After the Lend-Lease planes reached their Russian destinations, they did not always get the best of care. From his vantage point in Moscow, Deane concluded that the Soviets knew little and cared less about aircraft maintenance. "Pilots warm up their motors as they taxi to the take-off," he remarked. "There is never the slightest pause for 'revving-up' nor a final check between taxiing and departure." Russian pilots landed at whichever end of the field they arrived closest to and considered circling a field a "complete waste of time." Soviets loaded their aircraft by bulk, not weight, and wondered why they could barely clear the ground on take-off. Americans in Russia, said Deane, "were familiar enough with the life span of American aircraft . . . to know that maintenance consisted mainly of substituting new aircraft as the old ones wore out."[31]

The period of the last two Protocols, roughly the second half of the war, witnessed the steadily increasing ability of the Western allies to deliver the goods to Russia in quantities greater than promised, partly to offset the deficiencies that plagued the first two Protocols. The sinking of the *Scharnhorst* and the neutralizing of the remainder of Hitler's northern fleet signaled ultimate victory over the Nazi navy in the Arctic. Although fewer tons of Lend-Lease passed over that route than either the Persian Gulf or the Pacific, the fact remained that it was the most seriously contended of all and cost more in supplies and manpower sacrificed than any other. Completion of the highway and rail connections in the Persian Gulf area, as well as expansion of port facilities and the assembly of aircraft and trucks there, allowed impressive amounts of freight to pass to Russia in 1944,

[30] Carr, "Great Falls to Nome," 201–202; *Soviet Supply Protocols*, 96; Report on War Aid, 18.

[31] Deane, *The Strange Alliance*, 79.

making the Persian Gulf the single most important Allied-operated Lend-Lease route. Topping all routes in quantity carried, nearly one thousand Soviet vessels quietly plied the Pacific virtually unmolested, hauling record tonnages past the Japanese islands to Vladivostok. The complete story of this entirely Russian-operated route will necessarily await Russian naval historians.

CHAPTER NINE

Wheels, Wings, Wrenches, and Wheat

O N JUNE 22, 1941, War Department estimators pointed out that Germany had approximately 173 divisions available for use in Russia. The Red army deployed approximately 144 divisions of varying strength from the border inward. Faulty communication and co-ordination, low morale, and a degree of inept leadership allowed the Nazis to exploit the initial advantage of surprise. The Russian air force, which mustered 5,552 first-line planes in 346 squadrons, lost 1,800 in the first eight hours of the war, two-thirds on the ground. The Soviet navy suffered comparable losses in the Baltic Sea: 295 vessels were sunk (including two battleships, a cruiser, and sixteen destroyers), 201 damaged, and others put out of action (such as seventy-three seized by the Finns). By the time Lend-Lease included Russia, the Red army had lost over one million men to German prison camps, an unknown number of men killed and wounded, and a staggering material loss of nearly 80 per cent of the equipment on hand.[1]

During the summer of 1941, German strength grew with every fiery thrust into Russia. In order to delay the German Jugger-

[1] Roosevelt Library, President's Secretary's File, War Department, Box 27, code radiogram from Berlin, June 22, 1941; President's Secretary's File, Navy Correspondence, Box 21, bulletin to Roosevelt, July 3, 1941; bulletin to Roosevelt, October 20, 1941; bulletin to Roosevelt, November 4, 1941; Institut Marxizma-Leninizma, *Istoriia Velikoi Otechestvennoi Voiny Sovetskogo Soiuza, 1941–1945* (*History of the Great Patriotic War of the Soviet Union, 1941–1945*), Vol. I, 471, 472, 479, 481; Vol. II, 16. Hereafter cited as *Istoriia Velikoi Otechestvennoi Voiny*. This Russian source claims Germany had 190 divisions available for use in Russia.

naut, the Soviets transferred at least twenty thousand troops from Siberia to the front and mobilized worker battalions, all to little avail until that reliable old ally, winter, arrived. By the end of 1941 the Nazis controlled an area of Russia in which 45 per cent of the prewar Soviet population lived, an area that accounted for one-third of the gross industrial output, 38 per cent of the grain and cattle, 84 per cent of the sugar, and 60 per cent of the hogs. Manpower, trucks, tractors, and the like disappeared from rural areas as Soviet or Nazi armies found use for them.[2]

With Soviet farm manpower reduced by one-third and farm machinery and equipment by at least as much, the production of agricultural products dropped on the arable land that remained in Soviet control. In 1942 the gross output of all grains in the Soviet Union fell two-thirds, compared to 1940. Herds of cattle declined 48 per cent; milk production, 45 per cent; sheep and goat herds, 33 per cent; and hog production, 78 per cent. Although state stores held the official price of dark wheat flour to 2.4 rubles a kilogram (when available), the same amount brought 80 rubles on the open market. The price of beef inflated over 100 per cent and butter rose over 230 per cent, while inflated prices of milk, vegetable oils, and other commodities also reflected the restricted supply. Cities, factories, offices, schools, and other organizations resorted to mass gardening (comparable to a gigantic Victory Garden scheme), which doubtless prevented starvation in some urban areas during the summer of 1942.[3]

The Soviets asked for and received growing amounts of food supplies under the Protocols. *Pravda* claimed that the amount of foodstuffs sent to Russia as of April 30, 1944, amounted to

[2] Roosevelt Library, President's Secretary's File, Navy Correspondence, Box 21, bulletin to Roosevelt, November 4, 1941; *Istoriia Velikoi Otechestvennoi Voiny*, II, 46, 61, 166; G. I. Shigalin, *Narodnoe Khoziaistvo SSR v Period Velikoi Otechestvennoi Voiny* (*National Economy of the USSR During the Great Patriotic War*), 55–56, 188–89. Hereafter cited as *Narodnoe Khoziaistvo*.

[3] Naum Jasny, *The Socialized Agriculture of the USSR, Plans and Performance*, 523, hereafter cited as *Socialized Agriculture*. *Istoriia Velikoi Otechestvennoi Voiny*, II, 521, 523, 554; Shigalin, *Narodnoe Khoziaistvo*, 197.

2,805,472 tons. Using that figure as the total sent to Russia during the war, a Soviet economist (in 1961) dismissed this type of aid as "insignificant." Lend-Lease accounts show that by June 30, 1944, 3,406,524 tons of food had left the United States for Russia. By September 20, 1945, and the end of Lend-Lease, the amount sent had reached 5,000,774 tons of foodstuffs. More than one-quarter of the foodstuffs represented grains, wheat, wheat flour, other flours, grain cereals and finished grain products, dried peas and beans, and seeds. Of this category, 1,209,-211 tons left the Western Hemisphere under Lend-Lease, and 1,-154,180 tons arrived in Russia (the difference was lost en route by either enemy action or natural causes, was diverted to other Lend-Lease accounts, or remained in the pipeline as of September 20, 1945). The actual measure of foodstuffs by tonnage distorts the story of this type of assistance. Lend-Lease supplied 37,477 tons of seeds (only 40 tons were lost on the way), and United States Russian War Relief (a private, non-profit agency) provided another 2,307 tons. These seeds grew a lot of wheat, corn, and other vegetables and represented a very important commodity. The state of Soviet agriculture "necessitated economizing heavily on seed, at the expense of the following crop" even in 1945.[4] Unmeasurable but significant importations of items such as seed and the fact that very little of the Lend-Lease foods reached the civilian population (Soviet leaders intended it for the military) increased the importance of the amount of foodstuffs received by Russia. When the Soviets complain of the *insignificant* amount, they are lamenting that they asked for too little.

The decline of Soviet agriculture during the whole war, including 1945, "was probably more than three times as large, in percentage terms, as the decline in Russian farm output during the war of 1914-18." This occurred in spite of the attempt

[4] Shigalin, *Narodnoe Khoziaistvo*, 191; *Pravda*, June 11, 1944, p. 1; Report on War Aid, 1–7; Millard C. Faught, "Seeds are Bullets for the Allies," *The New York Times Magazine*, September 5, 1943, p. 12. All metric and long ton figures converted to short tons.

to increase the sown area of their own Far East by 30 per cent and of Middle Asia by 20 per cent, as compared with 1940. They also planted a much higher percentage of winter wheat than was customary. That they did not succeed in their plan to replace lost Ukraine crops with new areas planted is clear from the fact that their 1945 total agricultural output reached approximately 53,500,000 tons (barn crop, not biological crop), or little more than half as much as the present Soviet territory had before the war. In fact, even in 1945 the Russians planted only a total of 85,500,000 hectares (one hectare equals 2.471 acres), as against nearly 112,000,000 before the war. It is obvious that food of all descriptions, especially grains, remained in very short supply. United States officials in Moscow transmitted constant reports to that effect. In some areas, such as Leningrad, there was widespread starvation, and Soviet officials slowly instituted a nonuniform food rationing system in their urban centers. Even with rationing in operation, fats were not plentiful, and items such as meat and butter remained rare. On November 21, 1943, the Soviets reduced the bread ration, a move not announced in the Soviet press or abroad, since foreign newsmen were not allowed to report it. Harriman told Hull in late November, 1943, that United States food shipments in full accord with the Protocol were absolutely necessary. An Allied observer noted, "The urban population in general is suffering from undernourishment to such an extent as to hamper its normal capacity for work." The Red army seemed in good shape, however, and American embassy officials believed that actual starvation among the public could be avoided if the Lend-Lease food program was carried out as planned.[5]

In April, 1942, the newspaper *Krasnaya Zvezda (Red Star)* reported to the Red army that "at present the main grain regions

[5] Jasny, *Socialized Agriculture*, 69–70, 522–23; Alexander Baykov, "Agricultural Development in the U.S.S.R.," *Bulletins on Soviet Economic Development, Bulletin 2*, December, 1949, 12, 13; *Foreign Relations, 1942*, III, 412–13, 414, 420, 422–24, 430, 434–35, 441–42, 479–81, 487; *Foreign Relations, 1943*, III, 789–90.

of the R.S.F.S.R. [Russian Socialist Federated Soviet Republic] can satisfy the demands of the country and of the army in grain." There is little doubt that this overoptimistic statement was published as a morale booster, just as there is little doubt of its inaccuracy. On July 11, 1942, the Soviet government ordered the creation of a special grain fund for the Red army, amounting to 2,377,000 tons for the year 1942. This order was renewed in subsequent years and apparently remained operative as late as 1946. In October, 1942, Stalin told visitor Willkie that with the loss of the Ukraine, "the food situation therefore would be bad during the winter. The Soviet Union would need two million tons of wheat and a correspondingly large quantity of concentrated foodstuffs such as butter, condensed milk, lard, meat products, and so forth." Harriman estimated that the field production of wheat was greater in 1943 than in 1942, but because of losses from delayed harvesting and threshing, the total crop was slightly smaller. All of these factors serve to underline the precarious agriculture situation in the Soviet Union.[6]

To relieve this acute condition, or at the very least to keep the Red army in fighting trim, Lend-Lease sent 1,154,180 tons of grains; 672,429 tons of sugar; 782,973 tons of canned meats; 730,902 tons of smoked meats, sausages, fats, and oils (including butter and lard); 517,522 tons of vegetable oil and shortening; 362,421 tons of canned and dried milk, cheese, eggs, dehydrated vegetables, fruit and vegetable pastes and purees, and the like; and 61,483 tons of canned and fresh fruits and vegetables, vitamins, yeast, tea, coffee, salt, spices, nuts, and animal feed. In all, 4,291,012 tons of foodstuffs arrived safely in the Soviet Union. Again, tonnage alone does not disclose any index of either volume or value. Compression and dehydration of foods (removal of air and moisture respectively) reduced both weight and volume considerably. Volume reduction alone was estimated to be one-seventh of the original, resulting in a very sig-

[6] Jasny, *Socialized Agriculture*, 374; *Foreign Relations, 1942*, III, 434–35, 729; *Foreign Relations, 1943*, III, 789–90.

nificant saving in shipping space. If the Red army received all of the foodstuffs that arrived in Russia through Lend-Lease from the United States, and if the Red army averaged twelve million men, then by simple arithmetic Lend-Lease supplied each man with slightly more than a half of a pound of concentrated food a day. Obviously this "average" never really existed, but supplemented by the Soviet grain fund for the army, Lend-Lease food proved vital to maintain adequate nutrition levels for Russian fighting men.[7]

Soviet production of steel, which reached 20,166,600 tons in 1940, slumped to a mere 8,801,600 tons in 1942. Under Lend-Lease, the Soviet Union received 2,589,766 tons between 1941 and 1945. The tonnage, when compared with a Soviet output of 43,639,200 tons between 1942 and 1945, appears small, but again, appearances are deceiving. Most of the Lend-Lease steel comprised specialty steels such as high-speed tool steel, cold-finished bars, hot-rolled aircraft steel, tin plate, steel wire, pipe and tubing, and hot-rolled sheets and plates. More than one-fifth of the Lend-Lease steels included railroad rails and accessories. In other words, Russia imported specialty steels, freeing her mills from the expense and time involved in their production. Also, $13,200,000 worth of auxiliary equipment for Soviet steel makers enabled them to increase their output of carbon-steel ingots by an estimated 2,500,000 tons a year. Almost all of this equipment reached Russia before September 20, 1945, and if its impact on war production is not easily estimated, certainly its usefulness in reconstruction cannot be overlooked. On the other hand, Soviet production of aluminum, though on the increase between 1942 and 1945, remained small. From 1941 through 1944, Russian industry produced 285,418 tons of the metal, whereas they received, from 1941 through 1945, 261,109 tons from Lend-Lease. This amount equalled nearly four years of

[7] Report on War Aid, 21–22 (tonnages of all figures in the text are not total exports but total actually delivered); Stettinius, *Lend-Lease*, 104; *Istoriia Velikoi Otechestvennoi Voiny*, IV, 125; Deane, *The Strange Alliance*, 94.

their production. Since the fine Soviet T-34 tank, widely used, boasted an aluminum alloy engine, Lend-Lease aluminum proved a vital commodity. Copper shipments to the Soviet Union, excluding wire, amounted to 391,711 tons, an amount equal to three-quarters of the entire Soviet copper production for the years 1941–1944. Copper, so widely used in the production of weapons and ammunition, also figured quite significantly in Soviet war industries. The Lend-Lease contribution in this area is obvious.[8]

The total shipment of nonferrous metals (781,663 tons) such as magnesium, nickel, zinc, lead, tin, and others formed an impressive tonnage compared to Soviet production, but their uses are so great it is impossible to calculate any particular impact. Russian statistics often do not include categories that compare in any way with those kept by the Allies. One small example is Soviet production of ferro-alloys (generally used in the manufacture of various types of steel and iron), which is unknown, although the United States sent over sixteen thousand tons of various types of these alloys and a like amount of molybdenum concentrates (also used in steel making) over the several roads to Russia. A very large amount of metallic wire and cable found its way to Russia as well. Soviet signal services received 956,688 miles of field telegraph wire, enough to reach thirty-eight times around the world. The Red army also used 2,118 miles of marine cable and 1,136 miles of submarine cable. Red army ground communication suffered from the prewar notion that the Commissariat of Communication (civil agency) would serve to link the general staff with the fronts, so a military communications network did not exist. Since Soviet commanders preferred wire to radio, the need for a large amount of field telegraph wire is easily explained.[9]

[8] Shigalin, *Narodnoe Khoziaistvo*, 113; Report on War Aid, 17, 24–25; Dimitri B. Shimkin, *Minerals, A Key to Soviet Power*, 104, 114, 115, 136, 139. Hereafter cited as *Minerals*. Metric tons converted to short tons for consistency.
[9] Report on War Aid, 25; *Istoriia Velikoi Otechestvennoi Voiny*, I, 447, 455; and Shimkin, *Minerals*, 104, 114, 115, 136, 139.

Advancing German forces destroyed or carried away 175,000 metal-cutting machines and 34,000 forge and press machines. They destroyed, either wholly or in part, 31,850 industrial enterprises. United States Lend-Lease statistics measure the amounts of machinery and equipment in terms of dollars and not units, making comparisons unreal. Equipment worth $1,095,-140,000 was hauled to Russia, and this great total included $310,-058,000 worth of machine tools plus millions of dollars worth of military and marine generators, industrial furnaces, rolling-mill equipment, various types of metal working and forming tools, excavating and dredging machinery, and so on. Many of the lost Soviet industrial machines were obsolescent, while those replaced were modern, and productivity of the Lend-Lease equipment exceeded that which was replaced, again confounding any statistical comparison. Russian figures indicate more metal-cutting machines were received from abroad by spring, 1944, than the Russians had overoptimistically planned to produce for themselves in the year 1942. Certainly Russian war and postwar production owed a great deal to Lend-Lease machinery.[10]

The Soviets salvaged a great deal of factory equipment from under the guns of advancing Nazis. They managed to dismantle and move eastward part or all of 1,360 large industrial plants, some of the equipment from all aircraft, tank, and motor plants, 93 steel-working plants, 150 machine-tool factories, 40 electrical plants, and a variety of others. At the same time, ten million people were relocated in the Urals, Western Siberia, Kazakhstan, and the Volga basin. Russia put 2,250 large industrial units into operation during the war and restored another 6,000 in areas liberated from the retreating Germans. Even so, initial industrial losses were so great that the 1945 level of Soviet production remained below that of 1940.[11] To make up for these

[10] Report on War Aid, 22–24; Shigalin, *Narodnoe Khoziaistvo*, 101, 118; *Pravda*, June 11, 1944, p. 1; *Istoriia Velikoi Otechestvennoi Voiny*, II, 491.

[11] Shigalin, *Narodnoe Khoziaistvo*, 48, 49, 85, 88, 113.

great losses, the United States sent Russia a number of industrial plants and projects.

One of the earliest industrial projects that Russia received, the Ford Motor Company's tire plant, became one of the most controversial. Procured for $10,000,000 in November, 1942, it included a power plant to supply it with steam and electricity. Used for passenger car tires before the war, and idle from early 1942, experts estimated that it was capable of turning out one million military tires a year from Russian rubber. Although almost all of the plant had been shipped by the fall of 1944, construction delays prevented any production from it before the end of the war. General Sidney Spalding visited the plant site in Moscow in February, 1944, and because he was disappointed at the progress that Soviet technicians were making, he arranged for American engineers to travel to Russia in order to give technical advice. The Soviets virtually ignored them, so the United States technicians gave up and returned to the States. When the United States military mission in Moscow packed up and departed for home in October, 1945, the plant still lacked the necessary utilities (water, steam, electricity, compressed air), and there seemed no prospect of getting any production from it.[12]

In September, 1942, American officials approved shipment of another project, a petroleum refinery, to replace facilities destroyed by the Nazis. Four main plants and two subsidiary plants, designed to refine forty thousand barrels of crude oil a day into aviation gasoline, motor vehicle gasoline, and lubricating oils, cost $41,000,000. This equipment reached Russia by May, 1945, and fifteen United States technical experts came along to supervise construction. This project moved along considerably faster than the tire plant, and by September, 1945, two units were producing acceptable motor gasoline, though only 97 per cent and 98 per cent built. Russia reported that two other units of the six delivered were 80 per cent and 48 per cent

[12] Report on War Aid, 16; Stettinius, *Lend-Lease*, 223–24; Deane, *The Strange Alliance*, 100–102.

complete. In April, 1944, the Lend-Lease Office approved additional Soviet orders totalling $17,900,000 to increase the project. By September 30, 1945, 92 per cent of the additional equipment had been delivered in the United States but only 38 per cent exported. Russia included the remainder in the October 15, 1945, agreement that she made with the United States.[13] Like the tire plant, the petroleum refinery proved of little use in the war, but like the rest of the industrial equipment that Russia received, it provided a basis for postwar reconstruction.

Russia's petroleum output, which was vital to her mechanized army, ebbed sharply. Although the Soviet Union produced 34,272,200 tons of crude oil in 1940, output fell to 19,946,200 tons in 1943 and rose only to 21,378,800 tons by 1945—this at a time when Russia had large numbers of trucks, tanks, and aircraft in the field. The Soviet Union received 2,849,166 tons of petroleum from the United States, nearly half of the total in aviation gasoline (99 octane and over), and a large amount of gasoline blending agents, presumably to boost performance levels of Soviet refined products. The total tonnage of oil products lend-leased to Russia represented only a fraction of her total petroleum consumption, but again this is a misleading fact. Although north-route convoys suffered severe attacks and frequent suspensions, a substantial amount of petroleum arrived in Murmansk, which was close to the northern front, thus relieving painful shortages caused by the interruption of Soviet rail communciations with the Caucasus region. Also a little additive goes a long way, and many Russian aircraft flew on gasoline that was power-boosted in this manner; the hundreds of thousands of American-built trucks also consumed Soviet gasoline to which blending agents had been added.[14] Once again, comparisons between Lend-Lease shipments and Russian production serves no useful purpose.

[13] Report on War Aid, 16; Donald M. Nelson, "American Production—Russian Front," *Survey Graphic*, Vol. 33 (February, 1944), p. 57.

[14] Report on War Aid, 26; Shigalin, *Narodnoe Khoziaistvo*, 113. Metric tons converted to short tons for consistency.

Lend-Lease also provided Russia with the major part of a proposed $178,000,000 power program designed to produce 1,457,274 kilowatts of power. This included stationary steam plants (capable of 631,939 kw.), steam- and diesel-operated power plants mounted on railroad cars (with 370,000 kw. output), stationary diesel plants (327,498) kw.), trailer-mounted diesel plants (72,945 kw.), and hydro-electric stations (54,392 kw.). The mobile power equipment was designed to provide temporary sources of power in re-occupied devastated areas. By September, 1945, $135,000,000 worth of the equipment had been exported, $7,000,000 worth was diverted to other Lend-Lease recipients, $4,000,000 worth of equipment contracts were cancelled, and $32,000,000 worth was shipped under the October 15, 1945, agreement. According to Stettinius, some of the generating equipment powered Soviet factories in the trans-Ural region where the Soviets estimated a power shortage amounting to 300,000 kilowatts. Mikoyan believed hydro-electric equipment was vital for munitions industries in both the Urals and Central Asia and asked that it be given highest priority. Lend-Lease deliveries up to 1944 accounted for 20 per cent of the total Soviet power-equipment increase for the entire war period. Soviet industry lagged far behind its 1940 power-equipment-manufacturing level even in 1945. The $167,000,000 value of Lend-Lease electrical plants received by the Soviet Union was roughly equal to the cost of electrical energy purchased by the manufacturing industries in New Jersey, Connecticut, and New York in 1947. The total productivity of the plants approximately equals the capacity of Hoover Dam.[15]

A wide variety of mills were prefabricated in the United States and sent to bolster Soviet production in specific areas. An aluminum-rolling mill for aircraft sheeting, an eighteen-inch

[15] Report on War Aid, 16; Shigalin, *Narodnoe Khoziaistvo*, 113, 118; *Istoriia Velikoi Otechestvennoi Voiny*, II, 508; *Pravda*, June 11, 1944, p. 1; *Foreign Relations, 1943*, III, 764–65; *The World Almanac 1961*, 286; U.S. Bureau of the Census, *Annual Survey of Manufactures: Fuels Consumed and Electrical Energy Produced*, 1950, 13, 14.

"merchant mill" (capable of milling large-diameter steel bars), two pipe-manufacturing mills, a blooming mill, a rail and structural steel mill, and a railroad tie and fish plate mill all arrived too late to be of major value to the war effort, though certainly these were useful in subsequent reconstruction. Their combined value amounted to $26,119,000. Minor plants included a wallboard plant, a voltol plant, a nitric acid plant, several hydrogen gas plants, and the like, valued at $4,402,000. Those mills and plants not completely shipped prior to September, 1945 were contracted by the Soviets to be purchased under the October 15, 1945, agreement.[16]

The Soviet Union manufactured about 1,000 locomotives, 30,900 freight cars, and 1,051 passenger cars in 1940. Soviet production of railroad rolling stock of any kind virtually ceased during the war as plants capable of such production switched to weapons manufacture. Blitzkrieg or not, the Nazis failed to capture or destroy much rolling stock. By the end of 1942 the Soviets were still using 85 per cent of the number of locomotives serviceable in 1940 and operating only one-fifth fewer freight cars. Because of German occupation, rail lines had been shortened by 40 per cent, a factor that increased the ratio of rolling stock to mile of line. The rail system bore the brunt of the evacuation process and of a good share of the reoccupation traffic. Even so, the average daily carloading figure for the first half of 1941 was not again reached until four years after the war. Carloadings fell off 60.2 per cent in 1942 (from the 1941 peak) and by 1945 had recovered only 40.2 per cent. Obviously military freight accounted for a significant part of the traffic, amounting to about one-third of all freight carried by Soviet railroads in 1944. During the war years the Soviets built 11,000 kilometers of new railroad line, more than they had built between 1928 and 1939. Even this did not replace destroyed track, for the Nazis tore up 69,913 kilometers of line, demolished 2,323 bridges, and

16 Report on War Aid, 17.

destroyed large numbers of service installations, depots, and the like. Russian engineers had replaced 48,786 kilometers of track and 1,847 bridges by the war's end.[17]

To help the Soviet Union build and rebuild its railways, the United States supplied 1,900 steam locomotives, 66 diesel locomotives, 9,920 flat cars, 1,000 dump cars, 120 tank cars, and 35 heavy machinery cars, making a total of 13,041 units. If put together into one train, there would be over 130 miles between locomotive and caboose. Americans also sent enough rails and accessories to build nearly 7,669 miles of track. Over 110,000 tons of railroad wheels and axles assisted the Soviets in maintaining and rebuilding their own equipment. The United States included a complete railroad block system at a cost of $10,900,000 and capable of fully covering 3,000 kilometers of track. The amount of Lend-Lease rails received by Russia was enough to account for more than half of the Soviet Union's new wartime construction.[18]

Some of the tank cars carried certain of the 820,422 tons of Lend-Lease chemicals to their place of manufacture. Caustic soda, a versatile chemical, headed the list in quantity (98,210 tons). Ammonium nitrate (2,602 tons), a component of certain explosives, followed caustic soda in quantity among the inorganics. Ethyl alcohol topped the list of organic chemicals (379,742 tons). Extremely versatile, it could be used for many operations from solvent to liquor manufacture and was in great demand by Soviet munitions makers. Toluol (or toluene) trailed ethyl alcohol in amount sent through Lend-Lease (113,884 tons). This strategic chemical formed an important constituent of TNT (trinitrotoluene) and also was an important ingredient in high-octane aviation gasoline. Next among the organics came phenol

[17] *Narodnoe Khoziaistvo SSSR v 1960, Statistical Ezhegodnik* (*National Economy of the USSR in 1960, Statistical Yearbook*), 290; Holland Hunter, "Soviet Railroads Since 1940," *Bulletins on Soviet Economic Development, Bulletin* 4, 11–13, 30; *Istoriia Velikoi Otechestvennoi Voiny*, IV, 603.
[18] Report on War Aid, 17, 24, 28; *Eighteenth Report on Lend-Lease*, 20–21.

(38,549 tons), also known as carbolic acid, another chemical of many uses, but most useful during wartime for its trinitro derivitives.[19]

Textiles, though not as explosive as chemicals, found equally important work clothing the Red army. Cotton cloth was the largest single category of textile products shipped to Russia (102,673,000 yards). Corps of tailors could manufacture 34,-557,667 uniforms from that yardage. Working rapidly, Soviet seamsters could have cut 20,012,667 warmer uniforms from the 60,138,000 yards of woolen cloth. Essential to either operation were the $1,598,000 worth of buttons that accompanied the yard goods to the Soviet Union. Millions of G.I.-type belts, bandoliers, straps and the like (enough to stretch around the world at the equator with some overlap) came from 53,803,000 yards of webbing. Most Red army men were provided with one pair of the 14,572,000 army boots; others could pull on a pair of the felt or rubber boots or shoes included in the $4,378,000 shipment of "other types." It is not possible to assume that Soviet soldiers wore clothes cut from Lend-Lease cloth, but enough clothing and shoes for the entire Red army, with reserve stocks, arrived safely.[20]

In most categories of weaponry, the Soviets manufactured more than they received from their allies, although reliable statistics are scarce. Soviet military historians boast that Russia produced enough firearms and artillery by the end of 1942 to arm 535 infantry and cavalry divisions (during the war these divisions averaged 8,000 to 9,000 men—smaller than their United States counterparts), 342 artillery regiments, and 57 parachute units. Soviet military historians do not offer any more specific statistics than that, so what it meant in terms of up-to-date small arms and artillery is impossible to compute. In 1941, Stalin informed Hopkins of Soviet shortages in anti-aircraft weaponry

[19] Report on War Aid, 26–27; *Foreign Relations, 1943*, III, 773–74. See Table of Chemicals and their uses, Appendix.

[20] Report on War Aid, 28.

(he needed twenty thousand pieces), large-caliber machine guns, and rifles (he asked for a million). Of these arms, only anti-aircraft guns appeared on any of the Protocols. Although these guns were urgently needed by beleaguered Russia in 1941–1942, the allies had few to spare, and manufacture of them was slow at first. In the long run, 7,509 anti-aircraft guns, from 37 mm. to 4.7 inches, arrived in Russia. A non-protocol Russian request for automatic weapons brought 112,293 Thompson .45-caliber submachine guns (another 23,340 destined for the Soviets was lost en route). The Thompson guns moved in company with 11,500 pistols and revolvers that arrived safely, all on Lend-Lease accounts. Most of these small arms reached the Soviet Union in the winter of 1941 and the spring of 1942. In 1943, Soviet arsenals turned out 1,100,000 automatic weapons and 3,400,000 rifles and carbines, but in 1944 they cut back production in these lines as reserve stocks accumulated.[21]

The total number of Lend-Lease aircraft delivered to the Soviet Union, 14,018 of them, proved to be only a fraction of the 115,596 produced in Soviet plants from 1941 through 1944 (although prior to 1943 Russia produced many that were obsolete, prewar, one-engine wood and canvas models). The number of tanks and self-propelled guns sent to Russia (8,003 arrived, 860 were lost on the way) paled next to Soviet production of 84,200 such units between 1941 and 1944. But 362,288 Lend-Lease trucks and 47,238 jeeps accounted for most of the Red army's vehicles. Between 1942 and 1944 the Soviets produced only 128,000 trucks, or about one-third of the number received from the United States. Not included in the Lend-Lease truck totals were 2,293 ordinance service vehicles, 4,158 half-tracks and armored scout cars, 792 ten-ton Mack cargo trucks transferred from the Persian Gulf, or the two truck assembly plants also transferred from the Gulf. To enable the Russians to keep the

[21] *Istoriia Velikoi Otechestvennoi Voiny,* II, 512; IV, 8, 583; Sherwood, *Roosevelt and Hopkins,* 328; Roosevelt Library, President's Secretary's File, War Department, Box 27, production chart, September 5, 1941, and letter, Stimson to Roosevelt, November 12, 1941; Leighton and Coakley, *Global Logistics,* 559.

Lend-Lease vehicles running, 3,681,000 tires and 3,676,000 tubes, 1,807 tons of synthetic and crude rubber to make more tires, and the tire plant that never produced anything were received by the Soviet Union.[22]

The Soviets claimed to have solved their ammunition production problems by the end of 1942 and did not again experience a shortage of artillery shells as they had around Leningrad. In 1943, Soviet industry produced 175,000,000 rounds of bomb, mortar, and artillery shells and increased that figure to 184,-000,000 in 1944. Also in 1944 they manufactured 7,400,000,000 rounds of small-arms ammunition. The United States did not undertake to supply either kind of ammunition to the Soviet Union except as it was furnished with Lend-Lease weapons in standard United States Army ratios. The second Protocol, for example, noted "204 90-mm. anti-aircraft guns, complete with ammunition." In the Thompson machine gun category, suppliers observed, "Note. Ammunition for all weapons will be supplied in the same proportion as for United States troops, and, if practicable, in an amount equal to the accuracy life of weapons."[23]

Lend-Lease supplied Russia with a substantial amount of explosives and material to make explosives. Smokeless powder accounted for the greatest quantity among the powders, with all other varieties (including stick and cordite) amounting to only 3,000 tons out of a total of 132,959 tons. In addition, 139,186 tons of TNT and 53,639 tons of other explosives, mainly dynamite, arrived safely in Russia. The Allies lost 10,252 tons of explosives at sea while en route to the Soviet Union, nearly all from north-route shipments. The TNT tonnage alone provided enough powder to load 79,500,000 105-mm. high-explosive shells. Considering how the Soviets massed their artillery in

[22] Report on War Aid, 19, 28; *Istoriia Velikoi Otechestvennoi Voiny*, 11, 510; III, 171; IV, 8, 513; Shigalin, *Narodnoe Khoziaistvo*, 113. The compelete story of aircraft delivery is fully told elsewhere.

[23] *Istoriia Velikoi Otechestvennoi Voiny*, II, 212, 512; IV, 583; *Soviet Supply Protocols*, 19, 20.

offensives (250 guns per kilometer of front line), Lend-Lease TNT proved invaluable. The Soviets obtained enough Lend-Lease powder of various types to account for well over one-third of their 1944 bomb-, motar-, and artillery-shell production. Manufacture of sufficient munitions in the Urals and elsewhere did not insure their delivery to the front. Transportation difficulties caused Faymonville to tell Stettinius that the three-month lapse of convoys in 1942 had "seriously deranged" the supply of munitions to the front, and six months of 1943 elapsed without shipments on the north route. The "need for . . . munitions," Faymonville noted, "through northern ports is correspondingly greater" than last year.[24]

The Soviet navy, not ranked among the world's large ones, boasted few capital ships. Motor torpedo boats, submarines, minelayers and minesweepers, and destroyers formed the bulk of this primarily defensive arm. The British and American navies needed little help from Russia, except in the Barents Sea where Soviet sailors remained conspicuous by their absence until late in 1943. With British and American help, the Russian navy assumed part of the convoy protection load by 1944. In all, Lend-Lease sent the Soviet navy 556 vessels. These included 205 motor torpedo boats, 140 submarine chasers, 77 minesweepers, a variety of landing craft, 15 river tugs, 4 repair barges, 2 icebreakers, and miscellaneous smaller craft. The United States asked for the return of many of these ships after the war but met with Soviet refusal to return them. They became a pawn in the post-war Lend-Lease settlement game.[25]

Lend-Lease also provided a large amount of construction equipment ($10,792,000 actually received); technical equip-

[24] Report on War Aid, 20; *Foreign Relations, 1943*, III, 775. Computation is based on the formula that the explosive weight of a shell is 10 per cent of its total weight (except for armor-piercing shells). A 105-mm. shell weighed about thirty-five pounds.

[25] Report on War Aid, 21; *Department of State Bulletin*, Vol. 24 (February 19, 1951), 302–303; *Istoriia Velikoi Otechestvennoi Voiny*, III, 217–18, 407; IV, 448, 462, 465. See Chapter VII for the story of the ships and the settlement.

ment such as radio stations, receivers, locators, direction finders, altimeters, beacons, and compasses (valued at $7,526,000); repair facilities such as 2,293 ordinance service vehicles; link trainers; paper products; photographic material; and so on.[26] In the absence of Soviet statistics, the contributions of Lend-Lease aid in many areas remains unknown. The unappealing and imperious Soviet wartime attitude that the materials were needed if Russia requested them persisted as the only gauge to Soviet requirements. However critical Russia may later have become regarding Lend-Lease, the fact remains that *Soviet* leaders *requested* not only the items that appear on the four Protocols but also a variety of other materials that fell into the Lend-Lease category. Russian leaders did not allow Lend-Lease officials to investigate their requests or to evaluate the effectiveness of the aid. Therefore, Lend-Lease officials—and history—must conclude that although the totals were not large in terms of tonnages, the materials were strategic, useful, and vital to Soviet success.

Military historians agree that Stalingrad marked the turning point in Red army fortunes during World War II. Russian soldiers employed 27,000 trucks in the area to carry men and supplies. In September and October, 1942, as the Soviets prepared for their November counter-offensive, the high command rushed ten infantry divisions from distances of 200 to 250 kilometers by truck to the battleground. By June 30, 1942 the United States had delivered 36,865 trucks to Russia (out of 71,584 available), or 25 per cent more than the number employed on the Stalingrad front. At Stalingrad, as the Russian counter-offensive began, the Red air force concentrated 1,115 aircraft. At the same time, 1,285 (out of 1,727 available) Lend-Lease war planes reached the Soviet Union by all routes prior to July 1, after which 286 more came in through the Persian Gulf and another 92 came over the new ALSIB route before the end of October. The 1,663 American-made aircraft included P-39 and P-40 fighters and

[26] Report on War Aid, 20, 21, 28.

A-20 attack bombers, more than equalling the number of modern aircraft that the Soviets employed at Stalingrad.[27]

Although American trucks and planes may not have made up the vital percentages of that equipment on the field at Stalingrad, their presence in Russia permitted Red army and air force concentrations that otherwise would have been impossible. A communications system, so necessary for effective military co-ordination, would not have existed in any efficient way without the 56,445 field telephones and the 381,431 miles of field telephone wire that arrived in the Soviet Union before Stalingrad. While Stalingrad's liberators probably did not carry all 81,287 Thompson submachine guns or use all the 6,823 jeeps, these too reached Russia before the counteroffensive.[28]

In the summer and fall of 1943 the speed of Red army advance doubled over any previous offensive progress. Soviet mobile units averaged thirty to thirty-five kilometers a day, and even other units increased their pace to ten to twenty-five kilometers. The 148,286 trucks, jeeps, and motorcycles received in the Soviet Union by June 30, 1943 certainly contributed greatly to Soviet speed. The daily average speed of offensive advance remained unchanged in 1944, but the Red army liberated large areas in bigger sweeps. And well they might stretch farther easier: between June 30, 1943, and June 30, 1944, they had received 154,675 trucks, jeeps, and motorcycles, bringing the total of these vehicles to 302,961. The overwhelming number of these were trucks, 236,383 of them. Red army units that captured Bucharest arrived there on the eleventh day of an advance that averaged thirty kilometers a day. Soviet mechanized units soon "out-panzered" their Nazi teacher. Often Red army mobile units reached German troop concentration areas before the Nazis did,

[27] *Istoriia Velikoi Otechestvennoi Voiny,* III, 21, 24, 26; Leighton and Coakley, *Global Logistics,* 559; Motter, *Persian Corridor,* 498; Carr, "Great Falls to Nome," 192.

[28] *Istoriia Velikoi Otechestvennoi Voiny,* II, 174; Leighton and Coakley, *Global Logistics,* 559.

disorganizing the enemy and inflicting heavy casualties. Soviet soldiers sped into Brandenburg Province early in 1945, surprised the enemy, and captured 288 Nazi aircraft on the ground. Subsequent Russian lightning-like advances in Manchuria reflected the effectiveness of the three-month build-up following the end of the war in Europe, a build-up made possible by Lend-Lease stock-piling of 46,140 vehicles (42,599 trucks) between May 13 and September 3, 1945. In that Far Eastern campaign, Red army units moved an average of fifty kilometers a day. Thus Lend-Lease aid, including the 416,769 trucks and jeeps, supplied the transportation for the rapid Russian advances that put the Soviets across the Balkans and into Austria, and indeed across more than half of Europe before they met other Allied troops advancing from the west.[29]

American officials, whose duties took them to the Soviet Union, frequently discovered evidences of American Lend-Lease.[30] Standley, who frequently went out of his way to unearth evidence of Lend-Lease aid, spoke with Molotov on the subject. "Even the man on the street," Molotov boasted, "knows we are getting Lend-Lease supplies from our Allies." Standley retorted, "That may be so Mr. Molotov. But we have no contact with the man in the street. . . . The man in the street does not dare talk to us." Molotov protested that Standley was mistaken. At Kuibyshev, Standley discovered "the ever-present Lend-Lease Studebaker truck bringing grain, wood, and ice from across the river." He also talked to a man on the street at Kuibyshev, a thin, young, Red army soldier who liked Americans and had "ridden your fine Studebaker." In addition, Standley watched ten Lend-Lease Aircobra fighters take to the air to escort Churchill's plane from

[29] *Istoriia Velikoi Otechestvennoi Voiny,* III, 598; IV, 293, 303, 503; S. Golikov, *Vydaiushchiesia Pobedy Sovetskoi Armii v Velikoi Otechestvennoi Voiny (Outstanding Victories of Soviet Armies in the Great Patriotic War),* 265–67; Report on War Aid, 2, 3, 4, 6, 19; *Izvestiia,* June 27, 1944, p. 3; February 1, 1945, p. 1, February 10, 1945, p. 2.

[30] The Soviet Union carefully restricted the travel of American and foreign officials. What such officials could notice that the Soviet bureaucracy did not intend them to see is a matter of speculation.

Moscow in August, 1942. Although Standley inspected the factories in the Ural region he made no comment about the presence of Lend-Lease machinery.[31]

In September, 1942, Angus I. Ward, American consul general at Vladivostok, reported "the appearance of American flour, sugar, and lard on the Vladivostok market several months ago," which "evoked many gratifying expressions" by the local populace to Ward. In a visit to the Caucasus front in December, 1942, General Patrick J. Hurley observed American A-20's and B-25's on several Soviet air fields. Ensign J. Leonard Bates, U.S.N.R., stranded in North Russia for eight months in 1943, noted that the Soviet fleet commander "said Lend-Lease naval craft and planes had proven very effective against the submarine." As the Russians unloaded the merchant ship, *Israel Putnam*, which brought him to Arctic Russia, Bates observed. "The Russians don't waste a thing. In several of the holds a bit of the bean cargo had spilled. Do they leave it? . . . I'll say not! A woman scoops up the beans, puts them into a sack, and sews it up." Bates also looked over "tanks, jeeps, trucks, cranes, tin, iron, planes, cordage, ammunition, and various foodstuffs . . . awaiting shipment."[32]

General John R. Deane, recalling a trip to Minsk and Vilna in July, 1944, remarked about the "preponderance of [Russian] motorized and mechanized equipment" with which they outmaneuvered the Nazis. "Here again," Deane added, "one could see the results of American assistance. Besides the motor trucks already referred to, there were scattered through the city innumerable American Sherman tanks which had been disabled by German artillery fire." Along with General Sid Spaulding, Deane used the occasion of his field visit to quiz Soviet field commanders "on the use and effectiveness of American equipment. As was the case with all the field commanders," Deane

[31] Standley and Ageton, *Admiral Ambassador*, 133.

[32] *Foreign Relations, 1942*, III, 458, 679; J. Leonard Bates, "The Arctic Life Line," unpublished master's thesis, 36, 71, 85.

235

remembered, "they were enthusiastic about the supplies that were being sent from America." And small wonder. As Deane observed, "except for American trucks there did not appear to be enough of any one kind [of Russian vehicle] to set up convoys which could be moved as units."[33]

Vice-President Henry A. Wallace traveled to the Soviet Union in May and June, 1944, confining his visit largely to Soviet Asia. At Seimchan, Wallace found "Penick and Ford corn oil from Cedar Rapids and Pillsbury enriched flour from Minneapolis. The food," Wallace supposed, "had been transferred under lend-lease." Conducted through a locomotive works at Ulan Ude, Wallace noticed "lend-lease wheels and a heavy press." In Seattle, on his return, Wallace summed up his impressions of Lend-Lease to Russia on a nationwide radio hook-up. "In factories everywhere I found American machinery.... I found ... American aluminum in Soviet airplane factories, American steel in truck and railway repair shops, American machine tools, . . . American compressors and electrical equipment, . . . electric shovels, . . . core drills, . . . trucks and planes."[34]

Just because Lend-Lease equipment arrived in Russia, no guarantee existed that the Soviets would make the best use of it. An American naval officer sent to advise Soviet technicians on installation of diesel engines in naval patrol boats found over seventy Lend-Lease diesel engines "deteriorating from rust in open storage." Another United States naval officer complained that inadequate railway transportation in North Russia meant large amounts of supplies had to wait months before being moved out. Soviet difficulty with the Ford tire plant has already been noted. On the other hand, Soviet air ace Alexander Pokryshkin used a Lend-Lease Aircobra to shoot down forty-eight of the fifty-nine Nazi planes credited to him.[35]

[33] Deane, *The Strange Alliance*, 207–208, 211.

[34] Wallace, *Soviet Asia Mission*, 32, 56, 190–91.

[35] Deane, *The Strange Alliance*, 96, 101; Bates, "Arctic Life Line," 85; *Sixteenth Report on Lend-Lease*, 28.

From all of this, a number of obvious conclusions appear. Lend-Lease food shipments alleviated serious Soviet shortages. Russian steelmakers concentrated on basic types of steel while Lend-Lease supplied specialized steels and alloys. Lend-Lease aluminum and copper shipments occupied a vital spot in Soviet industry. Lend-Lease field telephones and wire rebuilt shattered Red army communications. American Lend-Lease petroleum products, such as gasoline, blending agents, and additives, either boosted the octane of Soviet gasoline or powered American Lend-Lease aircraft, tanks, or trucks. Lend-Lease power-generating equipment accounted for one-fifth the total Russian increase of such equipment during the entire war period. Over 130 miles of Lend-Lease rolling stock glided over nearly 7,700 miles of Lend-Lease railway track, more than half of the Soviet Union's new line construction. Red army soldiers marched in American shoes and boots and wore uniforms from Lend-Lease wool and cotton. The Red army fired Lend-Lease explosives, equal to one-third of their 1944 production, at the Nazis and Nipponese.

The timely arrival of Lend-Lease tanks and planes helped stem the German tide and boosted the morale of Soviet fighting men. The total number of these weapons, although small compared with Soviet production, nevertheless contributed to eventual Russian superiority over the Nazis. The tremendous number of trucks, jeeps, motorcycles, and other vehicles comprised the very basis of Soviet mobility, making possible the rapid advance into Central Europe. It should also be remembered that by the time the Red army reached the peak of its mobility, Nazi mobility had been nearly destroyed by the strategic bombing of the United States and Britain against Nazi fuel production. Because the Soviet Union could de-emphasize vehicle construction, it could concentrate on the manufacture of planes and tanks. Lend-Lease factories contributed importantly to Russia's postwar reconstruction, in some instances more than to the war effort. The Ford tire plant, auxiliary equipment for Soviet steel mills, six

THE ROADS TO RUSSIA

refinery units, the 1,500,000 kilowatt power program, seven smaller metal mills (including the $6,000,000 aluminum rolling mill), and a variety of lesser plants remained only partly completed at war's end.

What the Soviets themselves wasted or ruined through unfamiliarity or neglect is not possible to conjecture and, while perhaps an important factor, cannot enter into the conclusion. The judgment must be that United States aid to Russia played a much more vital war role than it would appear from the cold statistics. *Newsweek* correctly claimed that although the United States "provided only a small part of the equipment and supplies used by the Russians," nevertheless it supplied, "in large quantities, critical items."[36]

The $11,047,488,792.47 worth of defense aid provided to the Soviet Union under Lend-Lease included only the cost of the delivered items. To this figure there should also be added substantial outlays in lives and equipment. The disbursement for Russian aid did not include $11,000,000 worth of construction in the Persian corridor and over $53,000,000 worth along the ALSIB route, or the loss, along with Great Britain and other Allies, of eighty-five merchantmen and twenty warships on the North Russian route, with corresponding casualties. Thousands of Allied soldiers and sailors and millions of Allied civilians strained to make Lend-Lease to Russia a reality. Underscoring the vital nature of the aid, one editor wrote that "seldom has so much been done with so little [money]," while another reflected the unselfish nature of the program when he admonished that "common victory in a common cause is the only possible settlement for Lend-Lease accounts."[37]

[36] Ernest K. Lindley, "We Gave the Red Army its Speed," *Newsweek*, Vol. 25 (February 12, 1945), 54.

[37] *Forty-Third Report on Lend-Lease*, 17; Motter, *Persian Corridor*, 501; Carr, "Great Falls to Nome," 232; Roskill, *The War at Sea*, III, Pt. II, 432–35; *Saturday Evening Post*, Vol. 218 (October 13, 1945), p. 124; Ernest K. Lindley, "Lend-Lease, Enthralling Enterprise," *The Virginia Quarterly Review*, Vol. 20 (Spring, 1944), p. 285.

Viewed from another angle, Lend-Lease to Russia made up slightly more than one quarter of the total Lend-Lease bill. The British Empire reigned as the chief beneficiary, with a share that amounted to $31,610,813,206.15. Russia followed next with its more than $11,000,000,000, and thirty-eight other governments shared the remaining $5,400,000,000. Lend-Lease expenditures ranged from 12 per cent of the total United States war expenses in 1941 to 17 per cent in 1944, averaging, Lend-Lease officials calculated, 15 per cent. The stature of the aid programs, with Russian included, is not the least diminished by this comparison, but placed in better perspective. The raising, equipping, transporting, and supporting the United States armed forces around the world, shipping facilities that never stretched far enough, natural and enemy constructed hazards, and the demands of other Lend-Lease recipients meant that Russian aid had to be vital and selective.[38]

[38] *Forty-Third Report on Lend-Lease*, 17; *Twenty-Second Report on Lend-Lease*, 19; *Twentieth Report on Lend-Lease*, 40–42.

CHAPTER TEN

Soviet and American Viewpoints and "End-Lease"

Soviet Communists, directing Russian reflexes, reacted to Western aid and alliance in a manner predictable only in the eccentric semi-phantasy land of Soviet historiography, where truth twists to conform to fashionable patterns of dialectics. As distorted through Soviet rose-colored glasses, Russian history since the 1930's reflected capitalistic persecution. In the late thirties, aggressive, hostile, imperialistic nations surrounded Russia, with the single exception of China, already at war with Japan. Tiny Latvia, Estonia, and Lithuania supported puppet governments of Western imperialist states (England, France, and Germany). Rumania and Poland hungered for Soviet territory. Finland built fortifications to ready itself for war with Russia. English and American monopolists helped German capitalists to install Hitler and the Nazis in power in Germany. England, from 1937 on, tried to direct Nazi aggressions eastward and would come to no defensive agreement with the Soviet Union. Nor would France or the United States join such an accord. In spite of the breach in capitalist ranks that occurred in the 1930's, with England, France, and the United States facing Germany, Italy, and Japan, an anti-Soviet front developed from the time of Munich. A Nazi attack on Russia in 1939 could have become a capitalistic crusade against communism.[1]

According to this perverted Soviet version, Russia turned the

[1] *Istoriia Velikoi Otechestvennoi Voiny*, I, 5, 21, 30, 31–36, 109, 133–34, 176–77, 251, 259, 278.

tables on the Western capitalists with the non-aggression pact of August 23, 1939, made with Germany. In one stroke, Soviet leaders broke the anti-Soviet front, forestalled the aggressive designs of the West, and bought time to improve its defenses. In September, 1939, the inevitable clash between the Western capitalist powers reflected classic Leninist dogma that World War I would be repeated if the imperialists and bourgeoisie remained in power. In 1947, N. A. Voznesenski, then deputy premier of the Soviet Union, wrote that "the main fascist states, Germany, Japan, and Italy, acting in the interests of one group of capitalist countries, attempted, by means of armed force to change the prevailing world system of capitalism into their favor." The Soviets divided the war itself into two periods, the "imperialist's war," from September, 1939, to June 22, 1941, and the "great patriotic war," which began with the attack on Russia on June 22, 1941 and ended with Japan's defeat.[2]

According to Moscow's interpretation, the Nazis broke the ten-year non-aggression pact when they struck Russia. Italy tore up a 1938 treaty, and Finland renounced the truce of 1940. Spain, Portugal, Turkey, Sweden, and Japan, although officially neutral, actually assisted Nazi Germany. Even the Vatican, the Soviets claimed, obliged its clergy to support Germany. American monopolists, greedy, profit-minded, and haters of communism, supplied vital materials to Germany through Switzerland, Vichy France, Spain, and Portugal. Their factories in Germany made weapons for the Nazis. However, fascist aggression threatened not only American and English workers, but also some of their capitalist rulers. This explained why many prominent industrialists and statesmen desired to ally with Russia if the Soviet Union suffered German attack. Thus a common enemy provided a basis for an alliance of the United States, England, and Russia.[3]

[2] *Ibid.*, I, xix–xxii, 3, 5, 176–77; N. A. Voznesenski, *The Economy of the U.S.S.R. During World War II*, 1.

[3] G. A. Deborin, *Vtoraia Mirovaia Voina* (*The Second World War*), 120, 121, 133; V. L. Israelian, *Diplomaticheskaia Istoriia Velikoi Otechestvennoi*

Immediately after the Nazi attack, England and the United States talked about helping Russia but did very little because the Western powers feared Russia would not survive the German attack. That reason, observed Soviet historians, prevented Lend-Lease from being immediately extended to Russia. Also, American monopolists intended to exploit Russia's gold reserves and enrich themselves on the Soviet Union's plight. Finally, as a result of the Moscow Conference (1941), the United States extended Lend-Lease to the Soviet Union and thus strengthened the anti-fascist coalition. Lend-Lease goods came slowly, at best. Russians became indignant whenever their Western allies could not fill a "modest request." The Soviet concept of Lend-Lease remained quite simple: they forwarded their requirements, and the Anglo-Americans filled them.[4]

In the beginning the Soviet press reacted a little differently. As Red army troops staggered from the violent Nazi onslaught, leading communist organs sought to bolster Russian spirits. *Pravda*, for example, on June 26, 1941, published a front page account of British air raids on Germany. On July 3, 1941, in a radio address to his people, Stalin observed that Anglo-American pledges of aid "can only evoke a feeling of gratitude in the hearts of the people of the Soviet Union." *Pravda*, on July 31, used heavy type on page one to announce Hopkins' arrival in Moscow, and in the same issue an editorial writer described the "United Front of Freedom-loving People." On August 1, *Pravda* ran a large picture of Hopkins and Stalin on the first page, while page 4 (of this four-page paper) carried tributes to the Red army reprinted from New York newspapers. In fact, throughout the remainder of 1941 the Soviet press devoted an unusual amount of space to foreign news, diplomatic conferences, foreign sym-

---

Voiny 1941–1945 (Diplomatic History of the Great Patriotic War), 9, hereafter cited as *Diplomaticheskaia Istoriia.*

[4] Israelian, *Diplomaticheskaia Istoriia,* 9, 13, 15, 34; Deborin, *Vtoraia Mirovaia Voina,* 138, 139; *Istoriia Velikoi Otechestvennoi Voiny,* II, 179–80, 188–90.

pathy meetings, Allied military and industrial potential, and the like. The theme that echoed throughout this orchestration stressed Anglo-American help and the idea that Russia did not fight alone.[5]

In October and November, *Pravda* (faithfully echoed by *Izvestia* and *Krasnaia Zvezda* [*Red Star*]) laid the groundwork for United States Lend-Lease with an October 9 (page 3) account of American industry that assured Russians that "the American arsenal has started. . . . [It] began putting its production on the balance scale of countries . . . fighting against fascism." Exactly one month later *Pravda* printed part of Roosevelt's letter that offered Stalin $1,000,000,000 in long-term interest-free credits and Stalin's agreeable reply. Meanwhile, *Pravda* and *Krasnaia Zvezda* featured pictures and articles dealing with Allied aid. In *Krasnaia Zvezda*, page 1, November 13, the editors published a photograph of British fighter pilots fighting in the Soviet Union; on November 14, page 1, American fighter planes arrived for a "Soviet air regiment" (another picture); on November 21, page 1, a photograph of English tanks used by the Red army; and on November 25, page 3, a glowing account of English heavy tanks. *Pravda*, on October 4, published pictures of tanks in England destined for the Soviet Union, and on December 22, page 2, it described how quickly Russian soldiers "learned how to operate these complicated machines."

Stalin, who spoke on the twenty-fourth anniversary of the October Revolution (on November 6, 1941), injected a jarring note into this rare atmosphere of good comradeship maintained by the Soviet press. Pleading for a second front, Stalin lamented that there were "no armies of Great Britain or the United States on the European continent at present," which left Russia to wage "the war of liberation alone without anyone's military aid." Before he finished, however, Stalin acknowledged that Britain

[5] Joseph Stalin, *The Great Patriotic War of the Soviet Union*, 16, hereafter cited as *The Great Patriotic War*.

and America "decided systematically to assist our country with tanks and aircraft," and as his listeners knew, such shipments had already begun.[6]

During the winter of 1941–42 this first wartime period of Soviet press attention to Allied affairs tapered off. Pictures of Allied weapons and equipment disappeared from the publications (although American motor vehicles appeared, they appeared unlabelled as such). Almost all other Allied war news wound up on page 4, except for diplomatic affairs. Soviet Washington correspondents reported on Lend-Lease to Russia as each quarterly Lend-Lease report appeared, and *Pravda* dutifully mentioned this news throughout the war, on page 4. The Soviet press warmed up again briefly in June, 1942, as Britain concluded a treaty of alliance (May 26, 1942) and Hull and Litvinov signed the Lend-Lease Master Agreement in Washington on June 11. *Pravda*, on June 13, page 1, referred to the Master Agreement as "another" concerning delivery of "arms and other war materials" from the United States. On June 14, *Pravda* ran editorials about "The Undefeatable Alliance" and on June 17 quoted United States production statistics with the observation that "America became an arsenal for democratic states of anti-Hitlerite front." On June 18 in *Pravda* a noted Soviet economist (E. Varga) commented very favorably on the "Military Potential of the United States of America." *Pravda* carried, on June 19, Molotov's speech to the Supreme Soviet that described the June 11 agreement with the United States. *Pravda* noted casually that the Supreme Soviet ratified the government's foreign policy.

On June 20, *Pravda* stated on page 1 that the "growing flow of armament supplied to our country by our allies is an important and necessary addition to the armament being forged in overwhelming quantity in Soviet plants for the dear Red Army." On June 21, *Pravda*, in a third page article headed "America Picks up the Tempo," noted an increase of aid deliveries over 1941. Using more United States production figures, the writer observed

[6] Stalin, *The Great Patriotic War*, 24, 25, 32.

that the combined output of the United States, the United Kingdom and the Soviet Union would provide Hitler's death sentence. By July 1, *Pravda* promised its readers (on page 4) that "The Anti-Hitlerite coalition is Undefeatable," described the strength of the Allies, and told how the second front was coming. But this summer warmth faded with the onset of fall and the failure of a second front to materialize. Both *Izvestia* (August 2, 1942) and *Pravda* (August 5, 1942) took pains to inform their subscribers that the idea of a second front was popular in England and the United States.

The Soviet press cooled off in its enthusiasm for its Western allies and became critical of them and their efforts, even resorting to cartoon ridicule (although mild in form). Now the demand for a second front built up and recurred more and more frequently. *Pravda*, on November 8, 1942, reported unenthusiastically, on page 4, the Allied North African landings. The Soviet press remained cool to Allied war efforts throughout 1943, as Standley discovered early in the year. Only once in a while did a favorable article appear, and Soviet diplomats abroad gave more credit to Lend-Lease than Russian newspapers conceded. On March 13, 1943, *Pravda* (page 4) printed a summary of speechmaking furnished to it by its Washington correspondents at a breakfast commemorating the "Second Anniversary of the American Law about Lend-Lease." Litvinov, *Pravda* reported, remarked that although it was "hardly possible" to conceive the great consumption of material by the Red army, mostly provided by the Soviet Union, "the materials, received under the Lend-Lease law, and the weapons provided tremendous help, deeply appreciated by the people of the Soviet Union who know all about the scale of this help." The Red army's mobility "was substantially assisted by American trucks." Food deliveries assumed "great importance" because the Ukraine "is still in the hands of the enemy and the newly liberated Northern Caucasus is still devastated." He also lauded Aircobra fighters and B-25 bombers. Another island of acknowledgment in the 1943 press came in *Pravda* on

245

October 6, 1943, again on page 4. The new ambassador to the United States, Gromyko, told Roosevelt that the Soviet people valued American support and expressed their "warm gratitude" for it.

Stalin, this time on the occasion of the twenty-sixth anniversary of the October Revolution on November 6, 1943, credited Allied bombing of Germany with weakening Nazi military might and noted, "To all this is added the fact that the Allies are regularly supplying us with various munitions and raw materials, [and] it can be said without exaggeration that by all this they considerably facilitated the successes of our summer campaign." The Moscow papers published, on January 3, a digest of Crowley's statement of January 2 concerning Lend-Lease for the first ten months of 1943. They published figures on planes, tanks, trucks, field telephones, wire, and the like. Harriman noted that they devoted four inches of newsprint to the subject on that occasion. On May 1, 1944, Stalin again acknowledged Allied help. "A considerable contribution to these successes [of the Red army in the winter-spring of 1944] has been made by our great Allies . . . [who] supply us with very valuable strategic raw materials and armaments," who fight in Italy, and who bomb Germany. By November of 1944, Stalin remarked how "the workers in the Soviet rear won economic victory over the enemy in their lone fight against Hitler." Although he complimented Allied military successes after the May Day, 1944, speech, no similar pronouncements followed for Soviet consumption.[7]

The Allied landing in Normandy brought a brief thaw in the Soviet press's attitude. On June 11, 1944, *Pravda* editorialized on page 1 about "Two Years of Soviet-American Agreement." Although friendly, the article emphasized the vital role of the Red army and underplayed American aid. But on the same page in the same issue, the Soviets printed their first—and last—release about the actual deliveries to the Soviet Union by the United

[7] Stalin, *The Great Patriotic War*, 103, 122, 133–34; *Foreign Relations, 1943,* III, 798.

States, Great Britain, and Canada. In a report from The People's Commissariat of Foreign Trade, "About the Deliveries to the Soviet Union of the Weapons, Strategic Raw Materials, Industrial Equipment, and Foodstuffs," *Pravda* set down a fairly accurate summary of deliveries through April 30, 1944. Although Russian newspapers often printed stories about Soviet industry, reconstruction, and the like, they seldom disclosed any idea of the role played by Lend-Lease material. *Izvestia*, on January 4, 1944, described Russian industrial successes in Siberia and restoration of industry in the Don Basin as a purely Soviet achievement. *Izvestia*, on November 11, 1944, discussed Soviet industrial expansion especially in metallurgy and power generation without a word of American aluminum or American generating equipment. On February 21, 1945, *Izvestia*, page 3, discussed electric-power advances in detail, including the use of mobile power stations (on railroad cars). A Soviet citizen, if alert, might have noticed that *Pravda*, in a report released in the United States by Crowley and picked up by *Pravda* reporters, had disclosed twelve days earlier that sixty rail-mounted mobile power units had been sent to the Soviet Union.

As with Crowley's reports, mentioned above, the nationally important Soviet presses of *Pravda*, *Izvestia*, and *Krasnaia Zvezda* also summarized Lend-Lease news made by Roosevelt, Stettinius, Churchill, and Beaverbrook. These items, too, always appeared on page 4, the last page of all three papers. Local Russian newspapers seldom reprinted news of that sort. No Russian paper published information about Allied supply routes or convoy arrivals. So while not completely uninformed about Lend-Lease, the Soviet people learned little about it since it received very little attention in the Red press. Soviet citizens did not have the advantage of Red army soldiers, who at least saw and used Lend-Lease trucks and other weapons. The American consul at Vladivostok worried because he felt the Russians did not know the terms of Lend-Lease but felt it to be a big-business monopoly administered for gain by the United States. The consul added that the people of his area knew that if it were not for American aid they would be starving, no matter how America ran the program.

At the end of the war, Russia took care to disregard the role of Lend-Lease. "Although we went through exceptional economic difficulties in the first years of the war," Molotov recalled on November 7, 1945, "our country nevertheless supplied the needs of our heroic army with all essentials, including first-class weapons, qualitatively superior to those of the enemy." Two years later, Deputy Premier Voznesenski observed, "Comparing the amount of Allied deliveries of industrial goods to the U.S.S.R. with the amount of industrial production in socialist enterprises of the U.S.S.R. during the same period, it appears that the ratio of such deliveries to domestic production . . . comprises only about 4 per cent." The 4 per cent figure then became a standard and was repeated by other Soviet sources.[8]

After the war, through the curious looking-glass of Soviet historiography, the average Russian citizen learned that militarily the United States and Great Britain had the strength to open a second front by the end of 1941 in spite of Pearl Harbor and the new Pacific war. But the capitalistic ruling circles of the United States and the United Kingdom, maneuvering for more advantageous world positions, protracted the war for the exhaustion of both Germany and the Soviet Union. Naturally then, the two governments did not strain themselves to send supplies to the Soviet Union. They even "systematically wrecked" deliveries during the most critical times. Although transportation difficulties provided the Western powers with excuses for slowness in delivery, they never were the actual reasons. The Lend-Lease agreement struck a blow, nevertheless, at Anglo-American reactionaries, who conspired with the Nazi imperialists to isolate the Soviet Union. The government of the Soviet Union, ever alert, carefully defended its national independence and sov-

[8] *Foreign Relations, 1943*, III, 760–61; *Pravda*, November 7, 1945, p. 2; Voznesenski, *The Economy of the U.S.S.R.*, 40.

ereign rights against the imperialistic side of Lend-Lease, which took the form of military bases and political and economic dependence.[9]

In one instance, Soviet historians have decided, United States and United Kingdom leaders attempted to "blackmail" the Soviet Union when they exposed convoy P.Q. 17 to disaster by withdrawing its escorts and scattering it. Subsequent losses became excuses for reduced deliveries. In addition, the leaders of the United States and Great Britain used "second front" promises for both 1942 and 1943 to entice the Soviet Union. Besides their sabotage of the second front and their failure to complete scheduled deliveries, the "ruling circles" of England and the United States conducted secret negotiations with Hitlerite Germany. Pope Pius XII and Francisco Franco, noted reactionaries, worked as mediators. American and British supplies, sighed a Red historian, would have helped achieve a Soviet economic victory over the enemy. The "working masses" of the Western powers knew this, but the profit-seeking, imperialistic, capitalistic, "ruling classes" would not allow it. They kept all scientific and technical information secret from the Soviet Union, although they shared these secrets with American corporations that belonged to German cartels. As a result, the help, the insignificant 4 per cent, forced the Soviets to wage their economic struggle with the Nazis single-handed.[10]

Speaking to Rumanian workers on June 19, 1962, Khrushchev asserted that during World War II American monopolists made "billions of dollars on war deliveries. They fattened themselves on the blood of the people lost during two world wars." That is how, Khrushchev continued, "American industry has risen to such a high level. That is why today the United States of America has the opportunity to produce and consume more goods." The

[9] *Istoriia Velikoi Otechestvennoi Voiny*, II, 363–65; Deborin, *Vtoraia Mirovaia Voina*, 148, 172.

[10] Deborin, *Vtoraia Mirovaia Voina*, 200–201, 239, 414; *Istoriia Velikoi Otechestvennoi Voiny*, 503.

chunky Soviet leader made it clear that Soviet and Rumanian blood provided American fat.[11]

If it occurred to Soviet citizens at all, they might have asked themselves how it was that bourgeois Nazi Germany came so close to victory in the Soviet Union, and why wartime allies sought to weaken one of their number by providing only token aid and postponing a second front. The answer to the first question was found in Stalin's claim that peace-loving states, such as the Soviet Union, are always weaker than aggressor states, such as the capitalist ones. Russia could not trust her "democratic" but also capitalist allies, allies that needed her help but did not wish to see her emerge from the war as a strong power. Obviously it proved a simple task to slough off Russia's reverses in the war by blaming Russian mistakes on her lukewarm allies. In such a situation the Soviet Union could not publish full data about the critical amounts of aid received under Lend-Lease without giving the lie to her own propaganda. Although Americans expressed a degree of enthusiasm for their Soviet ally, they did not imagine Russia would shrug off Lend-Lease as an insignificant 4 per cent and as an attempt to ensnarl the Soviet Union in the political machinations of the capitalist world (which shrewd Russian diplomats had carefully avoided, according to the official propaganda line). All of which meant the Soviet Union had fought virtually alone. Settlement of the account would to some degree expose the extent of the aid, inconsistent with the aims of Soviet propaganda.

In the United States there was little reaction to Russian conceptions during the war. By January, 1944, the American war machine was racing along in high gear. President Roosevelt, in the thirteenth report on Lend-Lease, told the nation how American-built equipment played a major role in the Red army's offensive against retreating Nazis. More American-made aircraft flew with Soviet markings than any other kind, except the United States (7,000 since October, 1943). Russian soldiers rode in

[11] *Pravda,* June 20, 1962, p. 2.

195,000 Lend-Lease vehicles, attacked with 3,500 Lend-Lease tanks, and consumed 343,000 tons of Lend-Lease wheat and 341,000 tons of Lend-Lease canned meat. This type of aid for the Soviet Union soared in 1943 to 63 per cent above a comparable period in 1942. *Pravda,* impressed with the report, reproduced lengthy extracts from it, "probably the greatest amount of space devoted to any Lend-Lease report since the program was begun." At the same time this enthusiastic report appeared, as well as other glowing statements from the Foreign Economic Administration office, the Russian Embassy published an article titled, "The War Economy of the U.S.S.R. in 1943," which credited the Red army's success to Russia's industrial progress but which included no mention of Lend-Lease aid.[12]

Also in January, the Soviets sent Stalingrad veteran Lenoid Rudenko to the United States to take over as chairman of the Russian Purchasing Commission. Rudenko early expressed the high regard that the Soviet Government and the Red army had for Lend-Lease assistance. More of this assistance got through to Russia unscathed: Crowley announced that although the tonnage shipped to Russia nearly doubled in 1943, the shipping losses dropped from 12 per cent to 1 per cent. In fact, the War Food Administration reported that Russia received 51 per cent of United States food shipments abroad, and the British Empire was second with 42 per cent. Crowley's announcement of these figures was again fully reported in the Soviet press. In March and again in April the Foreign Economic Administration took care to point out that aid continued to pour into Russia at greatly accelerated speeds, well ahead of the monthly schedules.[13]

In April, Victor Kravchenko, chief of the metals section of the Soviet Purchasing Commission, announced his resignation and asked for political asylum. A member of the Communist party and a responsible Soviet industrial manager, Kravchenko ac-

[12] *The New York Times,* January 7, 1944, pp. 1, 8; January 11, p. 2; January 19, p. 1.

[13] *The New York Times,* January 20, 1944, pp. 1, 4; February 28, p. 6; March 1, p. 4; March 18, p. 2; April 3, p. 3.

cused Russia of conducting a two-faced foreign policy, which, on the surface, reflected collaboration, but which in fact remained unchanged from basic prewar Soviet goals. Kravchenko decried the absence of basic political liberties in the Soviet Union and announced that Russian plans for the Balkans and Poland did not include the free reconstructions that Soviet leaders promised. Sensational as it was, this condemnation of the Soviet system failed to dampen the House of Representatives' enthusiasm for the annual extension of Lend-Lease. It passed easily on April 19, 334 to 21. One jarring note came with the Wadsworth amendment, which in fact restricted the President from assuming any obligations under the Lend-Lease law "except in accordance with established constitutional procedure." The object of the amendment was to head off any executive postwar foreign economic or military commitments that Congress felt fell normally within its purview.[14]

On May 17, Roosevelt signed the Lend-Lease extension after the Senate, a week earlier, had passed it 63 to 1. "Victory will come sooner, and will cost less in lives and materials," the President announced, "because we have pooled our manpower and material resources, as United Nations, to defeat the enemy." As if to give point to this pooling, the Soviets decorated twenty-nine officers and four enlisted men of the Persian Gulf Service Command, which afforded "great assistance to the Red Army in its struggle with the Nazi German invaders." In subsequent weeks, Harriman, Crowley, Eric Johnson (president of the United States Chamber of Commerce), and representatives of the *NAM News* (National Association of Manufacturers) all discussed various facets of the Lend-Lease to Russia program. The *NAM News* saw the Soviet Union as a tremendous postwar market, especially if it received American loans.[15] The Allied landing in France and the subsequent campaigns connected with it occupied most of the news space in American papers, making

14 *The New York Times*, April 4, 1944, p. 1; April 20, pp. 1, 18.
15 *The New York Times*, December 26, 1944, p. 17; December 27, p. 3.

Lend-Lease seem much less vital now that the Yanks had landed.

After leaving the Lend-Lease Administration, Stettinius wasted no time in rushing into print with *Weapon For Victory*, a history of Lend-Lease. Ernest K. Lindley, in a review for *The Virginia Quarterly Review*, observed that a "more effective instrument of national policy seldom has been devised." This was true because "seldom has so much been done with so little [money]." Leo M. Cherne, in the *Saturday Review of Literature*, did not feel so charitable. He accused the administration of doing "a bad job of informing the public as to the real nature of lend-lease" and reproached Stettinius for missing the "chance to drop the dollar sign" in the book. Repayment, Cherne admonished, "is in the damage done by the British or Russian or Chinese soldiers shooting American rifles." Howard P. Whidden, Jr., writing in *Foreign Policy Reports*, agreed with Cherne that the United States proved inept at keeping its citizens informed on Lend-Lease. The concept, Whidden noted, obviously aimed at preventing another war-debt quarrel. Yet American opinion in recent months indicated to him that the issue remained unclear in the public mind. "Both the administration and Congress have apparently decided that the benefits to be gained from the re-establishment of multilateral trade would be much greater than any to be obtained from an effort to collect payment for war aid." Whidden concluded that the Allies who signed mutual aid agreements "accepted a broad political obligation to join with the United States in seeking to free the channels of world trade. The next step," he added, "would appear to be a general cancellation of obligations with respect to Lend-Lease and reverse lend-lease materials consumed in the war."[16]

In a report marked "Confidential, For Limited Circulation," New York's Council on Foreign Relations published a mimeo-

[16] Lindley, "Lend-Lease, Enthralling Enterprise," *The Virginia Quarterly Review*, Vol. 20 (Spring, 1944), pp. 281–85; Leo M. Cherne, "The 'Double L' Arsenal," *Saturday Review of Literature*, Vol. 27 (January 22, 1944), pp. 3–4; Howard P. Whidden, Jr., "Reaching a Lend-Lease Settlement," *Foreign Policy Reports*, Vol. XX (April 15, 1944), pp. 22, 27.

graphed critique on Lend-Lease, "Its Nature, Implications, and Settlement." The Council claimed that "popular opinion toward lend-lease shows ill-informed, contradictory and controversial attitudes. Most Americans feel that something is owed us in repayment," as a national public opinion poll showed in February of 1942. In January, 1943, 25 per cent of those polled "did not know what lend-lease was," while 54 per cent of those interviewed felt that recipients should pay for the aid received. A large group, 58 per cent, thought the United States would not be so repaid. The danger here, the report pointed out, was that "any propaganda group" would be in an excellent position to muster support for a strong stand on repayment and to claim that "failure to collect is a betrayal of American interests." This attitude would seriously impair any settlement at all. The Council observed that a November, 1943, Truman Committee report to the United States Senate asserted that "lend-lease was never intended as a device to shift Allied war costs to the United States," and concluded with a proposal that if "the benefited nations could not repay in dollars they might transfer some of their internationally held assets to this country, such as oil reserves and metal deposits." An observer who remembered Roosevelt's homely garden hose analogy of only four years earlier might well have wondered what happened to the concept.[17]

In February, 1945, Crowley appeared before the House Foreign Affairs Committee to dispel a number of "fictions" about Lend-Lease which were being spread with the help of enemy propaganda. Most of them concerned Britain, although Crowley pointed out that the Soviets did not trade American aircraft to Japan for rubber. Stimson followed Crowley into Congress to advocate yet another extension of the Lend-Lease Act. "We are at the crisis of the war," the Secretary claimed, with the beginning of the assault on Fortress Germany and with Japan's main

17 Council on Foreign Relations, "The Problem of Lend-Lease: Its Nature, Implications, and Settlement," *American Interests in the War and the Peace,* mimeograph, 8–9.

armies still intact. Stimson vowed that Lend-Lease was the most powerful factor in creating co-ordinated strategy. Lend-Lease, he pointed out, "almost certainly [has] done more than any other one instrument" to break down Soviet suspicions of the West. Stimson believed Lend-Lease to be "one of the foundation stones of the new union of nations." After Stimson's statements, wrote a reporter, the extension of Lend-Lease for another year appeared assured.[18]

In April, Harry S Truman, the new President, signed the extension of Lend-Lease. In May, Crowley reported that even though the Protocol remained without formal signature, shipments ran nearly 110 per cent of the volume scheduled. On the heels of that announcement came the news of May 13 that Lend-Lease shipments to Russia had been suspended the day before. Although they were resumed soon after, it appeared that matters were serious enough to warrant another trip by Hopkins to Moscow, this time on behalf of Truman. When Hopkins resigned from government service on July 3, the press took note of his recent mission to Moscow to "save the United Nations" but revealed very little about Hopkins' war role.[19]

In the summer of 1945 the capitulation of Japan and an end to the war in the Pacific finally came. At the same time, the National Defense Investigating Committee of the Senate, formerly headed by Truman, but then by Harley M. Kilgore (West Virginia), blasted the Lend-Lease administration for its lack of planning and poor administration. After visiting thirty cities and supply posts in six European countries, the Senators criticized everything about the program from poor accounting for reverse Lend-Lease to indifference among the beneficiaries. Following V-J Day, Truman listened to his advisers advocate peacetime extension of Lend-Lease for reconstruction. Unalterably opposed to this, Truman asked that the program be liquidated as soon as

[18] *The New York Times*, February 11, 1945, IV, p. 8; February 15, p. 7; February 16, p. 22.

[19] *The New York Times*, April 18, 1945, p. 15; May 10, p. 13; May 13, I, p. 1; June 1, p. 10.

possible. The President felt other means of postwar rebuilding should be worked out. Early in September, *Newsweek* ran, under the headline, "End-Lease," an account of the termination. It quoted Britain's new prime minister, Clement Atlee, as protesting Britain's "very serious financial position." Leo Crowley, holding the first open press conference in years, pointed out that $1,500,000,000 worth of goods was piled up in Lend-Lease stockpiles abroad or was in transit and that another $2,000,000,000 remained under contract. Crowley would not comment on the subject of Lend-Lease indebtedness. If Crowley would not, the *Saturday Evening Post* would. In an editorial, the *Post* lamented that the dollar sign Roosevelt had tried to eliminate remained to distort the true picture of Lend-Lease. "Nobody," the editor wrote, "intended to collect dollars for the tanks which helped to save Stalingrad." A "common victory in a common cause is the only possible settlement for Lend-Lease accounts."[20]

Not very many Americans agreed with the *Post*. Elmo Roper, who directed a survey on the subject in December, 1945, found that 49 per cent of those questioned believed Lend-Lease should have been stopped when it was (Truman, at least, appeared to have popular support in his decision), while only 19 per cent thought Lend-Lease should have been extended for another year, apparently for reconstruction. Roper also discovered that 58 per cent of his respondents believed that the United States should make Lend-Lease settlements satisfactory to both sides, which would give the United States concessions, services, and perhaps some goods in repayment. Over 27 per cent felt the United States should hold out for full payment in either goods or money—Whatever happened to that eliminated dollar sign?—

[20] *Newsweek*, Vol. 26 (July 16, 1945), pp. 31–32; Vol. 26 (September 3, 1945), pp. 38–40; *Time*, Vol. 46 (August 27, 1945), p. 20; *Saturday Evening Post*, Vol. 218 (October 13, 1945), p. 124. Byrnes, Crowley, and Vinson acted as an advisory subcommittee to make recommendations to Truman in connection with problems concerning the termination of Lend-Lease. Truman Library, Lend-Lease, letter, Truman to Vinson, August 24, 1945.

but only 5 per cent believed that the account ought to be cancelled completely.[21]

Whatever Americans believed, Lend-Lease proved to be a convenient source of much needed industrial equipment as valuable for Russia's reconstruction as for the war (more so, considering the fate of the Ford Tire plant, for example). Under the Fourth Protocol, Group V, Machinery and Equipment, $482,-000,000 worth of long-term equipment had been contracted under an optional purchase agreement, not directly under Lend-Lease, but apparently in accord with the stipulations for Section 3-C of the amended Lend-Lease Act, conditions the Russians had refused a year earlier. Desire for the equipment prompted Rudenko to seek an explanation from Crowley as soon as Crowley and Grew received Truman's signature on the executive order ending Lend-Lease on May 8. Truman reacted to Allied screams of pain at the abrupt ending of Lend-Lease by ordering all promises previously made to be honored. Crowley, in a reply to Rudenko on May 30, 1945, assured him that this equipment would indeed be delivered.[22]

[21] *Fortune*, Vol. 32 (December, 1945), p. 310. The *Fortune* Survey directed by Elmo Roper asked first this question (results are indicated): "Which one of these comes closest to your idea of how lend-lease should have been handled?" (1) Lend-Lease should have been stopped when it was and in the way it was, 49.4 per cent; (2) should not have been stopped so suddenly, 18.4 per cent; (3) Lend-Lease should have been extended up to a year, 19 per cent; (4) Don't know, 13.2 per cent. Second, Roper's pollsters asked this question: "What do you think the U.S. should do about what other countries received from us under Lend-Lease?" (1) Hold out for full payment in either goods or money, 27.4 per cent; (2) make settlements satisfactory to both sides that will give us concessions, services, and perhaps some goods, 58.1 per cent; (3) cancel all they owe us, 5.2 per cent; (4) Don't know, 9.3 per cent. Roper concluded, "It is obvious that any reasonable propositions to pay off in facilities or in 'cultural currency' would be seriously entertained." Of the White House mail concerning the termination of the program by Truman, most was in support of the President. Many wanted to know the precise figures on Lend-Lease to the penny. Truman Library, President's Official File No. 356, Box 1038.

[22] *Soviet Supply Protocols*, 111–12; *Twenty-First Report on Lend-Lease*, 48–53; letter, Leo T. Crowley to Lt. Gen. L. C. Rudenko, May 30, 1945, from Foreign Economic Administration files in the State Department.

In addition, much of the other equipment destined for the Soviet Union under the Fourth Protocol but stalled with the end of Lend-Lease had been contracted by Russia for purchase. According to instructions from Truman, governments that desired to purchase material in the pipeline would be allowed to do so on mutually agreeable terms. The Office of Lend-Lease understood that these terms were to be similar to the pattern of agreement already entered into by France, Belgium, and Holland under Section 3-C of the Lend-Lease Act. On October 15, 1945, Russia signed a pipeline transfer agreement with the United States. The price charged for material therein was generally the United States purchasing agency contract price, F.O.B. point of origin, or in the case of foodstuffs, the "fair value" of the articles plus certain storage and transportation costs. The total bill was to be paid in twenty-two annual installments beginning July 2, 1954, and ending July 1, 1975. The interest or carrying charge agreed upon was $2\frac{3}{8}$ per cent, commencing July 1, 1946 and payable annually, beginning July 1, 1947.[23]

An important exception to the end of Lend-Lease occurred in shipping. Foreign Economic Administration officials feared that an abrupt termination of the aid program would disrupt the international shipping pool and complicate the job of supply for Allied armies of occupation. So Foreign Economic Administration officers agreed that Lend-Lease would pick up the shipping tab for essential supplies for the various Lend-Lease governments for a period of sixty days following V–J Day. This procedure underwent some modification after November 1, 1945, by allowing Lend-Lease to carry the freight charges on certain undertakings with the understanding that the extended service would eventually be repaid. Following December 21, 1945, all Lend-Lease ocean freight halted except in cases of pipeline transfers and goods shipped at the direction of the Joint Chiefs of Staff. Even the last-mentioned pipeline shipping charges were

<hr>

[23] *Twenty-First Report on Lend-Lease,* 7, 8, 48–53. According to the *Forty-Third Report on Lend-Lease,* 13, the actual total was $11,047,488,792.47.

marked for repayment according to the terms of the pipeline agreements, such as the October 15 agreement with Russia. In a report to Truman on February 20, 1946, Crowley mentioned that the Foreign Economic Administration had made "every effort" to see that the pipeline goods would continue to be available to the Allies on mutually satisfactory financial terms. He noted that through the United Nations Relief and Rehabilitation Administration, the Bretton Woods legislation, and the increased lending authority of the Export–Import Bank (especially helpful) many of the Allies had been assured of an uninterrupted flow of supplies necessary to their economy. "We must recognize," Crowley concluded, "that it will not be possible for our Allies to pay us dollars for the overwhelming proportion of lend-lease obligations which they have incurred."[24]

The Comptroller General of the United States upset the delicate pipeline agreement network by ruling that Lend-Lease deliveries, even under the agreements, had to cease after December 31, 1946. The ruling followed Congressional action in passing the Third Deficiency Appropriation Act, 1946, approved in July. The monies appropriated to the Agriculture and Treasury departments for delivery completion could not be so used after December 31, 1946. To insure continued delivery, the foreign governments involved were asked, in accordance with Section 3-C of the Lend-Lease Act, to deposit in escrow sufficient funds to cover expenses for which appropriated monies could not be used. The comptroller general then ruled that even those deposits could not be used unless Congress stipulated that their use would not violate the intent of the Third Deficiency Appropriation Act. Subsequently, State Department officials urged Congress to clarify the intent of the law, and Truman proposed the necessary legislation in a message to Congress in June, 1947. Finally the Supplemental Appropriation Act, 1948, provided $500,000 for liquidation expenses to the Treasury Department.

[24] *Twenty-First Report on Lend-Lease*, 7, 8. Truman Library, President's Official File 356, Box 1038, letter, Crowley to Truman, February 20, 1946.

This included completion of pipeline deliveries to Australia, Belgium, China, France, Saudia Arabia, Guatemala, Brazil, Peru, the United Kingdom, and the Netherlands. Obviously not included was $19,372,000 worth of pipeline material that could not be sent to the Soviet Union to complete the October 15, 1945, agreement. With $482,000,000 worth of supplies contracted under the optional clauses of the Fourth Protocol and $222,494,547.01 contracted under the October 15, 1945, accord (of which $19,372,000 remained unshipped), the pipeline stoppage dashed any real hope that payments that began on July 1, 1947, would be continued. Before negotiations fell through, the Soviet Union had paid $11,126,765.24 against the principal of the pipeline account and was credited with $10,036,257.58 on various other cash accounts.[25]

Congressional action in the Third Deficiency Appropriation Act, 1946, and the Supplemental Appropriation Act, 1948, ended any chance of continuing the agreements then in force and doubtless hurt negotiations for a general Lend-Lease settlement. Congress, however, reflected national disenchantment with the United States' former Soviet ally. After the victory in Europe, the uneasy alliance fell apart. The Russians sealed their occupation zones, ringing down Churchill's famous "iron curtain," and proceeded to reconstruct Eastern Europe as they saw fit. Many aspects of the Yalta and Potsdam agreements broke down as the Soviet Union stripped Eastern Europe of industrial and agricultural materials for reparations. Failure to get United States loans or credits meant that this harsh Soviet policy "be-

[25] *Twenty-Fourth Report on Lend-Lease*, 11–12, 20, 21; *Forty-Third Report on Lend-Lease*, 8–10. The various pipeline agreements with all concerned Lend-Lease nations totaled $1,200,000,000. Roughly $30,000,000 of the total remained to be shipped by December 31, 1946. Two-thirds of this remainder, $19,372,000, had been earmarked for Russia. Clark M. Clifford, presidential assistant, deleted from the State Department draft of Truman's letter of transmittal (the foreword) in the *Twenty-Fourth Report on Lend-Lease* (October 10, 1947) the following sentence: "The material held for delivery to the Soviet Union under the agreement of October 15, 1945, which Congress decided should not be transferred, is being disposed of in accordance with applicable law and procedures." Truman Library, President's Official File 356, Box 1038.

came a matter of paramount importance to Russia."[26] Failure of economic agreement between the Soviet Union and the United States, however, loomed more as a symptom of deteriorating relations than a cause. Russia negotiated a series of mutual assistance pacts with Eastern Europe and built the Cominform (designed to take up where the Comintern left off in 1943). At the same time, Truman's "Doctrine" heralded a firm American foreign policy line toward Russia, and the primarily humanitarian Marshall Plan helped European nations help themselves recover and at the same time provided a bulwark against communism. Under the circumstances of this new "cold war," Congress could hardly be blamed for terminating the pipeline and other purchase agreements with the Soviet Union. Congress traded the prospect of Lend-Lease settlement for a firm diplomatic policy.

Nevertheless, lukewarm negotiations for a Lend-Lease accord to close the books continued. In April, 1951, the State Department observed that the United States had furnished Russia with Lend-Lease supplies and services worth $10,800,000,000 and had requested payment for only the civilian-type articles remaining in Soviet custody at the war's end. Allowing for depreciation and loss, American officials calculated the value of those items at $2,600,000,000. The United States offered to settle for $800,000,000, but Russia offered only $240,000,000 (less than the amount involved in the Fourth Protocol option alone). Russia refused a United States offer to submit the settlement to arbitration. Other factors involved the return of Lend-Lease naval and merchant vessels (672, in all) and compensation to American firms for use of their patented oil refinery processes supplied by Lend-Lease (the Soviets settled with only one of seven American firms involved). In 1954 and 1955 the Soviet Union returned 127 of the vessels lend-leased to them. In 1956 the United States Navy sent observers to watch the Russians destroy 79 additional ships, too rickety to make the ocean crossing. Again, in 1960, 10 more aged and unserviceable vessels went

[26] George Vernadsky, *A History of Russia*, 454.

to the bottom by mutual consent and under the eyes of United States Naval observers (another sank before it could be towed to the destruction rendezvous). The Soviets offered to purchase 87 merchant and thirty-one naval vessels, but until an over-all settlement could be reached, the United States refused. In all, that left 279 Lend-Lease vessels unaccounted for in Russian hands, and a total of 397 (as of 1962) to be included in a final accounting.[27]

[27] *Department of State Bulletin*, Vol. 24 (May 7, 1951), 744–46; (February 19, 1951), 302–303; (January 15, 1951), 94; (April 23, 1951), 647–48; Vol. 26 (June 2, 1952), 879–81; and *Thirty-Sixth, Thirty-Seventh, Thirty-Eighth,* and *Forty-Second Reports on Lend-Lease Operations, passim.*

CHAPTER ELEVEN

What Ever Happened to the Garden Hose?

Franklin D. Roosevelt gambled three times and lost only once, a reasonable record in the international game he played. He wagered on Britain's survival and won. He bet against long odds that Russia would remain in the war against Germany, and he won again. He further speculated that by not attaching political strings to Russian aid, he could secure their friendship and assure their co-operation in the peace, but this time he lost.

The very gambles Roosevelt made, win or lose, showed him to be a leader willing, in these instances, to take responsibility and make decisions that were essentially his own, decisions that were contrary to the advice of some of his most trusted advisers. Perhaps this is nowhere better illustrated than in the concept and execution of Lend-Lease. With the United Kingdom staggering from the powerful Nazi lunge that had buried France, and Germany and Russia bound together in trade agreements and pledged not to attack each other, it appeared that Britain's wake had begun. Haunted by the specter of old war debts implicit in the Johnson Act (that outlawed loans to those who defaulted on World War I debt payments) and further circumscribed by the Neutrality Act, Roosevelt determined to find a way to bolster Britain. The result was the conception of Lend-Lease, his insistence on a broad and general law that in fact allowed him great powers over type and extent of aid, and his successful efforts to keep control of the entire Lend-Lease program in his own hands.

Responsible for the decision to help first Britain and later Russia, Roosevelt, the resourceful administrator, naturally took the necessary steps to control the program designed to implement those decisions. Thus the Division of Defense Aid Reports, which after the Lend-Lease Act passed succeeded the President's Liaison Committee, was created within the Executive Office and housed as unobtrusively as possible as part of the Office of Emergency Management.

Although the decision to help Russia was made by Roosevelt and Churchill prior to the Nazi attack, Roosevelt the politician cleverly shepherded the necessary appropriations and other United States defense measures through Congress before including Russia in Lend-Lease—a move that prematurely made could very well have jeopardized not only Russian aid but the rearmament program itself. Roosevelt's willingness to put the Soviet program on the basis of formal protocol agreement, thus giving it a stature that other participants in the mutual aid pool did not have, and his resolution to honor that accord even at the expense of his own rearmament program and Britain's Lend-Lease priorities displayed his sincere purpose of gaining Soviet friendship and winning Soviet co-operation.

The office of the President, being the complex and involved agency that it is, has made it necessary for the Chief Executive to have advisers not directly connected with any specific branch of the government. "Kitchen cabinets" of such trusted men have long been a feature of the executive branch, but probably no President had a more intelligent and more selfless counselor than Roosevelt did in Harry Hopkins. Roosevelt placed the major responsibility for the execution of the Lend-Lease program and for Lend-Lease to Russia safely in Hopkins' hands. Major General James H. Burns (executive officer of the Division of Defense Aid Reports) and later, when the Office of Lend-Lease Administrator was created, Edward R. Stettinius, Jr. (Administrator), headed their offices and handled the daily routine, dealt with congressmen and other officials, and executed policy transmitted to them by Hopkins. Roosevelt's confidence in Hopkins is illustrated over and over again, as Hopkins headed not only Lend-Lease but later the President's Soviet Protocol Committee and the Munitions Assignment Board. In key chairs such as those, Hopkins was in a position to translate any Presidential aid directive into immediate action. In addition, because of the President's trust, his own keen mind, and the energy that sprang from his chronically ill body, Hopkins was able to exert considerable influence on both Churchill and Stalin. They could talk to and communicate with Hopkins at least as frankly as they might with Roosevelt, and they knew it. Adviser, troubleshooter, eyes and ears for the President—this was Hopkins. Hopkins also provided an alternative target for Roosevelt's detractors, although he did not relish that role. Through his activities in Lend-Lease, Hopkins' abilities came into sharp focus and revealed him as the second most important man in the administration of the United States' World War II effort.

Roosevelt decided and Hopkins concurred that in total war it was necessary to put the nation's resources to work where they would do the most good and to persuade America's allies to do the same. Lend-Lease, as a mutual aid concept, proved to be an excellent answer that fitted within the framework of United States law and at the same time gave Britain and other opponents of aggression access to United States industry on a scale that they could never purchase. Within the broad scope of Lend-Lease the United States would help her allies win the war; by having removed the dollar sign from the aid, the United States would not complicate postwar settlements with burdensome debts that might imperil the Alliance's solidarity at the war's end and divide it in the pursuit of peace. No concessions were to be wrung from American allies as a price of aid during the war, and especially did this rule apply to the Soviets. If they were grateful for the unstinting help during the war, they could co-operate at the peace table. Roosevelt aimed for this factor to be a decisive weapon in the settlement.

The failure of this "no-concessions" policy proved to be one of the tragedies of the war. This gamble of Roosevelt's failed partly because he could not control as many of the variables surrounding it as he could concerning the operation of the Lend-Lease program itself, partly because he did not realize that the objectives of Communism could not be changed by all the sincerity and good will he might ever command. On this point Soviet leaders were more realistic than those of the Western allies. They were as intransigent to deal with when the fortunes of war frowned upon them as they were a couple of decades later. The dealings with Russia on the Lend-Lease level illustrate as clearly as any other example that the Soviets never gave their allies any real reason to believe that a beautiful friendship was in the making.

In the beginning, Allied aid to Russia was partly a selfish necessity, a part of the realistic prerequisite for the defeat of Germany. The precarious military situation in the Soviet Union throughout 1941 and 1942 necessitated placing high priorities on shipments of war material to Russia, even when these same shipments disrupted urgent aid schedules for Great Britain or for United States military build-up, or both. Even Pearl Harbor brought only a slight pause to the Soviet program undertaken by United States industry. The aircraft program was realigned to include substantial deliveries to Russia at the expense of previous British–American agreements; Britain virtually stripped her Middle East command of tanks, and the United States shipped almost all of her medium tank production of November, 1941, through January, 1942, to the British in the Middle East to replace those sent to Russia. Armored trainees in the United States had to find substitutes to use in maneuvers. In March, 1942, all gasoline-powered light tanks were requisitioned from American and British schedules in order to meet the Soviet Protocol. All field telephone wire produced in the United States in January, 1942, and 90 per cent of that produced in February and March, was sent to Russia. Requisition of shipping facilities for the Russian deliveries further pinched the Anglo-American build-up in Britain and in the Pacific. In the manner of carrying out their aid promises to the Soviets, both Britain and the United States unstintingly did their best even to the point of severely hampering their own programs.

By the time of the Stalingrad victory, the danger that the Soviet Union would crumble under Nazi pressure became more and more remote. At the same time, the United States industrial program had picked up considerable momentum, and although the shipping situation remained stringent, Soviet aid demands caused less disruption of Anglo-American schedules than in the preceding year. At this point, on both counts, aid to Russia ceased to be a selfish necessity and became instead an act of unselfish generosity. Roosevelt and Hopkins maintained their decision that no political or economic concession should be wrung from the Soviet Union in return for Lend-Lease and continued to insist that Lend-Lease be continued and even expanded, not stopped or tapered off as some officials advocated. In fact the Third and Fourth protocols showed overages in some categories.

At all stages, the Americans, the British, and the Canadians carried the program through at far greater risks than the Soviets were willing to take to make it succeed. The Soviets refused to permit their Western allies to send military observers to the Eastern front as Britain and the United States wished to do in order to better determine Soviet needs. Although the Allies did work out the details of the ALSIB air delivery route, the Soviets initially resisted its establishment. The Soviets quarreled about delivery schedules and railroad allocations in the Persian Gulf. Soviet officers, often unrealistically, insisted upon more rigid specifications for the war equipment than did the war offices of Britain and the United States. The Soviets fussed about British personnel stationed in North Russia, closed down British radio stations there, allowed R.A.F. units to operate only sporadically, and never provided fighter cover for north-route convoys as they had promised. And yet the Soviets insisted that the north route provided the most useful and most direct delivery of all.

The Soviet leaders never understood, or at least never appeared to understand, the natural limitations on Lend-Lease exports. From the time of the Second Protocol on, an ever increasing share of United States production was devoted to the program, and if delivery had not been contested by the Nazis and unlimited shipping space had been available, a much larger share of United States production could possibly have been sent to Russia. The total tonnages exported to the Soviet Union under Lend-Lease amounted to relatively small percentages of total United States production, but total production grew fantastically, making percentage figures more deceptive. For example, in 1944, 2 per cent of the United States food supply was exported to the Soviet Union (13 per cent exported to United States Armed Forces, 4 per cent to other Lend-Lease beneficiaries, and 1 per cent in commercial export), but United States food production was up 35 per cent over the 1935–1939 average. Also in 1944, 20 per cent of the United States petroleum supply, 6 per cent of the metals, and 11 per cent of the munitions were exported, and all but a fraction of these transfers went to Great Britain and Russia, "the British predominating in a ratio of two to one."[1] Yet by 1944, United States industrial production was up about 280 per cent over the 1935–1939 average. Had greater shipping facilities, in particular, been available, it is likely that larger percentages of American production might have been exported to the Soviet Union. For one thing, they would not have had to select a certain tonnage from a larger offering that would be available; the entire offering would have been shipped. Had United States military advisors in the Soviet Union been permitted to estimate Red army needs more closely, this too would likely have resulted in a greater variety or a larger amount, or

[1] *19th Report on Lend-Lease,* 29, 47; (Julius A. Krug) *War Production in 1944, Report of the Chairman of the War Production Board,* 21.

both, of exports from American production. Yet Soviet leaders never admitted that any limitation existed, although they did agree to select urgent items from the total projected-aid lists.

All of the efforts of the Western allies to build up the Soviets to withstand and turn upon the Nazis, to carry out as carefully as possible, often under impossible conditions, their aid commitments, and to keep these commitments free from political entanglements in the hope that the Soviets would reciprocate at the peace table proved vain. It was not possible to purchase good will in the Soviet Union.

From the story of Lend-Lease to Russia emerges a narrative of unfettered aid to a suspicious ally, of a Red army given mobility that made it an incredible striking force, and of a shattered nation that received unquestionably valuable industrial potential to spark her reconstruction, all with virtually no attempt to credit her allies in any more than the most grudging way. Lend-Lease speeded the end of the war for the Russians and for the Western allies alike and, in that way, served its purpose well. As Stettinius wrote, it was a "weapon for victory." But because it enabled the Soviet Union to swallow much of Eastern and Central Europe, it did not prove to be a tool for peace. The Soviet outlook, as determined by its anti-Western orientation, was not modified by the wartime experience or by Lend-Lease. Roosevelt's garden hose helped put out the fire and served to splash a little water on the Soviet garden of reconstruction, but it did not make friends out of the intransigent neighbors.

"We cannot measure the sacrifice and heroism," wrote Truman, "of . . . the men and women on the production front here at home. Nor can we measure the contribution to victory of those allied fighting men who, with their own and lend-lease weapons fought and fell. . . . Each . . . has contributed to the pool of fighting power in accordance with [his] . . . abilities and capacities."[2]

[2] *19th Report on Lend-Lease*, 5.

APPENDIX A

TABLE I

Lend-Lease Shipments to the Soviet Union by Time Period, Cargo Type, Route, and Tonnage*

1. June 22, 1941–Sept. 30, 1941. Not shipped under Lend-Lease, but under $10,000,000 Treasury Department advance, the $50,000,000 Defense Supplies Corporation advance, and other arrangements.

Type of cargo	Atlantic	Pacific	Total	Distribution of total tonnage, percentage
U.S. supplies				
R.R. transportation equip.	0	0	0	0
Trucks and other vehicles	1,561	14	1,575	1
Metals	1,251	3,404	4,655	3
Chemicals and explosives	1,033	3,693	4,726	3
Petroleum products	9,500	120,854	130,354	79
Machinery and equip.	280	15,575	15,855	10
Food	19	3,899	3,918	2
Other U.S. supplies	1,258	1,365	2,623	1
Canadian and British supplies	0	0	0	0
Other Sources	0	2,494	2,494	1
TOTAL	14,902	151,298	166,200	100

2. Oct. 1, 1941–June 30, 1942, First Protocol period.

	Atlantic	Pacific	Total	Distribution of total tonnage, percentage
U.S. supplies				
R.R. transportation equip.	0	0	0	0
Trucks and other vehicles	214,148	16	214,164	15
Metals	411,619	12,906	424,525	30

Chemicals and explosives	55,542	465	56,007	4
Petroleum products	132,459	35,536	167,995	12
Machinery and equip.	29,116	576	29,692	2
Food	129,999	175,038	305,037	22
Other U.S. supplies	74,281	1,943	76,224	5
Canadian and British supplies	137,841	8,770	146,611	10
Other sources	0	0	0	0
TOTAL	1,185,005	235,250	1,420,255	100

3. July 1, 1942–June 30, 1943, Second Protocol period.

U.S. Supplies

R.R. transportation equip.	0	0	0	0
Trucks and other vehicles	308,919	139,569	448,488	15
Metals	460,874	289,016	749,890	24
Chemicals and explosives	70,697	110,669	181,366	6
Petroleum products	54,331	159,157	213,448	7
Machinery and equip.	28,604	139,864	168,468	5
Food	294,236	703,547	997,783	33
Other U.S. supplies	167,657	70,119	237,776	8
Canadian and British supplies	45,898	11,142	57,040	2
Other sources	0	0	0	0
TOTAL	1,431,216	1,623,083	3,054,299	100

* Report on War Aid, 1–8; all tonnages are in long tons.

Type of cargo	Atlantic	Pacific	Total	Distribution of total tonnage, percentage
4. July 1, 1943–June 30, 1944, Third Protocol period.				
U.S. supplies				
R.R. transportation equip.	39,455	31,011	70,466	1
Trucks and other vehicles	641,618	100,719	742,337	13
Metals	699,971	312,430	1,012,401	18
Chemicals and explosives	288,848	219,301	448,149	8
Petroleum products†	45,272	401,434	446,706	8
Machinery and equip.	182,335	305,166	487,501	8
Food	936,541	798,260	1,734,801	30
Other U.S. supplies	350,517	122,451	472,968	8
Canadian and British supplies	31,741	298,652	330,393	6
Other sources	0	0	0	0
TOTAL	3,156,298 [3,216,298]‡	2,589,424	5,745,722	100
5. July 1, 1944–May 12, 1945,§ Fourth Protocol period.				
U.S. supplies				
R.R. transportation equip.	146,901	208,838	355,739	6
Trucks and other vehicles	531,235	114,035	645,270	12
Metals	654,164	468,432	1,122,596	20
Chemicals and explosives	206,670	192,676	399,346	7
Petroleum products‖	250,455	498,285	748,740	13
Machinery and equip.	232,585	243,060	475,645	9

Food	553,674	603,699	1,157,373	21
Other U.S. supplies	188,986	121,515	310,501	6
Canadian and British supplies	51,863	265,707	317,570	6
Other sources	0	0	0	0
TOTAL	2,816,533	2,716,247	5,532,780	100

6. May 13, 1945—September 2, 1945, Operation *Milepost* period.

U.S. supplies

R.R. transportation equip.	9,067	32,313	41,380	3
Trucks and other vehicles	28,353	209,764	238,117	15
Metals	37,988	211,214	249,202	16
Chemicals and explosives	7,279	50,509	57,788	4
Petroleum products	34,496	371,670	406,166	26
Machinery and equip.	30,465	38,073	68,538	4
Food	22,594	235,607	258,201	17
Other U.S. supplies	13,972	103,235	117,207	8
Canadian and British supplies	7,613	97,487	105,100	7
TOTAL	191,827	1,349,872	1,541,699	100

† The United States sent 166,359 additional long tons from Abadan.
‡ The apparent discrepancy in arithmetic appears in the tables in Report on War Aid. There is no way of knowing if these are actually errors or if an unknown factor was involved. The figure in brackets appears to be correct.
§ The German surrender on May 8 brought a new policy of aid on May 12, with the discontinuation of the European front. By May 12, 95 per cent of the tonnage scheduled under the Fourth Protocol had already been exported.
‖ The United States sent 388,843 additional long tons from Abadan.

7. Sept. 3, 1945—Sept. 20, 1945, period of termination.

Type of cargo	Atlantic	Pacific	Total	Distribution of total tonnage, percentage
U.S. supplies				
R.R. transportation equip.	0	947	947	2
Trucks and other vehicles	0	879	879	2
Metals	2,801	9,014	11,815	30
Chemicals and explosives	39	343	382	1
Petroleum products	0	0	0	0
Machinery and equip.	819	1,330	2,149	5
Food	1,989	5,875	7,864	20
Other U.S. supplies	1,325	2,683	4,008	10
Canadian and British supplies	2,331	9,603	11,934	30
Other sources	0	0	0	0
TOTAL	9,304	30,674	39,978	100

SUMMARY: 17,500,900 long tons shipped from the United States. 16,429,800 long tons (94 per cent) shipped from the Western Hemisphere. Of the supplies sent to the Soviet Union from the Western Hemisphere from June 22, 1941 to September 20, 1945, 98 per cent was of Lend-Lease origin. The total value of these shipments is reported at approximately $10,200,000,000. In addition, supply services such as ocean transport on American vessels, repairs to Soviet ships, ship supplies, bunkers, port dues, training of Soviet crews for Lend-Lease aircraft, and ships were valued at approximately $700,000,000.

TABLE II

Aircraft Deliveries to the Soviet Union (by route)
June 22, 1941–September 20, 1945*

	ALSIB	S. Atlantic to Abadan	Water to N. Russia	Water to Abadan
Delivered at factories	8,058	1,055	1,543	4,142
Lost in the U.S.	74	17	0	0
Lost in Canada and Alaska	59	0	0	0
Departed N. America	7,925	1,038	1,543	4,142
Lost after departure	0	43	310	231
Arrived at destination	7,925	994	1,232	3,911
Delivered to U.S.S.R. at destination	7,925	993	1,232	3,868

TOTALS

   Delivered at factories: 14,798†

   Lost en route: 734

   Arrived at destination: 14,062

   Delivered to U.S.S.R. at destination: 14,018

* Report on War Aid, 18. This does not include deliveries destined for Britain but retransferred to the Soviet Union.
† This does not include PBN and PBY patrol planes.

TABLE III

Aircraft Deliveries to the Soviet Union (by type and route)
June 22, 1941–September 20, 1945*

Type	ALSIB	Water to N. Russia	Water to Abadan	S. Atlantic to Abadan	Total
Pursuit					
P-40	48	910	1,090	0	2,048
		49†	300†	0	349†
P-39	999	50	2,020	0	3,069
	1,592†	30†	961†		2,583†
	27‡	28‡			55‡
P-47	3	4	188	0	195
P-63	2,312				2,312
	85†	3†	0	0	85† [88]
					9,438 [13,014]
Light bomber					
A-20	1,363	126	550	869	2,908
Medium bomber					
B-25	733	5	0	124	862
Heavy bomber					
B-24	1§	0	0	0	1§

TOTAL

Cargo					
C–46	1	0	0	0	1
C–47	707	0	0	0	707
Observation					
O–52	0	19‖	0	0	19‖
Trainer					
AT6-c	0	8	20	0	28
AT6-F	54	0	0	0	54
				TOTAL	4,580

PBN and PBY navy patrol: 185, some delivered from North Carolina, some from Kodiak, Alaska.

* Report on War Aid, 18. This does not include deliveries destined for Britain but retransferred to the Soviet Union.

† Delivered on British account.

‡ Delivered on other Lend-Lease accounts (besides Britain and the Soviet Union).

§ This bomber carried a United States mission and was stranded in Siberia and then transferred to the Soviet Union.

‖ Thirty sent, eleven lost.

TABLE IV

Vehicles Delivered to the Soviet Union Under the Lend-Lease Program[*]

Items	Lend-Lease Export	Total Exports	Arrived	Lost En Route	Diverted[†]
Trucks					
Jeeps					
¼ ton 4×4	47,993	48,993	43,728	3,657	1,378
amphibious	3,510	3,510	3,510	0	0
Trucks					
¾ ton	25,240	25,240	24,564	78	598
1½ ton	153,415	159,494	148,664	6,660	1,826
2½ ton	190,952	193,603	182,938	4,300	1,130
2½ ton amphibious	589	589	586	3	0
5 ton and over	852	858	814	0	0
special purpose	2,792	2,792	2,784	8	0
Truck tractors (w/o trailer)	1,941	1,960	1,938	6	0
TOTAL	427,284	437,039	409,526	14,712	4,932
Trailers (w/o tractors)	102	105	105	0	0
Truck Engines	2,000	2,000	2,000	0	0

Ordnance Service Vehicles

Field repair trucks	1,543	1,543	1,534	9	0
Tank recovery units	130	130	130	0	0
Tank transporters	655	655	629	26	0
TOTAL	2,328	2,328	2,293	35	0

Combat Vehicles

Light tanks	1,682	1,682	1,239	443	0
Medium tanks	5,374	5,374	4,957	417	0
Self-propelled guns					
AT 75 mm.	5	5	5	0	0
AT 57 mm.	650	650	650	0	0
AT 3 in.	52	52	52	0	0

* Report on War Aid, 19–21. The total exports are sometimes greater than the total Lend-Lease exports because some items were shipped prior to Lend-Lease or on Soviet purchase orders. There are some further discrepancies in the figures from this report. For example, total jeep (¼ ton, 4x4) exports amount to 48,993, but the total found by adding arrivals + lost + diverted equals 48,763 (130 jeeps unaccountable). There is no way of knowing if these are actually errors or if an unknown factor was involved. The correction for one seemingly obvious error is shown in brackets.

† This column refers to orders that were originally destined for the Soviet Union but for certain reasons (rerouting of a ship, reduction of unshipped backlog) were diverted to another Lend-Lease account.

Items	Lend-Lease Export	Total Exports	Armored	Lost En Route	Diverted
AT 37 mm.	100	100	100	0	0
AA 50 cal.	1,000	1,000	1,000	0	0
Half-tracks	1,158	1,158	1,104	54	0
Armored scout cars	3,282	3,282	3,054	288	0
TOTAL	13,303	13,303	12,161	1,142 [1,202]	0
Motorcycles	35,170	35,170	32,200	1,870	1,100
Track-laying tractors	8,071	8,074	7,570	253	0
Engines for tractors	3,282	3,282	3,216	66	0
Railway Units					
Steam locomotives	1,911	1,911	1,900	11	0
Diesel-electric locomotives	70	70	66	4	0
Flat cars	10,000	10,000	9,920	80	0
Tank cars	120	120	120	0	0
Dump cars	1,000	1,000	1,000	0	0
Heavy machinery cars	35	35	35	0	0
TOTAL	13,136	13,136	13,041	95	0

TABLE V
Random Exports to the Soviet Union Under the Lend-Lease Program*

Items	Lend-Lease Export	Total Exports	Armored	Lost En Route	Diverted
Weapons					
Guns					
AA 90 mm.	270	270	241	9	0
AA 40 mm.	5,595	5,595	5,399	196	0
AA 37 mm.	424	424	340	16	0
AA 50 cal.	1,925	1,925	1,925	0	0
AA 4.7 in.	4	4	4	0	0
AT 27 mm.	63	63	35	28	0
Submachine guns, 45 cal.	131,633	135,633	112,293	23,340	0
Pistols and revolvers	13,000	13,000	11,500	1,500	0
Mortars	30	30	30	0	0
Smoke pots (1000 units)	1,423	1,423	1,423	0	0
Rocket launchers	3,000	3,000	3,000	0	0
Explosive (tons)					
Smokeless powder	140,531	140,531	129,667	4,909	0
Stick powder	2,210	2,210	2,210	0	0

* Random selection by the author from Report on War Aid, 19–26, 28. The total exports are sometimes greater than the total Lend-Lease exports because some items were shipped prior to Lend-Lease or on Soviet purchase orders. There are some further discrepancies in the figures from this report. For example, total gun (AA 90 mm.) exports amount to 270, but the total found by adding arrivals + lost + diverted equals 250 (20 guns unaccountable). There is no way of knowing if these are actually errors or if an unknown factor was involved.

Items	Lend-Lease Export	Total Exports	Armored	Lost En Route	Diverted
Other powder	18	57	55	2	0
Cordite powder	927	1,027	1,027	0	0
TNT	136,335	136,335	129,138	3,848	250
TNT (from U.K. acc't.)	10,048	10,048	10,048	0	0
Dynamite	46,153	46,153	46,153	0	0
Picric acid	1,649	1,649	1,411	92	0
Colloyxlin (nitrocellulose in alcohol)	7,864	7,864	6,075	1,401	86
Radio					
Stations†	35,941	36,871	35,800	966	32
Receivers†	5,898	5,968	5,899	69	0
Locators†	380	380	348	32	0
Direction finders	705	705	705	0	0
Altimeters	538	538	538	0	0
Beacons	63	63	63	0	0
Compasses	800	800	800	0	0
Parts, etc. ($1,000)	7,577	7,620	7,526	59	0
Construction machinery (road, aircraft, railway, mixers, pavers) ($1,000)	10,910	11,038	10,792	144	0
Foodstuffs (tons)					
Wheat	55,713	55,713	55,713	600	0

Wheat flour	659,051	659,051	638,796	8,827	5,062
Other flour	40,121	40,121	40,121	0	0
Other finished cereals and products	112,550	112,550	109,629	1,065	528
Dried peas and beans	270,514	270,514	239,429	7,905	23,138
Seeds‡	37,477	37,477	37,437	40	0
Sugar, U.S. stocks	532,845	532,845	502,195	18,285	12,364
Sugar, other sources	170,234	170,234	170,234	0	0
Canned dehydrated meat	14,942	14,942	14,942	0	0
Canned Tushonka	272,009	272,009	265,569	2,904	0
Other canned meat	485,181	485,181	452,084	17,497	15,422
Fatcuts	299,758	300,230	292,742	3,328	4,142
Butters§	69,772	69,772	67,876	1,010	735
Lard	316,824	317,908	293,210	7,833	16,846
Vegetable oil, shortening oleo, and other oils	520,800	521,195	517,522	1,533	2,140
Canned milk	31,021	31,021	30,727	282	0
Dried milk	77,352	77,352	71,410	1,145	4,394
Dried eggs	121,144	121,144	110,651	4,949	5,296
Soya flour and grits	71,075	71,075	66,504	0	0
Coffee	10,581	10,910	10,350	0	560
Feed	33,631	33,631	28,417	5,214	0

† Incomplete accounting as of the date of the report.

‡ Russian War Relief, a private agency, sent 2,307 tons of seeds on Lend-Lease ships.

§ The Soviet Union was the *only* recipient of butter under the Lend-Lease program.

Items	Lend-Lease Export	Total Exports	Armored	Lost En Route	Diverted
Tools, machinery, and telephone equipment ($1,000)					
Generator sets, military, marine, and other	175,804	175,900	173,745	1,123	0
Machine tools	305,899	323,895	310,058	8,607	0
Secondary metal-forming machinery	59,215	68,738	66,567	995	27
Metal-cutting tools	34,736	34,936	34,878	55	0
Excavating and dredging machinery	33,443	34,241	31,050	2,036	1,005
Field telephones	19,272	19,552	16,968	1,850	26
field telephone units	415,426	422,426	380,135	39,238	—
Other telephone and telegraph equipment	14,324	14,572	14,419	59	0
Steel (tons)					
Hot-rolled aircraft steel	237,580	237,580	233,170	3,401	0
Cold-finished bars	171,555	171,555	160,248	7,407	671
Cold-rolled sheets	100,681	100,681	68,582	29,697	1,709
Tin Plate	169,616	169,953	153,971	11,696	2,871
Rails and accessories	721,047	721,047	685,740	25,835	1,421
Hot-rolled sheets and plates	393,052	393,052	365,612	19,693	2,357
Steel pipe and tubing	244,096	244,096	222,107	17,320	1,654
Steel wire	123,975	123,975	115,555	6,289	673
Tool steel	43,396	43,609	40,766	1,640	48
High-speed tool steel	15,065	15,065	14,203	554	0

Bimetal	44,544	44,544	1,093	0
Stainless steel	13,156	12,822	98	0
Armor plate	8,950	5,786	2,897	267
Alloys (tons)				
Ferro-silicon	8,028	7,174	1,050	0
Ferro-chromium	4,197	3,703	494	0
Ferro-molybdenum	2,906	2,906	0	0
Molybdenum concentrates	15,850	16,949	1,430	0
Cable and wire (miles)				
Marine cable	2,339	2,118	129	0
Submarine cable	1,186	1,136	50	0
Field telegraph wire	1,105,024	956,688	134,684	197
Metals (tons)				
Copper				
base alloys	356,523	359,599	17,510	0
tubes, etc.	35,751	34,168	1,193	36
electrolytic	17,944	17,944	0	0
Aluminum ingots and bars	193,163	189,237	5,293	0
Fabricated aluminum	68,320	71,872	2,393	0
Zinc	57,148	54,826	2,323	0
Lead	20,145	20,139	0	0
Pig nickel	14,671	13,843	828	0
Magnesium	9,060	9,060	0	0
Petroleum products (tons)				
Gasoline blending agents||	729,225	732,295	17,236	12,373

|| An additional 102,132 tons of blending agents sent to Russia were charged to Lend-Lease from the Abadan refinery.

Items	Lend-Lease Export	Total Exports	Armored	Lost En Route	Diverted
Aviation gasoline over 99 octane	602,949	628,134	590,434	0	37,650
Aviation gasoline, 87–99 octane#	18,220	148,949	122,415	2,069	24,465
Aviation gasoline, 87 octane and under	19,269	19,690	19,690	0	0
Automotive gasoline	207,222	278,770	267,088	0	11,682
Kerosene	16,864	16,870	16,870	0	0
Fuel oil	269,639	288,661	287,262	0	0
Lubricating oil and grease	104,841	114,919	111,676	1,678	0
Aviation gasoline over 99 octane from other accounts**	572,979	572,979	572,979	0	0
Cloth, rubber, leather					
Cotton cloth (1,000 yds.)	106,893	106,895	102,673	2,662	0
Woolen cloth (1,000 yds.)	62,485	62,748	60,138	1,258	0
Webbing (1,000 yds.)	55,843	58,257	53,803	2,427	0
Tarpaulin (1,000 yds.)	13,432	13,667	13,528	74	0
Cordage and twine (tons)	14,805	15,582	15,356	90	0
Leather (tons)	49,861	51,815	46,161	4,861	469
Rubber (tons)					
crude	269	269	269	0	0
Vistanex (synthetic rubber)	998	1,012	984	28	0
other synthetic rubber	10,221	10,224	9,825	0	0
Tires (1,000 units)††	3,775	3,786	3,606	110	61
Tubes (1,000 units)††	3,813	3,824	3,640	111	63

Rubber hose ($1,000)	7,888	7,939	7,784	155	0
Other rubber items ($1,000)	21,114	21,118	20,843	174	0
Boots (1,000 pair)					
army	14,704	15,417	14,572	578	6
ski	225	225	221	0	0
Chemical products (tons)					
Caustic soda	99,052	99,075	98,210	707	0
Ammonium nitrate	3,394	3,394	2,602	113	0
Acetone	12,977	12,977	12,264	654	0
Ethyl alcohol	388,449	388,449	379,742	159	0
Toluol	116,619	119,246	113,884	3,192	359
Phenol	40,453	40,901	38,549	1,732	171
Methanol	28,070	28,070	23,774	3,242	371
Paper					
Parchment (tons)	4,208	4,221	4,201	0	0
Map (tons)	9,277	9,280	8,835	265	0
Cigarette (tons)	1,055	1,055	987	68	0
Photo film ($1,000)	1,684	1,703	1,631	59	0
Miscellaneous ($1,000)					
Asbestos material	478	491	483	4	0
Buttons	1,647	1,647	1,598	49	0

An additional 14,718 tons of 87–99 octane sent to Russia were charged to Russian Lend-Lease from the United Kingdom account.

** The other accounts were the United Kingdom and the Abadan refinery.

†† There were 75,000 tires and 36,000 tubes transferred by the United Kingdom to Russia and charged to the United States.

TABLE VI

Distribution of Tonnage* by Ship Registry†
(Vessels involved in the transfer of Lend-Lease to the Soviet Union)
June 22, 1941–September 20, 1945*

Category	Tonnage	Percentage
United States ships	8,199,000	46.8
United States ships transferred to Soviet registry	5,367,000	30.7
Soviet ships	3,401,000	19.4
Others	534,000	3.1

* Gross long tons.
† Report on War Aid, 10.

TABLE VII

Cargo Shipped from the Western Hemisphere to the Soviet Union
June 22, 1941–September 20, 1945*

Route	Amount shipped (gross long tons)	Arrived %	Lost %	En route %
North Russia	3,964,000	93	7	0
Persian Gulf‡	4,160,000	96	4	0
Black Sea	681,000	99	0	1
Soviet Far East	8,244,000	99	0	1
Soviet Arctic	452,000	100	0	0

TOTALS

Amount shipped: 17,501,000
Arrived in Russia: 16,587,000 (83)†
Discharged in Britain: 343,000§
Lost: 488,000

* Report on War Aid, 15, 29.
† En route September 20, 1945.
‡Shipment to the Gulf by several routes; the tonnage includes all routes.
§ The major portion was discharged in the United Kingdom in 1942–1943 and reshipped to North Russia without any loss.

TABLE VIII

Possible Wartime Uses of Inorganic and Organic Chemicals
Lend-Leased to Russia in Largest Quantities*

Inorganic

Caustic soda: rayon, chemicals, soap, petroleum refining
Ammonium nitrate: explosive and plant food
Boric acid: antiseptic
Calcium chloride: concrete, dust preventative for roads and mines
Phosphorus: fire bombs
Potassium dichromate: tanning, dyeing, waterproofing fabrics
Potassium nitrate (saltpeter): nitric acid, high explosives, black powder
Soda ash: glass, washing compound, soap, and many other uses
Sodium bromide: photography, source of bromine for tear gas or dyes
Sodium dichromate: same as potassium dichromate (above)

Organic

Acetone: high explosives (cordite and smokeless powder)
Ethyl alcohol: many uses (including drinking)
Ethylene glycol: antifreeze, nitroglycerine and dynamite
Glycerine: explosives, nitroglycerine and dynamite
Methanol: solvent (shellac and varnish), antifreeze, source of formalde-
    hyde for plastics
Phenol: plastic (bakelite), or picric acid (explosive)
Toluol: explosive–TNT
Aniline Oil: black dye source
Butyl acetate: lacquer thinner
Butyl alcohol: solvent
Camphor: plasticizer for smokeless powder and celluloid
Casein: glue, plastics
Citric acid: medicine and beverages
Dibutyl phthalate: plasticizer for lacquers, etc.
Diethylene glycol: wetting agent
Dimethyl aniline: explosive ingredient of Tetryl (tetryl is shock sensitive
    and used for detonators)
Diphenylamine: stabilizer for cordite and smokeless powder

* Analysis through the courtesy of Eli W. Blaha, Ph.D., research chemist.

Ethyl acetate: lacquer thinner
Ethylene dibromide: lead scavenger for gasoline
Furfural: plastics (durite)
Hexamine (hexamethylene tetramine): ingredient of hexogen, explosive similar to tetryl

APPENDIX B

ATOMIC ESPIONAGE AND LEND-LEASE

MAJOR GEORGE RACEY JORDAN, a veteran air force officer stationed during part of the war at Great Falls, Montana (an ALSIB terminal), charged various United States officials (including the Lend-Lease Administration and, specifically, Vice-President Henry Wallace and presidential assistant Harry Hopkins) with aiding and abetting Soviet espionage by allowing the export of atomic materials and tons of classified documents over ALSIB to Russia. In a series of postwar radio broadcasts (1949) with commentator Fulton Lewis Jr. and in a book devoted to the subject, Jordan presented his case. The House Un-American Activities Committee and the Joint Committee on Atomic Energy examined Jordan's allegations.[1]

Jordan observed the transfer of large amounts of documents, blueprints, drawings, and technical information on B-25's and other aircraft bound for the Soviet Union. He was convinced, partly by the guard posted over the material, partly by his suspicious attitude of the Soviet officials, and partly by his own unauthorized inspections, that military secrets were being shipped out of the country in large batches. In the years following the war, when the knowledge of the Manhattan District project became generally known, Jordan believed that his worst suspicions had been confirmed. He thought that the Soviets had smuggled atomic materials and other related information from the United States to Russia, using the ALSIB connection at least in part.

When Jordan appeared before the Joint Committee on Atomic En-

[1] George Racey Jordan, *From Major Jordan's Diaries, passim*; U.S. Congress, Joint Committee on Atomic Energy, *Soviet Atomic Espionage, 184.*

ergy in 1950, he put eight specific charges before them. The committee conducted a careful investigation into Jordan's accusations. The committee had little difficulty explaining the amount of paper shipped to Russia. "The documents . . . [specifications for a B-25, for example] would make a stack 3 feet high. A large volume of blueprints, documents, and papers was required for such Lend-Lease items as the oil refinery and the synthetic rubber plants shipped to Russia." The heavy flow of paper, the committee observed, "also suggests the difficulty of definitely establishing that no single piece of paper relating to the atomic energy program was surreptitiously taken or sent out of the country." Also it was a simple matter to include all sorts of materials in diplomatic pouches, of which there was a great volume and which, by their nature, enjoyed immunity from search.[2]

Various materials on facets of atomic research as carried on by the universities of the country were not secret, and prewar investigations into and the construction of particle accelerators, such as cyclotrons, could have been carried out of the country. The Soviets built at least one such machine. Uranium, a by-product of radium production, had been known since the turn of the century, and was used in coloring ceramics, in photography, and in the laboratory (as an analytical agent). It was quite expensive since the demand always exceeded the supply. "Before January 26, 1943," the Joint Committee reported, "there were no unusual United States Government controls on delivery, price, or use of uranium; but on that date its ceramic and photographic uses were forbidden by WPB Order No. M–285. Other legal restrictions were not applied as the Manhattan District did not wish to call attention to this material." The result was that 200 pounds of uranium oxide, 220 pounds of uranium nitrate, and less than 25 pounds of impure uranium metal were shipped to Russia under export license. In addition, a Canadian corporation sold Russia 500 pounds of ura-

[2] *Soviet Atomic Espionage*, 185. Members of the Joint Committee were: Brien McMahon (D), Connecticut, chairman; Carl T. Durham (D), North Carolina, vice-chairman; Richard B. Russell (D), Georgia; Edwin C. Johnson (D), Colorado; Tom Connally (D), Texas; Clinton P. Anderson (D), New Mexico; Bourke B. Hickenlooper (R), Iowa; Eugene D. Millikin (R), Colorado; William F. Knowland (R), California; John W. Bricker (R), Ohio; Chet Holifield (D), California; Melvin Price (D), Illinois; Paul J. Kilday (D), Texas; Henry M. Jackson (D), Washington; W. Sterling Cole (R), New York; Charles H. Elston (R), Ohio; Carl Hinshaw (R), California; James E. Van Zandt (R), Pennsylvania.

nium oxide and 500 pounds of uranium nitrate in 1943. Heavy water, "a scientific curiosity" with no industrial or military use (before 1943), also moved unrestricted. The Soviets received 1,100 grams, a shipment cleared by Lend-Lease, the War Production Board, the State Department, and Manhattan District officials. "The records indicate . . . refusal to ship might have been more informative to the Russians than any help they could derive from the small quantities of materials requested." Subsequent Soviet requests for nine long tons of uranium nitrate were rejected because the material was not available.[3]

The committee queried officials of the Manhattan District, officials of various other government agencies, former Vice-President Wallace, and close associates of Hopkins. They could find no basis for Jordan's charges against the individuals. Jordan himself told the committee, that "he was uncertain" of the details relating to his Hopkins charge, which he had made on Fulton Lewis' radio program. The committee found no indication that any unauthorized documents or other important papers were sent over ALSIB, but they took note of the volume and observed that they must "preclude any positive statement that nothing ever went to Russia without approval." The committee concluded that the shipments of atomic materials were made with the full knowledge and consent of the United States government.[4]

The same Joint Committee report, which gave Lend-Lease a clean bill of health, also reported on Soviet espionage in the United States, its structure, and something of its history. One Russian involved was connected with Amtorg, in New York, and directed the courier Harry Gold, who in turn had contact with Klaus Fuchs, David Greenglass, and the Rosenbergs. Although the Rosenbergs were not suppliers of atomic information, a theoretical physicist such as Fuchs and a bomb mechanic such as Greenglass certainly furnished the Soviets with valuable atomic bomb information.[5]

Since Semen M. Semenov in Amtorg and Anatoli Yakovlev in the Russian consulate in New York City were procuring information from experts in atomic research, the possibility is increased that some of this might have been in the volume of papers or the diplomatic pouches that traveled over ALSIB. That is, however, vastly different from laxity, permissiveness, or corruption of Lend-Lease officials.

[3] *Soviet Atomic Espionage,* 184–87.
[4] *Ibid.,* 190–92.   [5] *Ibid.,* 1–4.

APPENDIX C

CHRONOLOGY OF EVENTS

1939

Aug. 23	Russo-German Non-Aggression Pact.
Sept. 1	German invasion of Poland.
Sept. 3	France and the United Kingdom declare war on Germany.
Sept. 5	United States invokes Neutrality Act against belligerents.
Nov. 4	Arms embargo to belligerents lifted but exports limited to cash and carry.
Nov. 30	Russia attacks Finland.
Dec. 6	President's Liaison Committee established to oversee aid to Allies.
Dec.	U.S. places moral embargo on strategic material shipments to U.S.S.R.

1940

March 12	Russo-Finnish armistice.
May 10	Germany invades the Netherlands, Belgium, and Luxembourg. Churchill becomes prime minister.
May	U.S. "Rainbow 4" plan for hemispheric defense prepared. Approved by the President in July.
	U.S. Army and National Guard strength increased.
	U.S. Navy begins Atlantic "Neutrality patrol."
May 29	President reactivates Advisory Commission to the Council on National Defense.

June	Russia occupies Estonia, Latvia, and Lithuania.
June 10	Italy attacks France.
June 17	France sues for peace.
June 22	Surplus military supplies sold to Britain.
June	Wendell Willkie nominated by Republicans for President.
July	Democrats nominate Roosevelt for third term.
Aug.–Sept.	German air assault on Britain.
Sept. 3	Destroyers for bases deal consummated.
Sept.	R.A.F. regains control of British skies.
Sept.	U.S. begins first peacetime military draft in history.
Oct. 21	Roosevelt establishes Priorities Board within the Advisory Commission to the Council on National Defense.
Nov.	Roosevelt elected to third term as President.
Dec. 18	Roosevelt's "garden hose" speech.
Dec. 29	Roosevelt's "Arsenal of Democracy" fireside chat.

1941

Jan. 6	Roosevelt's State of the Union message stresses aid to Britain.
Jan. 10	Lend-Lease bill introduced into Congress.
Jan. 21	Moral embargo on U.S.S.R. lifted.
March 1	Soviet ambassador informed of planned Nazi invasion of Russia.
March 2	Bulgaria joins Axis.
March 11	Lend-Lease Act passed and signed by Roosevelt. Great Britain and Greece brought under Lend-Lease.
March 27	Congress appropriates $7,000,000,000 for Lend-Lease.
April 6	Nazis invade Yugoslavia.
April 10	Greenland occupied by U.S. "Neutrality Zone" extended eastward to longitude 25° west.
April 14	German African troops cross into Egypt.
April 23	Nazis occupy Athens.
April 24	Navy extends patrols to 26°west longitude.
April–June	Wolf packs of Nazi submarines cause heavy Allied

	losses in Atlantic; Nazi surface fleet threatens Atlantic shipping.
May 2	Division of Defense Aid Reports established in Office of Emergency Management to handle Lend-Lease.
May 6	Major-General James H. Burns named executive officer of the Division of Defense Aid Reports.
May 27	Roosevelt proclaims an unlimited national emergency.
June 14	U.S. freezes assets of all continental European powers including Russia.
June 21	Germany invades Russia.
June 24	Roosevelt promises aid to Russia; Soviet assets in the U.S. unfrozen.
June 25	Roosevelt refuses to apply provisions of Neutrality Act to Russia, thus keeping Far Eastern supply lines open.
June 30	First Soviet arm request made to U.S.
July 1	Iceland occupied.
July 9	Roosevelt orders all possible aid sent to Russia before October 1.
July 11	Division of Defense Aid Reports establishes special section to take care of Soviet aid.
July 13	Hopkins flies to Britain to confer with Churchill.
July 28	Hopkins flies on to Russia to confer with Stalin.
Aug. 9	Atlantic Charter meeting begins.
Aug. 12	Military draft in U.S. extended by one vote.
Aug. 28	Supply, Priorities, and Allocations Board established.
Sept. 11	U.S. begins to escort shipping to Iceland.
Sept. 12	Defense Supplies Corporation agrees to purchase $100,000,000 of strategic materials from Russia.
Sept. 13	U.S. moves into Iran and extends Lend-Lease to Iran.
Sept. 16	U.S. Navy escorts American shipping to 22° west longitude; Edward R. Stettinius Jr. appointed Lend-Lease administrator.

Sept. 28	U.S., U.S.S.R., and U.K. supply conference opens in Moscow.
Oct. 1	First Soviet Protocol signed in Moscow.
Oct. 28	Second Lend-Lease appropriation, $5,985,000,000; Office of Lend-Lease Administration established.
Oct. 30	Roosevelt credits $1,000,000,000 to Russia under Lend-Lease.
Nov. 7	Defense of Russia declared vital to defense of U.S., formally bringing Russia into Lend-Lease.
Dec. 4	Victory Program feasibility report completed.
Dec. 7	Japanese attack Pearl Harbor; Lend-Lease shipments suspended.
Dec. 8	U.S. declares war on Japan.
Dec. 11	Germany and Italy declare war on U.S.; U.S. declares war on Germany and Italy.
Dec. 22	*ARCADIA* conference begins in Washington.
Dec. 28	Lend-Lease shipments ordered resumed as planned; deficits to be wiped out by April 1.

1942

Jan.–March	Nazis build up sea and air strength in northern Norway.
Jan. 16	Roosevelt creates the War Production Board.
Feb.	Roosevelt extends a second $1,000,000,000 credit to Russia for Lend-Lease.
March 1	Nazis attack northern-routed Allied convoys to Russia in force.
March 5	Third Lend-Lease appropriation, $5,425,000,000.
April 7	Standley, new U.S. ambassador, arrives in Russia.
May 7	Draft of Second Soviet Protocol readied by U.S. planners.
May 26	Litvinov given draft of Lend-Lease Master Agreement.
May 30	Molotov given draft of Second Protocol.
June 11	Soviets sign Lend-Lease Master Agreement; which supersedes all previous Lend-Lease financial agreements with Russia.

July 1	Second Protocol goes into effect although not signed.
July 4	North route Convoy P.Q. 17 broken up by Nazi sea and air attack, future convoys suspended on North route.
Sept. 2	North route convoys resumed.
Sept. 3	The Alaska-Siberia route for flight delivery of aircraft to Russia (ALSIB) opened.
Sept. 5	North route convoys suspended again; "trickle" method (independent sailings) used until convoys resume.
Oct. 1	U.S. takes command of Persian Gulf route operations.
Oct. 6	Second Soviet Protocol signed.
Oct. 30	Roosevelt establishes the President's Soviet Protocol Committee with Hopkins as chairman to co-ordinate Soviet aid.
Nov. 1	U.S. begins transfer of fifty-nine cargo ships to Russia, for use on Pacific route.
Nov. 8	*TORCH* (Allied North African) landings.
Dec. 15	North route convoys resumed.

1943

Jan. 14–24	Casablanca meeting of Roosevelt and Churchill.
March	North route convoys suspended.
March 8	Ambassador Standley accuses Soviets of not telling Russian people of Lend-Lease aid.
March 11	Lend-Lease Act extended for one year.
May	First Allied convoy through Mediterranean since 1941.
May 3	Standley resigns as ambassador to Russia.
May 11	*TRIDENT* conference of Churchill and Roosevelt begins in Washington.
June 14	Fourth Lend-Lease appropriation, $6,273,629,000, passes Congress.
July 1	Third Soviet Protocol goes into effect.
July 9	Allied forces land in Sicily.

Aug. 11–24	*QUADRANT* Conference of Roosevelt and Churchill at Quebec.
Sept. 25	Foreign Economic Administration, with Leo T. Crowley as administrator, created by Roosevelt; absorbs Office of Lend-Lease Administration. Stettinius appointed under secretary of state.
Oct. 18	Harriman, new U.S. Ambassador, arrives in Russia; Secretary of State Hull also arrives in Russia for meeting of Foreign Ministers.
Oct. 19	Third Soviet Protocol is signed.
Nov. 1	North route convoys resume.
Nov. 22–27	Cairo Conference of Roosevelt, Churchill, Chiang Kai-shek.
Nov. 28–Dec. 1	*EUREKA* conference of Roosevelt, Churchill, Stalin at Teheran.
Dec. 26	British navy destroys *Scharnhorst* as it attempted to break up a north route convoy.

1944

Jan. 20	Red army breaks siege of Leningrad after twenty-nine months.
May 1	North route convoys suspended.
May 17	Lend-Lease Act extended for one year.
June–Sept.	U.S. shuttle-bombing bases in Ukraine operate for seven missions.
June 4	Rome liberated.
June 6	D-day; Allied forces land in France.
June 30	Fifth Lend-Lease appropriation, $3,538,869,000.
July 1	Fourth Soviet Protocol goes into effect.
July	Peak month for discharge of cargo at Persian Gulf ports.
Aug. 15	North route convoys resumed.
Sept. 11–16	Second Quebec Conference between Roosevelt and Churchill.
Oct. 20	American forces land in the Philippine Islands.
Nov.	Roosevelt elected to a fourth term as President.
Dec. 16	Battle of the Bulge begins.

1945

Jan.	Black Sea supply route to Russia opened.
Feb. 4–11	*ARGONAUT* Conference of Roosevelt, Churchill, Stalin at Yalta.
April 1	American forces land on Okinawa.
April 12	Roosevelt dies; Truman becomes President.
April 16	Lend-Lease extended to July 1, 1946.
April 17	Fourth Soviet Protocol signed.
April 25	United Nations Conference convenes at San Francisco.
May 8	V–E Day; Crowley cuts Lend-Lease.
May 12	Fourth Protocol ends, but deliveries to Russia under *MILEPOST* agreement and "pipeline" continue.
July 5	Sixth Lend-Lease appropriation, $2,475,000,000.
July 17–Aug. 2	Potsdam Conference.
Aug. 6	Atomic bomb dropped on Hiroshima.
Aug. 8	Russia enters war against Japan.
Aug. 9	Atomic bomb dropped on Nagasaki.
Aug. 14	Japan surrenders.
Aug. 21	Truman orders Crowley to end Lend-Lease.
Sept. 2	V–J Day.
Sept. 20	End of all Lend-Lease to Russia; President's Soviet Protocol Committee dissolved.
Oct. 15	Russia signs pipeline agreement to purchase all Lend-Lease materials under contract or in storage.
Oct. 20	Foreign Economic Administration abolished; Lend-Lease matters transferred to State Department.

1946

Dec. 31	All pipeline agreements ended by controller general (all except Russia's resumed in 1948).

BIBLIOGRAPHY

Bibliographical Note

Important primary manuscript materials included *Report on War Aid Furnished by the United States to the U.S.S.R.*, made available by the Department of State's Research Guidance and Review Division, along with George M. Fennemore's *The Role of the Department of State in Connection with the Lend-Lease Program.* A number of items from the Franklin D. Roosevelt Library, such as various segments of the *President's Official File*, proved of obvious value, as did similar items from the Harry S Truman Library. Publications of the Civilian Production Administration (such as *Industrial Mobilization for War: History of the War Production Board and Predecessor Agencies, 1940–1945*), minutes from various agency meetings (such as those of the Advisory Commission to the Council of National Defense, the O.P.M., the S.P.A.B., and the W.P.B.), and the War Production Board's special studies, (such as Chaikin and Coleman's *Shipbuilding Policies of the War Production Board, January 1942–November 1945*) were of basic value. Census Bureau reports, Treasury Department reports, Department of State publications, such as the *Soviet Supply Protocols,* were very useful. The President's (quarterly) *Reports to Congress on Lend-Lease Operations* and various publications of the Office of Lend-Lease Administration itself were especially valuable.

The Hopkins papers remain the most significant "closed" records (closed except as noted among the Roosevelt items). Even the material available to Robert E. Sherwood for his monumental *Roosevelt and Hopkins* is not cleared for the historian to use. Therefore,

Sherwood's book has to stand as a source in itself until the Hopkins files are opened. Much the same comment applies to various army records. Leighton and Coakley's *Global Logistics* and Motter's *Persian Corridor,* along with other of the War Department official histories, fall in the same category as *Roosevelt and Hopkins.* Personal accounts, such as Deane's *Strange Alliance* (and his personal comment to the author), Ickes' *Secret Diary,* Stimson's *Memoirs,* and others are important biographical materials. *Correspondence Between the Chairman of the Council of Ministers of the U.S.S.R. and the Presidents of the U.S.A. and the Prime Ministers of Great Britain During the Great Patriotic War of 1941–1945* comes from untouchable Kremlin archives, but it can be frequently cross-checked in Churchill's history of World War II and the published volumes of the *Foreign Relations of the United States* series. A doctoral dissertation, Carr's "Great Falls to Nome: The Inland Air Route to Alaska, 1940–1945," was originally prepared as part of the air force history and proved quite valuable, as was Bates's "The Arctic Life Line," an M.A. thesis based on a personal diary.

In nearly the same category as the War Department histories is Samuel Eliot Morison's naval history. I leaned heavily upon and am much indebted to his colorful account. Much more recent is Stephen W. Roskill's *The War at Sea,* part of the official British history of World War II. Roskill offers a wider variety of statistics than does Morison, but he had the advantage of later publication. By using both Morison and Roskill, superb, detailed accounts of the sea action can be obtained.

BIBLIOGRAPHY

Manuscript Sources

Fennemore, George M. The Role of the Department of State in Connection with the Lend-Lease Program. Department of State, Division of Research and Publication, April 3, 1943, typescript.

Lend-Lease Clinic. Office of Lend-Lease Administration, June 2, 1942, mimeographed.

Report on War Aid Furnished by the United States to the U.S.S.R. Department of State, Protocol and Area Information Staff of the

U.S.S.R. Branch, and Division of Research and Reports, November 28, 1945.

Roosevelt, Franklin D. (Records from the Franklin D. Roosevelt Library, National Archives and Records Service, Hyde Park, New York.)

President's Official File 4193, Lend-Lease Agreement, 1941–1945, Boxes 1–8.

President's Official File 4559, Office of Lend-Lease Administration, 1941–1945.

President's Official File 173, Transportation, 1940–1942, Box 2.

President's Official File 173–B, Transportation Miscellaneous, through 1944.

President's Official File 220, Russia, 1941–1945, Box 2.

President's Official File 220–A, Russia Miscellaneous, 1942–1943, Box 7.

President's Official File 25, War Department, 1941–1945, Boxes 8, 9.

President's Official File 21, Treasury Department, 1940–1945.

President's Official File 4529, Isador Lubin, 1937–1945.

President's Official File 4725–H, Isador Lubin, 1945.

President's Secretary's File, Box 32, Harry Hopkins.

President's Secretary's File II, Departmental Correspondence, Navy Department, 1936–1945, Boxes 20, 21.

President's Secretary's File, Russia, Box 14.

President's Secretary's File, War Department, Box 27.

President's Secretary's File, Henry L. Stimson, Box 27.

President's Secretary's File, Henry Morgenthau Jr., 1939–1944.

President's Personal File 4096, Harry Hopkins.

President's Personal File 2987, Sir Stafford Cripps.

President's Press Conferences, Volumes 16 and 17, Boxes 236, 237.

Truman, Harry S (Records from the Harry S Truman Library, National Archives and Records Service, Independence, Missouri.)

President's Official Files, 349–356, Box 1037.

President's Official Files 356–357, Box 1038.

Also, file folders bearing the following designations:

Lend-Lease.

Lend-Lease Operations.

Lend-Lease Report.
Lend-Lease (Only). [Letters to Truman from citizens.]

Public Documents

Jones, S. Shepard, and Denys P. Myers, eds. *Documents on American Foreign Relations.* Vol. III, July 1940–June 1941. Boston, World Peace Foundation, 1941.

Stettinius, Edward R., Jr. *Report to the 78th Congress on Lend-Lease Operations.* Bound with *President's Reports on Lend-Lease Operations,* following Seventh Report, see U.S. President.

U.S. Bureau of the Budget, War Records Section. *The United States at War. (Historical Reports on War Administration: Bureau of the Budget,* No. 1.) Washington, D.C., Government Printing Office, 1947.

U.S. Bureau of the Census. *Annual Survey of Manufactures: Fuels Consumed and Electrical Energy Produced, 1950.* Washington, D.C., Government Printing Office, 1953.

U.S. Civilian Production Administration, Bureau of Demobilization. *Chronology of the War Production Board and Predecessor Agencies, August 1939 to November 1945. Historical Reports on War Administration: War Production Board, Miscellaneous Publication* No. 1. June 20, 1946. Multilith.

——. *Industrial Mobilization for War: History of the War Production Board and Predecessor Agencies, 1940–1945.* Washington, D.C., Government Printing Office, 1947.

——. *Minutes of the Advisory Commission to the Council of National Defense. (Historical Reports on War Administration: War Production Board, Documentary Publication* No. 1.) Washington, D.C., Government Printing Office, 1946.

——. *Minutes of the Council of the Office of Production Management. Historical Reports on War Administration: War Production Board, Documentary Publication* No. 2. Washington, D.C., Government Printing Office, 1946.

——. *Minutes of the Supply Priorities and Allocations Board. Historical Reports on War Administration: War Production Board, Documentary Publication* No. 3. Washington, D.C., Government Printing Office, 1946.

———. *Minutes of the War Production Board. Historical Reports on War Administration: War Production Board, Documentary Publication* No. 4. Washington, D.C., Government Printing Office, 1946.

———. *Minutes of the Planning Committee of the War Production Board. Historical Reports on War Administration: War Production Board, Documentary Publication* No. 5. Washington, D.C., Government Printing Office, 1946.

———. *Historical Reports on War Administration: War Production Board, Special Study.*

No. 22. Charles M. Wiltse. *Aluminum Policies of the War Production Board and Predecessor Agencies, May 1940 to November 1945.* July 15, 1946, multilith.

No. 23. Richard J. Purcell. *Labor Policies of the National Defense Advisory Commission and the Office of Production Management May 1940–April 1942.* October, 1946, multilith.

No. 26. William Chaikin and Charles H. Coleman. *Ship-building Policies of the War Production Board January 1942–November 1945.* April 15, 1947, multilith.

U.S. Congress. Joint Committee on Atomic Energy. *Soviet Atomic Espionage.* 82 Cong., 1 sess., Joint Committee Print, Washington, D.C., Government Printing Office, April, 1951.

U.S. Department of State. *Foreign Relations of the United States, Diplomatic Papers, 1940.* Department of State *Publication 6638,* Washington, D.C., Government Printing Office, 1957, Vol. III.

———. *Foreign Relations of the United States, Diplomatic Papers, 1941.* Department of State *Publication 6642,* Washington, D.C., Government Printing Office, 1958, Vol. I.

———. *Foreign Relations of the United States, Diplomatic Papers, 1942.* Department of State *Publication 7165,* Washington, D.C., Government Printing Office, 1961, Vol. III.

———. *Foreign Relations of the United States, Diplomatic Papers, 1943.* Department of State *Publication 7601,* Washington, D.C., Government Printing Office, 1963. Vol. III.

———. *Foreign Relations of the United States, The Conference at Malta and Yalta, 1945.* Department of State *Publication 6199,* Washington, D.C., Government Printing Office, 1955.

———. *Foreign Relations of the United States, The Conference of Ber-*

lin (Potsdam) *1945.* Department of State *Publication* 7165, Washington, D.C., Government Printing Office, 1960.

――. *Peace and War: United States Foreign Policy 1931–1941.* Washington, D.C., Government Printing Office, 1943.

――. *Soviet Supply Protocols.* Department of State *Publication* 2759, *European Series 22,* Washington, D.C., Government Printing Office, n.d.

U.S., President. *Reports to Congress on Lend-Lease Operations.* No. 1–43. Washington, D.C., Government Printing Office, 1941–1960. Titles vary.

U.S.S.R., Ministry of Foreign Affairs. *Correspondence Between the Chairman of the Council of Ministers of the U.S.S.R. and the Presidents of the U.S.A. and the Prime Ministers of Great Britain During the Great Patriotic War of 1941–1945.* 2 vols., Moscow, Foreign Languages Publishing House, 1957.

Books: Including Biographies and Memoirs

Beard, Charles A. *President Roosevelt and the Coming of the War, 1941.* New Haven, Yale University Press, 1948.

Churchill, Winston S. *Closing the Ring.* Boston, Houghton Mifflin Co., 1951.

――. *Their Finest Hour.* Boston, Houghton Mifflin Co., 1949.

――. *The Grand Alliance.* Boston, Houghton Mifflin Co., 1952.

――. *The Hinge of Fate.* Boston, Houghton Mifflin Co., 1950.

Cline, Ray S. *Washington Command Post: The Operations Division.* Washington, D.C., Government Printing Office, 1951.

Columbia University, Russian Institute. *The Anti-Stalin Campaign and International Communism, A Selection of Documents.* New York, Columbia University Press, 1956.

Craven, Wesley Frank, and James Lea Cate, eds. *Services Around the World* (*The Army Air Forces in World War II,* Vol. VII). Chicago, University of Chicago Press, 1958.

Davies, Joseph E. *Mission to Moscow.* New York, Simon and Schuster, 1941.

Dawson, Raymond H. *The Decision to Aid Russia, 1941.* Chapel Hill, University of North Carolina Press, 1959.

Deane, John R. *The Strange Alliance.* New York, Viking Press, 1947.

Deborin, G. A. *Vtoraia Mirovaia Voina* (*The Second World War*). Moscow, Voennoe Izdatel'stvo Misisterstva Oborony Souiza SSR, 1958.

Djilas, Milovan. *Conversations with Stalin.* Michael B. Petrovich, trans. New York, Harcourt, Brace and World, 1962.

Feis, Herbert. *Between War and Peace: The Potsdam Conference.* Princeton, Princeton University Press, 1960.

————. *Churchill-Roosevelt-Stalin: The War They Waged and the Peace They Sought.* Princeton, Princeton University Press, 1957.

Golikov, S. *Vydaiushchiesia Pobedy Sovetskoi Armii v Velikoi Otechestvennoi Voin* (*Outstanding Victories of Soviet Armies in the Great Patriotic War*). Moscow, Gosudarstvennoe Izdatel'stvo Politichesskoi Literatury, 1954.

Hancock, W. K., and M. W. Gowing. *British War Economy.* London, His Majesty's Stationery Office, 1949.

Hull, Cordell. *The Memoirs of Cordell Hull.* New York, Macmillan Co., 1948.

Ickes, Harold L. *The Lowering Clouds, 1939–1941* (*The Secret Diary of Harold L. Ickes,* Vol. III). New York, Simon and Schuster, 1954.

Institut Marxizma-Leninizma. *Istoriia Velikoi Otechestvennoi Voiny Sovetskogo Souiza, 1941–1945* (*History of the Great Patriotic War of the Soviet Union, 1941–1945*). 5 Vols., Moscow, Voennoe Izdatel'svo Ministerstva Oborony Souiza SSR, 1960–1963.

Israelian, V. L. *Diplomaticheskaia Istoriia Velikoi Otechestvennoi Voiny 1941–1945* (*Diplomatic History of the Great Patriotic War 1941–1945*). Moscow, Izdatel'stvo Instituta Mezhdunarodnykh Otnoshenii, 1959.

Jansy, Naum. *The Socialized Agriculture of the USSR, Plans and Performance.* Stanford, Stanford University Press, 1949.

Jones, Jesse H., with Edward Angly. *Fifty Billion Dollars, My Thirteen Years with the RFC.* New York, Macmillan Co., 1951.

Jordan, George Racey. *From Major Jordan's Diaries.* New York, Harcourt, Brace, 1952.

Kerr, Walter. *The Russian Army: Its Men, its Leaders, and its Battles.* New York, Alfred A. Knopf, 1944.

Lane, Frederic C., with Blanche D. Coll, Gerald J. Fischer, and David B. Tyler. *Ships for Victory: A History of the Shipbuilding Under* the *U.S. Maritime Commission in World War II. Historical Reports on War Administration: United States Maritime Commission,* No. 1. Baltimore, The Johns Hopkins Press, 1951.

Langer, William L., and S. Everett Gleason. *The Undeclared War, 1940–1941.* New York, Harper and Bros., 1953.

Leighton, Richard M., and Robert W. Coakley. *Global Logistics and Strategy, 1940–1943.* (Department of the Army, Office of the Chief of Military History, *United States Army in World War II: The War Department*) Washington, D.C., Government Printing Office, 1955.

Matloff, Maurice. *Strategic Planning for Coalition Warfare, 1943–1944.* Washington, D.C., Government Printing Office, 1959.

———, and Edwin M. Snell. *Strategic Planning for Coalition Warfare, 1941–1942.* Washington, D.C., Government Printing Office, 1953.

Millett, John D. *The Organization and Role of the Army Service Forces.* Washington, D.C., Government Printing Office, 1954.

Morison, Samuel Eliot. *The Battle of the Atlantic, September, 1939–May, 1943.* Boston, Little, Brown and Co., 1947.

———. *The Atlantic Battle Won.* Boston, Little, Brown and Co., 1956.

Motter, T. H. Vail. *The Persian Corridor and Aid to Russia.* Washington, D.C., Government Printing Office, 1952.

Narodnoe Khoziaistvo SSR v 1960, Statistical Ezhegodnik (National Economy of the USSR in 1960, Statistical Yearbook). Moscow, Gosstatizdat, Tsentral'noe Statisticheskoe Upravlenie pri Sovete Ministrov SSR, 1961.

Roosevelt, Elliott, ed. *F.D.R., His Personal Letters, 1928–1945.* New York, Duell, Sloan, and Pearce, 1950, Vol. II.

Roskill, Stephen Wentworth. *The War at Sea, 1939–1945.* 3 Volumes in 4. London, Her Majesty's Stationery Office, 1954–1961.

Sayre, Joel. *Persian Gulf Command.* New York, Random House, 1945.

Sherwood, Robert E. *Roosevelt and Hopkins: An Intimate History.* New York, Harper and Bros., 1948.

Shigalin, G. I. *Narodnoe Khoziaistvo SSR v Period Velikoi Otechestvennoi Voiny (National Economy of the USSR During the Great Patriotic War).* Moscow. Izdatel'stvo Sotial'no-Ekonomicheskoi Literatury, 1960.

Shimkin, Dimitri B. *Minerals, A Key to Soviet Power.* Cambridge, Mass., Harvard University Press, 1953.

Smith, R. Elberton. *The Army and Economic Mobilization.* Washington, D.C., Government Printing Office, 1959.

Stalin, Joseph. *The Great Patriotic War of the Soviet Union.* New York, International Publishers, 1945.

Standley, William H., and Arthur A. Ageton. *Admiral Ambassador to Russia.* Chicago, Henry Regnery Co., 1955.

Statistical Digest of the War. London, His Majesty's Stationery Office, 1951.

Stedman, Murray Salisbury, Jr. *Federal Arms Exports Administration, 1935–1945.* New York, Kings Crown Press, 1947.

Stettinius, Edward R. Jr. *Lend-Lease, Weapon For Victory.* New York, Macmillan Co., 1944.

Stimson, Henry L., and McGeorge Bundy. *On Active Service in Peace and War.* New York, Harper and Bros., 1947.

Truman, Harry S. *Year of Decisions* (*Memoirs,* Vol. I). Garden City, Doubleday and Co., 1955.

Vandenberg, Arthur H. Jr., ed. *The Private Papers of Senator Vandenberg.* Boston, Houghton Mifflin Co., 1952.

Vernadsky, George. *A History of Russia.* New Haven, Yale University Press, 1961.

Voznesenski, N. A. *The Economy of the U.S.S.R. During World War II.* Washington, D.C., Public Affairs Press, 1948.

Wallace, Henry A., and Andrew J. Steiger. *Soviet Asia Mission.* New York, Reynal and Hitchcock, 1946.

Watson, Mark Skinner. *Chief of Staff: Prewar Plans and Preparations.* (Department of the Army, Historical Division, *United States Army in World War II: The War Department*), Washington, D.C., Government Printing Office, 1950.

Welles, Sumner. *The Time for Decision.* Cleveland, World Publishing Co., 1944.

Articles

Baykov, Alexander. "Agricultural Development in the U.S.S.R.," *Bulletins on Soviet Economic Development, Bulletin* No. 2, Faculty of Commerce and Social Science, University of Birmingham, England, (December, 1949).

"Cash-Register Spirit," *Nation,* Vol. 157 (October 30, 1943), pp. 487–88.

Cherne, Leo M. "The 'Double L' Arsenal," *Saturday Review of Literature*, Vol. 27 (January 22, 1944), pp. 3–4.

Condliffe, J. B. "Implications of Lend-Lease: Economic Problems in the Settlement," *Foreign Affairs*, Vol. 21 (April, 1943), pp. 494–504.

Council on Foreign Relations. "The Problem of Lend-Lease: Its Nature, Implications, and Settlement," *American Interests in the War and the Peace*. New York, Council on Foreign Relations, 1944, mimeograph.

Diebold, William, Jr. "Implications of Lend-Lease: Political Dangers in the Settlement," *Foreign Affairs*, Vol. 21 (April, 1943), pp. 505–12.

Hunter, Holland. "Soviet Railroads Since 1940," *Bulletins on Soviet Economic Development, Bulletin* No. 4, Faculty of Commerce and Social Science, University of Birmingham, England (September, 1950).

"Lend-Lease," *Time*, Vol. 42 (September 6, 1943), p. 25.

"Lend-Lease," *Time*, Vol. 42 (November 22, 1943), pp. 18–19.

"Lend-Lease to Date," *Fortune*, Vol. XXVI (October, 1942), p. 108f.

Lindley, Ernest K. "Lend-Lease, Enthralling Enterprise," *The Virginia Quarterly Review*, Vol. 20 (Spring, 1944), pp. 281–85.

———, "We Gave the Red Army its Speed," *Newsweek*, Vol. 25 (February 12, 1945), p. 54.

Nelson, Donald M. "American Production—Russian Front," *Survey Graphic*, Vol. 33 (February, 1944), pp. 56–59.

Saturday Evening Post (Editorial), Vol. 218 (October 13, 1945), p. 124.

Whidden, Howard P., Jr. "Reaching a Lend-Lease Settlement," *Foreign Policy Reports*, Vol. XX (April 15, 1944), pp. 22–31.

Periodicals

Department of State Bulletin. Volumes 24, 26, 29.

Fortune. Volumes 26, 32.

Izvestia. 1941–1945.

Krasnaia Zvezda (Red Star). 1941–1945.

Newsweek. Volumes 25, 26.

Pravda. 1941–1946.

Time. Volumes 42, 46.

The New York Times. 1941–1945.

Theses and Dissertations

Bates, J. Leonard. "The Arctic Life Line." Unpublished master's thesis in the University of North Carolina Library, Chapel Hill, 1946.

Carr, Edwin R. "Great Falls to Nome: The Inland Air Route to Alaska, 1940–45." Unpublished doctoral dissertation in the University of Minnesota Library, St. Paul, October 1946.

Gardner, John Frederick. "The Lend-Lease Program of World War II: Analysis and Appraisal." Unpublished doctoral dissertation in the University of Pittsburgh Library (on film at the Franklin D. Roosevelt Library, Hyde Park, N. Y.), 1946.

Other Works Consulted

Annual Report (U.S. Army) *Services of Supply for the Fiscal Year Ending June 30, 1942.* No publication data, 1942.

Army Service Forces Annual Report for the Fiscal Year 1943. No publication data, 1943.

Army Service Forces Annual Report for the Fiscal Year 1944. Washington, D.C., Government Printing Office, 1944.

Army Service Forces Annual Report for the Fiscal Year 1945. No publication data, 1945.

Bailey, Thomas A. *A Diplomatic History of the American People.* 4th ed. New York, Appleton-Century-Crofts, Inc., 1950.

———. *America Faces Russia.* Ithaca, Cornell University Press, 1950.

Brown, William Adams, and Redvers Opie. *American Foreign Assistance.* Washington, D.C., The Brookings Institution, 1953.

Byrnes, James F. *Speaking Frankly.* New York, Harper and Bros., 1947.

Crocker, George N. *Roosevelt's Road to Russia.* Chicago, Henry Regnery Co., 1959.

Dennet, Raymond, and Joseph E. Johnson, eds. *Negotiating With the Russians.* Boston, World Peace Foundation, 1951.

Goodrich, Leland M., ed. *Documents on American Foreign Relations: Volume IV, July 1941–June 1942.* Boston, World Peace Foundation, 1942.

———, and Marie J. Carroll, eds. *Documents on American Foreign Relations: Volume V, July 1942–June 1943.* Boston, World Peace Foundation, 1944.

313

————. *Documents on American Foreign Relations*: Volume VI, July *1943–June 1944*. Boston, World Peace Foundation, 1945.

————. *Documents on American Foreign Relations*: Volumes VII, July *1944–June 1945*. Princeton, Princeton University Press, 1947.

Dymshits, A., and others. *Podvig Lenningrada 1941–1944* (*The Exploit of Lenningrad 1941–1944*). Moscow, Voennoe Izdatel'stvo Ministerstva Oborony SSR, 1960.

Eremenko, A. I. *Stalingrad*. Moscow, Voennoe Izdatel'stvo Ministerstva Oborony Souiza SSR, 1961.

Isakov, I. S. *The Red Fleet in the Second World War*. Jack Hural, trans. London, Hutchinson and Co., Ltd., 1947.

Koenig, Louis William. *The Presidency and the Crisis*. New York, King's Crown Press, 1944.

Leahy, William D. *I Was There*. New York, Whittlesey House, 1950.

"Lend-Lease." *Bol'shaia Sovetskaia Entsiklopediia* (*The Great Soviet Encyclopedia*). 2d ed. Vol. XXIV, 1954. 490–91.

McNeill, William Hardy. *America, Britain and Russia. Their Co-operation and Conflict, 1941–1946*. London, Oxford University Press, 1953.

Millis, Walter, ed. *The Forrestal Diaries*. New York, Viking Press, 1951.

Notter, Harley A. *Postwar Foreign Policy Preparation, 1939–1945*. Department of State *Publication* 3580, General Foreign Policy Series 15. Washington, D.C., Government Printing Office, 1950.

Rosen, S. McKee. *The Combined Boards of the Second World War*. New York, Columbia University Press, 1951.

Robinson, Edgar Eugene. *The Roosevelt Leadership, 1933–1945*. New York, J. B. Lippincott, 1955.

Schuman, Frederick L. *Soviet Politics at Home and Abroad*. New York, Alfred A. Knopf, 1947.

Tel'pukhovskii, B. S. *Velikaia Otechestvennaia Voina Sovetskogo Soiuza 1941–1945* (*The Great Patriotic War of the Soviet Union, 1941–1945*). Moscow. Gosudarstvennoe Izdatel'stvo Politicheskoi Literatury, 1959.

Timokhovich, I.V. *Sovetskaia Aviatsiia v Bitve Pod Kurskom* (*The Soviet Air Force in the Kursk Battle*). Moscow, Voennoe Izdatel'stvo Ministerstva Oborony Souiza SSR, 1959.

U.S. Bureau of the Census. *United States Exports of Domestic and*

Foreign Merchandise Under the Lend-Lease Program . . . Commodity by Country of Destination. Washington, D.C., Department of Commerce, *Report* FT 415, January, 1945–April, 1946.

———. *United States Exports of Domestic and Foreign Merchandise Under the Lend-Lease Program, Calendar Year 1944, Commodity by Country of Destination.* Washington, D.C., Department of Commerce, *Report* FT 415, August, 1945.

———. *United States Exports by Air of Domestic and Foreign Merchandise . . . Commodity by Country of Destination.* Washington, D.C., Department of Commerce, *Report* FT 731, June 1946.

U.S. Department of Commerce. *Foreign Aid by the United States Government, 1940–1951.* Washington, D.C., Government Printing Office, 1952.

U.S. Office of Lend-Lease Administration. *All for One; One for All, The Story of Lend-Lease.* Washington, D.C., Government Printing Office, June 1943.

U.S. Office of Lend-Lease Administration. *Lend-Lease and Us.* No publication data.

U.S. Senate. *A Decade of American Foreign Policy, Basic Documents, 1941–1949.* Senate *Document* 123, 81 Cong., 1 sess. No publication data.

U.S. Treasury Department. *Report on Lend-Lease Fiscal Operations.* No publication data. June 30, 1947.

U.S. War Department, *Report of the Chief of Transportation Army Service Forces World War II.* Washington, D.C., November 30, 1945.

War Production in 1942. [Report by the Chairman of the War Production Board, Donald M. Nelson]. Washington: War Production Board, no date.

War Production in 1944: Report of the Chairman of the War Production Board [J. A. Krug]. Washington: Government Printing Office, 1945.

Wartime Production Achievements and the Reconversion Outlook: Report of the Chairman of the War Production Board [J. A. Krug], October 9, 1945. Washington: Government Printing Office, 1945.

Welles, Sumner. *Where are We Heading?* New York, Harper and Bros., 1946.

INDEX

Acheson, Dean: 36, 120
Agricultural production, Soviet: 215, 217–19
Agriculture Department: 20, 259
Alabama (ship): 189
Allies: 5, 14, 18, 25, 81–82, 84, 88, 126, 128–29, 133–34, 136–38, 146, 150, 153, 165–69, 173, 176, 181, 188–89, 196, 201, 205, 209–10, 213–14, 230, 234, 250, 252–54, 257–59, 265–67, 269
ALSIB (Alaska-Siberia Air Ferry route): 92–93, 111–12, 127, 138, 155–56, 158–60, 210–12, 232, 267, 293, 295
American embassy in Moscow: 48, 135
American Red Cross: 76
Amtorg (Russian trading company): 26, 28, 30, 36, 52, 114, 295
Anglo-French Purchasing Board: 8
Anson (British battleship): 143, 145
ANVIL (code name for invasion of Southern France): 165
ARCADIA (Anglo-American conference in Washington, D.C., 1941): 81f.
ARGONAUT (code name for Yalta conference): *see* Yalta
Arkhangelsk (Russian warship): 197
Army and Navy Munitions Board: 36n.
Arnold, General Henry H.: 156, 158–59, 176, 211
"Arsenal of Democracy": 13–14, 23, 47, 71

Asia: 27, 30
Associated Press: 129
Atlantic Charter: 53, 65, 81, 95–96
Atlantic neutrality patrol: 5
Atlantic Neutrality Zone: 18
Atlee, Clement Richard: 256
Atomic Energy, Joint Committee on: *see* United States Congress
Augusta (U.S. cruiser): 53, 189
Aurand, Colonel Henry S.: 74n., 78
Australia: 260
Austria: 3
Avenger (British escort carrier): 145, 147, 150
Axis: 6, 13–14, 17, 24, 28, 34, 56, 80, 84, 177
Azores: 165

Badoglio, Marshal Pietro: 165
Balkan states: 252
Baltic states: 5, 25–27, 30, 37–38, 179
Barnes, Joseph: 126
Bates, Ensign J. Leonard: 235
Batt, William L.: 12, 58, 62–63, 75n.
Beaverbrook, Lord (William Maxwell Aitken): 53, 58–62, 81–82, 247
Belfast (British cruiser): 195
Belgium: 4, 258, 260
Bellingham (American merchantman): 150
Belyaev (head of Purchasing Commission of the Soviet Union): 114, 117–18, 155–56, 158
Bermuda: 18
Bessarabia: 5

Bickerton (British convoy frigate):
197
Biggers, John: 12
Bismarck (German battleship): 23
Black Sea route: 84, 206–207, 209–210
Blitzkrieg: 8
Bloom, Congressman Sol: 92
Bohlen, Charles E.: 184
BOLERO (U.S. buildup in Britain):
91–93, 115, 140
Bracken, Brendan: 55
Bradley, Major General Follett: 130,
156
Brazil: 6, 158, 260
Brett, Major General George H.: 58
Bretton Woods legislation: 259
British air force: 7, 47, 102, 144–45,
147, 153, 197, 267
British army: 4, 74, 137, 165, 179, 209
British navy: 18, 23, 65, 93, 102–109,
143–53, 194–97, 209, 231
British Purchasing Commission: 8, 14
Bulgaria: 17, 27, 38
Bureau of Research and Statistics: 72
Burnett, Rear Admiral R. L.: 145, 150,
152, 194
Burns, Major General James H.: 20–21,
41, 44, 46, 58, 115–16, 118, 120,
130, 138, 140, 156, 264
Butler, Senator Hugh: 162
Byrnes, James F.: 179

Cairo conference: 139
Campbell, Sir Ronald I.: 118
Canada: 6, 46, 53, 76, 163, 184, 267,
294
Cape Corso (British merchantman):
103
Casablanca conference: 132–34, 188
Cash and carry: 5, 36
Cassidy, Henry: 129
Chamber of Commerce, United States:
12
Chaney, Major General James E.: 60
Cherne, Leo M.: 253
Chiang Kai-shek: 78–79
Chicago Sun: 73n.
Chicago Tribune: 70, 73n.
China: 27, 41, 55, 57, 77–79, 126, 137,
160, 171, 260

Churchill, Winston: 5, 11, 17–19, 21,
30–35, 46–47, 49, 51, 53–54, 58,
80–81, 90–91, 93, 97, 108–109,
124–26, 132–34, 137–38, 150, 165,
171, 174, 179–80, 182, 192–93,
195–96, 234, 247, 260, 264–65
Ciliax, Vice-Admiral Otto: 102
City of Joliet (American merchantman): 104
Combined Chiefs of Staff: 87–88, 97,
133, 172, 183–84
Cominform: 261
Comintern: 137, 169, 261
Communist Party of the United States:
22 & n., 23, 32
Comptroller General of the United
States: 259
Connally, Senator Tom: 92
Connolly, General Donald H.: 139
Conscription Act: 7, 55
Convoy: 16, 18, 24, 40, 46, 65, 86, 88,
92–93, 100, 102, 108, 116, 118, 120,
125, 144–47, 151, 153, 188–89,
192–93, 195–96; PQ-QP series,
102–108, 124, 126–27, 144–45, 147,
150–51, 154, 249; JW-RA series,
152–53, 193–95, 197, 201
Council on Foreign Relations (New
York): 253
Council on National Defense, Advisory
Commission: 6, 8, 10
Cox, Oscar: 14–15, 21–22
Coy, Wayne S.: 44
Crete: 23
Cripps, Sir (Richard) Stafford: 49, 53,
58
Crowley, Leo T.: 164, 170, 175, 184,
187, 246–47, 251–52, 254–57, 259
Curtis, Charles, Jr.: 36–37
Czechoslovakia: 3, 38

Daily Worker: 32
Danzig: 3
Davies, Joseph E.: 39, 136–38, 160
Deane, Major General John R.: 92n.,
170–77, 180, 213, 235–36
Defense production, American: 14, 16,
20
Defense Supplies Corporation: 52–53,
64

De Gaulle, Free French General
    Charles: 170
Democratic Party: 10, 178
Denmark: 4
Destroyers-for-bases deal: 9, 10, 197
Dewey, Thomas: 177–79
Division of Defense Aid Reports:
    19–21, 36n., 41, 44, 46, 64, 97, 264
Doenitz, Admiral Karl: 153, 193, 195
Douglas, Lewis: 108n., 109
Douglas Aircraft Company: 208
Douglas Oil Refinery: 98
Dowding, Commodore J. C. K.: 150
Draft: see Conscription Act
Draftees: 40
DRAGOON (code for invasion of
    Southern France): 165
Duke of York (British battleship): 143,
    145, 193–94
Dunkirk: 9

Eden, (Robert) Anthony: 75, 137,
    171, 193
Edinburgh (British cruiser): 103
Effingham (American merchantman):
    102
Egypt: 17, 126
Eisenhower, Brigadier General Dwight
    D.: 112, 170
Election of 1940: 10
Election of 1944: 177–79
Ellender, Senator Allen J.: 162
Embrick, Lieutenant General Stanley
    D.: 58
Emmons (U.S. destroyer): 144
England: see Great Britain
Espionage, Russian: 38, 293–95
Estonia: see Baltic states
EUREKA: see Teheran conference
Europe: 3–4, 8–10, 18, 26, 28, 31, 36,
    57–58, 61, 81, 94, 165–66, 177,
    179–80, 183–84, 206, 210, 212, 234,
    260–61, 269
Export Control, Administrator of: 36n.
Export Control Act of 1940: 27
Export-Import Bank: 259
Expositor (American merchantman):
    102, 107

Far East, 180, 185

Faruk I, King of Egypt: 170
Faymonville, Brigadier General Philip
    R.: 41–42, 58, 62–63, 89, 114,
    116–17, 124, 128–31, 136, 139, 164,
    171–72, 231
Fifth Protocol (proposed): 212
Finland: 4–5, 25–26, 29, 38, 100
First (Moscow) Protocol: 62–63, 70,
    73–77, 79, 81, 84–87, 89, 90n., 94,
    98, 107, 109, 112, 115, 120–21,
    127, 166, 213, 266
Foley, Edward H.: 14–15
Ford, Henry: 22
Ford Motor Company: 98, 223
Foreign Economic Administration:
    164, 170, 175, 181–82, 184, 187,
    251, 258–59
Foreign Ministers Conference at
    Moscow, 1943: 169, 171, 173, 193
Foreign policy, United States: 17, 20,
    75, 127
Foreign Policy Reports: 253
Forrestal, James: 92, 183
Fortune: 99
Fourth Protocol: 166–68, 175, 181–82,
    184–85, 208, 210, 212–13, 255,
    257–58, 260–61, 267
France: 3, 5–6, 8, 58, 165, 174, 196,
    258, 260, 263
Franco, Francisco: 249
Frankfurter, Supreme Court Justice
    Felix: 15
Fraser, Admiral Sir Bruce Austin: 189,
    192–95
French navy: 7
French Provisional Government-in-
    Exile: 137
Fuchs, Klaus: 294

General Motors' Overseas Division:
    208
Geneva (Prisoner of War) Convention
    of 1929: 91
George, Senator Walter F.: 161
George II, King of Greece: 170
German air force: 7, 32, 48, 60, 100–
    108, 124, 144–150, 154, 188–196,
    201, 215
German army: 3–4, 6, 17, 23–25, 28,
    32, 34, 36, 57–58, 60–61, 82, 111,

126, 129, 134, 138, 210, 215–16, 233

German navy: 7, 18, 23, 99, 100–106, 109, 124, 134, 143–47, 150–51, 152–53, 188–89, 192–97, 201, 213

German-Russian Non-aggression Pact of 1939; *see* Non-aggression Pact of 1939

German-Russian Trade Agreement of 1941: 27

Germany: 3, 6, 22, 25, 27–32, 35–36, 39–40, 50, 54, 60, 74, 78, 80–81, 91, 100, 113, 165–66, 171, 173, 176, 184–86, 250, 263, 266

Gneisenau (German battle cruiser): 18, 23, 99

Goebbels, Joseph: 32, 61

Gold, Harry: 294

Golikov, Lieutenant General Filip R.: 42, 56, 70

Göring, Marshal Hermann: 150

Great Britain: 3, 5–14, 17–19, 21–25, 27–30, 32–33, 35, 39–47, 50–51, 53–55, 57–62, 65, 70–71, 74–80, 86, 94–95, 98–99, 107–108, 110, 114, 116–18, 120, 123–24, 127, 132, 135, 138, 140, 142, 154, 171, 176, 182, 184, 193, 196, 251, 254, 260, 263–68

Greece: 17, 179

Greenglass, David: 294

Greenland: 18

Greer (U.S. destroyer): 65

Grew, Joseph C.: 184, 257

Gromyko, Andrei: 36, 164, 181–82, 246

Guatemala: 260

Halifax, Lord (Edward F. L. Wood): 46

Harriman, W. Averell: 12, 21, 46–47, 53, 58, 60–63, 86, 89, 112, 124–26, 130, 136–37, 140, 142, 170–72, 173n., 174–77, 180, 182, 184, 218–19, 246, 252

Harvey, Colonel Alva L.: 156

Hawaii: 6

Hawkins, Harry C.: 94

Hazard, John N.: 41

Henderson, Leon: 22, 63, 72, 82n.

Henderson, Loy: 37–38

Hillman, Sidney: 22, 46, 72, 82n.

Hipper (German cruiser): 23, 99, 105–106, 143, 145–46, 152–53, 195

Hitler, Adolf: 3, 5, 13, 17, 23–26, 29–30, 32–34, 44, 47, 50, 54, 58, 62, 70, 73, 75, 99, 104–106, 143, 146, 150–51, 181, 186, 189, 194, 201, 210

Holland: *see* Netherlands

Hood (British battle cruiser): 23

Hoover, Herbert: 35

Hopkins, Harry: 11, 19–23, 39, 41, 43–56, 58–60, 63–65, 71–72, 82 & n., 88, 89, 91, 93–94, 97, 108–109, 112, 114–15, 118, 120, 122, 124–25, 127–28, 130, 132–33, 136–37, 139, 155–56, 159–60, 165, 167, 174–76, 178–80, 183–87, 209, 211, 242, 255, 264–65, 267, 292, 294

Hull, Cordell: 11, 15, 21, 26–27, 29, 31, 34, 58, 65, 80, 91, 95, 117, 130, 132, 156, 169–71, 179, 218, 244

Hungary: 38, 179

Hurley, General Patrick J.: 235

HUSKY (code for invasion of Sicily): 133, 188

Iceland: 18, 24, 40, 65, 102–105, 108, 151, 144, 193

Ickes, Harold: 10–11, 28, 34, 43, 56, 64

Ile de France (Allied troop transport): 142

India: 110

Indo-China: 6

Industrial production, American: 12–13, 22–23, 44, 56, 70–71, 73–75, 77–79, 81–82, 86–87, 120, 250, 267–69

Industrial production, Soviet: 220–29, 232

Internationalism: 127

International law: 3

International Red Cross: 91

Interventionism: 35

Iran: 49, 65, 110–11, 124–26, 139–40, 143, 203, 205–206, 208–209

Iraq: 110–11, 126, 140

Ireland: 146

Ismay, Major General Sir Hastings: 108
Isolationism: 14–15, 22–23, 30, 35, 40, 45, 54–55
Israel Putnam (U.S. merchantman): 235
Italian army: 4
Italy: 3, 6, 61, 80, 165, 176, 196, 210
Izvestia: 243, 245, 247

Jamaica (British cruiser): 152, 193–94, 197
Japan: 3, 5–6, 25, 27, 30, 41, 49, 53, 61, 73–74, 79–80, 84–85, 91, 111, 113, 162, 166, 171, 176–77, 180, 183, 186–87, 209–10, 214, 254–55
Johnson, Eric: 252
Johnson Act: 263
Joint Chiefs of Staff: 92, 115, 125, 132, 134, 168, 171–72, 175–76, 258
Jones, Jesse H., 52, 59, 64, 82n.
Jorden, Major George Racey: 293–95

Kearney (U.S. destroyer): 68
Khrushchev, Nikita S.: 32 & n., 249
Kilgore, Senator Harley M.: 255
King, Admiral Ernest J.: 91–93, 115, 124
King George V (British battleship): 143, 145
Kitchener, Lord (Horatio Herbert): 60
Kite (British convoy sloop): 197
KNIGHT'S GAMBIT (German operation against North Russian route convoys): 105
Knox, Frank: 10–11, 34, 41, 56–57, 71–72, 80, 82n., 120, 137
Knudsen, William S.: 11–12, 41, 56, 71–72, 82n.
Koln (German light crusier): 143, 146
Krasnaya Zvezda: 218, 243, 247
Kravchenko, Victor: 251–52

Land, Admiral Emory S.: 22, 88–89, 90n., 120, 142
Latin America: 6, 9, 24, 77
Latvia: *see* Baltic states
League of Nations: 4

Leda (British minesweeper): 150
Lend-Lease Act: 257, 259, 263–64; passage of, 16; Master Agreement, 94–96, 98, 168, 181; food shipments, 217–20; industrial shipments, 220–29, 232; munitions shipments, 228–29, 231; effect of, 232–34, 237–38; evidences of, 234–36; cost of, 238–39; Soviet view of, 242–50; pipeline agreements, 258–60; settlement, 261–62
Lend-Lease Act: 257, 259, 263–64; 89–90, 97, 114, 118, 129, 164, 170, 172, 175, 181, 224, 253, 293, 295
Lewis Fulton, Jr.: 293, 295
Lindley, Ernest K.: 253
Lithuania: *see* Baltic states
Litvinov, Maxim: 62, 91, 93, 95, 112, 117–18, 120, 132, 137, 171, 244–45
Loans to Russia, billion-dollar interest-free: 68, 70, 75, 88, 94–95
London (British heavy cruiser): 60
Lubin, Isador: 22, 178
Luetzow: (German battleship): 99, 151–53, 188–89, 195
Luftwaffe: *see* German air force
Lukashev, Konstantin I.: 114
Luxembourg: 4
Libya: 17
Lyttelton, Oliver: 196

McCabe, Thomas B.: 116–17, 124
McCloy, John J.: 74n.
Maginot Line: 4
Maisky, Ivan: 171
Manhattan District: 292–94
Maritime Commission: 20, 22, 36n., 46, 71–72, 88–90, 90n.
Marshall, General George C.: 6–7, 43, 78–80, 85, 87–89, 91–92, 94, 115, 124, 128, 137, 139, 168, 171–73, 175–76
Marshall Plan: 261
Martin, Congressman Joseph: 17
Mary Luckenbach (American merchantman): 147
Mauretania (Allied troop transport): 142
Maxwell, General Russell L.: 125
May, Stacy: 22

Michela, Colonel Joseph: 156, 172
Middle East: 46, 65, 78, 88, 126, 208, 266
Mikoyan, Anastas I: 225
MILEPOST (code for Lend-Lease stockpile in Siberia): 180, 183–84, 234
Milwaukee (U.S. cruiser): 195
Mobilization, American: 6–7, 10
Molotov, Vyacheslav: 27, 29, 36–37, 49, 62, 90–95, 114–16, 135, 171, 174, 193, 234, 244, 248
Moral embargo: 26–28
Morgenthau, Henry L., Jr.: 8, 12, 14, 19n., 28, 43, 52, 59, 64, 120
Morison, Admiral Samuel E.: 201–202
Moscow press: 163
Munitions Assignment Board: 84, 97, 115, 120, 160, 175, 209, 265
Munitions Control Board: 27
Munitions industry, American: 5, 7
Munitions production, Soviet: 228–31
Munitions Program of 1940: 7
Mussolini, Benito: 24

NAM News: 252
Nathan, Robert: 22
Nathaniel Green (American merchantman): 147
National defense: 44–45
Nation magazine: 162
Navy department: 8, 20, 42, 72, 90n., 98–99
Nazi Germany: see Germany
Nelson, Donald: 11–12, 72, 81–82, 89, 90 n., 120, 164
Netherlands: 4, 77, 258, 260
Netherlands East Indies: 41, 76, 79
Neutrality Act of 1939: 5, 36, 40, 65, 263
Neutrality pact of 1941: 40
Newfoundland: 18
Newsweek: 256
New York Herald-Tribune: 126
New York Times: 54, 98, 99, 160–61, 163–64
Non-aggression pact of 1939, German-Russian: 3, 25, 29, 30n., 241
North Africa: 134–35, 137, 142, 151

North Atlantic War Zone: 18
North Russian route: 84, 89, 92–93, 99, 106–107, 109, 116, 118, 120, 124–25, 127–28, 134, 144, 146, 150–51, 153–55, 188–89, 192, 195–96, 201, 207, 224, 230, 268
Norway: 4, 23, 48, 92, 99–100, 106, 112, 146, 151, 188–89, 194, 197
Nürnberg (German cruiser): 151, 195
Nye, Senator Gerald: 17, 162

Office of Economic Warfare: 164, 170
Office of Emergency Management: 19, 44, 170, 264
Office of Foreign Economic Co-ordination: 170
Office of Foreign Relief and Rehabilitation: 164, 170
Office of Lend-Lease Administration: see Lend-Lease Administration
Office of Price Administration: 22
Office of Production Management: 22, 36n., 41–42, 56, 58, 63, 71–72
Office of War Information: 126
Olsen, Rear Admiral Clarence E.: 172
"Operation Barbarossa": 29
Oumansky, Constantin: 26–31, 36–39, 42–45, 51–52, 56
OVERLORD (code name for invasion of Northern France): 137, 165, 174, 196

Panama Canal: 6
Patterson, Robert P.: 21
Pearl Harbor: 73–74, 80–81, 85, 98, 113, 164, 266
Persian Gulf: 40, 79
Persian Gulf route: 84, 107, 109–11, 113, 116, 118, 120, 124–27, 134, 139–43, 155, 163, 174, 178, 202–209, 213–14, 229, 232, 267
Persian Gulf Service Command: 139–42, 204–205, 252
Peru: 260
Peter II, King of Yugoslavia: 170
Philadelphia Record: 178
Philippine Islands: 76
Phoenix (American cruiser): 170
"Phoney War": see Sitzkrieg
Poland: 3, 24, 32, 38, 176, 179, 186,

252; corridor, 3; partition of, 1939, 4–5
Pope Pius XII: 249
Portugal: 165
Post-war settlement: 38, 231, 250
"Pot of Gold" plan: 6
Potsdam Conference: 187, 260
Pravda: 30, 129, 215, 242–47, 251
Preparedness program, American: 40
President's Executive Office: 170
President's Liaison Committee: 8, 19, 20–21, 74, 264
President's Soviet Protocol Committee: 120–22, 160, 167, 175, 183, 187, 265
Prince of Wales (British battleship): 51, 53
Prinz Eugen (German cruiser): 23, 99
Production Planning Board: 71
Protective Mobilization plan: 7
Public opinion: 13, 18, 24, 26, 36, 45, 55, 61, 74, 97–99, 161, 254, 256
Purchasing Commission of the Soviet Union: 114, 117–18, 212, 251
Purvis, Arthur B.: 8, 44

QUADRANT: see Quebec Conference
Quebec Conference: 165–66, 169, 174
Queen Mary (British transport): 137
Quincy (U.S. cruiser): 180

Raeder, Admiral Erich: 146, 153
"Rainbow 4" plan: 6
Ranger (U.S. aircraft carrier): 189
Rayburn, Sam: 15
Rearmament, American: 6, 7, 26, 40–41, 78–79, 264, 266
Reconstruction Finance Corporation: 52–53: *see also* Defense Supplies Corporation
Red Army: *see* Russian army
Red Sea: 18
Red Star: see Krasnaya Zvezda
Reinhardt, G. Frederick: 118
Renown (British battleship): 143
Republican Party: 10, 177–78
Reynolds, Quentin: 60
Robin Moor: 23
Rodman (U.S. destroyer): 114
Rommel, Marshal Erwin: 134

Roosevelt, Franklin D.: 6–21, 23–24, 26, 28–29, 31–47, 49, 51–53, 55–57, 59, 61, 63–65, 68–69, 71–72, 73n., 80–82, 84–86, 88–94, 97–99, 108, 111–12, 114–16, 120, 125–27, 130–34, 136–38, 150, 154, 156, 158n., 159–60, 163–65, 169–71, 211, 243, 246–47, 250, 252, 254, 256, 263, 265–67, 269; death of, 183–84
Roper, Elmo: 256
Rosenbergs, the (Julius and Ethel): 295
Roskill, Captain Stephen Wentworth: 201
ROUNDUP (plan for cross-channel attack in 1943): 91, 133
Royal Air Force: *see* British air force
Rudenko, General Leonid G.: 212, 251, 257
Rumania: 5, 28, 29
Russian air force: 100, 153–54, 156, 215, 233
Russian army: 29, 31, 39, 46–47, 53, 57–58, 74, 82, 109, 123–24, 126, 134–35, 138, 165, 173, 175, 179, 183, 186, 197–201, 210, 215–16, 218, 220, 228–29, 232–34, 237, 250–52, 268–69
Russian-German Non-aggression Pact of 1939: *see* Non-aggression Pact of 1939
Russian Military Mission to the United States: 42–43
Russian navy: 100, 108, 144, 150, 197, 215, 231
Russian Shipping Board: 90
Russo-Finnish War of 1939: 4
Russo-Japanese Neutrality Pact of 1941: *see* Neutrality Pact of 1941

Saudi Arabia: 126, 260
Saturday Evening Post: 256
Saturday Review of Literature: 253
Scharnhorst (German cruiser): 18, 23, 99, 153, 188–89, 193, 213; sinking of, 194–95
Scheer (German battleship): 99, 105–106, 143–44, 146, 151, 195
Schoemann (German destroyer): 103
Scylla (British destroyer): 145

Second (Washington) Protocol: 92–93, 114–20, 122, 124, 127–28, 130, 132–34, 138, 143, 154–55, 159–60, 163, 166, 168, 175, 211, 213, 230, 268

Second front: 82, 91, 92 & n., 94–95, 98, 114, 127, 134, 138, 246, 249–50

Security, American: 13, 34, 56

Semenov, Semen M.: 294

Sheffield (British cruiser): 152

Sherwood, Robert E.: 13, 15, 19, 24, 32, 60, 113, 127, 178

Sicily: 137, 165

Silver Sword (American merchantman): 150

Sitzkrieg: 4–5

Slavin, Lieutenant General N. V.: 173

SLEDGEHAMMER (plan for limited cross-channel attack in 1942): 91

Somali (British destroyer): 150

Somervell, General Brehon B.: 122, 174

Soong, Dr. T. V.: 79

South Dakota (U.S. battleship): 189

Soviet Arctic route: 84, 107, 144, 155, 210–11

Soviet Far Eastern (Pacific) route: 84, 89, 107, 113, 119, 122–24, 134, 154–55, 163, 209–10, 213–14

Soviet Foreign Military Liaison Office (O.V.S.): 173

Soviet Purchasing Commission: *see* Purchasing Commission of the Soviet Union

Spalding, Brigadier General George R.: 21

Spalding, Brigadier General Sidney P.: 20, 41, 118, 124–25, 139–40, 142, 172, 223, 235

Stalin, Joseph: 5, 34, 39, 43, 47–51, 53–54, 58–63, 68, 70, 82, 88, 91–92, 108–109, 111–12, 125–32, 134, 137–38, 154, 156, 158n., 164–65, 169, 171, 174, 179, 181, 183–86, 192–93, 195–96, 211, 219, 242–43, 246, 250, 265

Stalingrad, Russia, battle of: 138, 232–33, 256, 267

Standley, Admiral William H.: 60–63, 110–12, 126, 128–32, 135–38, 156, 162, 167, 170–71, 234–35, 245

State Department: 9, 15, 21, 28, 31, 34, 37–39, 42–43, 45, 52, 94, 96. 112, 118, 120, 130, 132, 135, 164, 169–70, 182, 184, 187, 206, 259, 261, 295

State of the Union address: 13–14

Steinhardt, Laurence: 25, 29–31, 36–37, 39, 48, 51, 57–58, 63

Stettinius, Edward R., Jr.: 11–12, 20, 64, 70, 89, 90n., 97, 120, 123, 137, 160–61, 164, 169–70, 175, 179, 182, 225, 231, 247, 253, 264, 269

Stimson, Henry L.: 10–12, 18, 34, 38, 41, 43–44, 56–57, 63, 71–72, 74n., 80, 82n., 85–86, 120, 132, 137, 179, 183, 254–55

Supplemental Appropriation Act of 1948: 259–60

Supply, Priorities, and Allocations Board: 63, 72, 81–82

Supply Protocols, Soviet: 232, 264; *see also* First, Second, Third, Fourth, and Fifth (proposed) Protocols

Supply routes, Soviet: *see* Black Sea, North Russian, Persian Gulf, Soviet Arctic, and Soviet Far Eastern routes

Sweden: 29n.

Syria: 126

Tass (Soviet News Agency): 30n.

Teheran Conference: 174

Third Deficiency Appropriation Act of 1946: 259–60

Third Protocol: 122n., 163, 165–69, 175, 207–208, 210–13, 267

Thurber, James: 205

Time magazine: 161–62

Tirpitz (German battleship): 99, 102, 105–106, 143, 147, 153, 188–89, 195–97, 201

TORCH (invasion of North Africa): 125–26, 132, 140, 151

Tovey, Admiral Sir John Cronyn: 145, 151, 153, 189, 192

Treasury Department: 4, 8, 14, 20–21, 55–56, 64, 182, 259

Trident (British submarine): 99

TRIDENT (Roosevelt-Churchill meet-

ing in Washington, D.C., May, 1942): 137–38.
Trinidad (British cruiser): 18, 102
Truman, Harry S: 176, 179, 183–85, 255–59, 269
Truman Doctrine: 261
Turkey: 29
Tuscaloosa (U.S. cruiser): 11, 102, 144–45, 189

Ukraine: 61
Ulm (German minelayer): 144
Ulster Queen (British anti-aircraft ship): 147
United Kingdom Commercial Corporation: 202, 208–209
United Nations: 180, 184, 186, 252, 255; Relief and Rehabilitation Administration, 259
United States Army: 5–9, 16, 57, 59, 71, 74, 77–78, 80, 85, 87, 109–10, 115, 133, 137, 140, 142, 165, 174, 202, 207–10, 230; air force, 7, 48, 60, 77–78, 111, 128, 145, 154, 156, 158–59, 176–77; Army Service Forces, 20 n., 122; General Staff, 34; War Plans Division, 79; Quartermaster General, 90; Services of Supply, 139; Munitions Assignment Committee (Ground), 140; Air Transport Command, 159; Motor Transport Service, 202–204, 206
United States Congress: 4, 6–9, 13–16, 28, 40, 51, 54–55, 57, 63–65, 68, 80, 97, 127, 132, 135–36, 160, 162–63, 182, 252, 254, 259–61, 264; House of Representatives, 15–16, 28, 162, 252, 254, 293; Senate, 15–16, 162, 252, 254–55; Joint Committee on Atomic Energy, 193–95
United States National Guard: 5–6, 40
United States Navy: 5, 7–8, 16, 65, 71, 80, 102, 107, 112, 115, 143–44, 189, 192, 209, 231, 261–62
United States Steel Export Corporation: 9

Van Buskirk, Arthur: 118

Vandenberg, Senator Arthur: 17
Vandenberg, Arthur H., Jr.: 17
Vandenberg, General Hoyt S.: 172
Vickery, Admiral Howard L.: 46
Victorious (British aircraft carrier): 105
Victory Program: 72–73, 81
Virginia Quarterly Review: 253
Vishinsky, Andrei: 171
Voroshilov, Marshal Klementy: 173
Voznesenski, N. A.: 241, 248

Wallace, Henry: 72, 82n., 92, 236, 293, 295
Ward, Angus I.: 235
War Department: 8–9, 15, 20–21, 42–43, 57, 64, 72, 85–87, 90 n., 98–99, 112, 114–15, 122, 124, 170, 176, 215; Defense Aid Requirements Committee, 20; Division of Defense Aid, 20
War Food Administration: 251
War Production Board: 22n., 82, 114, 164, 170, 177, 293–94
War Shipping Administration: 90 & n., 108n., 109, 120, 134, 142–43
Washington (U.S. battleship): 102
Wasp (U.S. aircraft carrier): 102
Watson, General Edwin M.: 42, 178
Weapon For Victory: 253
Wehrmacht: *see* German army
Welles, Sumner: 26–30, 33–34, 36–39, 41, 44, 46, 52–54, 118, 136, 169, 179
Western Europe: *see* Europe
West Point (U.S. troop transport): 142
Wheeler, Senator Burton K.: 14–15, 17, 35, 162
Wheeler, Colonel Raymond A.: 65, 110, 124
Whidden, Howard P.: 253
Wichita (U.S. cruiser): 102
Willkie, Wendell: 10, 16, 126–31, 136, 219
Wilson, Charles E.: 177
Winant, John G.: 21, 25, 31
Woodring, Henry: 8–9
Woods, Sam E.: 29
World War I: 3

World War II: outbreak of, 3; Soviet view of, 240–42

Yakovlev, Anatoli: 294
Yalta meeting: 180, 182–83, 260
Yeaton, Major Ivan: 63

Young, Philip: 21–22, 41, 73–74
Yount, Brigadier General Paul F.: 205
Yugoslavia: 17, 38, 179

Z–26 (German destroyer): 102

THE ROADS TO RUSSIA was set in Linotype Caledonia, a typeface designed by the American designer W. A. Dwiggins from Scotch typefaces that have served the printing craft for hundreds of years.

Display lines are set in Bodoni, a face distinguished by its mechanical precision and contrasting thick-and-thin strokes.

The paper on which this book is printed bears the watermark of the University of Oklahoma Press and is designed to have an effective life of over three hundred years.

UNIVERSITY OF OKLAHOMA PRESS

NORMAN